E. P. Thompson and the Making of the New Left

E. P. Thompson
and the Making of the New Left

Essays & Polemics

Edited by CAL WINSLOW

MONTHLY REVIEW PRESS
New York

Library of Congress Cataloging-in-Publication Data:

Thompson, E. P. (Edward Palmer), 1924–1993.
[Essays. Selections]
E.P. Thompson and the making of the new left : essays and polemics /
edited by Cal Winslow.
pages cm
ISBN 978-1-58367-443-7 (paperback) — ISBN 978-1-58367-444-4 (cloth) 1.
Socialism—Great Britain. 2. Working class—Great Britain 3. Labor
movement—Great Britain. 4. Right and left (Political science)—Great
Britain. I. Winslow, Calvin, editor. II. Title.
HX244.T56 2014
335—dc23
                                    2014017249

Monthly Review Press
146 West 29th Street, Suite 6W
New York, New York 10001
www.monthlyreview.org

UK ISBN: 978-1-909831-07-0 (paperback)
PUBLISHED IN THE UK BY:
Lawrence & Wishart
99a Wallis Road
London E9 5LN
www.lwbooks.co.u

Typeset in Arno Pro

5 4 3 2 1

Contents

Acknowledgments

First, I thank Faith Simon for her collaboration in every stage of this project. This is found "not in this or that particular" but in the entire project, start to finish.

I want also to thank David Howell, Joseph Matthews, and Iain Boal for their support and encouragement, above all for generously reading, commenting on, and correcting drafts. I thank them too for their many years of friendship.

I thank Michael Watts and the Geography Department at the University of California, Berkeley, for support.

Acknowledgment is due to the staffs at the Brotherton Library, the University of Leeds, the Hull History Centre, the Modern Records Collection, Warwick University, the Stanford University Libraries, and the University Library at the University of California, Berkeley.

I must thank Rosalie Winslow and also the staff at the University of Edinburgh for helping to find and retrieve a copy of "Through the Smoke of Budapest."

I am indebted to Andrew Gordon, Sven Beckert, and Jessica Barnard for the kind invitation to address the the Global E. P. Thompson Conference held at the Weatherhead Center, Harvard University, October 3–5, 2013. It inspired me to think harder, and introduced me again to Edward's international world.

I would like to thank Fred Inglis, Trevor Griffiths, Hilary Rose, Michael Barrett-Brown, and Marion Kozak, all of whom knew Edward back in the day, for taking time to speak with me and offering invaluable recollections and reflections on the issues and events that are the subject here.

I have had the invaluable assistance of friends and former students of Edward's: Judith Condon, Julian Harber, Paul Smith, Anna Davin, and Hugo Radice. I thank them for support, for their hospitality, for helping me to try to make Edward come alive once more, and for the opportunity to reflect on our own experiences with history from below, our work in adult working-class education, and with (the struggle continues!) the future of socialism! All of us, in one way or another, have been inspired by Edward.

Richard Taylor, Roger Fieldhouse, and David Goodway all generously shared their histories of the Extramural Department at Leeds University, including drafts of chapters, then unpublished, from *E. P. Thompson and English Radicalism.*

I have also benefited greatly from the encouragement of Marcus Rediker and Eric Hoddersen, as well as the advice and criticism of Laurie Flynn, Madeline Davis, Sheila Rowbotham, Kate Soper, John Grayson, Joseph White, Gillian Boal, John Gillis, Stephen Roberts, Pete Clarney, and Michael Rustin, as well as support from Will Smith, Jean Corston, and Summer Brenner.

Tim Clark and Anne Wagner opened their home and library to me, and also reopened for me the world of L. S. Lowry, while giving me in London a home and "office" away from home at a time when this was sorely needed.

Kate Thompson and the late Dorothy Thompson encouraged and supported me in the earliest stages. I regret that Dorothy, who always insisted that people *read* Edward, will not see the outcome of this project.

Of course, Michael Yates, Martin Paddio, and the staff at Monthly Review Press are to be thanked, above all for their patience, collaboration, and dedication to work in publishing, a vocation Edward knew well and documented in the many histories he produced.

The Introduction that follows I offer as my thanks and tribute to Edward Thompson. It has been a great pleasure for me to write which is, all at once, stirring, difficult, emotional, inspiring *again*. It has allowed me a chance, in a small way, to repay a great debt, too late of course, but such is the nature of things. I hope the errors will be few; they will in the event be my responsibility alone.

Finally, I must thank Jessie Winslow, Samantha Winslow, Rosie Winslow, and Matthew Winslow—and again, Faith—for the love without which work and life could have little meaning.

ĕ

IT IS NEVER SAFE TO ASSUME THAT ANY
of our history is altogether dead. It is more often
lying there, as a form of stored cultural energy. The instant
daily energy of the contingent dazzles us with its brightness.
What passes on the daily screen is so distracting, the presence
of the status quo is so palpable, that it is difficult to believe that
any other form of energy exists. But this instant energy must
be reproduced every moment as it is consumed; it can never
be held in store. Let the power be cut off for a while, then
we become aware of other and older reserves of energy
glowing all around us, just as, when the street-lights
are dowsed, we become aware of the stars.

—"A Special Case"
Writing by Candlelight

Edward Thompson and the Making of the New Left

I f many of the Yorkshire young people had in fact got socialism 'inside of them,' then something of its quality—the hostility to Grundyism,[1] the warm espousal of sexual equality, the rich internationalism—owed much to Tom Maguire."

The late Edward Thompson paid special tribute to only a few individuals. Tom Maguire was one. Maguire was a young Leeds socialist (1865–1895); he was a member of the Socialist League and a founder of the Yorkshire Independent Labour Party (ILP). Thompson immortalized him in his 1960 essay "Homage to Tom Maguire," reprinted in this book.

Maguire personified the tradition of northern socialism for Thompson and connected him and his own comrades to that tradition. Thompson clearly felt a deep admiration for the young socialist (Maguire died at thirty). It was not that he idealized Maguire, but he did see in him the best of the working class, the kind of person the socialist movement needed. Maguire, semi-employed, of poor Irish-Catholic parentage, became a socialist at sixteen; he joined the Social Democratic Federation (SDF) a year later. When the split in the SDF took place in 1884, he sided with William Morris, artist and revolutionary socialist. This, for Thompson, was not simply an episode of historical interest. Rather, it was a link in a chain; and this took him right back to the origins of British Marxism and its since-forgotten fusion with English Romantic socialism, with Morris, his circle, and the Socialist Federation.[2]

Edward Thompson was one of the great figures of the post–Second World War left.[3] He is remembered best as a historian, the author of a biography of William Morris,[4] and then, most famously, for his magisterial history of the Industrial Revolution in England, *The Making of the English Working Class* (1963).[5] He was, of course, much more than this. He was a veteran of the war; he served as a tank commander in North Africa and the Italian campaign. He thought of himself as a poet first, also as a writer; visiting New York, in 1946, "an aged war veteran of 22," and the author at that time of just one short story, he was thrilled at the "misrecognition" of being "taken to be a writer."[6] Indeed, as a writer, his style, wit, and eloquence were rivaled by few; as a political prose writer probably none. He was a lifelong poet, the author of a novel, and an orator capable of commanding the attention of thousands.[7]

In the years 1948 to 1965, Edward Thompson lived with his family in Halifax in the north of England. Edward and Dorothy Thompson had been Communist Party members; they joined in the war years, horrified by Hitler but critically ill-informed in regard to the Soviet Union and Stalin. In the crisis of 1956 (Hungary and Suez), they rebelled, left the Party, and became founders of a New Left, a British movement in an international current of dissident Communists. This movement was as well an early manifestation of the youth rebellions of the decade to come.

In the 1960s, Thompson created and then directed the prestigious Centre for the Study of Social History at the new Warwick University (1965–1970), where he was a labor historian, best known for "history from below," and a founder of the "new social history." In 1970, the Thompsons left Warwick for rural Worcestershire. He worked there as a free scholar, an independent writer, and a public intellectual, a critic of "the secret state" and a thorn in the side of Labour and Tory alike.[8] During these years, Thompson completed a series of magnificent essays on eighteenth-century England.[9]

In 1980, Thompson, alarmed by the late-1979 NATO decision to deploy Cruise and Pershing II missiles in Britain and across Western Europe, turned to full-time peace/anti-nuclear activism. He became a founder, then best-known spokesperson of END (European Nuclear Disarmament), a movement unique and distinct in that it linked its work with dissidents in the Soviet Union and its East-Central European Communist states. This last project reflected Thompson's lifelong antipathy to the Cold War and the division of Europe. END would attract millions, and, though ultimately unsuccessful in resisting the missile deployment, did much to undermine authority both in the East and West. And it accomplished this on the basis of a mass movement from below.[10]

The essays in this collection reflect Thompson and his work in the late 1950s and early 1960s when the Thompsons lived in Halifax. This was for Thompson a period of intense activity, editing, writing, and peace/political organizing, all the while raising a family and working full-time as a teacher in adult working-class education. This place and these years are the setting for the essays; they are the essential background for our subject, *E. P. Thompson and the Making of the New Left*. The essays reflect his work, his experience, and his outlook in a time perhaps not so well known as others in his life; yet these years were crucial in terms of the development of his teaching, writing, and political activism. They culminated, fifty years ago, in the publication of *The Making of the English Working Class*, an achievement that would at once overshadow virtually all his other work.

The Making came to have a life of its own, separate from this background and sometimes separate from Thompson as a real, living, working person. Perhaps this can be corrected—it needs to be. *The Making*, after all, was more than a history. It was, he insisted, a political work as well, "a polemic" and a call to arms. It was the result, in part, of a decade of work in the peace movement, then nearly another decade in the New Left. *The Making* was aimed not at the academy but principally at "his students, the Campaign for Nuclear Disarmament (CND), the Left Clubs," and those young workers, indifferent to the trade unions and the Labour Party, radicalized yet watching from the fringes of these movements.[11] It was, then, also a work of the *moment*. It was to be a sort of platform for the New Left. It was meant to connect his movement to that "long tenacious revolutionary tradition of the British commoner."[12]

The New Left, the *first* New Left, was born in 1956, the year that commenced with Nikita Khruschev's "secret speech" and ended jolted by the twin crises of Suez and Hungary.[13] The October-November Suez debacle in Egypt began with the British, French, and Israeli plot to seize the Suez Canal—just nationalized by the Egyptian president Gamal Abdul Nasser—then to overthrow his regime. Simultaneously, Soviet tanks crushed a workers' rebellion in Budapest, the Hungarian capital. "These two events," Stuart Hall, another founder of the New Left, recalled, "whose dramatic impact was heightened by the fact that they occurred within days of each other, unmasked the underlying violence and aggression latent in the two systems that dominated life at that time—Western Imperialism and Stalinism."[14] Hall himself was then "dragged backwards into Marxism, against the tanks in Budapest."[15]

In a complacent Britain, where the approved discourse fixed on apathy and affluence, the New Left was something new—a new movement, a "milieu."[16] It championed free, open discussion, debates, participation, demonstrations, marches, and sit-downs. Hilary Rose, the historian of science, remembers "the ferment" of the time, the "searching for a new kind of politics. New Left Clubs sprang up as places to debate ideas, rather than expound the correct line."[17] It advanced a socialism that considered cultural and social, as well as economic and political issues. It campaigned for a non-aligned left, independent of and in opposition to the two superpowers. In addition, it joined with the Campaign for Nuclear Disarmament (CND) in its campaigns against nuclear weapons and nuclear war. It was a revolutionary socialist movement, active in the trade union and labor movements.

The New Left, however, cast aside much of what then defined the revolutionary left. This included, first of all, abandoning traditional Communist norms, the consecration of the experience of the Russian Revolution, that is, the "road map" to revolution. It also rejected fetishizing the form and role of organization, that is, of Leninism and "The Party." Edward Thompson savaged this tradition, above

all Stalinism and its ideology, its determinism and cruel anti-humanism, its turning "men into things." The New Left was instead decentralized, non-hierarchical,
creative, experimental, and humanist.[18] It was a movement from below and its
intention was for socialism from below. Thompson's "Socialist Humanism" set
many of the political signposts for this movement, yet this was just one essay, one
in an outpouring of writing by his and others. The articles, books, and journals
that would come from this movement reveal an astonishing array of talent and
commitment: Thompson; Doris Lessing, writer; Stuart Hall, founder of cultural
studies; Christopher Hill, historian of the English Revolution; Paul Hogarth,
illustrator; Raymond Williams, historian of culture: John Saville, labor historian;
Lawrence Daly, coal miner; Ralph Miliband, political theorist; Raphael Samuel,
founder of the History Workshop; and many others.

Thompson's New Left essays illuminate this movement, its ideals, its causes,
and its practice, all invaluable for the historian of these years. They bring it back
to life, but they are of more than academic interest. Today we see a resumption
of a global resistance to capitalism—a resistance to its neoliberal armies and its
reinvigorated imperialism, its staggering inequalities, and its war on our planet.
This has inspired a new generation of activists. The essays here represent an
offering as well, a political gift to the new generation as it confronts capitalism
and empire. Confrontation, of course, brings questions that every generation
inevitably must face, questions the first New Left faced. Hard questions. What
is to be done? What are the alternatives? And also older ones: What is socialism? What are its values? How to get there, how to organize? The 1950s New
Left pursued a socialist renewal. What went wrong? What did they get right?
Our own traditions remain hidden, fractured, and incomplete. They too demand
rethinking, reworking, and renewal. Perhaps some guidance will be found here.

THE EXPERIENCE OF TOM MAGUIRE and his place in the history of northern
socialism present a rewarding introduction to Edward Thompson in these years.
"Homage to Tom Maguire" reveals not just what Thompson meant by "socialism
from below" but anticipates, as all these essays do, *The Making,* and it explains
by historical example the sort of socialist movement he wanted. Thompson saw
in Tom Maguire the potential of working people, the kind of young worker he
looked for in his own efforts in the first New Left. Maguire was the product of
the mills, brickyards, and gasworks of the West Riding, of communities where
squalid back-to-backs, open-privy middens, and "infant mortality rates (in some
districts) of over one in four" persisted. Children went into the mills at the age
of ten.[19] But also it was a place where memories were long and communities—
the Colne, Calder, and Holme valleys—were close-knit. Here "an 'alien agitator'
from outside would make little headway; but once the local leaders moved, the
whole community might follow."[20] This seems to have been the case in the West

Riding strikes of 1889, the great gas workers' victory in Leeds, and the defeated 1890 Mannington Mills strike in Bradford. Maguire was a poet as well ("Machine Room Chants"), but first of all a socialist, and, in what was the highest praise from Thompson, a socialist with "his boots on."[21] The Leeds strikes, in which Maguire played a critical part, were "a groundswell . . . at the rank-and-file level." They were "bottom-up" strikes, of the kind that Thompson had celebrated, as had Morris when he wrote of the 1889 London dockers: "They have knocked on the head the old slander against the lower ranks of labour."[22] The strikes embodied what Thompson valued in provincial socialism—the roots in community, the commitment to class struggle, and the thirst for political organization. These were the sorts of movements, Thompson believed, upon which a "socialism from the bottom up" might be built.

The 1890s were not the 1840s; there had been "improvements" since "the Hungry Forties." More had changed when the Thompsons moved to Halifax in 1948. Nevertheless, older conditions survived, both in memory and in fact. Poverty remained widespread in postwar Britain; it was a hard place for millions, even at the "end of austerity." It remained so, despite what the Tories said about abundance. The academy's "affluent worker" misleads us.[23] It's not surprising that Labour Party "statesmen" happily joined in this chorus.[24] But the fact was, as sociologist Peter Townsend would reveal, that poverty actually increased in the 1950s. He and Brian Abel-Smith, practitioners of a new, committed sociology, were relentless in exposing widespread deprivation; Townsend's work was just the beginning of a lifetime of challenging the official myths of an abolished poverty.[25]

The Thompsons' friend Richard Hoggart, author of *The Uses of Literacy*, the classic account of class and culture, said this of his native Leeds: "To a visitor, they are understandably depressing, these massed proletarian areas; street after regular street of shoddily uniform houses intersected by a dark pattern of ginnels and snickets (alleyways) and courts; mean, squalid and in a permanent half fog; a study in shades of dirty grey, without greenness or the blueness of sky. . . . There are houses fitted into the dark and lowering canyons between giant factories and the services which attend them; the barracks of an industry."[26]

The Thompsons came north to learn about class and working-class movements, thus the northern context demands emphasis. This is often dismissed, more often ignored, yet here were Labour's strongholds, where deprivation remained pervasive and class was ubiquitous.[27] Edward and Dorothy Thompson settled in Siddal, a working-class district on the edge of the Halifax. Dorothy had joined the Communist Party as a schoolgirl in Kent; Edward, following the example of his older brother, Frank, joined in 1942 at Cambridge, just before enlisting in the armed forces. They met at Cambridge and were reunited after the war, together joining international volunteers in the Yugoslav Youth Railway, working with a wide assortment of young people to build a crucial link in the national rail network. The project, they believed, represented "a new spirit in Europe," and an alternative to division and war. They would later reject the "Communism" that took them to the Balkans, but not the spirit they found there, which would inform their commitments right through their lives.[28]

The Thompsons started their family in Halifax with three children—Ben, Mark, and Kate. They were not like George Orwell, just passing through, on assignment.[29] They would stay well into the 1960s. Years later Dorothy would tell friends they regretted having left the West Riding. Their home, "a large, cold, hospitable gritstone house in the dark town of Halifax,"[30] became a vital center of activism, an "open house" for comrades and kids. Their friend Trevor Griffiths remembers that "the energy of the discussions in that house was palpable; you could smell the sweat from the arguments."[31] It was also a place for working-class neighbors. Some years later, in an editorial dispute with John Saville over a question of education policy, Edward in his defense responded, "Since the children of manual laborers [have been continuously] in and out of our house for the past ten years, I know something about this."[32] At issue was Thompson's dissatisfaction with socialists who confined educational policy to "provisions" and "equality of opportunity." He asked Saville, "What is education for?" and "What sort of life do we educate for?"[33] The Thompsons' door was open there in Halifax as well as in Leamington and later in Wick Episcopi; Julian Harber, a student and lifelong friend, remembers their "legendary hospitality"[34] and that this was their intention, to provide an open place for discussion, argument, and camaraderie.[35]

The Making of the English Working Class is dedicated to Dorothy Greenald, born in Hartshead, West Yorkshire, the daughter of a coal miner. She was among his first students: "Edward was almost working class, really, in his attitudes and warmth and friendliness. . . . I don't think I've ever had as long and close and warm a relationship with anyone than we had with Edward."[36] Hilary Rose attributed this to the anthropologist in him: "Listen, listen, listen . . ."[37]

Thompson wasn't working class, of course, far from it. He was raised in Boars Hill, at Oxford, educated at Kingswood School, Bath, and Cambridge (Literature). His father, also named Edward ("a tough liberal"), a missionary in India, a poet and writer, was a prominent anti-imperialist of his time, a leading advocate of independence for India. He taught Indian history at Oxford and lived Indian history in India. Edward Sr. was fluent in Tamil and Urdu; he lectured in Bengali and Sanskrit at Oriel College, Oxford. Edward's mother, Theodosia, an American, was also a missionary; she was teaching Arabic and French at an orphanage in Jerusalem when they met.[38] The gift for language was passed on to Frank, their elder son, allegedly favored and more gifted.[39] He is said to have mastered a score of tongues. India was ingrained in the Thompson home: its history and culture, its freedom fighters, its heroes. Edward the younger recalled he found it no surprise to learn that a visiting honored guest might just have been released from prison. On one such visit, he was given instructions in cricket batting by Jawaharlal Nehru.

Dorothy Thompson was also a historian; she and Edward were both associated with the now celebrated Communist Historians' Group,[40] organized by Dona Torr. "We were or tried to be good communists," writes Eric Hobsbawm, recalling the Group, "though only E. P. Thompson (who was less closely associated with the Group than Dorothy Thompson) was politically important enough to be elected to his District Party Committee."[41] The Group included not just the Thompsons but Hobsbawm, Christopher Hill, Victor Kiernan, R. H. Hilton, Maurice Dobb, James B. Jefferys, George Rudé, John Saville, and an assembly of others who in important ways rewrote English history. Thompson, first a poet and writer, must nevertheless have picked up some history in the Group. He also, at Torr's insistence, got the habit of getting things right empirically and learned the value of collective work. Thompson would recall "all the healthy ideas of collective intellectual work which we learned from Dona."[42]

In family history, it was agreed that, in addition to political work—he would chair the Halifax Peace Committee; he was secretary of the Yorkshire Federation of Peace Organizations; and he was editor of the *West Riding Peace Journal*—Edward would take full-time employment teaching. Dorothy would raise the children, as well as teach part-time (adult education), work in the Historians' Group, and continue political organizing. In the late 1940s she organized campaigns in the West Riding to keep wartime nurseries open.[43] She also worked in the peace movement, which in the early 1950s meant opposition to the U.S. role in the war in Korea, and began research on her lifetime interest, Chartism. Such arrangements were not so unusual in the forties,[44] but they were easier said than done, surely in the chaos of the Thompson house. It meant, among other things, that Dorothy's writings would be considerably postponed. In 1970, with the children mostly grown, she took a position as full-time lecturer at Birmingham University where she confirmed an esteemed place in her field and a permanently secure position in the historiography of Chartism.[45]

Edward Thompson in turn taught adult education, crisscrossing the heavily populated West Riding to meet small groups who signed up for courses on offer from the Leeds University Extramural Department and the Workers Education Association (WEA). The Leeds University Extramural Department's terrain was extensive, covering not only the densely populated West Riding of Yorkshire but also the huge, then remote and sparsely populated North Riding, stretching as far north as Middlesbrough on Teeside.[46] Thompson's home in Halifax was fifteen miles from Leeds, seventy-five miles from Middlesbrough. Most often these were three-year courses, twenty-four weeks per term and simply to learn, with no degrees, no certificates, and no promise of future employment.

Thompson was one in a generation of socialist educators—young people, nearly all veterans—who *chose* workers' education as an active alternative to elite education, just as the Thompsons chose to live in the provincial West Riding, purposely far from the metropolis. Workers' education was seen not just as avocation but as a movement for social change. These veterans turned teachers had been radicalized in the military; many had participated in the Cairo Parliaments and the shipboard assemblies. They had also participated in the politicized education on offer from the Army Bureau of Current Affairs, an official wartime incarnation of adult education, but one that Churchill suspected of spreading socialist ideas. It did. Frank Thompson had been a Unit Education Officer. His superior in Cairo Special Operations was fellow Communist James Klugmann.[47] Edward fought in North Africa and in the Italian campaigns; he was a tank commander in the terrible siege of Cassino (100,000 Allied casualties). One finds no hints of Soviet chauvinism in his writings; nor was he a patriot, and clearly he was not anti-British. The war for him was an anti-fascist crusade; he was, like his brother, a pan-European and internationalist.[48] The Thompsons shared the hopes of 1945: the idea was that there would be no going back to the old Britain and that they could do something about it. The hope was that "the old social class horribleness would be broken up forever."[49]

In a shabby old Rover, or sometimes on the bus, Thompson, carried with him books and papers, making his way to some village hall or schoolroom to meet with a dozen or fifteen people in order to talk about Wordsworth and Blake, Lawrence and Shakespeare, or the future of socialism, but especially the inheritance of these people and their West Riding communities: the connections between his students and their forebears—the weavers, spinners, miners, the Luddites, Chartists, and utopians.

Thompson taught in a score of towns and villages, including Cleckheaton, "one of Gradgrind's fortresses,"[50] a textile town in the Spen Valley, best known now as a setting for Charlotte Brontë's *Shirley* and for its history of Luddite risings. He taught in Shepley, a village in Kirklees that was home to four woolen mills in the nineteenth century and a place where Joseph Radcliffe from Milmsbridge House had been Lord of the Manor (he was knighted for his role in suppressing the Luddites in Huddersfield following the murder of a Marsden mill owner). He taught in Hemsworth, a mining village on the eastern border of the West Riding, the place with the biggest Labour majority in the country, where ballots for Labour were "weighed not counted," and where, he wrote to Saville in 1958, "The miners spit when they hear their MP and councilors mentioned."[51] Halifax itself was then a town of 80,000 in Calderdale in the South Pennines; its industries included woollens, carpets, machine tools. It was an important center of the early Independent Labour Party (ILP).[52]

The past may be another country, but not here, not this past. These towns, communities, even streets, remained close-knit; memories were long, old traditions persisted, and so much seemed never-changing. On this moor the Luddites drilled. In this valley, the Chartists assembled. Thompson found that in Maguire's Leeds "a quite remarkable proportion of the young men and women prominent in the early Yorkshire I.L.P. claimed Chartist forebears or the influence of Chartist's traditions in their childhood."[53]

The Industrial Revolution in Yorkshire was tangible, ever present. Saville, teaching at Hull, remembered an early trip to visit the Thompsons: "I took the train to Halifax, changing at Leeds. It was a journey that has remained in my mind. I was steeped in Chartist history and now here I was, seeing the towns and villages where I knew there had been Chartist meetings and gatherings, with wonderful names such as Sowerby Bridge, Hipperholme and Luddenden Foot. Edward met me at Halifax station and took me up to their house which overlooked part of the town."[54] Edward and Dorothy worked to make themselves part of this history; they passed it on as well, and not just in writing. Shelia Rowbotham, a pioneer in feminist history, was twenty-one when she first explored the Thompsons' library and learned from them the stories of Maguire, Alf Mattison, and Edward Carpenter. She soon began her own life of recovering hidden histories. "Through Dorothy and Edward Thompson there was a living connection to those early days of West Riding socialism. . . . Edward Thompson [told] . . . me about that northern socialism, how for a time preoccupation with changing all forms of human relationships had been central in a working-class movement."[55]

THE NAME EDWARD THOMPSON came to be synonymous with "history from below," a way of practicing and understanding history that became important in the 1960s and 1970s. "Edward didn't invent 'history from below,'" Dorothy Thompson told our memorial meeting at New York's Ethical Culture Center in late 1993. "He was just one of the best practitioners of it."[56] The "practitioner," however, did not just write about workers' history. He lived it as teacher, neighbor, friend, comrade. He lived with workers, he learned from workers, and it is this that made *The Making* unique, timeless. It was also the fact that Thompson was a master of the archives, the records, the citation; and it was this genius, fused with his perspectives, that enabled him to recover "forgotten evidence of class struggle" and the "invisible rules that govern behavior." In Britain, he argued, "an immense amount of existing historiography . . . has seen society within the expectations, the self-image, the apologetics, of a ruling class: 'the propaganda of the victors.'"[57] So to counter this, it was necessary to find not just what is "hidden in history" but also to challenge the official records, rebutting the lies of the record-keepers and giving a voice to those who had none. This was one of Thompson's great contributions.[58]

Moreover, Thompson's example encouraged in others a new freedom, surely for those of us working beyond the confines of the typical historians' hedges, seeking new ways of understanding the actualities of eighteenth- and nineteenth-century life.[59] His reach carried well beyond his initial discoveries, into innumerable new areas of investigation, clearing a path for working-class studies, women's history,[60] black history, cultural studies, and even the world of painting.[61] Here, as John Barrell has suggested, the "voices" of the painters—Gainsborough, Morland, Constable—could be extraordinarily powerful in shaping what we might call the official memory of the period, *the tradition* of Happy Britannia with "its good, deserving poor."[62] And yet, as Barrell wrote in *The Dark Side of the Landscape*, this freedom opened entirely new dimensions of work, among other things, by demanding research *against* that tradition and understanding the *"constraints"*— "often apparently aesthetic but in fact moral and social—that determined how the poor could, or rather how they could not be represented."[63] Further, this freedom challenged the way in which the tradition was used "to resist or to deny the creation of that consciousness," that is, that working-class consciousness revealed in *The Making.*[64]

Adult education was not easy work. It required discipline and a certain zealous commitment. As a young tutor, Thompson would explain that, on more than one occasion, "his aim was to make socialists, create revolutionaries and transform society."[65] Over time this was tempered, but teaching, like everything else for Thompson, was always political. It had its frustrations and disappointments. One class in Middlesbrough was a problem: "Two steelworkers (it is true) were on the provisional register, but despite the friendly atmosphere of the class, they did not appear to be at home, and did not go beyond the sixth meeting. . . . The tutor, who drove over eighty miles to the illuminated sky and glaring furnaces of the steel centers, found this disappointing."[66] A closer look, however, reveals that such complaints, his "disappointments," most often contain a core of self-criticism. What had he done wrong? How had he failed his students? What adjustments must he make? This is seen in his persistent appeals that even the least successful classes must not be cancelled. When his class at Hemsworth caused considerable administrative problems, Thompson stated that it was "important . . . that a branch of this quality, with a good tutorial record, should be kept alive in the heart of the Yorkshire coalfield."[67] Whatever the problems, they could be resolved; they must be kept going because "the alternative was surrender, surrender to false standards, surrender to the pressures of elitism."[68]

And how was this a problem? Just what were the "pressures of elitism"? As an example, Roger Fieldhouse tells us that in July 1950, Thompson submitted a paper to the Extramural Department, "Against University Standards," a twenty-five-page polemic, a critique of what he saw as the mistaken direction of the department.[69] It was not an argument contesting the aim of high-quality in-class work; it was not against excellence in teaching tutors or against the pursuit of good outcomes. Rather, it challenged what Thompson considered "a theory hostile to the healthy development of working-class adult education." The paper referred to a colleague's uncritical reference to John Henry Newman's[70] conception of the mission of the university, that is, as a place with the aim of fostering "a pure and clear atmosphere of thought . . . habits of mind formed to last through life, of which the attributes are, freedom, equitableness, calmness, moderation, and wisdom" often translated, Thompson explained, as "tolerance."[71] Thompson contested this notion of "tolerance" as an aim of education. He advanced this response: "A student, let us suppose, joins the class with a burning sense of class injustice or an attitude of compassion to his fellow workers. He desires to study economics in order to find the means of righting this injustice: or literature in order to enrich his life and that of his fellows." But, we are told, his process of study must aim to make an effective change in his "attitude." Thus, it follows, Thompson contended, that "we must deny the validity of the student's experience, and assert that the tutor, by virtue of a university education, is better fitted to judge both matters of fact and matters of attitude and behaviour." But "to prescribe an attitude of calmness, or moderation, or tolerance toward a society or social problems is to pre-judge that this attitude is an appropriate one. The exponents of this theory of 'objectivity' are not only agreeing to make available facts about society to their students, but are also claiming to dictate the students' response, and therefore, behaviour in relation to these facts."[72] In this case "the student is to change his persistent attitude from one of indignation or compassion to one of tolerance, only on the grounds that he was mistaken before and that the facts of society are such as merit toleration. And to do this we must deny the validity of the student's experience and assert that the tutor, by virtue of a university education is better fitted to judge both matters of fact and matters of attitude and behaviour." It seems, Thompson concluded, that the pursuit of the theory of "objectivity" and "tolerance" as the decisive aim of adult education "leads in the end to a theory of indoctrination" and that "this is a typical form of class indoctrination."[73]

This dispute seems not to have interfered with Thompson's teaching nor to have produced negative consequences. He would remain in the department for seventeen years. Most of Thompson's classes were in fact successful, both in themselves and in his pursuit of the history of the Industrial Revolution. Sometimes a class member was able to provide indirect, but personal, links to the period. At Cleckheaton the great-grandfather of a student had been named Feargus O'Connor after the Chartist leader.[74] At Batley a student "revealed herself in the last evening to have been a lifelong collector of old songs and ballads," and in his report Thompson quoted in full an example taken down "fifteen to twenty years ago" from "a blind workhouse inmate (who thought the song 'Chartist')," but which he himself judged plausibly as "an early (eighteenth century?) song—possibly sung at primitive trade-union ceremonies."[75]

"The mixture of students, old, young, verbose, garrulous, set the stage for an evening—unpredictable—exciting, anything could happen."[76] One student recalls, "I was struck by his sheer enthusiasm, also a little bit awed by his undoubted intellect, which, combined with his humor, and his articulate & graphic method of expression, made his classes fascinating."[77] Quite early on, he came to be seen as one of the Extramural Department's outstanding tutors. Bill Baker, a senior member of staff at Leeds, observed a 1949 class in Cleckheaton. He expected to find Thompson ill at ease because of his "lack of knowledge of the character of WEA classes." Instead, he was impressed "by the way the class participated with freedom and abandon."[78] This free expression was to be valued, above all by the tutor, the educator who, Thompson insisted, had as much to learn from the student's experience as to teach. In November Baker visited another of Thompson's classes, at Bingley. He reported, "In many respects this was one of the most satisfactory classes that I have ever visited. Thompson's work was quite first-class, both in his introduction of the subject (Dickens's *Hard Times*) and in stimulating the discussion."[79]

"I WENT INTO ADULT EDUCATION," Thompson recalled, "because it seemed to me to be an area in which I would learn something about industrial England and teach people who would teach me."[80] He did, and they did. It was in Halifax that both *William Morris* and *The Making* were written. *The Making*, Thompson wrote, was "written in Yorkshire, and is coloured at times by West Riding sources."[81] Originally, *The Making* was intended simply as a modest "industrial and social history" of West Riding, a guide for his students. He would sometimes refer to it as "my West Riding book." It was in the West Riding that he worked to rescue the forgotten histories, and to implant these in a tradition right up to the present, fusing that tradition with the movement for socialism in his own time. He wrote for his students, for the young trade unionists, the CND, and the New Left. He also wrote, in Morris's sense, to "make socialists," showing, as Hobsbawm once observed, "little distinction between how the world is *and* how it ought to be." Thompson moved easily to what needs to be done.[82]

The Making of the English Working Class, a 900-page volume, was completed in less than three years. This astonishing accomplishment remained something of a puzzle of "just how the book got itself written" even to Thompson himself. In 1980, looking back, he explained, "In 1959–62 I was also heavily engaged in the work of the first New Left, the Campaign for Nuclear Disarmament, and so on. The writing was only possible because some part of the research had already been laid down during the previous ten years in the course of my work as a tutor in extramural classes in the West Riding."[83]

Published to great acclaim, *The Making* was instantly recognized as a classic. It is now in its fiftieth year of uninterrupted publication. In an editorial, *The Guardian* of 26 December 2013 recalled its "elegance and dedication." "No historian of British society has since produced a book to match E. P. Thompson's *The Making of the English Working Class*. . . . The book crackles with energy, as it uses *scraps of evidence* such as popular songs and workshop rituals to paint a picture of workers' lived 'experience'" (emphasis in original).[84] It is no surprise, thinking back, that *The Making* came as something of a shock in its field. It was written by a virtually unknown lecturer in adult education; its author was self-taught, without an advanced degree, with no attachment to a prestigious institution or department. His use of poetry, song, broadsheets, made academics flinch. Indeed, *The Making* quite literally burst the complacency of history departments. Iain Boal has written that it sent "shock waves" through "the polite smoking rooms" of quiescent universities and "permanently changed the landscape of that epoch."[85] *The Making* was a defiant *challenge* to academic history, a counternarrative to the official record—for example, his contention that "the Industrial Revolution was imposed not on raw material but on free-born Englishmen."[86] Thompson's humanism transformed social history, and the history of the Industrial Revolution has never been the same since. Nor has the conclusion to the school days' debate "progress or poverty" been more contested. Progress? he asked. "I do not mean to deny the positive evidence," he wrote, but "growth can be a misleading term. Suffering is not just wastage on the margin of growth: for those who suffer it is absolute."[87] Assessing the period, Thompson wrote, "There was intensified exploitation, greater insecurity, and increasing human misery. By 1840 most people were 'better off' than their fore-runners had been fifty years before, but they had suffered and continued to suffer this slight improvement as a catastrophic experience."[88] Thompson had a keen sense of the heavy price of progress. *The Making* placed Edward Thompson with Dickens and Engels and Gaskell as a chronicler of one of history's great transformations.

On this side of the Atlantic, *The Making* helped clear a path in a widening challenge to the nation's official record of compromise, consensus, and conservatism. Of course, the civil rights movement was the major force in exploding all this. But *The Making* added to the progress achieved in our understanding of just how debilitating, how disarming the ideology of classlessness, or "we're all middle class," was then, and is now. Thompson raised the forbidden banners of class, banners then half-buried in the wreckage of post-McCarthy America. These were not just the banners of old, however; they were not those that upheld the deterministic categories of the Old Left. Thompson's notion of class was set free of these. He argued that class was not a "thing"; it was a "historical phenomenon . . . that must be embodied in real people and in a real context." Thompson's assertion that the working class "made itself as much as it was made" was a provocation and also a revelation.[89] It raised the question of "agency," and from this followed "self-activity." This renewed, deeper vision of class was indispensable if a new generation was to make any sense at all of the conflicts and new movements of the 1960s.[90]

"I COMMENCED TO REASON in my thirty-third year, and, despite my best efforts, I have never been able to shake the habit off."[91]

> I first acquired the habit in 1956, when, with John Saville and others, I was involved in producing a duplicated journal of discussion within the Communist Party, *The Reasoner*. Reasoning was disliked by the leadership of the Party, and the editors were suspended from membership. Since this suspension coincided with the repression of the Hungarian revolution (October/November 1956)—and the exodus of some 10,000 members from the British Communist Party—it was decided that our offensive activities might be continued outside the structure, and, with the aid of other comrades, *The New Reasoner* was founded in 1957. This quarterly journal continued for 2 ½ years.[92]

Thus the immediate origins of the *first* New Left. Saville recalls, "We were highly committed Party members who had come through the tough and difficult years of the Cold War—more difficult than is often appreciated." He recalled "personal experiences" with others "who had left the Party to cultivate their own gardens, or of those who had left to become, in our eyes, renegades."[93] At the same time, he remembers, "we had both been emotionally, politically and morally shocked at the revelations of what Stalinism really meant, and as Communists and historians we saw clearly that we were obliged to analyze seriously the causes of the crimes which in the past we had defended or apologized for."[94]

The first issue of *The Reasoner* sold out in a few weeks. The second issue was published twenty-four hours before the September meeting of the CP Executive Committee, a meeting for which the agenda included the demand that Thompson and Saville cease publication immediately or be suspended. The production of *The Reasoner* was no small task; it fell largely on Saville, Dorothy Thompson, and Edward Thompson. Nevertheless, a third issue was scheduled for November. "Edward typed all the stencils—in a note to a correspondent I [Saville] remarked that Edward had typed nearly 40,000 words on stencils . . . in five days' time; and he similarly typed the whole of the longer third issue."[95]

It was the rebellion and then the bloody repression in Hungary that stunned the Thompsons and shook the world of Communism. "Stalinism has sown the wind," Edward Thompson responded, in an emotional appeal to his movement, "and now the whirlwind centers on Hungary. As I write the smoke is still rising above Budapest."[96] He asked, rhetorically, "Where is my party in Hungary?" but there was no answer from King Street, the Party headquarters in London; instead, "by an angry twist of history, it seems that the crop is coming up as students', workers' and soldiers' councils, as 'anti-Soviet' soviets."[97] The news of the rebellion, of the tens of thousands of workers and students taking to the streets, the scenes of the street battles, now to be seen on television, the spectacle of unarmed workers and students confronting Soviet tanks, then, two days after Suez, the bloody repression, all this could mean only one thing: "This was the end." "It meant a profound break," recalled Dorothy Thompson. "It was the finish of old-style politics, the old block of ice."[98] And for Edward Thompson, "No chapter would be more tragic in international socialist history, if the Hungarian people, who once before lost their revolution to armed reaction, were driven into the arms of the capitalist powers by the crimes of a Communist government and the uncomprehending violence of Soviet armies."[99]

The events in Budapest, staggering as they were, found the Thompsons not entirely unprepared. Dorothy Thompson suggested that "most of those who left the Party in 1956 also had a name within for being critical,"[100] and "the Reasoners," as journal supporters called themselves, "none of [us] came from Communist families, all had joined the party in the late thirties or early forties as a conscious choice. These were the years of the failed defense of the Spanish government and the attempts at building a Popular Front against fascism in Europe."[101]

The Thompsons had been committed Party members; they followed the line. They believed in the values of loyalty and discipline. Still, they were critics; one need not look far for the evidence of this. Thompson's long 1950 poem, "A Place Called Choice," concludes, "I declare that man has choice," a conviction he would make prominent in the New Left outlook; his second contribution to *The New Reasoner* was titled "Agency and Choice."[102] Thompson had not been a Party puritan; his bohemian Boars Hill youth was never quite forgotten. He shared much with his beloved brother Frank Thompson, whose biographer tells us that Frank joined at a time when "idealism, romanticism and a passionate anti-fascism came together to move the best of a generation leftwards. . . . His pull towards Communism lay in its promise of universal brotherhood, an imaginary politics of kindness, caring and compassion and the belief in a utopian future to stand against the evident bankruptcies of capitalism and the nightmare world of Fascism." He joined when "Iris [Murdoch] showed [him] how gentle and artistic communists could be." The young brother, also the writer and poet, under the spell of Wordsworth, Blake, Morris, could hardly have been immune to this.[103]

The Suez adventure ended in ignominious retreat, forced by the Americans and marking yet another blow to Britain's illusions of Empire. Only for the Israelis was the operation a success, inspiring both its military and enhancing its appetite. The Tories muddled through, but Labour's opposition, tortuously arrived at, gave space for a growing youth opposition, which would be a factor in the early successes of the Campaign for Nuclear Disarmament (CND) and the New Left. "The events of 1956 in the Eastern bloc," according to historian and peace activist James Hinton, "opened the way for a younger generation of socialists to take up once again the abandoned search for a third way between Stalinist authoritarianism and American hegemony. Khrushchev's denunciations of Stalin in 1956 threw the world communist movement into crisis." Hinton suggests that "the Hungarian revolution lifted the spell of 'Nineteen Eighty-Four,' reviving the possibility of building a genuinely democratic socialism in Eastern Europe."[104] In a February 1957 letter, Doris Lessing, who had joined the Communist Party as a young girl in Southern Rhodesia, wrote Thompson, "I feel as if I've been let out of a prison."[105]

Thompson's own retrospective (from 1960) was this: "1956 marks the watershed. In the first place, since 1956, there has been a world-wide and continuing movement of Communist dissidence which (if we overlook—as we should—Mr. Howard Fast) has not entered into the worn paths of traumatic anti-communism, God-That-Failedism, Encounterism, and the rest; but which has, on the contrary, sought to affirm and develop the humane and libertarian features of the Communist tradition."[106]

Thompson's "reasoning" was political and always practical.[107] It began with the appeal addressed to the world of "dissident communism." It then became a keystone in the collective project to create a New Left. By the spring of 1957, the Thompsons and Saville had published the first issue of the *New Reasoner*, "a quarterly journal of socialist humanism," based in the industrial North. There was from the start a North/South issue in the New Left, the North always closer to the trade unions and the labor movement. *The New Reasoner* editorial board included Doris Lessing, Ken Alexander, Peter Worsley, and Malcolm MacEwen. In succeeding issues contributors would include Ralph Miliband, Ronald Meek, Tibor Dery, G. D. H. Cole, Claude Bourdet, Raymond Williams, Tom Mboya, Dora Scarlett, Christopher Hill, C. Rajagopalachari, Michael Barrett-Brown, Alasdair MacIntyre, Victor Kiernan, and Dorothy Thompson.

That same spring a group of independent socialists at Oxford, including Stuart Hall and Raphael Samuel, produced the first issue of *Universities and Left Review*.[108] These two journals, along with the emergence of the CND in early 1958, became the institutional foundations of the new movement. Together they sought to rekindle the "moral imagination" of the British people. They developed, of course, in the midst of Britain's wider cultural revolution—*Look Back in Anger, Room at the Top*, and similar plays and films—in the late 1950s and early 1960s. And in this context, the New Left "displayed an expansive and apparently tireless dynamism, accumulating an imposing set of political properties and insignia, the tokens and titles of an estate of presumable substance."[109] In 1960 the two journals merged to form the *New Left Review*.[110]

Thompson, describing *The New Reasoner* as a journal of dissident Communists, remained for a time reluctant to abandon the term Communist. One reason was to make it clear that any new movement would have nothing whatsoever to do with "the God that failed" phenomenon, that is, the parade of notable ex-Communists entering service for the West. Richard Crossman's 1949 anthology of that name included Arthur Koestler, Richard Wright, André Gide, Louis Fisher, and Stephen Spender. Another reason was his insistence on what he then believed to be loyalty to a Communist tradition, a tradition reaching back not only to Marx and Engels but also to Morris and the first English socialists.

Thompson saw *The New Reasoner* as "polemical, engaged intellectual work," not as "a political ginger group in the labour movement" but as a vital part of a new, independent left; a broad but revolutionary left, committed to socialist renewal, and independent of but not hostile to the labor movement and the Labour Party.[111] The main enemy became the "Natopolitans."[112] Thompson was no anarchist, but neither was he sympathetic to Trotskyism, believing correctly, I think, that, though critics of Stalinism, the Trotskyists carried over into opposition much of its baggage, "the same false conceptual framework and attitudes—the same economic behaviourism, cult of the elite, moral nihilism."[113] The *New Reasoners*, in Hinton's words, "were frankly revisionist and uninterested in a return to Leninist purity. Harking back to the days of the Left Book Club—and, less explicitly, to the socialist revival of the 1880s and 1890s— Thompson urged the 'active minority of convinced socialists' not to lock themselves up in a new 'vanguard' or in the mere resolution mongering within the Labour Party."[114] He wrote to Saville, concerned that "we [not] just jump from one cozy in-group to another."[115]

Edward Thompson was not "the leader" of the first New Left; by definition it had no leader. Nevertheless, he played a critical role, as thinker—"reasoner"— writer, organizer, and foot soldier. Certainly his piece "Socialist Humanism," though subject of fierce debate in the New Left, including in the pages of *The New Reasoner* itself, was central in defining the political parameters of the movement. The New Left was diverse; it had neither a single political line nor a particular agenda. It was organized largely around its publications, *The New Reasoner* and the *Universities and Left Review*, and *The New Left Review*. The anthology *Out of Apathy* (1960), a symposium of ideas and ideals edited by Thompson, was an intellectual *tour de force*. Contributors were Thompson, Ken Alexander, Stuart Hall, Ralph Samuel, Peter Worsley, and Alasdair MacIntyre. The best-known New Left ventures, aside from those of the journals, involved the creation of the Left Clubs and participation and influence in the CND, where it pressed for unilateralism and independence from the Labour Party.

The clubs (by 1960, there were thirty or forty of them scattered across the country) became the real centers of radical thinking and activity in these years. The Partisan Café in Carlisle Street, Soho, the first of the radical coffeehouses in London, was especially significant. It was largely the creation of Raphael Samuel, one of the "younger" generation. In 1962, Samuel began what became a life of teaching adult education at Ruskin College, Oxford. In the early years, the London Club attracted several hundred people to its weekly meetings.[116] Hilary Rose recalls "the Partisan" and still identifies "as one of the enthusiastic youth who flocked to the Left Clubs in the early sixties." She remembers "the excitement, hearing speakers like Tom Mboya and Desmond Bernal, people she never thought she'd hear in person."[117] One club campaigned against "ugly" buildings. Another, Stuart Hall records, concerned "the deep involvement in 1958 with the race riots in Notting Hill and with the anti-racist struggles of the period around North Kensington." The clubs worked to establish tenants' associations and "helped to protect black people who, at the height of the 'troubles,' were molested and harassed by white crowds."[118] Dorothy Thompson remembers "the arguments and discussions which went on in and around the clubs about the family, open marriage, child rearing, and such matters were often too intense to be reduced to print, although some interesting fragments remain."[119] The writer and filmmaker Trevor Griffiths attended a 1961 summer school held just outside Otley, in the Yorkshire Dales: "Peter Worsley was there, so was John Rex, Ken Coates, Anderson came, so did Stuart Hall and Edward, of course. It was a terrific school; there was a striking lack of pomposity in the New Left, also a detestation of rank. The school was full of arguments, we argued about everything; in the end no one was right, no one wrong. And we played bad table tennis."[120]

The CND emerged in 1957 in reaction to Prime Minister Harold Macmillan's announcement of the development of a British thermonuclear arsenal, then the testing of a British hydrogen bomb at Christmas Island. It was founded in 1958 by a group of intellectuals, including Bertrand Russell, Julian Huxley, and A. J. P. Taylor. Its first rally that spring was the hugely successful Central Hall meeting (5,000 attended with a 1,000-person overflow); this was followed by the first of the Aldermaston marches. Thousands walked for four days to the Atomic Weapons Research Establishment at Aldermaston in Berkshire. The *Mail* ran this firsthand account: "I am writing this sitting on a grass verge of a country lane in Berkshire. During the past forty-five minutes nearly 5,000 people in a marching column three miles long have trudged past on this, the first day of the anti–H bomb march from Aldermaston to London. These marchers—men, women, and children—have come from all over Britain and many parts of Europe and the Commonwealth. And at late evening it looked like [it was] developing into the biggest single demonstration since the war."[121]

Subsequent marches increased in size and were welcomed by tens of thousands in London; by 1960 100,000 Easter demonstrators had gathered in Trafalgar Square.[122] The relationship between CND and the New Left was deep; Thompson believed that many of the thousands of those "left homeless" became CND stalwarts.[123] Within CND, Thompson argued for "a dynamic movement outside the Labour Party and free from its bureaucratic gags and tactical chloroform.[124] The sit-downs, like the Aldermaston marches, take the issues beyond conference halls and committee rooms to the 'arena of the whole nation.'"[125] CND declined in the early 1960s, though antiwar sentiment continued to define left-wing thinking and activity.[126]

In retrospect, the CND's significance is difficult to exaggerate, as is the New Left's influence within it. The CND's decentralized structures (in spite of its "leaders"), its grassroots formations, direct action, sit-downs, mass marches, and political independence—some of these forms borrowed from the civil rights movement in the United States—came to characterize the New Left movements nearly everywhere. It prefigured the social movements to come. CND has been represented as a "middle-class" movement; this was true only to a degree. Its base, as Thompson, anticipating the 1960s, and others were quick to see, included thousands of young workers, blue-collar as well as white. These people were representatives of a generation of young people who would, in time, move beyond the parameters established by the Labour Movement. "The young marchers of Aldermaston," Thompson wrote, "despite all immaturities and individualistic attitudes, are at root more mature than their critics on the Old Left. They have understood that 'politics' have become too serious to be left to the routines of politicians." And, he asked, "As for 'moral and spiritual values,' what can the Old left or Old Right offer, after all?"[127]

The British trade unions in the 1950s often tilted right. The Labour Party, led by Hugh Gaitskell, was divided; it exuded "the enfeeblement of the energies . . . [that] brought it to power in 1945."[128] The unions tended to be rigid, and entrenched leaderships were the rule, left and right. They were, however, well organized with strong militant currents within them; the 1956 shift to the left of the Transport Workers, led by Frank Cousins, though unexpected, would have long-term implications.[129] "Power at the Base," the title of an article by Ken Alexander, argued for a rejection of Fabianism, Labourism, and reformism.[130] Thompson granted the influence of Labourism: "The workers, having failed to overthrow capitalist society, proceeded to warren it end to end."[131] But he detected fractures within "the rank-and-file mood," "unofficial strikers," the "blue union" of the docks, and the rebellion led by the shop stewards at Briggs Motor, Dagenham.[132]

The Left Clubs, for Thompson, were to be "discussion-centers . . . places beyond the reach of the bureaucracy, where the initiative remains in the hands of the rank-and-file. If the bureaucracy reacts by anathemas and prescriptions, the clubs and publications will continue, staffed by socialists who are members of no party, but who intend to provide service to the whole movement."[133] And this indeed was the case with the clubs and CND; Thompson himself was one such socialist—teacher, writer, and activist. However, he was not without complaints. He wrote to Raphael Samuel:

> I have also SIX CLASSES, plus additional teaching for hospital adminis-trators (NINE classes this week) plus being on four Department Com-mittees, plus three children who keep having Guy Fawkes and birthdays, plus a miraculous growth of YCND (Youth CND) and CND in Hali-fax this past two months—which after so many dead years we can't just ignore (from nought to 150 YCND in two months!)—plus the corre-spondence of Chairing a Board (of New Left Review) you may have heard of. My only affinity to Marx is that I get boils on my neck.[134]

THOMPSON WAS GUARDED in assessing perspectives, yet optimistic as well—too optimistic, as things turned out. In his May 1959 New Reasoner article, "The New Left," he wrote that it was "scarcely identifiable in terms of organization—a few journals, several clubs, successful educational work." Yet he saw openings in Britain, "a mood which is very widely diffused both within the traditional labour movement and outside it." The "mood" expressed itself in "participation in the nuclear disarmament movement, which may soon precipitate in more specifi-cally socialist form." Then he was inspired by the participation of young people, both in CND and in response to the New Left movement. He also believed that in Britain "the 1956 dissidence with the Communist movement coincided with Mr. Bevan's accommodation with Mr. Gaitskell and the disorientation of the tra-ditional Labour left."

In these circumstances, he set some parameters, argued for and against poli-tics and forms, and for the New Left he envisioned. This included the recurring theme of the fight for socialism, for socialist renewal, he argued, must be in the here and now. The New Left "must not wait hopefully for the old disasters and repressions to engender the old defensive responses." On the contrary, its task is "to discover the new frustrations and potentials within contemporary life, the new growing-points. The way forward for Socialism lies not in frightening the children of the 1950s with the Ogre of the 1930s (although, true enough, he may still be lurking around), but in pointing the way to the great enrichment of social life potential within our society today. Enduring militancy is built not upon neg-ative anxieties but upon positive aspirations." At the same time, he contested Crosland's U.S.-inspired politics of affluence and consumption, arguing that Crosland had capitulated to the "mythology of prosperity" and was in reality offering up "the American tourist's dream" replete with "open-air cafes, brighter and gayer streets, later closing hours for public houses." Instead, Thompson contended, "Men do not want only the list of things which Mr. Crosland offers; they want also to change themselves as men. However fitfully and ineffectively, they want other and greater things: they want to stop killing one another: they want to stop this pollution of their spiritual life which runs through society as the rivers carried their sewage and refuse through our nineteenth century industrial towns; side by side with their direct economic interests, they would like to 'do benefits' to each other."

He challenged the Old Left argument that "apathy" in the labor movement was due exclusively to the machinations of the bureaucracy (either Transport House or King Street) and the treachery of the leaders. "This convenient excuse enables the Old Left to fall back upon the old repertoire of militant slogans, and to evade the labour of analysing the actual social forces which have contributed to the rise of bureaucracy and which enable the leadership to maintain its power." This permits the Old Left "to idealize a mythical militant working class . . . a working class which is far more a construct from passages of Lenin and/or Trotsky than a derivation from actual observation of the real tensions and conflicts of contemporary working-class life."

Thompson's prescriptions for the trade unions and the labor movement translated into a "bottom up" perspective for socialists. Their task was not to "lead" the workers—he had no time for "vanguards"—but to "assist in the education of a new generation of dedicated socialist leaders in the trade union and labour movements" who "must be dedicated to the enlistment of the people, in the participation, at every level of the exercise of power."

A democratic, revolutionary strategy, Thompson argued, would demand "a common strand of wage and ethical demands"; it would be built on education and research, with journals, books, Left Clubs. It would demand "the exchange of ideas between specialists and those whose experience—in nationalized industry or in local government—enables them to see more clearly than the theorist the limits of the old system, the growing-points of the new."[135]

Most of all, he believed, it would demand "a brake with parliamentary fetishism which supposes that all advance must wait upon legislative change." Most "popular gains," he argued, "have been won, in the first place, by direct action: direct action to increase wages, improve working conditions, shorter hours, build co-ops, found nursery schools."[136] And they have been won by struggle.

The club of the greatest interest, perhaps the one closest to Thompson's own perspectives, was not a club at all, but the Fife Socialist League. It was founded by Lawrence Daly, the coal miner and the League's chief spokesperson. In 1956 Daly publicly tore up his CP card; in 1959, he founded the League as a political discussion forum from which it could launch independent candidates. He joined CND in 1957. (In 1968 Daly would become the National Secretary of the National Union of Mineworkers (NUM); he steered the union through the great strikes of 1972 and 1974.[137])

Daly was on the board of both New Left journals; he was a contributor as well. In 1957 he became an independent county councillor in Fife.[138] In the 1959 general election he contested West Fife, the seat held by the CP between 1935 and 1950. Thompson and John Saville managed his campaign.[139] The campaign was independent, grassroots, and socialist, exactly, one suspects, what Thompson wanted. He, Dorothy Thompson, and the Dalys were personal friends; in Scotland the Thompsons stayed at Glencraig with Daly and his wife, Renee, on both private and political visits, and the Thompsons reciprocated. An anecdote, retrieved by historian David Kynaston, captures Thompson, the activist, "with his boots on." Responding in Halifax to a request from Daly, Thompson writes: "It's just possible we might find a speaker for you. But not a van. People just don't have vans to lend around." He could offer, however, some help: "Look," he wrote, "this Ernest Rodker is a first-class lad. He is what a young socialist comrade ought to be heart, soul and body in the cause. He has imitative and good ideas. He is willing to listen and learn. He has proved himself an organizer—did most of the publicity in London for the first Aldermaston. It would be good for him. The only problem? A beard. I have written to him and suggested to him he takes off his beard. If he does, I am telling you Bro., you will damn well have him for your campaign and you will thank us all afterwards."[140]

Nationally, the elections produced a heavy defeat for Labour; in Fife, Daly finished third, with 5,000 votes, well ahead of the Communist Party candidate.[141]

THE THOMPSON FAMILY PAPERS remain closed at their request and will be closed for some time to come. On this subject, Dorothy Thompson routinely advised, "If you want to know about Edward, you had best read his writing."[142] The articles collected here are presented in that spirit and with the hope they fill a gap; these New Left writings have until now been scattered, unpublished, or difficult to retrieve. This book represents just a selection of Thompson's many New Left writings; in the years 1956–62 he was prolific as always. The book begins with his appeal to fellow Communists, "Through the Smoke of Budapest," published in the mimeographed *Reasoner,* and concludes with three historical pieces: a lecture on William Morris, whose spirit informs all of Thompson's writings: "The Free-born Englishman," published first in the *New Left Review,* later in revised form as an important chapter in *The Making of the English Working Class.* Here he finds Thomas Paine, the champion of an ideal he himself cherished: "It was Paine who put his faith in the free operation of opinion in the 'open society': mankind are not now to be told they should not think or they should not read."[143] The third historical piece, "Homage to Tom Maguire," "the poet, propagandist and sagacious organizer," was first published in a collection honouring the historian G. D. H. Cole. Here Thompson anticipates the Preface to *The Making* with insistence on history from the bottom up. Maguire, Thompson argues, represents "the provincial leaders, commonly denied full citizenship . . . the marginalized and the hidden from respectable history."[144]

These pieces bookend a set of polemics from *The New Reasoner, The Universities and Left Review,* and the *New Left Review. The New Reasoner* essays are "Socialist Humanism" and "The New Left." *The Universities and Left Review* pieces presented here are "Socialism and the Intellectuals" and "Commitment in Politics," in which Thompson addresses "classlessness" but also offers a critique of tendencies to sentimentalize the old working class, misusing, he argues, Richard Hoggart's *The Uses of Literacy.* He worries about "an evasion of class struggle" and is skeptical about theories of "consumer capitalism." While praising *ULR* writers and readers, and the young middle-class activists of the day, he responds: "Let us keep steadily in view the realities of class power in our time: the community to which we look forward is potential only within our working-class movement."[145] From the *New Left Review* we have "Revolution Again" and "The Long Revolution," I & II, Thompson's review of Raymond Williams's classic *The Long Revolution.* Thompson discusses various "notions of revolution," while keeping his distance from the "cultural critique," that is, Williams's idea of "a whole way of life," counterposing to this "a whole way of struggle."[146] From *Out of Apathy* we have "At the Point of Decay," and "Revolution." And finally, unpublished until now, is "Where Are We Now?," Thompson's reflections on the state of things in 1963, the year of crisis for the first New Left.

"Socialist Humanism" continues to be the essential document for these years. It (and the continuation in "Agency and Choice") came to define the core politics of the first New Left; Dorothy Thompson described it as "a first attempt to anatomize Stalinism and the policies of the non-Soviet communist parties by someone who had only just come up for air."[147] It is still the most discussed (and criticized) of his contributions in these years.[148] Readers will judge its merits for themselves, but this might be the place to acknowledge the important cautionary recommendations made by Madeleine Davis, a leading historian of the British New Left: "We should be careful not to abstract 'socialist humanism' from the political context and purpose of Thompson's writing at this time and from the collective project of the New Left. . . . In keeping with Thompson's view of 'theory as provisional' and as polemic, socialist humanism is better viewed less as a fully articulated position than as a polemical and provisional starting point, as an ethical sensibility rather than a theory. . . . It is not one static position but rather describes the developing project that Thompson said ran through all his work, an attempt to recover and claim for socialism a 'lost vocabulary' of agency and moral choice. He pursued this through his histories."[149]

In this context, "Socialist Humanism" is an extraordinary document. It is an indictment that sweeps through the basic tenets of a whole worldview, one that, in theory, was representative of half the globe. It is also, importantly, a redefinition of socialism, and, however provisional, a beginning of perspectives, of a platform, for a new left. The background to this, of course, is the Khrushchev revelations, the purge trials, forced collectivization, the famines, and all the unfolding realities of the barbarities of Soviet rule. Thompson's subject here, however, is Stalinism as *ideology*, its anti-humanism, its projection, for example, of the idea that socialism can be defined and evaluated in terms of industrial output, its success or failure measured in tons of steel. Yet also, and not coincidentally, one finds in these pages the themes and arguments that are the foundation upon which *The Making*, and virtually all of Thompson's writings, are built. There is, for example, the idea that socialism is "not only economically practicable" but also "intensely *desirable*" and that socialism "would revolutionize human relationships, replacing respect for property by respect for man, and replacing the acquisitive society by the common weal."[150]

At the same time, Thompson asserts, "a long derided trend within the socialist movement appears to be reviving Utopian (or 'Socratic') socialism, that is, the vindication of the right of the moral imagination to project an ideal to which it is legitimate to aspire; and the right of the reason to enquire into the aims and ends of social arrangements, irrespective of questions of immediate feasibility: in brief, to ask questions of the order of 'Why?' and not only 'How?'"[151] At the same time, he offers a critique of "extravagances of utopianism," warning that "the value of utopianism is to be found not in raising banners in the wilderness, but in confronting living people with an image of their own potential life, in summoning up their aspirations so that they challenge the old forms of life, and in influencing such social choices as there are in the direction that is desired. Utopianism and realism should not form into rival contingents; they should quarrel in a constructive way in the heart of the same movement."[152]

WHAT HAPPENED? LOOKING BACK, 1959–60 was the heyday of both the New Left and the CND; the early 1960s brought decline in the clubs, then the disappearance of the New Left as a visible, tangible phenomenon. Its diversity, so vital in its early success, might have become a burden. Its financial resources were never adequate; then there was the organization issue, and the ever-present Labour Party conundrum: in or out or what? How to assess this? Dorothy Thompson, in "On the Trail of the New Left," takes issue "with the repeated suggestion that the New Left somehow 'failed.'"[153] She suggests that "in the long run, these years can be seen as the beginning of a long political rethinking of the problem of approaching the ideal of a just society."[154] Many of the themes and perspectives developed in the pages of New Left journals certainly persisted.

Edward Thompson's writings are among the best examples. The attempts at a unified movement, of permanent organization, with the Left Clubs in particular, never really got off the ground. The idea of a nonaligned left, however, endured, "in organizations like the Institute for Workers Control, CND and some parts of the Labour Party and the trade-union movement, where [the New Leftists] fought for a non-aligned position against the communists and fellow-travellers, on the one hand, and the Natopolitan social democrats, on the other."[155]

But if the "movement" disappeared, the *New Left Review* did not. The new editor of *New Left Review*, Perry Anderson, and the editorial "team" he constructed in 1963 would have disagreed with the above assessment, I think. Certainly one sees in the journal a dramatic revision in style, perspectives, and politics. Anderson himself, reflecting in 1974, wrote: "The mainstream of '56 proved in the end surprisingly thin, and left rather little trace."[156] I have included "Where Are We Now?" partly in response to this but also because it represents critical arguments in the political divide that is commonly seen to separate the New Lefts, first and second. It should be read along with "The Peculiarities of the English," Thompson's best-known assessment of these disputes. That essay is not included here due to its length and also because it has been reprinted and is easily available.[157]

"Where Are We Now?" was no doubt left unpublished for obvious reasons: it is a difficult piece and publishing it might have been seen as contrary to the notion that these were disputes best left buried and reconciliation sought. It is an angry piece; at the time Thompson believed the journal had been captured in a "coup." Over time, fences were mended. The team refused to publish "Peculiarities of the English," but later would carry articles by Thompson. Robin Blackburn was a member in 1963 of the Anderson team; his 1993 obituary, "Edward Thompson and the New Left," is a moving and thought-provoking reconsideration of both Thompson and the issues of the divide. It deserves the appreciation of all concerned.[158] "Where Are We Now?" is included here not to rekindle the flames. Rather, reading it today, it seems relevant and important, its points of contention were crucial then; it suggests fundamental issues for the New Left to come: the Third World, the meaning of "internationalism," violence, the role of socialists, theory and practice. Certainly, these issues, however controversial, came to bewitch much of the "new" New Left, and in truth, this "new" New Left was tripped up by most of them. "Where Are We Now?," then, fills an important gap in assessing the left, not just the first New Left, but that of the whole period, including the New Left of the 1960s. It remains of interest. As for the *New Left Review*, its appeal was reduced to a rather limited audience and it is still with us today. Theory, often originating on the continent, became its mainstay; practice was abandoned altogether. The writers and readers of the old *Review* withdrew and were scattered; the movement of the 1960s would have no journal to educate, activate, and unite it.

FINALLY, I SHOULD REPEAT HERE, there was more than one Edward Thompson. He was a poet, tank commander, Communist, teacher, historian, founder of the New Left, public intellectual, spokesperson for END, and an active socialist for more than fifty years. People expecting a political consistency, therefore, will inevitably be disappointed—there were indeed transitions. I have deliberately avoided the issue of his larger transitions, aside from his departure from and dispute with the Communist Party, and focused only on the New Left years.[159] But the fact is he moved from being quite orthodox as a Marxist to, at the end of his life, not really a Marxist at all. In the essays here, he worked, as he would say later, "within the Marxist tradition," but the keen observer will no doubt find revisions right along. But wouldn't this be expected? In context, the important thing is that "theory" (a term always problematic for him) was to be related to circumstances and practice. His ideas would over time be modified and reformulated, according to the nature of the struggle.[160] They were to be guides to action. They enabled him to connect the enclosing of the commons, the despoliation of the Dales, the pollution of the industrial cities, world war, and the threat of nuclear war with our concerns for the environment and the fate of the earth. I am afraid all this imprecision will be unsatisfactory to some; for my part I find many of the disputes of academia and of the left, the nitpickery and the scholastic antiquarianism, to be of little interest or significance. Edward Thompson was, and this is what is important to me, a lifelong socialist—a socialist interested in changing all forms of human relationships. Socialism was "inside him," as it had been for Maguire and Morris. Thompson was a person of the long tradition of "the left" in the old-fashioned sense. He was a person who fought for that tradition, he deeply believed in it, and in doing so he became a part of it, the ongoing tradition he did so much to chronicle. And in this his most lasting contributions may be his demand that we see things "from the bottom up"; for this he wrote "history from the bottom up" and pursued a socialism from the bottom up, a socialism for "real people." Thus he insisted that socialists must be willing to put on their boots and "walk among the people, to listen to them . . . and have a touch of humility before their experience."[161]

Did Thompson always get it right? Surely not. Were there times when he "sulked in his tent"?[162] Yes, but he was the first to say so. Could he be harsh, too harsh? Yes, but he fought tough battles, important battles, battles that needed winning and sometimes in his own camp. I will remember the Edward Thompson who excoriated the authorities at Warwick University; the Thompson who celebrated *not* the darkness brought on by the miners' strike in 1972, but rather the "incandescence."[163] Then, too, for his (to some) infamous discussion of "arbitrary power and the rule of law."[164] How is this last to be read today, I wonder, in an era of Abu Ghraib, Guantánamo, Fallujah, the NSA, and the war on terror? His 1976 piece, "The Secret State," reads like a defense of Manning and Snowden.

Thompson gave his life campaigning against nuclear weapons and nuclear war, and against the regimes that brandished them; in this he remained true to the values that carried him through life.

"I am not, I think, betraying a closely guarded state secret," Edward Thompson wrote to C. Wright Mills, "when I say that the movement which once claimed to be 'The New Left' has now, in this country, dispersed itself both organizationally and (to some extent) intellectually. We failed to implement our original purposes, or even to sustain what cultural apparatuses we had."[165] That was so, but we need still to remember Dorothy Thompson's qualifications. Edward Thompson was never afraid of failure; that would seem self-evident in a veteran of Monte Cassino. It seems equally doubtful that even as a young Communist, however full of hubris, he could have believed "success" as in any way guaranteed. And let us recall his targets: fascism, Stalinism, NATO, the secret state, Thatcher, Reagan, the Gulag, and Brezhnev. The movement, then as now, had lost as many battles as it had won. The idea of an end of history appalled Edward Thompson, as did any notion that the pursuit of a just society could be in any way time-bound. And so in concluding I will return to *The Making*: "Our only criterion of judgement should not be whether or not a man's actions are justified in the light of subsequent evolution." After all, "we are not at the end of social evolution ourselves." We now face our own "exterminisms," in the form of permanent war, the enduring curse of class, the ravaging of our environment, and the issue of the very survival of our earth as we know it.

—DECEMBER 2013
MENDOCINO COUNTY, CALIFORNIA

THIS IS AN APPEAL TO THE WORLD COMMUNIST MOVEMENT, above all to the British Communists, supporting the rebellion of the workers and students of Budapest and savaging the quiescence of his Party's leaders. Edward Thompson, then thirty-three and teaching adult working-class education in the West Riding of Yorkshire, was still a member of the Communist Party, having followed the footsteps of his brother Frank during the Second World War. He wrote this article, smoke literally still in the air, typed the stencils himself, and with Dorothy Thompson, his partner and comrade, and John Saville, the Hull historian, distributed it to an ever-widening world of Communist dissent. Within a year, 10,000 would leave the British CP. "No chapter," Thompson wrote, "would be more tragic in international socialist history, if the Hungarian people, who once before lost their revolution to armed reaction, were driven into the arms of the capitalist powers by the crimes of a Communist government and the uncomprehending violence of Soviet armies."

Through the Smoke of Budapest

Stalinism has sown the wind, and now the whirlwind centres on Hungary. As I write the smoke is still rising above Budapest.

It is true that dollars have also been sown in this embittered soil. But the crop which is rising will surely not turn out to be the one which Mr. Dulles expected—some new Syngman Rhee for Eastern Europe, backed by a fraudulent Chancellory and a Papal Junta?

By an angry twist of history, it seems that the crop is coming up as students', workers' and soldiers' councils, as "anti-Soviet" Soviets.

I do not know how things will be when this is published. Will Russian troops withdraw soon enough to prevent the country from being engulfed in waves of nationalist fury and anarchy? Will a new, honest government of Communists and others succeed in wresting calm from the passions of the moment—calm enough to ensure some justice, more mercy, and that the will of the people finds expression?

It is all that we dare hope for. But—leaving aside such groups of counter-revolutionaries as there must have been—those youths and workers of Budapest who first threw up barricades against the Soviet tanks, surely they did not wish to embrace the "American Century"? Nor can they then, unless in desperation, have found comfort in the hypocritical appeal to the Security Council of governments blooded to the elbow from their exploits in Kenya, Cyprus, Algeria—and now Egypt.

No chapter would be more tragic in international socialist history, if the Hungarian people, who once before lost their revolution to armed reaction, were driven into the arms of the capitalist powers by the crimes of a Communist government and the uncomprehending violence of Soviet armies.

And so I hope that the Communist Party, my party, will regain the support of the working people. But *where* is my party in Hungary? Was it in the broadcasting station or on the barricades? And *what* is it? Is it a cluster of security officials and discredited bureaucrats? Or is it a party "rooted in the people" of town and countryside, capable of self-purification and new growth?

We will read the answer in its actions. I hope we will hear less about "rooting out" this and that, "ruthlessly smashing" this and that, and more about learning from the people, serving the people, and honouring Communist principle.

I know that our Hungarian comrades will recall the prayer of their great patriot, Kossuth, over one hundred years ago:

Send, O God! the genial rays of the sun, that flowers may spring from this holy blood, that the bodies of my brethren may not perish in lifeless corruption . . . As a free man, I kneel on the fresh graves of my brethren. Sacrifices like these sanctify the earth; they purge it of sin. My God! a people of slaves must not live on this sacred soil, nor step on these graves!

I HAD INTENDED in this article to attempt some definitions of Stalinism, to enter into some questions of theory which our British leadership refuses to discuss, and to consult with readers upon the best way to rid our own party of Stalinist theory and practice.

But these points of theory have now found dramatic expression in the great square of Warsaw and amid the smoke of Budapest. It is difficult to speak at all in the teeth of a whirlwind. And if we have helped, in small degree, to sow that wind, do we have the right to speak?

And yet someone must speak. The *Daily Worker*, in its editorial columns, has done nothing to express our thoughts or to assert our honour in the past few weeks.

One week before the fighting commenced in Hungary, it published an editorial, "No Vengeance." This declared that "the difficulties created by the past violations of Socialist legality are being patiently solved." A crowd of 200,000 had attended the reburial of Laszlo Rajk, and voices were raised calling for the trial and punishment of those responsible for his executions:

"The anguish of the kinsmen and friends of these dead Communists is understandable; but it would be distressing to Hungary's friends throughout the world if new trials were to disturb the life of the Hungarian people and blot the "clean, new page" that their Party has now embarked on. Surely the time has come to temper justice with mercy and to look, not to the past, but to the bright future that a hard-working people and a Party united as never before can build together."

Good little hard-working people! We do not wish to "disturb" your life. Your Party has embarked you on a new page. You may rest content.

But the population of Hungary is nine million. And a crowd of 200,000 does not often assemble from the whole of Britain.

What thoughts passed through the minds of these people as they stood by this seven-year-old grave at this strange funeral?

Did they recall that Bela Kun, leader of the Hungarian Soviet Republic of 1919, had found an obscure and wretched death in the Soviet Union in the

1930s? That the Comintern had acquiesced in this betrayal and laid its botching hand upon their revolutionary movement while Horthy's White Guards stamped through their capital city?

Did they wonder how it was possible for their leaders—Rakosi, Gero, Farkas and the rest—to allow their comrade Laszlo Rajk, ex-International Brigader and victim of Nazi concentration camps, to be dragged through public execration to a traitor's shameful death?

"One cannot plan human consciousness," says our Comrade Gomulka. I think that this is a good thing, despite the tragic outcome in this case. Certainly, the same men cannot switch off "violations of Socialist legality" and switch on a "clean, new page" like an electric light. Nor can the moral responses of a people be switched by government edicts.

And what is "Socialist legality," by the way? Is it justice? Or is it as much justice as is expedient when the people are very angry?

Apart from the Poznan trials, I cannot remember any recent examples of "Socialist legality" which can be recognised as acts of justice.

And what was this justice which (in the editorial view of the *Daily Worker*) had been so stern and unrelenting that "the time has come" to temper it with mercy? I do not recall any trials of those responsible for "violations of Socialist legality" in Hungary or elsewhere, although Beria seems to be dead and I have read of some cursory shootings in Azerbaijan. Whether these were just or not, neither I nor the Editor of the *Daily Worker* know.

And why should the *Daily Worker* assume that any *just* trial would *blot* any "clean, new page"? And why should Hungarian party members assume that their Party *had* embarked on such a page, when they had not been consulted through any Congress? Why should it assume that the Party was "united as never before" when the members had recently learned that one part of its Central Committee had butchered the other part to placate a man whom we are now told was all along the agent of the "Mussavat intelligence service"?

And why should the Hungarian people be confident that such a leadership was about to build them a "bright future"?

And why should the *Daily Worker* call for "no vengeance," in the interests of hushing up truth and perverting justice in a case where the facts were becoming unpleasantly clear, when—so far as my memory goes—it had never before called for "no vengeance" in any of the more dubious trials in Socialist countries?

Why—and this is the real question—did the *Daily Worker*, which has for so long rejected letters and trimmed editorials to ensure that we do not "intervene" in the affairs of a brother party, suddenly speak in the name of British Communists to assure the Hungarian authorities that "it would be distressing to Hungary's friends throughout the world" if these guilty men were brought to trial?

I do not want to see vengeance. We have all had our fill of executions. But justice demands that criminals are tried for their crimes, and their associates shown out of public life.

I know very well that the knots tied by Stalinism cannot be untied in a day. But the first step on the road back to Communist principle is that we tell the truth and show confidence in the judgement of the people. After the 20th Congress (said Gomulka) "people began to straighten their backs, silent enslaved minds began to shake off the poison of mendacity. Above all the working people wanted to know all the truth, without embellishments and omissions." Our own need for truth is no less.

On October 29th, almost a week *after* the Budapest rising, the *Daily Worker* found a new editorial explanation:

"It is a tragedy that the leadership of the Party and the Government did not act more promptly in putting right those economic and political wrongs that were causing such deep discontent among the masses."

Too true. And if the Stalinists in Hungary attended to the advice given to them by the *Daily Worker* ten days before, it will have contributed to that fatal delay which triggered the revolt. And in that case, a part of the blood shed in Budapest lies on British heads.

IN THE NEXT FEW DAYS, with the dramatic events in Poland, the *Daily Worker* sat awkwardly on the fence, with its editorial legs on the wrong side.

I can think of few moments so moving, so significant for the future of the international working-class movement, as those when our courageous comrade Wladyslaw Gomulka emerged from gaol and calumny and found for the Polish people a narrow passage through to a creative future, between the rocks of counter-revolution on the one hand and of armed intervention on the other. All honour to the maturity, self-discipline, and confident initiative of the Polish people!

But the *Daily Worker* could see none of these things. It could not (editorially) even see the excellent reports of Gordon Cruickshank in its own columns. For two days running it could see nothing but speeches by Eisenhower, "wild rumours ... in the capitalist Press," "divisions in the popular ranks," new "Pilsudskis": "The imperialists may see some cause for rejoicing, but they might well be seeing things, things that are not there. Time, of course, will resolve doubts as it will dispel hopes. We are not astrologers, but we have faith in the working class, and that includes the working class of Poland." (23 October)

Time (of course) has dispelled doubts in the shape of half a million people demonstrating peacefully in Warsaw's greatest square. Time has not yet dispelled doubts as to the competence of our Editorial Department of Failed Astrology.

The only serious doubts (apart from these) of that weekend have now been partially dispelled: would the Soviet Union commit the crime of launching a cold or hot war against the new Polish Communist government? If the *Daily Worker* had advice to give, it should have sent it to this quarter. Editorials in the international Communist press, calling for restraint from the Soviet Party, might have had a salutary effect, here and on events in Hungary. Such advice would have been endorsed by the great majority of British Communists.

But from start to finish, our paper—in the name of all of us—has sent the *wrong* advice and sent it to the *wrong* address.

BACK TO HUNGARY. On Tuesday night, October 23rd, demonstrations by students and others led on to general rioting and bloodshed in Budapest. No facts were clear. Had counter-revolutionary groups, aided from outside, laid sparks on the tinder of an embittered population? Where did the working class of Budapest stand? We anxiously awaited information.

On Thursday morning the answers were given:

"Counter-revolution in Hungary staged an uprising in the hours of darkness on Tuesday night. The Hungarian working class rallied around its Government and Party and smashed this attempt to put the clock back. The capitalist Press rejoiced too soon and what it rejoiced about was the shooting of shop stewards, Socialists and Communists by armed detachments of terrorists." (25 October)

No evidence was given for these statements. Our Department of Failed Astrology had learnt nothing from the 20th Congress, Poznan, Warsaw in October.

It is a small point, but I cannot find in any reports references to the murder of shop stewards. Perhaps this was only a harmless device to rouse the indignation of British trade unionists?

It is also a pity that the *Daily Worker* showed few signs of editorial indignation when it was first revealed that under Rakosi's regime a great many Communists, Socialists and trade unionists were imprisoned and shot. "Soviet troops have answered the call of the Hungarian Government for assistance precisely because those troops are acting in solidarity with the Hungarian people to defend the Socialist system." (26 October)

It is comforting to know that history is always so "precise" in its movements. In fact, the Soviet intervention vastly aggravated the situation and greatly embittered the people. If we are to use Stalinist terms, the Soviet tanks were "objectively" inflaming "counter-revolution."

I find it a profound source of shame that a Communist government should have become so corrupt, so isolated from the people, that in a time of crisis it could find no protection in the arms of its own working class. "Let every local Labour Party and Communist Party branch, every trade union branch and executive committee, every Labour M.P., send telegrams to the Hungarian Government condemning the counter-revolutionary violence and standing by the Government and people . . . ." (25 October)

No, no, no, no! This is not work for us. Shame on this indecent haste, shame on this breach of solidarity, shame on those who wished to rush in the moral armaments of the British working class behind Gero's security police, to destroy these students and young workers in the streets!

Is our Party leadership bent on making a miniature Poland or Hungary out of our Party? How far from reality, from our Labour Movement, must they be to print such an appeal at such a time? Our membership has had enough.

IT IS TIME THAT WE had this out. From start to finish, from February onwards, our leadership has sided (evasively at times, perhaps) with Stalinism.

This is not to say that they have defended the memory of Stalin, or seriously questioned the dishonest attempt to make one man a scapegoat for the sins of an historical epoch.

On the contrary, they have run two lines of argument. First, all these "wrong things" (which we "could not know about") were associated with the influence of one man in Russia, and the "cult" of his "personality": second, Stalin's theory was admirable but (unknown to us) an alarming gap grew up between his theory and his practice.

Convenient arguments, these, for our leaderships since they absolve us from all responsibility for having passed "wrong information" and justified "wrong things": since they absolve them from all need to drive out the influence of Stalinism upon their own theory and practice, and that of our Party.

But there *is* one "wrong theory" of Stalin's which we are licensed to criticise: the theory of the intensification of the class struggle. All right, let us look at it. The theory derives, in fact, from Lenin—thrown out in a fluid situation of revolutionary crisis, and, like so much else, wrested out of context by Stalin and turned into a stone axiom:

"Certain comrades interpreted the thesis on the abolition of classes, the establishment of a classless society and the dying out of the state, to mean justification of laziness and complacency, justification of the counter-revolutionary theory of the subsiding of the class struggle and the weakening of state authority. Needless to say, such people cannot have anything in common with our Party. These are either degenerates, or double dealers, who must be driven out of the Party. The abolition of classes is not achieved by subduing the class struggle but by intensifying it. The state will die out not by the weakening of state authority, but by strengthening it to the utmost necessary for the purpose of finally crushing the remnants of the dying classes and for organizing defence against the capitalist environment." (Stalin, Report to January 1933 Plenum, CPSU (B))

Take out this one "wrong theory" and this whole passage falls apart, and shows itself to be corrupt. The theory of the all-powerful, centralised state is wrong—our comrades in Poland and Yugoslavia are proving this in life. The attitude towards the role of the Party, and towards party comrades, is wrong.

And the Stalinist theory of the dictatorship of the proletariat is wrong. Once again, Stalin made out of Lenin's words a stone axiom: "The dictatorship of the proletariat is the domination of the proletariat over the bourgeoisie, untrammeled by law and based on violence and enjoying the sympathy and support of the toiling and exploited masses." (Stalin, *Foundations of Leninism*)

As we learn from Hungary, such a dictatorship need not for long command the sympathy of the toiling masses: nor would it do in Britain. This is indeed a far cry from Engels' definition of the "two infallible expedients" which distinguish this phase of transitions: election to all positions by universal suffrage, with the right of recall residing in the electors: and all officials to receive workers' wages. (Introduction, *Civil War in France*)

And the identification of all disagreement, all opposition, all hesitation, with "objective" counter-revolution is wrong. It permeates Stalin's writings and the *History of the CPSU (B)* (upon which a generation of our full-timers have received their education) from end to end. "The opposition has ideologically broken with Leninism . . . and has objectively become a tool of counter-revolution against the regime of the proletarian dictatorship." "To attain victory, the Party of the working class, its directing staff, its advanced fortress, must first be purged of capitulators, deserters, scabs and traitors." (CPSU (B), 289, 360)

And the military vocabulary of Stalinism is wrong, and strange and offensive to the ears of the British working class.

And the attitude to discussion is wrong. This should have been clear when, in 1931, Stalin branded the editors of a journal which had permitted a discussion of certain pre-war theories of Lenin, for "rotten liberalism," for "stupidity bordering on crime, bordering on treason to the working class." "Slander must be branded as such and not made the subject of discussion."

And the theory of the Party is wrong, the theory that "the Party becomes strong by purging itself," the theory of the Party's paternal, self-appointed mission and infallibility, the "cult of the Party" which submerges all loyalty to people, to principle, to the working class itself in loyalty to the Party's "iron discipline."

And the mechanical theory of human consciousness is wrong: the theory that historical science "can become as precise a science as, let us say, biology," the subordination of the imaginative and moral faculties to political and administrative authority is wrong: the elimination of moral criteria from political judgment is wrong: the fear of independent thought, the deliberate encouragement of anti-intellectual trends amongst the people is wrong: the mechanical personification of unconscious class forces, the belittling of the conscious processes of intellectual and spiritual conflict, all this is wrong:

> "The superstructure is created by the basis precisely in order to serve it, to actively help it to take shape and consolidate itself, to actively strive for the elimination of the old watchword basis, together with its super-structure." "Desperately the old superstructure rallies to the defence of the basis that gave rise to it." (Stalin, *Marxism in Linguistics*; Klugman, *Basis & Super-Structure*)

All these theories are not altogether wrong. But they are wrong enough to have brought our movement into international crisis. And it was mechanical idealism such as this, mounted on Soviet tanks, which fired through the smoke at the workers and young people of Budapest.

STALINISM IS SOCIALIST THEORY and practice which has lost the ingredient of humanity. The Stalinist mode of thought is not that of dialectical materialism, but that of mechanical idealism. For example:

> "If the passing of slow quantitative changes into rapid and abrupt qualitative changes is a law of development, then it is clear that revolutions made by oppressed classes are a quite natural and inevitable phenomenon. Hence the transition from capitalism to Socialism and the liberation of the working class from the yoke of capitalism cannot be effected by slow changes, by reforms, but only by a qualitative change of the capitalist system, by revolution. Hence, in order not to err in policy, one must be a revolutionary, not a reformist." (Stalin, *Dialectical and Historical Materialism*)

The gap between Stalinist theory and practice is inherent in the theory. "Truth is always concrete," wrote Lenin; but from the fluid movement of Lenin's analysis of particular social realities, Stalin plucked axioms. Stalinism is Leninism turned into stone.

Instead of commencing with facts, social reality, Stalinist theory starts with the idea, the text, the axiom: facts, institutions, people, must be brought to conform to the idea. Wheat is grown in hothouses to "prove" a scientific theory:

novels are written to "prove" the correctness of the Party line: trials are faked to "prove" the "objective" treason of the victims.

Stalinist analysis, at its most degenerate, becomes a scholastic exercise, the search for "formulations" "correct" in relation to text but not to life. And how often is this "correct formulation" poised mid-way between two deviations one to the left, one to the right? "To the question, which deviation was worse, Comrade Stalin replied: 'One is as bad as the other . . .'" Do the real choices of life present themselves in this mechanical way?

"He had completely lost consciousness of reality," declares Khruschev. And he was not alone. This gap developed everywhere. It was this gap which defied Khruschev's analysis: "Not only a Marxist-Leninist but also no man of common sense can grasp how it was possible to make whole nations responsible for inimical activity." Precisely so. But this is the irony of Stalin's career. Emerging as the most "realistic," the "strongest" Marxist, he limited his vision to the single task of holding and extending the power of the Soviet State. Tearing his severe, textual path through unprecedented complexities and dangers, he allowed one part of reality to escape him—the thoughts, prejudices, aspirations, of living men and women. Stalinism is at the opposite pole to common sense.

But never free from the restraint of common senses rather, the Stalinist oscillates between the axiom and "realpolitik": dogmatism and opportunism. When the axioms cease to produce results, a "mistake" is "recognized," Khruschev's speech is made: the tanks withdraw from Budapest. But the theory is little changed. For Stalinism prevents a serious critique from emerging within the borders of its rule. And we, outside these borders, have also failed.

Stalinism was not "wrong things" about which "we could not know," but distorted theories and degenerate practices about which we knew something, in which, to some degree, we shared, and which our leadership supports today. Who does not know that our moral atrophy, our military vocabulary and structure, our paternalist outlook upon the people and their organisations, our taste for disseminating "wrong information," our fear of popular initiatives independent of our guidance, our dislike of criticism, our secrecy and occasional bad faith with our friends—all these have crippled our propaganda, isolated us, and robbed our work of its right reward? And who does not know that it was our rank-and-file that was tainted least with these things, and our leadership most?

Our leaders do not wish to discuss this because they do not wish to change. At heart, they have always feared the "thaw." Their hearts lie with the Soviet tanks. After all, tanks are mechanical things, which will answer to controls and can consolidate power. "Marxism-Leninism" is safe with them. But if people take initiative into their own hands . . . it is too great a risk.

And on the other side of the smoke, what do we hope for from the people of Poland, the workers and students of Budapest, when their wounds are healed and their national pride assuaged? First, I hope, a new respect for *people*, permeating the whole of society, its institutions, its social relations. And then, a new respect for truth, for principle. A democracy which does not limit its action within narrow limits defined by a paternal Party, pronouncing anathema on all who stray outside, but one based on real confidence in the peoples' initiatives. A new understanding of the continuity of human culture. And finally, a new internationalism, based (among Socialist countries) upon true independence and respects and (among Communist Parties) upon truthful exchanges and fraternal controversy—exchanges in which the membership, by personal and published contact, can take part.

THE POLISH AND HUNGARIAN people have written their critique of Stalinism upon their streets and squares. In doing so, they have brought back honour to the international Communist movement. These revolutions have been made by Communists: not it is true by those who arrogated to themselves all wisdom and authority, but by Communists just the same. Wherever this wind of Stalinism has been sown, Communists have also sown good Socialist seed. The crop of human brotherhood will prevail, when the winds have passed away.

I recall a "Christmas message" from my brother, which he wrote after meeting Communist partisans, in December 1943:

> "There is a spirit abroad in Europe which is finer and braver than anything that tired continent has known for centuries, and which cannot be withstood. You can, if you like, think of it in terms of politics, but it is broader and more generous than any dogma. It is the confident will of whole peoples, who have known the utmost humiliation and suffering and who have triumphed over it, to build their own life once and for all."

It is the crime of Stalinism that it crabbed and confined this spirit, while many of those who are now greeting, with complacent self-approval, the exploits of the Bolish and Hungarian peoples, themselves were feeding Stalinism with each strident anti-Communist speech, with the rearmament of Germany, with each twist of the Cold War.

Stalinism confined this spirit, but it was never killed. Today it walks abroad again, in full daylight, on Polish streets. It was present on the Budapest barricades, and today wrests with anarchy for the future of Hungary. Never was there a time when comrades of ours were in so great need of our solidarity, in the face of the blind resistance of Stalinism, the black passions of reaction.

This Socialism of free people, and not of secret speeches and police, will prove *more* dangerous to our own imperialism than any Stalinist state. Its leaders will make mistakes enough, but not such "mistakes" as destroy their own honour and the good name of the Party.

We British Communists have a right and duty to greet our comrades in these lands of reborn principle.

Shame on our leaders for their silence!

Greetings to the Polish people! Honour to the working people, and students, who shed their blood at Budapest! May they regain mastery over their own future, and curb the mob passions unloosed by their ordeal! And may it prove that Communist need never fire on Communist again!

"SOCIALIST HUMANISM: AN EPISTLE TO THE PHILISTINES,"
was the lead article in the first issue of *The New Reasoner*, published
in Summer 1957. It was, as Dorothy Thompson remarked, "a first
attempt to anatomize Stalinism and the policies of the non-Soviet
communist parties by someone who had only just come up for air."
It was a withering attack on Stalinism as an ideology, but it was also
much more. Here Thompson developed the core of ideas upon which
he would build all his writings. These included people as agents of
history, the importance and validity of human experience, the place
of choice and moral imagination, and the fallacy of determinisms.
He advocates a "socialist society that would revolutionize human
relationships, replacing respect for property by respect for man, and
replacing the acquisitive society by the common weal."

Socialist Humanism

AN EPISTLE TO THE PHILISTINES

"The standpoint of the old materialism is 'civil society'; the stand-point of the new is human society or socialised humanity."

—MARX, 10TH THESIS ON FEUERBACH

"The poet said to the bureaucrat: Man creates by the laws of beauty. The artist creates the heart's face: an image of all that's human. But he said: I've no time to argue—though it sounds like a deviation—Desk-deep in class war on the eighteenth floor I'm making the Revolution."

—TOM McGRATH

O ur island is one of the very few provinces of Europe which has not in this century suffered from civil or international war upon its own soil; and which has escaped the consequences—gas chambers, "quisling" regimes, partisan movements, terror and counter-terror—which have coloured the outlook of whole nations, East and West. It is very easy for us to fall into insular, parochial attitudes, and therefore necessary that we should commence any discussion of the future of socialism by reminding ourselves of some of the larger facts of our time. For two hundred years the pace of technological and social change has accelerated to an unprecedented degree, and nuclear fission and automation promise an even more rapid acceleration. In the past few years several continents which—fifty years ago—were on the periphery of civilisation, have entered the arena of international politics. In the past fifty years more human beings have been killed in war than in any comparable period. The fact that, in the past ten, these wars have abated in extent, although not in intensity (Korea, Indo-China, Kenya, Algeria), indicates less any change of heart than mutual fear of the overwhelming killing power of atomic weapons. The only reasonable deduction from all these facts is that mankind is caught up in the throes of a revolutionary transition to an entirely new form of society—a transition which must certainly reach its climax during this century.

This is confirmed by the emergence upon one quarter of the earth's surface of a new society, with a new economic structure, new social relations, and new political institutions. The fact that British socialists do not like all the features of this society has no bearing upon the fact of its existence. It was obviously only short-sightedness which ever led socialists to conceive of the new society stepping, pure and enlightened, out of the fires of the old. Who should be surprised, when we recall the tormented history of the past fifty years, that the new society has sprung from the fire, its features blackened and distorted by pain and oppression?

But the future of British socialism may be very much affected by the understanding of and feelings towards the new society of British socialists, since it has always been their faith that socialism was not only economically practicable but was also intensely *desirable*; that is, that socialist society would revolutionise human relationships, replacing respect for property by respect for man, and replacing the acquisitive society by the common weal. It was assumed that all forms of human oppression were rooted, ultimately, in the economic oppression arising from the private ownership of the means of production; and that once these were socialised, the ending of other oppressions would rapidly ensue. "So easily might men gette their living," wrote More, "if that same worthye princesse lady money did not alone stop up the waye betwene us and our lyving. . . . Thys hellhounde creapeth into mens hartes: and plucketh them backe from entering the right pathe of life."

If, then, British socialists find features of the new society in the East repugnant, and find in them evidence that new forms of oppression—economic, physical and psychological—can perfectly well take root in a socialist society, a number of consequences will follow. Some will cease to be socialists, or to desire to take any active part in working for the new society. Others will lose confidence in the revolutionary perspectives of socialism, take a more limited and humdrum view of human potentialities, and hence cease to struggle for that transformation in men's values and outlook which socialists once thought possible. If it is true that we are in a period of revolutionary transition, then such reactions are likely to strengthen capitalist society, prolong the transitional period, align the working-class movements in the West alongside the dying order and thus enflame international disagreements, and, as a consequence, harden and perpetuate the oppressive features of the new society. Moreover, it is evident that British socialists who see men who claim "Marxism" as their guide, banner, and "science" perpetrating vile crimes against their own comrades and gigantic injustices against many thousands of their fellow men, will assume—and have assumed—that the ideas of Marx and Engels are useless or even dangerous, that they leave out of account essential points, that they give a false view of "human nature," and that, although Marxism may have imparted a fanatic fervour to Russian and Chinese communists, a sense of acting as the instruments of destiny, nevertheless the ideas of Marx and Engels give as false a view of reality as did those of Calvin. But if this natural assumption is *wrong,* then British socialism is weakened at its weakest point. Pragmatism may take the British labour movement through another few years; but it will not prove adequate to dealing with the increasingly complex problems of this period of transition.

It is my contention that the revolt within the international Communist movement against "Stalinism," will, if successful, confirm the revolutionary confidence of the founders of the socialist movement. And if this is so, it must be of the profoundest importance to British socialists, since it will restore confidence in our own revolutionary perspectives.

Stalinism as Ideology

"STALINISM" IS, IN A TRUE SENSE, an ideology; that is, a form of false consciousness, deriving from a partial, partisan, view of reality; and, at a certain stage, establishing a *system* of false or partially false concepts with a mode of thought which—in the Marxist sense—is idealist. "Instead of commencing with facts, social reality, Stalinist theory starts with the idea, the text, the axiom: facts, institutions, people, must be brought to conform to the idea."

There is another approach to Stalinism, which sees it not as an ideology so much as an hypocrisy; that is, the largely hypocritical speeches and quite different practices of a bureaucratic caste in Russia, concerned with the maintainance and extension of their privileges and interests; and the similar speeches and actions of their "stooges," "dupes," etc., outside.[1]

This is a mistaken view. First, it underestimates the strength, inner logic and consistency of Stalinism, a common feature in all mature ideologies. In doing so, it fails to present a serious theoretical confrontation, and instead (as one must with a hypocrisy) decends to personalities or to abuse of "the personality."

Second, it overlooks the fact that many features of "Stalinism" antedate J. V. Stalin by many years, antedate the Russian Revolution and the emergence of the Russian bureaucracy. For example, the dogmatism which in the Soviet Union has taken on institutional form is kin to that with which Engels took issue in the British and American labour movement in the 1880s:[2] and anti-intellectualism finds its forerunner in the French *ouvrierisme.* Third, it fails to explain the way in which Stalinist concepts and practices have struck root in countries where—so far from drawing nourishment from the privileges of bureaucracy—the Communists who espoused them have had to face only ostracism, hardship, imprisonment, or death for their pains. And this is confirmed, not only by the pattern of orthodoxy, but also by the marked similarities in the forms of revolt against that orthodoxy, appearing during 1956 in America and Poland, in Hungary,

India, and in the Soviet Union itself. Fourth—and of most importance—such an approach tends to be infected by one of the cardinal false-hoods of Stalinism: the attempt to derive all analysis of political manifestations directly and ;in an over-simplified manner from economic causations, the belittling of the part, played by men's ideas and moral attitudes in the making of history.

Thus we must view Stalinism as an ideology—a constellation of partisan attitudes and false, or partially false, ideas; and the Stalinist today acts or writes in certain ways, not because he is a fool or a hypocrite, but because he is the prisoner of false ideas. But this is not to suggest that Stalinism arose just because Stalin and his associates had certain wrong ideas. Stalinism is the ideology of a revolutionary elite which, within a particular historical context, degenerated into a bureaucracy. In understanding the central position of the Russian bureaucracy, first in developing and now in perpetuating, this ideology, we have a great deal to learn, from the analyses of Trotsky and even more from the flexible and undogmatic approach of Isaac Deutscher and others. Stalinism struck root within a particular social context, drawing nourishment from attitudes and ideas prevalent among the working-class and peasantry—exploited and culturally deprived classes; it was strengthened by Russian backwardness and by the hostility and active aggression of capitalist powers; out of these conditions there arose the bureaucracy which adapted the ideology to its own purposes and is interested in perpetuating it; and it is clear enough now to most people that the advance of world socialism is being blockaded by this bureaucracy, which controls the means by which it is attempting to prevent—not a new ideology—but a true consciousness from emerging. In Russia the struggle against Stalinism is at one and the same time a struggle against the bureaucracy, finding expression in the various pressures for de-centralisation, economic democracy, political liberty, which are becoming evident. But—important as this—we must not allow the particular forms which this revolt is taking in Russia and in Eastern Europe to obscure the general character of the theoretical confrontation which is now taking place throughout the world communist movement. Stalinism did not develop just because certain economic and social conditions existed, but because these conditions provided a fertile climate within which false ideas took root, and these false ideas became in their turn a part of the social conditions. Stalinism has now outlived the social context within which it arose, and this helps us to understand the character of the present revolt against it.

This is—quite simply—a revolt against the ideology, the false consciousness of the elite-into-bureaucracy, and a struggle to attain towards a true ("honest") self-consciousness; as such it is expressed in the revolt against dogmatism and the anti-intellectualism which feeds it. Second, it is a revolt against inhumanity—the equivalent of dogmatism in human relationships and moral conduct—against administrative, bureaucratic and twisted attitudes towards human beings. In both sense it represents a return to man: from abstractions and scholastic formulations to real men: from deceptions and myths to honest history: and so the positive content of this revolt may be described as "socialist humanism." It is humanist because it places once again real men and women at the centre of socialist theory and aspiration, instead of the resounding abstractions—the Party, Marxism-Leninism-Stalinism, the Two Camps, the Vanguard of the Working Class—so dear to Stalinism. It is socialist because it reaffirms the revolutionary perspectives of Communism, faith in the revolutionary potentialities not only of the Human Race or of the Dictatorship of the Proletariat but of real men and women.

The "Disease of Orthodoxy"

THE REVOLT APPEARED first as a revolt against dogmatism. "Common meetings and political action of students and workers were the most outstanding feature of the October days in Poland," records Oscar Lange:

> "The students had read the classical works of socialist theory, the works of Marx, Engels and Lenin. The reformers in the 16th century compared the reality of the Papal Church with the teaching of the Bible; in the same way, our students compared the reality of the Stalinist version of socialism with the teachings of Marxism and Leninism. . . . That criticism was pretty devastating; the conclusion was the need for a new way of building socialism in our country." (*Monthly Review*, Jan. 1957)

Searching for the roots of dogmatism—the imposition of a system of authorised preconceptions upon reality rather than the derivation of ideas from the study of reality—the revolt (especially among the intellectuals) turned against institutional "Zhdanovism." The claims which reached their zenith in the period of Zhdanov's ascendancy can be recalled in the words of the *Modern Quarterly* (1947): "Zhdanov . . . speaks as a Marxist philosopher who has a world view embracing, not only politics and economics, but ethics, art, philosophy, and every phase of human activity." Since the Central Committee of the CPSU—or more accurately Stalin and Zhdanov—were the accredited masters of this "world view" it fell to them to exert a despotic authority upon the nation's intellectual and cultural life. The controlled intellectual life breeds dogmatic orthodoxy as a matter of course. "The establishment of an iron control not only over works of art, but over the very process of creation,, signifies a loss of confidence in the artistic intelligentsia"—so write two Soviet philosophers, in *Voprosy Filosofi*, November 1956:

Even now . . . confidence has not been fully restored. As in the past, it is only the officials of government departments, among whom there are numerous time-servers, who enjoy full confidence. It is true that of late there has been a slight change—theatres have been given the right to draw up their own repertory plans . . . but unfortunately this still applies only to the classics and not to works on contemporary subjects.

Clearly a society which inhibits the emergence of ideas in this way must find itself in increasing difficulties, economic, political, international. How does it come about that after forty years of "Soviet power" the seats of knowledge (except technological and related sciences) should be filled by placemen, scholastics, and—

> . . . the lofty, servile clown,
> Who with encroaching guile, keeps learning down.

Anti-intellectualism has deep roots within all working-class movements. It arises, first, from that intense loyalty to party or organisation (and consequent suspicion of the individualist or non-conformist), which is a necessary quality if the working class is to be welded into an effective political force. Second, from the hostility of revolutionaries to the ideas prevailing in the ruling class; and to those intellectuals who share its outlook and privileges and purvey its ideas. Moreover, in any socialist revolution there is bound to be a tension—and in a backward country like Russia an exceptionally acute tension—between the values of collectivism and individualism. Where the possibility for the free expression of the creative personality has existed only for the few, and has co-existed with the savage exploitation of the many, it is inevitable that the period of transition towards a fuller creative life for the many will at the same time limit the possibilities of life for the few. These tensions between individualist and social values, between collective discipline and that intellectual initiative which in the end must always arise from the individual, are inherent in the conflict between dying bourgeois and emergent socialist society. It is also to be expected that in any period of revolutionary change, the magnitude of the problems, the fervent inspiration of the times, will lead to the discouragement of speculative thought, to a literature of engagement, to a science with a practical utilitarian cast—such demands will inundate the socialist intellectual from outside, and he will feel the same promptings from within.

These tendencies, then, are to be expected in the phase of transition, although there are other, quite contrary, *tendencies both* within working-class life and within the socialist tradition. But the tendencies are present, can be enflamed within certain historical and social contexts, and therefore can the more easily be expressed in the initial stages of building socialist society in both institutional and ideological forms. Stalinism found the institutional forms by eliminating opposition, imposing bureaucratic control over all intellectual activities, and destroying (both within and without Russia) democracy within the Communist Party, under the rigid structure of "democratic centralism." At the same time Stalinism congealed into rigid ideological form those very partisan or fragmentary concepts which express the outlook of a revolutionary elite leading classes both bitterly exploited and culturally deprived. Lenin, in the aftermath of revolution, foresaw the dangers:

> People dilate at too great length and too flippantly on "proletarian culture." We would be satisfied with real bourgeois culture for a start, and we would be glad, for a start, to be able to dispense with the cruder types of pre-bourgeois culture, i.e. bureaucratic or serf culture, &c. In matters of culture, haste and sweeping measures are the worst possible things.

But in the process of transforming Russia's backward peasantry into an advanced industrial society, Lenin's warning was swept aside. Stalinism glories in partisanship, and prefers the ideology, the false consciousness, to the true consciousness which Marx and Engels devoted their lives to free from the trammels of the false. The struggle to attain towards an objective understanding of social reality was denounced as "objectivism," a betrayal of revolutionary class commitment. As we shall see, Stalinism converted the concepts of "reflection" and of the "superstructure" into mechanical operations in a semi-automatic model. The conscious processes of intellectual conflict were seen not as agencies in the making of history but as an irritating penumbra of illusions, or imperfect reflections, trailing behind economic forces. The ideas of critics or opponents were, and are, seen as symptoms of bourgeois conspiracy or penetration, targets for abuse, or fear, or suspicion. Hence it was easier to abolish the economic category from which the ideas arose—the old intelligentsia, the national minority—than to change their minds and their way of life. Hence, in the West, the intense self-distrust of the middle-class communist intellectual, the abasement before the "instinctive" lightness of working-class attitudes, which (commencing in a valid self-correction of attitudes arising from limited and partisan bourgeois experience) swings to its opposite and hangs like a smoke-pall of inhibitions preventing sturdy and confident intellectual growth. Hence also the most extreme, and almost pathological, forms of anti-intellectualism are found not among militant proletarians, but among middle-class intellectuals who have become self-twisted into Stalinist apologists. Stalin at least "believed in" his own ideology. Stalinism, in the era of Khruschev, has lost all confidence in itself. Thus *Pravda* (December 26th, 1956):

It would be a mistake to think that bourgeois propaganda does not influence the minds of Soviet people, notably those of the youth. Some comrades have misinterpreted the recent changes in the Party line. . . . Imperialist reaction mobilises the whole arsenal of lies and *calumny* for a fresh
crusade against the Marxist-Leninist world view. The reactionary press is
full of lying phrases about so-called national Communism, with the sole
aim of misleading the labouring masses. Under the influence of this propaganda, and from an un-willingness or inability correctly to analyse current events, some wavering elements are abandoning Marxism-Leninism
or trying to revise it.

But Stalinism no longer knows what "it" is. How much easier if *the* people
had no minds, if the "superstructure" was cut out and society was all "base": then
this clumsy business of reflection could be done away with. Ideas are no longer
seen as the medium; by which men apprehend the world, reason, argue, debate,
and choose; they are like evil and wholesome smells arising from imperialist and
proletarian cooking. One wonders whether the editors of *Pravda* ever speculate
upon what Marx was *doing* all his life, in his gigantic effort to bring his concepts
into rational order.

This economic automatism certainly is not Marxism. Over the years some
Western Marxists have developed a kind of split mentality. On the one hand they
have tried to develop creatively the flexible "ideas of movement" of Marx and
Engels; on the other, they have failed to face the fact that Stalinism spoke in a
different tongue. They have been aware (for example) that the Soviet Encyclo-
pedia is full of the most blatant distortions of history and crass reductions of
the ideas of outstanding thinkers and writers of the past into terms of their class
origin, etc.; but they have shrugged this off as the vulgarisation of a few hacks,
and refused to concede that this flowed from the essential character of the dominant ideology in Soviet society. We should reflect that ideas are handled roughly
by parties, institutions, social processes. The ideology of Victorian *laissez-faire*
mill owners was not the same thing as the thought of Adam Smith and Bentham; the middle class seized on certain ideas only—and these often imperfectly
understood—and adapted them to their own interests. Much the same has been
true of "Marxism" in Soviet society. The Soviet industrial manager is no more a
disciple of Marx than was Mr. Bounderby a disciple of Adam Smith.

But this is not only a question of the vulgarisation of ideas. Economic
automatism found increasing expression in Stalin's writings, and stands fully
revealed in his "Concerning Marxism in Linguistics." Marx derived from the
study of history the observation that "social being determines social consciousness." In class society men's consciousness of social reality, when viewed from
the standpoint of historical effectiveness, takes its form from the class structure

of that society; that is to say, people grow up within a social and cultural environment which is not that of "all men" but that of certain men with interests opposed to those of other men: they experience life as members of a class, a nation, a family. But this is not an automatic reflex in the individual's mind; he both experiences and—within the limitations of the cultural pattern of his class (traditions, prejudices, etc.)—he thinks about his experience. Obviously men with similar experiences think differently: all sorts of weird, crazy, remarkable ideas are thought up; outstanding individuals, like Shakespeare or Marx, certainly do not "reflect" their class experience only. "Reflection" (in this context) is a term describing social processes (and one with unfortunate connotations); it can be observed in history that men with the same economic interests and class experience sift and accept those ideas which justify their class interests, forming from them a system of partisan, partially false ideas, an ideology. Those ideas which do not suit the interests of any effective social grouping are either stillborn, or (like More's "Utopia") remain suspended, without social effectiveness, until new social forces emerge. But it is of first importance that men do not only "reflect" experience passively; they also think about that experience; and their thinking affects the way they act. The thinking is the creative part of man, which, even in class society, makes him partly an agent in history, just as he is partly a victim of his environment. If this were not so, his consciousness would indeed trail passively behind his changing existence; or he would cease to change:

> "The materialist doctrine that men are products of circumstance and upbringing and that, therefore, changed men are products of other circumstances and changed upbringing, forgets that circumstances are charged precisely by men and that the educator must himself be educated." (Marx, Third Thesis on Feuerbach)

In all their historical analysis Marx and Engels always kept in view this dialectical interaction between social consciousness (both active and passive) and social being. But in trying to explain their ideas they expressed them as a make-believe "model," the "basis" of social relations (in production) and the "superstructure" of various branches of thought, institutions, etc., arising from it and reacting upon it. In fact, no such basis and superstructure ever existed; it is a metaphor to help us to understand what does exist—men who act, experience, think and act again. It turns out that it is a bad and dangerous model, since Stalin used it not as an image of men changing in society but as a mechanical model, operating semi-automatically and independently of conscious human agency. Thus Stalin declared the "superstructure":

is connected with production only indirectly, through the economy, through the basis. The superstructure therefore reflects changes in the level of development of the productive forces not immediately and not directly, but only after changes in the basis, through the prism of the changes wrought in the basis by the changes in production.

This is, of course, ludicrous: it is scarcely translatable into human beings at all. An idea is not a reflex of a gasometer, no matter through what "prism." This reduces human consciousness to a form of erratic, involuntary response to steel-mills and brickyards, which are in a spontaneous process of looming and becoming. But men are conscious of themselves: this "economic base" is made up of human actions—labouring, distributing, selling—and if by their actions they change their relations with one another (some becoming owners, others serfs) they are bound to experience this too, and it will very much affect their ideas. But because Marx reduced his concept of *process* to a clumsy static model, Stalinism evolved this mystique wherein blind, non-human, material forces are endowed with volition—even consciousness—of their own. Creative man is changed to a passive *thing*: and things, working through prisms, are endowed with creative will. Man's role is to serve these things, to bring more and more productive forces into being: "The superstructure is created by the basis precisely in order to serve it, to actively help it to take shape and consolidate itself, to actively strive for the elimination of the old watchword basis, together with its superstructure."

How far we have come from real men and women, from the "educators and the educated"! Hence Stalin's statement that historical science "can become as precise a science as, let us say, biology." This is nonsense. Scientific techniques may be used in the study of history, we may speak of employing a scientific *method*, but we will never attain to a *precise* science of history, like a natural science, because of man's creative agency. No "basis" ever invented a steam engine, or sat on the National Coal Board.

It is, then, a poor model which in Stalin's hands led into dangerous abstractions. Ideas hostile to socialism or to Stalinism were seen as the last desperate rallying of an old "superstructure": it is far easier to be inhumane if one takes a non-human model. This gross fear of unorthodox thought informing a bureaucracy with the means at its disposal for manipulating opinion and eliminating dissent has brought some socialists to the point of despair. It seemed possible that the human potential of socialist society might be constricted into some monstrous bureaucratic-military form when men were on the very threshold of entering into the classless society; a constriction which might delay the human fruition of socialism for centuries, or even lead on to its own destruction. The dialectical interaction between men and their social environment which Marx saw as the dynamic force of history appeared to be frozen. But (Blake's warning):

"Expect poison from the standing water." "Our view shows that circumstances make men *just as much* as *men* make circumstances." (*German Ideology*) The creative act by which men, themselves the product of their circumstances, change these circumstances in their turn, and thus change themselves, was impeded by a false consciousness buttressed by the organs of state and involving a falsification of historical evidence upon a gigantic scale. Ideas were *explained away*, had *no reality*, except as *symptoms* (passive mirror-reflections) of class being—on the one hand, "weapons" of the proletariat; on the other, evidences of bourgeois penetration. If unorthodox ideas appeared, it was the business of the O.G.P.U. to furnish evidence of the "conspiracy" which they must "reflect." We learn to our cost that ideas are indeed real and material forces within society: that false, warped, fragmentary ideas can leave their evidence in the thronged corpses, the barbed-wire encampments, economic dislocation and international conflict. We re-learn (what Marx surely understood) that man is human by virtue of his culture, the transmission of experience from generation to generation; that his history is the record of his struggle truly to apprehend his own social existence; and that Marx and Engels, through their discoveries, hoped to assist in the liberation of men from false, partial, class consciousness, thereby liberating them from victimhood to blind economic causation, and extending immeasurably the region of their choice and conscious agency. Hence the concept of mankind *mastering* its own history, of socialism bringing "pre-history" to an end, and—by enabling mankind to approximate more closely than ever before to a true self-consciousness—enthroning for the first time the human reason and conscience:

man—
Equal, unclassed, tribeless, and nationless, Exempt from awe, worship, degree, the king Over himself...

And Marxism itself is not (as Stalin described it) "the scientific expression of the fundamental interests of the working class," but (in nature) "means no more than simply conceiving nature just as it exists without any foreign admixture" (Engels): and (in social reality) the struggle to attain towards a similar objective self-consciousness (without the foreign admixture of class ideology) by changing men of their own changing existence. The Soviet Encyclopaedists have forgotten the continuity of human culture, that man's true knowledge and self-knowledge has advanced through the zig-zags of the distorted and the partisan. What has advanced has not been a "weapon," or a dialectic, or a new class-bound ideology, but the sum of the knowledge of man.

What is a "Mistake"?

THE FIRST FEATURE of Stalinism, then, is anti-intellectualism, the belittling of conscious human agency in the making of history; and the revolt against it is not the revolt of a new ideology but the revolt of reason against irrationalism. A second feature of this revolt, equally challenging, equally hopeful, is the revolt against *inhumanity*, the revolt against the dogmatism and abstractions of the heart, and the emergence of a warm, personal and humane socialist morality—moral attitudes always present in the rank and file of the communist movement and within Soviet society, but distorted by Stalinist ideology, institutions, and bureaucratic practices.

Throughout the world, East and West, people are asking the same questions. By what vile alchemy do some communists, who spring from the common people, struggle, sacrifice, and endure incredible hardships on the people's behalf, become transformed into monsters of iniquity like Beria and Rakosi— lying, slandering and perjuring, destroying their own comrades, incarcerating hundreds of thousands, deporting whole nations? Communists are asking of their own leaders, the people are asking of Communist parties, would you also act like this if you were in power? Are those minor "mistakes" which we have witnessed—character assassination, dissemination of "wrong information," bad faith—signs that you also would follow the same pattern? Like old Lear in the storm, humanity regards the leaders of world communism and cries out: "Is there any cause in nature that breeds these hard hearts?"

Stalinism is incapable of giving any answers to these questions. The Stalinist apologist simply throws his hands across his eyes and refuses to recognise their existence. Thus George Matthews: "For Marxists every political decision is good or bad according to whether or not it serves the interests of the working people and the cause of socialism." ("World News," 30th June, 1956)

Thus John Gollan:

If you disagree with your opponent's political line, it is easy enough to call it immoral. But what has this to do with Marxism and the determining of a class position on events?

The moral estimation flows from, and cannot be separated from, the political estimation. ("World News," 9th March 1957)

How many and how unaccountable, it seems, have been the wrong "political estimations" in the past thirty years! And by what standard can we be sure that they are wrong? Can we be sure only by the evidence of "practice" which Rakosi—at length and after much diligence—procured: when the people are tormented and infuriated beyond endurance and break into revolt? Let us bring to these abstractions the criticism of life: for example, the trial of Traicho Rostov.

Rostov was born in 1897, shot in 1949, rehabilitated in 1956. Secretary of the Bulgarian CP both during the underground struggle early in the war, and in the three years after liberation, he was condemned to death as a traitor, saboteur, wrecker and agent of British intelligence. His trial differs from the general run, in that Rostov refused to plead guilty in court. A vignette from the trial sets the tone. In 1942 the leading members of the underground central committee in Sofia were arrested and condemned to death. Rostov's sentence was subsequently commuted to life imprisonment, although most of his comrades were executed. This fact was alleged as proof of his having broken under police methods and become an agent. Interrogated by the President of the Court, Rostov explained that Mladenov, the authority who had announced to him the commutation of his sentence, did so on higher orders:

> Rostov: "Mladenov stated . . . that the Minister of War . . . asked him 'How many death sentences were being provided for in the trial?' He replied that about 9 or 10, not definitely, were being provided for. The Minister of War had asked him: 'On Whom?' He had begun mentioning their names and having pronounced the first six names, coming to the seventh, i.e. to my name, the Minister of War had said that six were enough, but from the seventh on, i.e. from Traicho Kostov on . . .
> The President: "One moment, please. Do you know who might have taken steps before the Minister of War . . ."
> Rostov: "The Minister of War had stated that this was being done . . . on the order of the King."
> The President: "Do you know to what this care on the part of the then King might be due?"
> Rostov: "I did not ask, Comrade President. (*laughter in the hall*) I asked no one on this matter. I did not undertake any investigation."
> The President: "But you maintained now, that your conduct there was the conduct of a Communist?"
> Rostov: "Yes, it was."
> The President: "Why did the King then show this peculiar concern for you, but showed no concern for the other friends of yours, who, as you have said, were much less active than you? Have the Prosecutors any questions?"

"Have the Prosecutors any questions?" For, as the trial unfolds, all are prosecutors: the President, the co-defendants, the lawyers for prosecution and for "defence." Every random fact—a chance encounter with Tito in Moscow in 1933, an accidental visit to the house of the head of the British mission, past Party decisions—is woven into the fabric of a monstrous slander. Before the war "he advanced hostile, left-sectarian Trotskyist ideas in relation to the peasants . . . and helped the monarcho-fascist power." After the war, as Chairman of the Economic Planning Commission, he was responsible for every economic dis-location—the closing of a lemonade factory here and a bread shortage there— which might have aroused discontent among the people. The man who is thus robbed of his honour and accused of betraying his own life's work is excluded from the witness box, and his "defence" handed over to a counsel who com-mences by apologising for "defending" such a traitor, and concludes:

> Comrade Judges, it is my duty to declare before you in accordance with my conscience: as a lawyer, as a citizen of our Republic and as your true assistant, evaluating all these data. . . .
> I admit that indeed the facts of the indictment are proved. . . . This is the revealed truth.

The defendants are allowed a "last plea." One by one they come forward: "Citizen Judges, I plead guilty . . . I deeply repent." Once again, Rostov broke the pattern:

> Rostov: "I consider it the duty of my conscience to declare to the Court and through it to Bulgarian public opinion, that I have never been at the service of British Intelligence, that I have never taken part in the criminal conspiratorial plans of Tito and his clique . . ."
> The President: "What do you want of the Court?"
> Rostov: ". . . that I have always had an attitude . . ."
> The President: "What do you want of the Court?"
> Rostov: ". . . of respect and esteem for the Soviet Union."

A co-defendant is hustled forward to denounce Rostov once more as "the chief organiser and leader of the anti-State conspiracy . . . coward . . . traitor." This time the President does not intervene.

And what did Rostov "want of the Court"? Justice would have been too much to have asked for. What equal is there for the bitter irony with which this man, twice tried for his life before a court in which there was no justice to be found, replies to the Judge, "I did not undertake any investigation." But we—we surely must *undertake* some investigation into the moral conduct of his accus-ers? What moral touchstone impelled Rostov to defend, before a court of unjust Communists, the honour of his conduct as a Communist? Why should he feel it to be the "duty of my conscience" to uphold this honour, when all around him were conscienceless?

This is not a case of some chance injustice committed in the heat of revolutionary ferment. Excesses of violence in times of class confrontation, the vengeance of popular anger against quislings and collaborators—such actions can be understood, or justified, as the rough justice of the people. But the Rostov case—which is symptomatic of a thousand other actions—is a case of a deliberate, carefully conceived act of injustice. It is in no sense an accident of passion. Its intention is plain. The removal of a political opponent is only a minor objective. It is as important to rob him of his honour as of his life. The purpose, first, is to deceive the people. As such, the action corrupts not only all those who take part in the betrayal and the deception: it will result, also, in tendencies towards the corruption of society. Its further purpose is to create a climate of fear and suspicion, within which the manipulators of power can intimidate opposition; and especially opposition from within the ranks of the Communist Party, where many of the most principled and courageous socialists will be found.

Confronted by such facts as these, the Stalinist argument as to the identity of moral and political "estimation" falls to pieces. No doubt Rakosi or Beria may have "estimated" that such actions were "in the interests of the working class": they temporarily strengthened the power of the state, stampeded the people into "monolithic unity," drove terror into the hearts of opponents, and so on. But we are concerned not with the "estimations" of the initiators of these actions but with the moral degeneracy which such actions reveal. "Wrong theories" do not frame-up, slander and kill old comrades, but wrong men, with wrong attitudes to their fellow men. For Khruschev to tell us that Stalin "believed" he was defending the interests of the working-class is beside the point. The scourges of mankind, from Genghiz Khan to the agents of the Inquisition, believed themselves to be instruments of some ultimate good; history may bestow a tithe of its compassion upon them, but the rest is reserved for their victims.

We feel these actions to be wrong, because our moral judgements do not depend upon abstractions or remote historical contingencies, but arise from concrete responses to the particular actions, relations, and attitudes of human beings. No amount of speculation upon intention or outcome can mitigate the horror of the scene. Those moral values which the people have created in their history, which the writers have encompassed in their poems and plays, come into judgement on the proceedings. As we watch the counsel for the defence spin out his hypocrisies, the gorge rises, and those archetypes of treachery, in literature and popular myth, from Judas to Iago, pass before our eyes. The fourteenth-century ballad singer would have known this thing was wrong. The student of Shakespeare knows it is wrong. The Bulgarian peasant, who recalls that Rostov and Chervenkov had eaten together the bread and salt of comradeship, knows it is wrong. Only the "Marxist-Leninist-Stalinist" thinks it was—a mistake.

Questions of Morality

SURELY AFTER COMMITTING—and condoning—such "mistakes" as these, Marxism is condemned to the derision or disgust of history?

Professor G. D. H. Cole has drawn, once again, this conclusion. "The entire structure of Communist ideology rests," he declares, on the belief that "there is in the real world no morality except class morality":

> It was therefore justifiable and necessary for the proletariat to use any method and to take any action that would help it towards victory over its class-enemies. . . . If Communists abstained from certain kinds of action treated as "unmoral" by bourgeois moralists . . . they did so solely because they thought them more likely to harm than to further the revolutionary cause. (*New Statesman*, 20 April 1957)

Such events as the Rostov trial and the suppression of the Hungarian Revolution reveal "the foundations of Communist philosophy nakedly exposed in action." "Real" Communists may quibble about the tactical—or political—expediency of such actions, but they have no grounds for moral revulsion. Those who feel such revulsion are not "real" Communists, but are left-wing democratic socialists who do not, at bottom, accept Marx's ideas.

In phrasing his argument this way, I think that Professor Cole misstates the nature of the conflict now taking place within the world communist movement. The premise which he advances ("class morality") can certainly be derived from certain writings of Marx and Engels, and more especially of Lenin, but it is certainly not the whole of their meaning, implicit and explicit. And the conclusions derived from it are—it seems to me—an accurate summary, not of "real" Communism but of the partisan ideology of Stalinism, which emerged in particular conditions and which has never been co-terminous with the whole communist movement. Hence it may equally be said that this conflict is the revolt against the ideology of Stalinism, and a struggle to make explicit the true, humanist content of "real" Communism.

This distortion of moral values also finds a root in the conditions of revolutionary struggle. It is easy, in our parochial island, to forget these conditions: the repression of the Commune, 1905, civil war and famine, the massacre of Shanghai, the fascist terror. I recall the experiences of some of those Bulgarian partisans, with whom my brother fought. One—a young peasant—had had all his hair torn from his head, when beaten in the fascist police station; a friend had been thrown alive into the boilers of the Sofia police; another had disappeared, leaving no trace, until his signet ring and gold teeth had been found in the drawer of a police agent. This collaborator had poured acid into the wounds of partisans. That man had broken under indescribable torture and been forced to enter the service of the police. The movement was penetrated by agents. Men lived in exile, underground, in daily fear of arrest.

Such facts emphasise the crucible within which Stalinism—with its emphasis on hard, completely selfless, unbreakable, steel-like qualities—was cast. Stalin, over Lenin's bier, was engaging in neither rhetoric nor hypocrisy: "We Communists are people of a peculiar cut. We are cut out of peculiar stuff." Men were killed, betrayed, deserted: only the Party went on. The comrades themselves might be anonymous, unknown to each other. In storm and defeat, in concentration camp and partisan detachment, there grew up that intensity of self-abnegation, that sense of acting as the instrument of historical necessity, above all, that intense loyalty to the Party, as the summation of both personal and social aspirations. In Spain, in China, in Greece, in Yugoslavia, such Communist virtues signed the human record with nobility. Such virtues define the "conduct of a Communist."

But Stalinism, itself bred from such storm, turned these virtues into instruments of destruction. The centre of moral authority was removed from the community or the conscience of the individual and entrusted to the Party. Loyalty to Party bred hostility to all "factions" or non-conformists. A partisan ideology was buttressed by partisan moral attitudes: loyalty to Party and Cause displaced loyalty to particular human beings. Hence the phenomenon of the great purges when Stalinism found enemies in every street, and—in the name of the Party— friend denounced friend, husband denounced wife. Hence those victims who went to their deaths self-accused—even, in some cases, convinced of their own "objective" treason—in the name of loyalty to the Party. Hence, the demoralisation of Communist victims, who found the strength to endure fascist tortures but who entered the jails of the O.G.P.U. divided against themselves. And yet all this human oppression took place under the slogans of Communism. The victims were forced to confess to betrayals of communist principles and "communist conduct." By this alchemy human qualities were transformed into their opposites, loyalty bred treachery, self-sacrifice bred self-accusation, devotion to the people bred abstract, administrative violence.

This, then, is the soil of social reality which fostered the growth of those immoral features which have congealed in Stalinist ideology. Together with anti-intellectualism, they are embodied in institutional form in the rigid forms of "democratic centralism" of the Communist parties. These remove the centre of moral authority from the individual conscience and confer it to the leadership of the Party. Even in Britain, extremes of loyalty, identification of the Party with personal and social aspirations, reveal themselves in attitudes towards the critic who threatens to break the "unity of the Party" of intense hatred, which are rarely displayed towards the avowed enemy—the capitalist. Such attitudes are, of course, to be found in all factional squabbles in isolated religious or political sects; where—as in China or Italy—the parties have mass membership, so they are moralised or humanised by the moral attitudes prevalent among the masses of the people. But the most serious thing is that these humanist values (which always and in every country inform the feelings of the majority of the Communist rank and file) do not find expression in Communist orthodoxy; whereas destructive, partisan, anti-humanist and abstract attitudes have found sanction, perpetuation, and even glorification in Stalinist ideology.

Professor Cole has delineated this ideology in outline; although I think it is not so much an amorality (the ends justify the means) as an immorality (a predisposition towards morally repugnant means, an abstract instead of concrete attitude to men) which finds expression in Stalinism. Its ideological form arises, once again, from the mechanical expression of the "superstructure–base" relationship; because (Engels) "the economic movement finally asserts itself as necessary," Stalinism attempts to short-circuit the processes of social life by disclosing "economic necessity," by asserting economic, i.e. class, interests as the only "real" sources of human motivation.[3] This entirely mistakes man's nature, as revealed in his unfolding history. The Stalinist is fixated by Pavlov's dogs: if a bell was rung, they salivated. If an economic crisis comes the people will salivate good "Marxist-Leninist" belief. But Roundhead, Leveller, and Cavalier, Chartist and Anti-Corn Law Leaguer, were not dogs; they did not salivate their creeds in response to economic stimuli; they loved and hated, argued, thought, and made moral choices. Economic changes impel changes in social relationships, in relations between real men and women; and these are apprehended, felt, reveal themselves in feelings of injustice, frustration, aspirations for social change; all is fought out in the human consciousness, including the moral consciousness. If this were not so, men would be—not dogs—but ants, adjusting their society to upheavals in the terrain. But men make their own history: they are part agents, part victims: it is precisely the element of agency which distinguishes them from the beasts, which is the *human* part of man, and which it is the business of our consciousness to increase.

Nowhere is this deformation of thought seen more clearly than in the Stalinist attitude to the arts. At bottom, the Stalinist simply does not understand what the arts are *about*: he can see "good" or "bad" political ideas ("content") expressed in artistic form, but he is puzzled to understand why it is necessary to dress them up in this way—except as a kind of salad-dressing to make political theory more palatable, or else as forms of entertainment, amusement, relaxation. Thus the

Stalinist can make speeches about cultural amenities under socialism; there will be more three-decker concerts, more editions of the classics; these will "enrich" the people's leisure. But the understanding of the arts as the supreme expression of man's imaginative and moral consciousness, as media, through which men struggle to apprehend reality, order their responses, change their own attitudes and therefore change themselves—all this escapes from the categories of Stalinist mechanistic thought. Hence the enforced abasement of the moral and imaginative faculties before the seat of political judgment. Hence political judgment is not envisaged as the—unattainable but approximate—summation of those moral, imaginative, intellectual processes which are carried on throughout a society; but as the adjustment of human beings to the dictation of expediency or of "economic necessity." If their consciousness can be adjusted as well, so much the better; and this is the role assigned to the arts.

This, then, is the second decisive feature of Stalinist ideology: like all ideologies, it is a form of "self-alienation"; man forgets himself in abstractions, he is delivered over to the State, the Party, the sanctity of public property. Is Professor Cole right to say that this is "real" Communist theory, and can logically be derived from Marx? There is colour for this view to be found, first, in the failure of Marx and Engels to make explicit their moral concepts, and in the passive connotation sometimes attached by them to the concept of "reflection" (as opposed to "cognition"). Second, in the tone which they adopted within particular—and now easily forgotten—historical conditions in their polemics against various forms of "utopian" and "idealist" theories. But implicit within their historical method, explicit in their own moral evaluations, there is a total rejection of such moral nihilism.

Much confusion starts from Engels' statement in *Anti-Duhring*:

> As society has hitherto moved in class antagonisms, morality was always a class morality; it has either justified the domination and interests of the ruling class, or, as soon as the oppressed class has become powerful enough, it has represented the revolt against this domination and the future interests of the oppressed. That in this process there has been on the whole progress in morality, as in all other branches of human knowledge, cannot be doubted. But we have not yet passed beyond class morality. A really human morality which transcends class antagonisms and their legacies in thought becomes possible only at a stage of society which has not only overcome class contradictions but has even forgotten them in practical life.

It is important to realise that this statement commences with an observation derived from the study of history: it is not a statement about what morality is, or ought to be. Past moralities have not been the same thing as class interests;

they have justified or challenged these interests. It is self-evident that if the moral concepts dominant in a society challenge the interests of the ruling class, these concepts must either be without effect upon conduct (and express themselves in mysticism, retreat from action) or they must be revolutionary in implication. This then is a statement about the actually observed moral conduct of men in history; although as such it demands qualification in that men's moral consciousness may profoundly affect the form in which social antagonisms find expression, may mitigate or exarcerbate their conflicts, in the same way that the degree of approximation to reality of their intellectual concepts will affect the course of history.[4] "Timon of Athens" did not sway capitalism from its course, but it helped to ignite the mind of Marx; Blake's "Songs" did not end human exploitation, but may have influenced the treatment of children in industry. Moreover, only casuistry could argue that Shakespeare or Blake were "reflecting" the future interests of the working class. They were the tongues which—within the limitations of their time—spoke for *humanity*.

This is the source of Marx and Engels' humanism, which glows through all their writings and sustained them in their heroic intellectual discipline. It springs from anguish at man's self-divided, self-defeating history. "Everything civilization brings forth is double-edged, double-tongued, divided against itself, contradictory" (Engels). But throughout history, man, the undivided conscious agent, is emergent. It is not the same "man" at any point in history, though there are elements of human experience—before death and old age, birth, sexual experience—little influenced by class environment, and in this soil the arts take their root. But there is no quintessential "human nature," "no abstraction inherent in each separate individual," in all times and all societies. Rather, as history unfolds, as men make their own nature, there is a constantly developing *human potential*, which the false consciousness and distorted relations of class society deny full realisation. Hence Marx and Engels' constant reference to the powers "slumbering within" men; we know these powers to be present, from outstanding individuals, from periods of history in which creative energies or special aptitudes spring forth, almost without warning. Hence their repeated forecast of a "really human morality," "purely human sentiments," relations between men as opposed to relations between things. Hence their confidence that socialism—the abolition of classes—made possible the assertion of man's humanity, of his potential nature, of that which is specifically human in man: victim no longer of nature or of himself, but a conscious moral agent. "Man is the sole animal capable of working his way out of the merely animal state—his normal state is one appropriate to his consciousness, *one* to be *created* by *himself*." ("Dialects of Nature")

It is an axiom of some philosophy today that one cannot derive an "ought" from an "is," a moral imperative from a statement of fact. But from where else are moral concepts derived than from the "is" of man? Men's actions spring from the kind of people they are; they are what they are as a result of their environment and their ideas, including their moral ideas; judgments made on their actions are made by other, different, people. But men in class society are divided against themselves. They would like to have peace, but they get war; and so on. The quarrel between man's potential and his actual social existence expresses itself in frustrations, neuroses, moral corruption, if suffered passively. "He who desires but acts not, breeds pestilence," wrote Blake. In his youth he imagines himself adventurous, heroic, a passionate lover; he ends up reading the "News of the World" and watching Liberace on ITV. But if met actively, rebelliously, this quarrel is expressed in moral idealism, aspirations for a changed social existence, which gives rise to purposive social action.[5] Hence—as, again, Marx and Engels repeatedly asserted—moral judgments cannot be derived from abstract precepts and commandments, but only from real men and women, their suffering or well-being, frustrations and aspirations. Such judgments are bound to congeal into precepts, some of limited validity, and attaining towards a "universal" validity in class-less society. But the precept "Love One Another" did not prevent world war between Christian nations: and the precept "Interests of the Working Class" did not prevent tens of thousands of working people from being caught up in the great purge. What is important, in class society, is to judge *the men behind the precepts,* and the effect of their conduct upon other men. What does one judge *with?* One judges as a moral being: one responds with one's moral consciousness, itself the product of environment, of culture, and of agency. This is to say that moral judgments are never *easy;* because they are not abstractions, but are concerned with real men and women, they are as difficult as life. Nor is this relativism; man's moral consciousness has evolved in as real a sense as his intellectual consciousness. This consciousness comes to the point of expression, above all, in the direct and concrete perception of the artist; responding to the real quality of the life about him, evaluating this beside past culture, ordering his responses into forms which operate upon men, change their attitudes and their moral being in their turn. Thus the insights of William Morris, his discoveries about man's potential moral nature, were not icing on the Marxist gingerbread, but were complementary to the discoveries of Marx. Thus the Stalinist ideology, which reduces the moral consciousness to class relativism, or to Pavlovian behaviourism, forgets the creative spark without which man would not be man. By inhibiting the expression, at all levels of society, of this moral consciousness, Stalinism leads men to the denial of their own nature. The "end" of Communism is not a "political" end, but a human end; or rather, the end of man's transition from the animal, the beginning of man, the assertion of his full humanity. As such it is an economic, intellectual, *and* moral end; the conscious fight for moral principle must enter into every "political" decision; a moral end can only be attained by moral means. But this cannot be envisaged as taking place solely within the structure of "monolithic" party. The political leader may not have the gifts of the artist; the artist will make a poor political tactician. We must think less in terms of principles than in terms of social process. Stalinism will not be checked by electing poets to the Central Committee of the CPSU. The poet (let us say) must respond to the feelings of people, write poems which make them aware of their aspirations, change their attitudes, and thus colour the political conduct of the people. Such processes as these, side by side with institutions and legal codes, are guarantees of the liberties and moral health of a people. It is not without significance that the worst frenzies of the purge came after the deaths of Gorki and Mayakovsky. It is no accident that Stalinism reserved its special hatred for the artist. A Khruschev Constitution will indicate the end of Stalinism no more than did the Stalin Constitution. One Dudintsev and the response among the people to his work is a more potent sign.

Man's moral being cannot be sold into slavery to political expediency. The revolt against Stalinism is a revolt of the human conscience against this warped and militant philistinism. It is to be expected that it is through the conscience of the artist that this first finds expression. Thus Tibor Dery:

> As a writer my main concern is man. My criticism begins when I see man unhappy, especially when I see men and women suffer unnecessarily.... They [the Hungarian CP leaders] build and function on suspicion and distrust. They underestimate the people's sense of honour and its moral force; its capacity to think and to create.

In a thousand ways real life contradicts the empty exhortations of *Pravda*: "rotten elements" are seen to be men of integrity and courage, "enemies of the working class" to be honest students and working people, the paternal party functionary to be an ambitious, egotistical prig. Those pressures for conformity, in an exhausted, post-revolutionary, largely peasant society—symbolised in the appalling declension from Makarenko's early vibrant *Road to Life* to his later "Victorian," *Book for Parents*—and expressed in reactionary tendencies in education, social life and sexual morality—are beginning to break up. The fundamental moral consciousness of the people is unimpaired; the aspirations from which the socialist movement sprang grow stronger, not weaker. The relations of men in production are distorted by bureaucracy, but they do not conceal the potentials of socialist democracy. In Moscow and Leningrad the students and young people have found their rulers out. They have been given the jam of culture, in row upon row of "classics," and it has turned to ashes in their mouths. They can bring Aeschylus and Tolstoy into criticism of Khruschev, the clown who sits on history's steeple. They are turning to their own living writers, and the writers are turning to them, seeking a relationship no longer impeded by the monolithic party. Direct lines of communication are being laid. Thus Vasek Kana, the Czech writer, declared:

> The factory workers are my closest friends. I was born amongst them, I have remained loyal to them, and above all it is before them that I wish to ease my conscience. Did I help them when they needed my help? Did I protect them against those bureaucrats who sat round a green table and ordered them to produce absurd norms? Did I defend them when their criticisms brought down moral and material reprisals upon them? . . . Did I condemn a system of leadership based more often than not on lack of trust in the people? . . . Did I publicly condemn the self-styled "leading cadres" who behaved like lordlings? Did I stand up against those self-styled "organisers" who organised our life in such a manner that one could no longer live?

The people are beginning to heal themselves, and no amount of talk of "demagogy" and "revisionism" can halt the process, which will show itself in changed attitudes, changed relationships, changed responses, above all in changed men.

Stalinist ideology—this partisan consciousness of a revolutionary elite, born in conditions of indescribable hardship, encumbered by mechanistic errors to which Lenin contributed—arises from and perpetuates the class attitudes of hatred, and brings, in turn, hatred and suspicion into its own midst. Engels had confidence in "that morality which contains the maximum of durable elements . . . the one which, in the present, represents the overthrow of the present, represents the future: that is, the proletarian." (*Anti-Duhring*) The best features of the labour movement in his time, with its international outlook, its assertion of the brotherhood of man, its emphasis upon the dignity of labour, its pursuit of knowledge and culture, justified this confidence. "It has quickened and given life to feelings of a broader sympathy and brotherly trust, has increased the intelligence, elevated the moral tone, and brightened the life of all who, having regard for themselves and love for their fellows . . . have thrown in their lot in the battle of labour against capital." (Gasworkers' Address of 1889.) Such a morality, rooted in the strong social ties of the pit, the union, common industrial struggles, should lead on to the outlook of "socialised humanity." But such a morality contains also the attitudes of hatred to the enemy, utter repudiation from human fellowship of the blackleg or scab, vigilance against the agent or collaborator. Stalinism neglected the first group of attitudes, and exalted the second. Thus George Hardy, a British veteran of many bitter struggles, records in his memoirs a speech delivered in Shanghai in 1951:

As an old 'un I took the liberty . . . of reminding my hearers that the price of liberty is eternal vigilance. "The enemies," I said, "have not given up. They still exist in Shanghai and must be rooted out." This brought the audience to their feet, shouting slogans and raising their right hands.

Vigilance is necessary, and certainly in China, with Chiang-Kai-Shek and the U.S. Fleet off the mainland. But the constant heightened emphasis on vigilance, upon "ruthlessly smashing," "stamping out," etc., all opposition can—without effective institutional safeguards and freedoms—be used as a dangerous instrument of power to silence criticism, as Chinese leaders now admit. Tom Mann, on his many international missions, did not speak this language of "rooting out," "smashing," and "ruthlessness." He trusted the working people to display a morality superior to that of their oppressors. He—and others of his generation—were not afraid to speak, not only of the virtues of militancy, but also of fellowship, brotherhood, and even of love. After half a century of butchery, fascism, the betrayals of 1926 and 1931, this last word raises an immediate and cynical reaction even in Britain; but men have made this word also in their history, and there is no other which we can use. Socialism is the expression of man's need for his fellow men, his undivided social being, and hence it must find expression in love, even when attained only through the throes of class hatred and conflict. In the humanism of Marx's own writings there is an ultimate compassion, within which the partisan passions are contained. As he declared, in his Preface to *Capital*:

> Since I understand the development of the economic structure of society to be a natural process, I should be the last to hold the individual responsible for conditions whose creature he himself is, socially speaking, however much he may raise himself above them subjectively.

This is not to deny all moral criteria; for men have a region of moral agency, all the same. Nor can the compassion which flows from understanding have much influence upon action in certain historical contingencies—in war, confronted with fascism, in extreme industrial conflict—when men *must* be partisan. Nevertheless, the methods of violence inescapable in such contingencies must never be glorified; the Christian precept, "Forgive them, for they know not what they do," must reassert itself whenever and to the degree that contingencies allow. And the judgment on such "contingencies" is not a political judgment, but a moral judgment also. The political criminal (the fascist thug, the agent, the AVO torturer) must be tried for his criminality, not for his class origins or political affiliations. Those whose anti-social behaviour constitutes a danger to their fellow men must be re-educated, not left to rot in camps. Wrong ideas must be fought with right ideas, not by liquidating the men who hold them. Such attitudes of compassion did indeed find their expression in the early years of the Russian revolution; they find their expression in China today. This understanding that socialists work to liberate all humanity from the stunting antagonisms of class never left Marx or Engels' minds. I have before me the unpublished draft of the principles of the North of England Socialist Federation, annotated in Engels' hand. The original (by J. L. Mahon) reads: the Federation "aims at abolishing the Capitalist and Landlord class, and forming the workers of society into a Co-operative Commonwealth." But Engels amends it as follows: "aims at abolishing the Capitalist and Landlord class, as well as the wage-working class, and forming *all* members of society into a Co-operative Commonwealth." (My emphasis.) So slight a change, but so significant today! Socialist humanism places real people once again at the centre of its aspiration. It remembers the precept of Timon: "Men are born to do benefits." And what else is the "economic base" of socialism but men doing benefits to each other, and thereby enriching themselves? Stalinism seeks to freeze the "dialectic" into an orthodox, enforced collectivism. But social existence in the Soviet Union, people's new feelings and aspirations, conflict with this orthodoxy. New men and women are arising who seek to create a society, not of stagnation, but where the false dialectic of class is replaced by the human quarrel between the actual and the potential, between the boundless aspirations of life and the necessary limitations of the particular, the concrete, the personal. They seek to make men whole.

Contempt for the People

ALWAYS LIFE IS MORE unexpected, arbitrary, contradictory than the thoughts of the philosopher who abstracts and makes conceptual patterns, or the art of the poet who responds and organises his responses. But insofar as man is an agent, an "educator," he changes himself according to his thoughts and values; he tries to make his own history according to the laws of logic and the laws of beauty. If his concepts are false, do not correspond to social reality, he will cause himself suffering; hence Marx's insistence that theory finds its final test in action (a precept which demonstrates incontestibly the total corruption of Stalinist ideology). But also, if he fails to fashion coherent concepts at all, he abandons his own creative agency; he becomes a simple pragmatist, who muddles along in response to one social contingency after another. This is also likely to bring suffering onto his head.

This fashioning of concepts, this disposition to act by their laws, is not something which is carried on in society just by thinkers and poets, not something which is done for the rest of society by "intellectuals." We take examples from such people because it is in their activities—the systematised cultural disciplines within which they are engaged—that this human process (being—thinking and responding—becoming) finds its clearest point of expression. But every man is an intellectual and moral being. And here we come to a third distinctive feature of Stalinist ideology. Men, Marx held, develop their own nature in their labour, and in their relations with each other in the social act of labour:

> Labour is, in the first place, a process in which both man and Nature participate, and in which man of his own accord starts, regulates, and controls the material reactions between himself and Nature. He opposes himself to Nature as one of her own forces, setting in motion arms and legs, head and hands, the natural forces of his body, in order to appropriate Nature's productions in a form adapted to his own wants. By thus acting on the external world and changing it, he at the same time changes his own nature. He develops his slumbering powers and compels them to act in obedience to his sway.

Initiation, regulation and control demand intellectual and moral agency. Men must understand the seasons, plant their crops, store their seed, enter into relations with each other in the sowing and the harvest. Man's actions are human actions: and, also, "his own wants" are not purely animal wants, but human needs, physical, moral and intellectual. He needs clothes for warmth, and also for adornment; he needs shelter, but also "room to turn round in," privacy, etc. In this resides the dignity of human labour, which Marx explicitly dissociated from "those primitive instinctive forms of labour that remind us of the mere animal":

> We presuppose labour in a form that stamps it as exclusively human. A spider conducts operations that resemble those of a weaver, and a bee puts to shame many an architect in the construction of her cells. But what distinguishes the worst architect from the best of bees is this, that the architect raises his structure in imagination before he erects it in reality. (*Capital*, I, iii, VII)

At root the Stalinist does not recognise this central fact. When he reads that men "set in motion" their heads, he conjures up a picture of men butting their heads against trees, or jerking them about as they lift weights. He conceives of the "economic base" as made up of things—ploughs, spinning jennies, shipyards—to which men are appended, and which they affect only by technical innovations. Stalin finds it necessary to remind his readers that

> the development and improvement of the instruments of production was effected by men who were related to production, and not independently of men; and, consequently, the change and development of the

instruments of production was accompanied by a change and development of men, as the most important element of the productive forces.

But this grudging recognition of the agency—in a technological sense—of "the most important element of the productive forces" is sternly qualified: "The rise of new productive forces . . . takes place not as a result of the deliberate and conscious activity of man, but spontaneously, unconsciously, independently of the will of man." (*Dialectical & Historical Materialism*)

Stalin is led to this ridiculous conclusion by confusing the development of new productive forces (which is certainly the result of conscious, purposive action) with the compulsive social relations which arise involuntarily from this development. That is, Crompton and Watt and ten thousand others engage in deliberate and conscious activity; but they do not consciously will or foresee the train of social consequences which will flow from the changes they effect. But the Stalinist forgets that the "economic base" is a fiction descriptive not of men's physical-economic activities alone, but of their moral and intellectual being as well. Production, distribution and consumption are not only digging, carrying, and eating, but are also planning, organising and enjoying. Imaginative and intellectual faculties are not confined to a "superstructure" and erected upon a "base" of things (including men-things); they are implicit in the creative act of labour which makes man man.

From this flows that feature of Stalinist ideology which can best be described as anti-democratic, inherently bureaucratic, alternately paternalist or despotic towards the people. To understand the social environment within which this false idea took root we must turn to the experts on post-revolutionary Soviet society. It arises, surely, in part from the outlook of a revolutionary elite, desperately aware of its historical mission and almost impossible tasks, operating within a society without long democratic traditions or experience of democratic institutions, and with a large part of the people indifferent or actively hostile to its ideas. In this context we see the elite's self-identification with the "superstructure" operating upon a material base of economic (but not moral, intellectual) needs or discontents. Hence the fetishism of heavy industry, and neglect of consumer needs; hence the bureaucratic administration of industry, the central planning of economic life so minute that in Poland (for example) even the number of cucumbers to be pickled was included in the Five Year Plan. The desperate backwardness of Russia, the compelling need to force the pace of industrialisation, created the climate within which these practices and ideas grew up; but they led to the ultimate contradiction of a socialist economy which, instead of releasing the economic, the creative, initiatives of men, inhibits them and cramps them, and therefore slows down its own economic growth. Hence that whole tissue of bureaucraticism revealed so dramatically in the Polish 8th Plenum:

The working class was not master in its workshops, in its name control was exercised by the representatives of the state—a bureaucracy often indifferent to the needs of the masses. The needs of the masses, their standard of living, did not determine our economic planning—but, on the contrary, they were determined by plans, which often, at the expense of the masses, were based on wrong assumptions. This is why in spite of great successes in construction, the working class is so exasperated and disillusioned. (Arthur Starewicz, *The Polish Road*, p. 36)

But hence also a whole constellation of political attitudes, elitist, paternal, and anti-democratic, in Stalinist ideology. Hence the tone of Stalinist propaganda, throughout the world: the addressing of political demands almost exclusively to economic discontents, the belittling of the common sense, moral idealism, and political judgment of working people. Hence the ridiculous structure and strategy of the British CP which within the heart of an advanced political democracy, where above all it is the minds and consciences of the people which must be won for socialism, cannot help but foster within itself an elitist outlook. Despite all resolutions for building the "mass party," the masses refuse to be politically convinced by the most self-sacrificing of economic actions alone. The mind of the people lies open; but the Communist stubbornly addresses himself to the "economic base." The working man asks moral questions: the Communist only hands him a rent petition. Despite all the talk of "faith in the people," despite all the exaltation of the' "instincts" of the working class (as men-things, economic base), Stalinism conceals a colossal contempt, a vast all-embracing attitude of patronage, towards working men and women. This is the political expression of Stalinism: its veiled hostility to democratic initiatives in every form. Man is an appendage to the "instruments of production": the creative man at the heart of labour, from whom all instruments of production, all politics, all institutions flow, has escaped from the categories of Stalinist ideology.

Questions of Theory

THE IDEOLOGY OF STALINISM, then, has three distinctive features: anti-intellectualism, moral nihilism, and the denial of the creative agency of human labour, and thus of the value of the individual as an agent in society. This is not the same thing as saying that Stalinism is "Marxism with three mistakes"; at a certain point—related to the growth of the Russian bureaucracy, the Third International, and Stalin's own influence—dogmas and partisan class attitudes which had been present in different degrees in the working-class movement crystallised into a *systematised* ideology, held together within a false conceptual framework.

Although proclaimedly materialist, it partook of some of the characteristics of religion. Its symbol is the Lenin mausoleum. Its supreme ideologist was Stalin himself: and it found institutional expression in the CPSU and in the practices of "democratic centralism" in other CPs. Its most systematic exposition is to be found, perhaps, in Stalin's *Dialectical and Historical Materialism* (1938): its institutional justification was provided by the *Short History of the CPSU (B)*.

But the ideology of Stalinism cannot be laid at Stalin's door alone. Several of its features can be traced to ambiguities in the thought of Marx and, even more, to mechanistic fallacies in Lenin's writings. Marx used the word "reflection" in two quite distinct contexts. First, as a statement of the materialist standpoint: sense-impressions "reflect" external material reality which exists independently of human consciousness. Second, as an observation upon the way in which men's ideas and institutions have been determined by their "social being" in their history. But the second observation does not follow from the first premise. It is derived from the study of changing society, whose premises "are men, not in any fantastic isolation or definition, but in their actual, empirically perceptible process of development under definite conditions." Because a sense-impression may be described (metaphorically) as a "reflection" of material reality, it by no means follows that human culture is a passive mirror-reflection of social reality. Whenever Marx and Engels discussed the processes of social change they made it clear that this was not so. But (because scientific research had only begun to open up such questions) they tended to leap the gap between one and the other, and to enquire very little into the problem of *how* men's ideas were formed, and wherein lay their field of agency. The interaction between social environment and conscious agency (being—thinking—becoming) was central to their thought, and it was the neglect of agency which Marx saw as the weakness of mechanical materialism: "The chief defect of all hitherto existing materialism ... is that the object, reality, sensuousness, is conceived only in the form of the *object or contemplation* but not *as human sensuous activity, practice*, not subjectively. (*First Thesis on Feuerbach*)

This gap, between the raw material of experience and the processes of human culture, has increasingly been filled in during the past hundred years, by research into psychology, language, semantics, the sociology of culture, the nature of the arts, etc. Whereas Engels stated that "materialism must assume a new aspect with every new great discovery," Marxism in general has failed to take account of these advances, and—since the time of Lenin—has degenerated into ideology. For this, the uncritical acceptance of Lenin's *Materialism and Empirio-Criticism* must take some share of responsibility. Lenin's inspired political genius was not matched by an equal genius in the field of philosophy. In this work (now sanctified by Stalinism as a "basic text") his concern with the first premise of materialism led him into a number of fallacies. Among these (1) the repeated lumping together of ideas, consciousness, thought, and sensations as "reflections" of material reality. (But a sense-impression, which animals share with men, is not the same thing as an idea, which is the product of exceedingly complex cultural processes peculiar to men.) (2) The repeated statement, in an emotive manner, that material reality is "primary" and "consciousness, thought, sensation" is "secondary," "derivative." (Partially true: but we must guard against the emotional undertones that therefore thought is less important than material reality. Man is a conscious being, not an animal being with a "derivative" consciousness.) (3) Lenin slipped over from Marx's observation "social being determines social consciousness" to the quite different (and untrue) statement that "social consciousness reflects social being." (4) From this, he slipped over to the grotesque conclusion that "social being is independent of the social consciousness of humanity." (How can conscious human beings, whose consciousness is employed in every act of labour, exist independently of their consciousness?) (5) From this it was a small step to envisaging consciousness as a clumsy process of *adaptation* to independently existing "social being." "The necessity of nature is primary, and human will and mind secondary. The latter must necessarily and inevitably adapt themselves to the former." (S.W. 11, p. 248) "The highest task of humanity is to comprehend the objective logic of economic evolution . . . so that it may be possible to adapt to it one's social consciousness . . . in as definite, clear and critical a fashion as possible." (p. 376)

Thus the concept of human *agency*, of the "educators and the educated," became lost in a determinism where the role of consciousness was to adapt itself to "the objective logic of economic evolution." Human consciousness might thus be described as a form of innate behaviour pattern set in motion by economic stimuli, and with a very limited agency in making men conscious of their own innate adaptiveness. Such a pattern might be built within an electronic brain. Stalin's references to the "organising, mobilising and transforming role" of ideas are always framed within such a context of more or less efficient responses to stimuli. Hence Marx's commonsense view that man's freedom is enlarged by each enlargement of knowledge ("Freedom . . . consists in the control over ourselves and over external nature which is founded on knowledge of natural necessity," Engels) is transformed into the mystique of man's freedom consisting in his recognising and serving "the objective logic of economic evolution": his "freedom" becomes slavery to "necessity." Thus from one fallacy we slip to another: a passive "reflection" cannot initiate, plan, make revolutions; Lenin, absorbed in philosophical nuances, forgot that Marx and Engels held that social being determined social consciousness, not because of any automatic "reflection," but because in class society the compulsive nature of social relations gives rise to a conflict of wills, giving rise in turn to social changes which no one wills. In forgetting this he removed the cause of social change from the agency of men to the agency of economic necessity. But this led on (in Stalin) simply to a new form of dualism, in which man's conscious-ness is no more than the projection of a "soul" within matter, a "dialectic" within the instruments of production, the source of all change.

In a healthy socialist environment these fallacies would soon have been sifted out from the rich harvest of Lenin's political thought. But in fact the fallacies were seized upon by Stalin, systematised, and built into the framework of his thought. In *Dialectical and Historical Materialism* all sense of human agency, all understanding of the "educators and the educated," has disappeared.

If nature being the material world, is primary, and mind, thought, sec-ondary, derivative; if the material world represents objective reality exist-ing independently of the mind of men, while the mind is a reflection of this objective reality, it follows that the material life of society, its being, is also primary, and its spiritual life secondary, derivative, and that the material life of society is an objective reality existing independently of the *will* of men, while the spiritual life of society is a reflection of this objective reality.

The very mode of thought is idealist and mechanistic. Historical materialism is "the extension of the principles of dialectical materialism to the study of social life" (instead of the study of reality giving rise to, etc.); it is the "application of the principles of dialectical materialism to the phenomena of the life of soci-ety" (that is, the principles are imposed on the phenomena). The understand-ing of process ("our ideas of movement") is reduced to a vile physico-economic automatism: "Hence the practical activity of the party of the proletariat must not be based on the good wishes of 'outstanding individuals', not on the dictates of 'reason', 'universal morals', etc., but on the laws of development of society and on the study of these laws."

As if such "laws" of "society" exist independently of man's rational and moral being. But the whole structure of thought is corrupt. Stalin, trained in a Greek Orthodox seminary, was known as a "strong Marxist": and he had, indeed, an inexorable logic in leading from false premises to false conclusions. The honest Stalinist does not repudiate Stalin; he opens Stalin's works, is enmeshed in his logic, believes it, and then looks up and cannot understand the world. Surely Stalin's ideas are right: there must have been slips, "mistakes" in his practice? Let the reader return again to this work, and when amidst the blind automatism of productive forces, ask himself suddenly, "Yes, but where are *men*? Where is the man that Marx described, using his head and his hands in his labour?"

Such is the dependence of the development of the relations of production on the development of the productive forces of society, and primarily, on the development of the instruments of production, the dependence by virtue of which the changes and development of the productive forces sooner or later lead to corresponding changes and development of the relations of production.

The Khruschev Era

THE INSTITUTIONAL FORM—democratic centralism—has already been much discussed and well analysed.[6] Independent of arguments as *to* the validity of this or that type of organisation to particular contexts, we should view the CPSU and in varying degrees other CPs as institutions adapted to the needs of an ideological orthodoxy. It is in the nature of an orthodoxy that inhibits the emergence of unorthodox ideas, that it must have a source of infallibility, of revealed dogma, as the Catholic Church has its Pope. That is, someone must give the sign for change, someone must move on, or the institution will cease to respond to changing circumstances at all. If there is a lurch, or someone on the lower rung moves first, everything may be thrown into disorder, as after the Khruschev speech (Togliatti, Thorez, etc.). Thus the cult of the personality arose from the ideology of Stalinism, and not vice versa. So Party functions, Congresses, etc., assumed the form of devotional exercises, reaching their dizzy zenith in Stalin's reply to the debate at the 17th Congress (1934):

Comrades, the debate at this Congress has revealed complete unity of opinion among our Party leaders on all questions of Party policy, one can say. As you know, no objections whatever have been raised against the report. Hence, it has been revealed that there is extraordinary ideological-political and organisational solidarity in the ranks of our Party. (Applause) The question arises: Is there any need, after this, for a speech in reply to the debate? I think there is no need for it. Permit me therefore to refrain from making a speech in reply. (Ovation. All the delegates rise to their feet. Loud cheers. A chorus of cheers: "Long Live Stalin!" The delegates, all standing, sing the "Internationale," after which the ovation is resumed. Shouts of "Cheers for Stalin!" "Long live Stalin! Long live the C.C.!")

It is unfortunate that despite such unity it proved necessary that so many of these delegates should have to be shot. But it was through the denial of the role of individuals as agents in history, as initiators in the Party, that one individual took all of history as his role.

But false thinking on this scale repeatedly fails to produce results. The "social-fascists" turn out, after all, to be anti-fascists; Britain, after all, does not join hands with Germany in an anti-Communist crusade. Hence the constant "abrupt changes" in line. Stalin was not only an ideologist: he was also an extremely capable organiser and man of action, as his war leadership proved: indeed, in total war against the vilest expression of capitalism in *history*, ideology and reality were brought into a deceptive unity. But with the end of the war ideology no longer connected with real life. "The Stalinist oscillates between the axiom and 'realpolitik': dogmatism and opportunism. When the axioms cease to produce results, a 'mistake' is 'recognised.'" But the cornucopia from which "mistakes" flow in such abundance is never recognised. With Stalin's death the ideology sustained a tremendous blow. It is still intact, although infallibility attaches to an institution and not a man: the apex of the orthodoxy is now the C.C. of the CPSU. But since Stalin's death we have seen an almost manic oscillation between attempts to shore the dogma up, and concessions to reality. Khruschev is not a jolly pragmatist, doing what he thinks best by his own haphazard lights; he is the opportunist side of the Stalinist moon. The world is changing around him, and he does not understand why. He roars at Gomulka at the airport, and makes it up in Moscow. He denounces Stalin, and declares himself a Stalinist. He issues a statement on past "mistakes" in relations between socialist countries, and smashes the Hungarian rising before the ink is dry. Such actions precede the end of a dogma; but a dogma in its last days is also unpredictable, ill-tempered, dangerous. "We are not saints," declares Khruschev. That the world knows, but it indicates an advance in self-consciousness all the same. For Stalin believed in his own sainthood. Stalin viewed himself as the High Priest of historical necessity: Khruschev is too bothered patching up the holes to think sustainedly at all.

The world is changing because socialist people have changed. All this that I have described—the follies of thought and the corruptions of practice—were carried forward *in the name of Communism*. Stalinism has never been the same thing as the world Communist movement. The corruptions have enmeshed only those in the upper ranks of the inner bureaucracy. Stalinism has killed Communist thinkers, artists, and leaders of the working people, but it has never denied Communism. The precepts of Communism—in rigid and fragmentary forms— have been taught to children in school; voiced in dull lifeless novels; committed to memory by the rank-and-file Party member. The false consciousness was always encroaching: but it was always resisted by the people's traditions, their experiences in life. In those countries where the great purge could not reach, there has been constant conflict within the Communist movements between forces of health and corruption. Without the pressures of the OGPU and frame-ups, nothing could prevent practical experience, the humanist traditions of the socialist movement, the creative ideas of Marx and Engels, from resisting the spreading orthodoxy; only the inner Party bureaucracies, nourished on Stalinist texts and involved in the network of international deception, became true ideologists. But even from among these the pragmatic heretics—Gomulka, Tito, etc.—have constantly been thrown up. And in the Soviet Union new men and women have come on the scene. Where ideology, false consciousness, reigns, "the economic movement finally asserts itself as necessary." The instruments of production in the Soviet Union are socialised. The bureaucracy is not a class, but is parasitic upon that society. Despite its parasitism, the wave of human energy unleashed by the first socialist revolution has multiplied the wealth of society, and vastly enlarged the cultural horizons of the people; schools, books, concerts, technical institutes, art galleries—all these have multiplied also. The false consciousness of Stalinism now makes the bureaucracy—confronted by these enormous human energies—increasingly less capable of performing its function in planning and developing the national economy. On the one hand, economic and social frustrations develop; on the other, men and women struggle for a true, socialist consciousness, and seek to give it political expression. Throughout the Soviet Union people—and especially young people—are sick to the point of nausea with the mumbo-jumbo of *Pravda* and of "Marxism-Leninism-Stalinism." The "correct formulations" and ideological fatuities are contradicted by their living experience, and this gives rise to demands for common sense, decency, and humanity, such as find expression in Dudintsev's *Not By Bread Alone*. Throughout the international communist movement a similar ferment is in progress. The outcome in the Soviet Union cannot be forecast.

Under certain circumstances, the revolt might take the form of a limited political revolution. It must certainly give rise to changed institutions and patterns of social life. This, however, can be said with certainty. One thing only today holds Stalinism in power in the Soviet Union—the fear of war with the West. International relaxation following upon Geneva brought with it internal concession, the return of more prisoners from the camps, the Khruschev speech, the Polish events of October, the Hungarian revolution. Stalinism, bringing precept to fact, identifying all opposition to itself as "counter-revolutionary," crushed the Hungarian irevolt. But it could not crush the contradictions which gave rise to it. The hydrogen bomb, the soundly based fear of aggression from American imperialism (which every day announces new advanced bases for atomic missiles) strengthens the bureaucratic and military caste, gives to them their *raison d'être*, gives colour to Stalinist ideology, and at the same time weakens and confuses the fight against Stalinist ideology both in the Soviet Union and outside. The dismantling of Stalinism will not be assisted simply by swelling the chorus of anti-Stalinist abuse. We must understand—and explain—the true character of Stalinism, the new face of Soviet Society immanent within it. We must do what we can to dismantle the hydrogen bomb.

Men versus Things

SO BACK ONCE AGAIN to our parochial island. If this analysis is true, then the commonly found attitudes of British working people to the Soviet Union—that it is "going the right way" but has no democracy, "you can't speak your mind," and so on—have been more healthy than the uncritical allegiance of British-Communists. But this is not the whole truth. The rest lies in this. The Soviet Union is a socialist country, although this is not yet expressed in institutions, political conduct, or public morality. Out of storm, out of error, from a revolution that leapt a chasm of social development and encompassed a people without democratic traditions, there grew this ideology which has contorted the features of socialist man. But those features are human features; they are our features also; we see in them our own future. Hence the British Stalinist who accepts the contortions as "correct" and who distorts his own face into an imitative scowl: "There is no such thing as Marxism without the Communist Party." Hence the Communist who becomes enmeshed in Stalinist ideology simply because he dare not look at those features as they really are, he must idealise them—if he looked, he would lose hope for humanity. Hence also a certain spiritual despair, a paralysis of will, a lack of direction, in the British labour movement; it has seen the Gorgon's head and has lost the desire to move on.

Is it inevitable that the new society must be torn out of the old, with a partisan ideology such as Stalinism? It might be argued that the Bolsheviks would never have held power in Russia, in circumstances of inconceivable difficulty, if they had not strengthened the steel of endurance and summoned emotional energies by developing to their extreme point the partisan attitudes of the proletarian elite. But because Stalinism is the ideology of a proletarian elite in such a context, it does not at all follow that the inevitably partial and partisan outlooks of other working-class movements will give birth to new ideologies. False ideas there are bound to be during the transitional stage which Marx called the dictatorship of the proletariat. But if we learn the lesson of Stalinism, they need not grow into a self-perpetuating system of falsities. There might be some danger, in certain conditions and countries—and if the fall of the Soviet bureaucracy is long delayed—of the Trotskyist ideology taking root and, if victorious, leading on to similar distortions and confusions. Trotskyism is also a self-consistent ideology, being at root an "anti-Stalinism" (just as there were once anti-Popes), arising from the same context as Stalinism, opposing the Stalinist bureaucracy but carrying over into opposition the same false conceptual framework and attitudes—the same economic behaviourism, cult of the elite, moral nihilism. Hence the same desperate expectation of economic crisis, denunciation of movements—in the colonies or in the West—which find expression through constitutional forms, attacks upon the worldwide movement for co-existence. The best, most fruitful, ideas of Trotskyism—emphasis upon economic democracy and direct forms of political democracy—are expressed in fetishistic form: "worker's councils" and "Soviets" must be imposed as the only orthodoxy. But Britain teems with Soviets. We have a General Soviet of the T.U.C. and trades Soviets in every town: peace Soviets and national Soviets of women, elected parish, urban district and borough Soviets. Granted that these organisations must be transformed; but it is the people behind, or within, the institutions whom we must change.

The most striking thing about the British labour movement is that it cannot be said to have either a false consciousness or a true one: it has a hotch-potch, of capitalist ideas, humanitarian aspirations, working-class attitudes. We are a protestant people, distrustful of system-building: we have not suffered under an ideological orthodoxy, backed by the power of the state, for several hundred years. Our Labour movement, is guided, in the main, by pragmatism: which is not an ideology but a kind of fragmentary, piecemeal, fitful, true consciousness; it sees problems clearly, but not their relationship to each other. Therefore it tends to accept, or half-accept, a framework of capitalist ideas (the sanctity of NATO and the US alliance, the inevitability of the wages-prices-spiral, etc.) but to fight hard for certain principles and interests within it. It can at times see some problems very well, but cannot see how they arose, nor anticipate how they will change.

This pragmatism which, in a wry way, Engels admired, has served the British people a great deal better than most Marxists have been prepared to admit. Pragmatism combined with parochialism have served it least well in international affairs; and far more often than not they have served the colonial peoples very badly indeed. And yet even in international questions, Marxists tend to overstate the case; we should not forget that the British people played their part—with high and conscious morale—in turning the tide of fascism in Europe.

I am not dismayed, as some seem to be, by the refusal of a slump to develop. We should address ourselves as socialists to the context and people we find about us, and it is high time to get away from the idea that our views will only prevail, and the working class seize power, through a final cataclysmic confrontation of classes, preceded by economic ruin. It is true that Marx expected some such outcome; but, on the other hand, he hailed the 10 Hour Bill as "the first time that in broad daylight the political economy of the middle class succumbed to the political economy of the working class" ("Address to W.M.I.A.," 1864). Engels also encouraged the new unions to fight for the Legal Eight Hour Day and employ the machinery of State in the interests of the people; we have followed this road to the present day. The ferment of 1945 resulted in such victories for "the political economy of the working class" that the capitalist class was almost fought to a standstill and held prisoner within its own state machinery. The British working class finds itself in its present position not because we have the "oldest and most cunning capitalist class in the world," but because the capitalist class could not stop it. It has got no further because, being pragmatic and hostile to theory it does not know and feel its own strength, it has no sense of direction or revolutionary perspective, it tends to fall into moral lethargy, it accepts leaders with capitalist ideas. In Britain the new society is not—as in Russia—to be torn prematurely from the old, but is in many features formed within the old. I don't mean that we live in some half-way society, some "mutation" of capitalist society, some "late capitalist" phase which is almost socialism. We live in a capitalist society, there is no need for qualification. The ethos of capitalism is the same, the drive for profit is the same, the tendency towards war against backward peoples is the same, the debasement of cultural values into commodities, the elevation of property above men, the putting of things (bases on Cyprus, higher profits, etc.) before human beings—all these are the same; but between the Americans and the H Bomb abroad, and the constant, stubborn, determined pragmatic pressure of the people at home, our capitalist ruling class is hemmed in and cannot act as it would. Hemmed in, it could become dangerous, just as dying dogmatism is dangerous: Suez was a symptom: in the past few years irrationalism, religiosity, anti-humanist and vicious ideologies have been gaining ground among our middle-class. But the British capitalist class cannot do as it likes; however cunning, it has not got much left to give away, except the essential economic and political seats of its power. The working people of Britain could end capitalism tomorrow, if they summoned up the courage and made up their minds to do it. If they have lost the will, is it not just because there is full employment; it is also because, over thirty years, their hopes—and the hopes of many in the professional classes—in Russia have kept falling through. Working people in Britain still feel the social relations of capitalist society to be oppressive; but not so oppressive that they are willing to risk giving allegiance to a "Vanguard" which will establish a "Dictatorship of the Proletariat." They are better suited as they are; but remaining as they are leaves them as proletarians with bourgeois aspirations, exploited acquisitive men.

The militant philistinism of Stalinism is matched by our own muted and sterile philistinism. The new thinkers have little to offer. Man is the victim of the Dollar Gap, the wages-prices spiral; his aspirations must be fitted to his pocket. They feel, uneasily, that something is missing: Thus Mr. Crosland:

We need not *only* higher exports and old-age pensions, but more open-air cafes, brighter and gayer streets at night, later closing hours for public houses, more local repertory theatres, better and more hospitable hoteliers and restaurateurs, brighter and cleaner eating-houses, more local riverside cafes, more pleasure-gardens on the Battersea model, more murals and pictures in public places, better designs for furniture and pottery and women's clothes, statues in the centre of new housing-estates, better designed street-lamps and telephone kiosks, and so on. (*The Future of Socialism*)

Yes, we want some of these things; but let us look a little more closely. Look first at the slapdash writing and the sensibility revealed: "open-air cafes . . . public houses . . . hoteliers and restaurateurs . . . eating-houses . . . riverside cafes"; the American tourist's dream. It is nice for an MP to slip out of the House for a full meal in a pleasure-garden; but are we sure this is what socialists mean by the "full life"? This is a bit more middle-class life all round; there is no sense of a socialist community; redesigned street lamps and kiosks but not factories and cities. And then it is a list of things: it tells us nothing about people—the values of the men and women eating the food, walking under the lights, wearing the clothes; the quality of the plays, the murals, the statues. Meanwhile we are warned from many sources of the cultural and human pollution of the mass media of commercialism:

> Inhibited now from ensuring the "degradation" of the masses economically, the logical processes of competitive commerce, favoured from without by the whole climate of the time and from within assisted by, the lack of direction, the doubts and uncertainty before their freedom of working-people themselves . . . are ensuring that working-people are culturally robbed. . . . The constant pressure . . . becomes a new and stronger form of subjection; this subjection promises to be stronger than the old because the chains of cultural subordination are both easier to wear and harder to strike away than those of economic subordination.

Thus Mr. Hoggart (*The Uses of Literacy*, p. 200), and he concludes—addressing the working-class movement: "If the active minority continue to allow themselves too exclusively to think of immediate political and economic objectives, the pass will be sold, culturally, behind their backs." (p. 264) To which we may surely add this: Men do not want only the list of things which Mr. Crosland offers; they want also to change themselves as men. However fitfully and ineffectively, they want other and greater things: they want to stop killing one another: they want to stop this pollution of their spiritual life which runs through society as the rivers carried their sewage and refuse through our nineteenth-century industrial towns: side by side with their direct economic interests, they would like to "do benefits" to each other. Socialist humanism, East and West, is seeking to make apparent these aspirations, and to show the way to their fulfillment. Mr. Khruschev also promises the people more things: they ask for justice and reason, and he promises more automation. Like Mr. Crosland, talk of the full life makes him think of food: he is interested in brightening factory canteens. But creative men, their initiatives freed from slavery to profit or to bureaucracy, will soon enough see to their cafes and canteens. Philistinism, East or West, offers things but cannot satisfy men, because men are intellectual and moral beings. The ideologies of capitalism and Stalinism are both forms of "self-alienation": men stumble in their minds and lose themselves in abstractions; capitalism sees human labour as a commodity and the satisfaction of his "needs" as the production and distribution of commodities; Stalinism sees labour as an economic-physical act in satisfying economic-physical needs. Socialist humanism declares: liberate men from slavery to things, to the pursuit of profit or servitude to "economic necessity." Liberate man, as a creative being—and he will create not only new values, but things in super-abundance.

This case now has a greater significance, both terrible and hopeful. Philistinism and blind class interests have evolved the biggest Thing of all, a Thing to end all things. Today man and this thing face each other. This thing is there because both capitalism and Stalinism have reduced human being to things, commodities or appendages to machines. But now men must look to something else—not a thing at all, but to the reason "and conscience of man. Without that creative being, his hands outstretched against the bomb, humanity must fail and Marx's forgotten alternative be fulfilled: "the mutual ruin of the contending classes." And so throughout the world, men and women are growing angry at this culmination of four decades of war, gas chambers, concentration camps, napalm, political hypocrisy and arguments of expediency; the threat of this final thing is impelling into a new awareness man's own self-consciousness, his knowledge of his own undivided humanity. As Lysistrata cried out, "We are all Greeks!" so now humanity cries out, "We are all men!" And the barbarians who press against our frontiers are the blind clashing of interests and the arid abstractions which steal us from ourselves. The bomb must be dismantled; but in dismantling it, men will summon up energies which will open the way to their inheritance. The bomb is like an image of man's whole predicament: it bears within it death and life, total destruction or human mastery over human history. Only if men by their own human agency can master this thing will Marx's optimism be confirmed, and "human progress cease to resemble that hideous pagan idol, who would not drink the nectar but from the skulls of the slain."

THOMPSON WROTE THIS FOR THE FIRST ISSUE OF THE NEW *Universities and Left Review* of Summer 1957. Here he discusses what he sees as a "retreat from humanism," by intellectuals in particular, a retreat that was taking many forms: for some "a reluctant, apologetic shuffle; in some a jog-trot; in some, a shameless self-inflated gallop." He counterposes to this the possibility of "opening new circuits between the 'intellectual' and the people, in particular working-class people." As for his own commitment to "socialist humanism," he contends that this does not "imply Utopian myths of human perfectibility. A society without opposed classes will not be a society without social friction of many sorts; every vice, as well as every virtue, known to Shakespeare will still trouble the human soul ... but it will free the act of choice from the dictation of necessity, from the history-old inheritance of blind, involuntary oppression and wasteful contests of economic self-interest within which all choices have been made."

Socialism and the Intellectuals

The aftermath of resignation from the Communist Party is not the best time for writing articles. Silence would be more comfortable. For nearly a year I have found myself caught in the cross-fire of a divided world. In the last, not very genial, months of my Party membership, the positions which I was defending (and which others are still defending within the Communist Party) were under fire as "liberal," "idealist," "abstract," and so on. The fire which any Communist intellectual draws from the other side is well-known. It is because this predicament is of more than personal significance that I am writing this article.

First, I must seek to free myself from some of the clichés associated with "Resignation from the Party." Withdrawal from the extreme left has been a central motif within our culture ever since the French Revolution left the Solitary meditating upon a creed—

> That, in the light of false philosophy,
> Spread like a halo round a misty moon,
> Widening its circles as the storms advance.

Since the 1930s the motif has been repeated with monotonous insistence. The "rejection" of Communism, or Marxism, or Belief in Progress, is now a trivial routine affair.

The Resignee now has a shabby, walking-on part in the contemporary cast. It is assumed that he must make certain stylised gestures—loss of faith, anguished self-analysis, disillusion in political action. The routines are well-known, although the final postures are various; the inhabitant of political limbo, caught in a conflict between guilt and disgust; the strident anti-Communist, taking revenge upon his own youth, making good as a literary nark or Labour MP; the convert to Holy Church. For the onlookers (if I may change the image) the public resignation from "the Party" serves the functions of a ritual sacrifice in tribute to the liberal Gods. And the *Manchester Guardian* inscribes the blood upon its priestly tablets.

The liberal Gods—justice, tolerance, above all intellectual liberty; but not the humanist Gods of social liberty, equality, fraternity. These stubbornly remain on the Communist side. That is why—although I have resigned from the Communist Party—I remain a Communist.

The Logic of Anti-Communism

DOGMATIC ANTI-COMMUNISM, which begins by rejecting certain ideas or reacting against certain events, and which ends by rejecting or condemning hundreds of millions of *people*, is bound to lead on to despair. Analysis must commence with historical actualities; and first with the multitudes of human beings whose aspirations are expressed in terms of Communist thought and political organisation. Those who allow disgust with the illiberal and authoritarian features of orthodox Communism to dominate their outlook only too often end up by damming up within themselves the profound and active sympathy called forth by those epics of human achievement led by Communists in our time: the march of the Chinese 8th Route Army; the Yugoslav war of resistance; repeated feats of conscious social endurance and constructive labour; the real onslaught upon illiteracy and superstition, the first steps in the regeneration of peoples oppressed and anonymous through centuries.

The conflicts which matured within world Communism in 1956 are surely sufficient to have shattered the old simplified picture. It is no longer any good whatsoever to lump together all the contradictory phenomena of Communist-led societies as a Good Thing or a Bad Thing. But it seems to me that intellectuals in this country have been slow to grasp the inner significance of these events. The post-war generation is appalled at the carnage and confusion of the past two decades; it sees only—

the sacrificed of history's great rains, of the destructive transitions

and ignores the character of the transition itself. Too many are trapped in that movement of thought and sensibility which—commencing with the abstract rejection of Communism—leads on to the retreat from humanism.

This retreat from humanism is perhaps the most striking feature of our intellectual life today. It is already sapping our labour movement of vital intellectual and cultural energies. It could lead on to more serious consequences, which in turn could provoke a strong anti-intellectual current amongst our working class. Anti-Communism has inflamed international relations for long enough; but we have not yet begun to take stock of the damage which it has done to our own cultural and political life. And, to turn the coin over, the rejection of liberal values by the "Stalinists" has led the world Communist movement into crisis.

Retreat from Humanism

THIS RETREAT FROM HUMANISM takes many forms: in some, a reluctant, apologetic shuffle; in some, a jog-trot; in some, a shameless, self-inflated gallop ("Other people are the trouble"). The pace of all, the shufflers and the gallopers, seems to me to have accelerated significantly since the events in Hungary.

The ground-bass of this theme is sounded in a passage from a letter to the *New Stateman* last June, which I select not for its subtlety but for its self-revelation:

The example of Sweden, with its problems of excessive drinking and its high suicide rate, has shown that the introduction of the most advanced forms of welfare do not necessarily make man more content or better behaved. This is not used, of course, as an argument for abolishing all forms of welfare, but it would seem to indicate that welfare and equality on its own are not enough.

Experience of the last decade has shown that many of the rich and artisan and working classes are each out for all they can get, whether in the form of dividends, more wages, or subsidies.... The sufferers have, of course, been the traditional custodians of morality and unselfishness, the fixed income groups, who continue to live lives cramped and poverty-stricken in comparison with their fellows who wax rich on capital gains, swollen dividends, inflated wages, and overtime earnings.

What Sort of Life

SOME LINES OF THE MELODY are to be found in a letter which I received recently from a friend:

What sort of life will the scientific socialist life produce when it has "solved the problem of the means of production"? I don't suppose the socialist and communist leaders would have any better answer than the leaders of the T.U.C. if they were asked, "what is the good life?—when you have your automatic factories, atomic power, good plumbing, and a car for everyone and your seven hours leisure a day, *what do you do with your time?*" (In Sweden where they are very comfortable, the suicide rate is higher than the accident rate.)

It is difficult to know how to dig in one's heels on this muddy slope, whose grass has been rubbed off by the traffic of centuries. When Blake came across the line (in Bishop Watson's *Apology*), "The Wisdom and Goodness of God, in having made both Rich and Poor," he scribbled the annotation:

God made Man happy and Rich, but the Subtil made the innocent Poor. This must be a most wicked and blasphemous book.

It is difficult to *argue* about values: they are either affirmed or denied.

One might question the validity of conclusions based on the experience of *one decade*—although this is now being done on every side, from predictions as to the stability of capitalism, to conclusions as to the sinfulness of man.

Or one might enquire more closely into the mentality of the "traditional custodian of morality and unselfishness" who cannot conceal his envy at the improved material status of the working class, and who finds it difficult to refrain from advocating the abolition of "all forms of welfare." And what is the significance of the word "custodian"? It suggests that the subject is *guarding* morality and unselfishness, rather than practising these virtues in any active sense. If so, from whom is he guarding them? From the working-class? Or from materialism? And if from materialism, why should the custodian expect a hefty material reward for his services? Perhaps, after all, it is the "fixed income" and the pre-war wages-salary differential of which he is custodian?

The Suicide Rate in Sweden

SO LET US GET to the crux of the matter, which appears to be the suicide rate in Sweden. I don't know how long this colossal fact has been in circulation, but recently I have tripped over it in the most unlikely places.

Do we need to examine the credentials of such a shifty, scarcely literate fact as this? Who commits suicide in Sweden? Why? Is the suicide rate an authentic index of anything at all? What particular tensions exist within Swedish social and cultural life? How do we know that the suicide rate has got anything more to do with material well-being than the obvious fact that welfare services diminish the economic pressure upon the unhappy to continue the drudgery of bread-winning? Might it not equally be related to some spiritual exhaustion within Swedish culture, a shame-faced, parasitic well-being purchased while half Europe burned, a culture which has no heroic soil in which to take root?

I don't know the answer, and neither do those who throw this "fact" into the anti-humanist balance. But until this fact passes some such examination it is not a fact at all: it is a noise. The noise goes like this: Sweden's welfare state, wealthy working class, social-democracy = gin and suicide. Welfare = suicide. Wealthy working class = suicide. *Hydrogen-bomb.*

Human Condition

THE QUESTION OF PARTICULAR human beings taking their lives in particular circumstances in Sweden has nothing to do with the phrase. It is a noise made by people who are falling into certain contemporary attitudes; who oppose "life" to "politics," which is felt to be something other than life; who oppose the "good life," which is something inward and passive, to the outward life of social relationships; who are genuinely but confusedly repelled by the corruption of the human spirit by the mass-produced values of commercialism, but can see no social force strong enough to stem this corruption. Concern with the Swedish suicide rate is generally associated with a readiness to discourse on the Human Condition, but not to consider the conditions of any particular set of human beings; to talk of the Problem of Man at the same time as most of the problems of men acting in history are given up as irrelevant. As the slope becomes steeper, we find a wholesale dismissal of most human goings-on since the Renaissance. At the bottom we find Mr. Colin Wilson sitting beside Bishop Watson, up to their necks in metaphysical mire:

> Then, as the Outsider's insight becomes deeper, so that he no longer sees men as a million million individuals, but instead sees the world-will that drives them all like ants in a formicary, he knows that they will never escape their stupidity and delusions, that no amount of logic and knowledge can make man any more than an insect; the most irritating of the human lice is the humanist with his puffed-up pride in Reason and his ignorance of his own silliness.

Inhibitions of Kingsley Amis

I AM NOT GOING to argue with Mr. Wilson, since it is my silliness to seek the significance of man's life within terms of those human ends and values discovered by men in their own history; while it is his silliness to be interested in the reverberations of his own ego as he walks through a library. But I *am* concerned when I find Socialists gingerly setting foot on the upper slopes of the Bishop's glide; and such a one is Mr. Amis—the pamphleteer, I mean: the novelist is another matter.

There are parts of Mr. Amis's recent pamphlet which bristle with inhibitions against the affirmation of positive, humanist values. When he uses the words "hopes and aspirations" he must protect himself with a self-conscious giggle ("to coin a phrase"); slip, slap, slop go the frayed carpet-slippers as they shuffle away from the fire. But I feel it to be a *reluctant* shuffle, all the same. Mr. Amis would like to turn back and warm his hands—or at least the seat of his trousers.

Socialism and the Intellectual

THEN I AM A PREJUDICED witness, I am enough of a Party man still to be riled by the picture of Mr. Amis telling a Fabian, Week-End School that it is "too easy to laugh" at the intellectuals who went to fight in Spain. It appears that they were motivated by an amoral romanticism, "wicked out of a kind of folly." (See section, "Marxism and What It Meant.") This is supported by a line from Auden, and a gloss from Orwell. The line is out of its wider context, and the gloss is on Orwell's spleen and not on the poem. Auden was never in any serious sense a Marxist. As Mr. Amis points out, he did not fight in Spain. As for the Marxist's "taste for violence," are we not forgetting that violence, war, and terror were a condition of life, not only for Marxists, but for all who opposed fascism over a great part of Europe twenty years ago? My recollection is that those who went to Spain, and those who supported them in Britain, spent much of their time in warning of the dangers of a flood of violence if the Spanish lesson went unheeded. Further, if we are to talk in a large way about romanticism and irrationalism in the Thirties, it is worth recalling that intellectual liberty—highlighted by the murder of Lorca—was one of the first issues which intellectuals believed to be at stake in Spain.

I wish we could talk about things in the right context, and use the right terms. The Spanish war was a *war:* it is an event in history. There was a rebellion by a military junta. The country was flooded with Moorish soldiers, Italian and German troops and war material. The majority of the Spanish people took up arms, and appealed to the world for assistance. Our Government was for new assistance, but some hundreds of our people volunteered to go. No doubt there were as many motivations as there were volunteers, but most of them believed—or thought that they believed—that if Franco was halted, it would appreciably lessen the danger of world war. A few hours before Ralph Fox was killed he did not talk about his taste for violence or his old headmaster. He said: "If any of you get back, tell the people of England that the fight in Spain is not only Spain's fight, but England's." I think that this was true, and that Fox spoke not as a romantic, but as a political realist.

It is natural that Mr. Amis, the novelist, should be interested in questions of motivation. It is also true that "Spain" was a literary and political *symbol* of varying connotations. And I certainly think that political theory should

concern itself with personal motivations, and that the blind eye of orthodox Marxism in this respect has brought it to the verge of bankruptcy. In the
past few months I have had a stomach-full of the word "objective," now being
worked overtime by the Stalinist old-guard to defend the *status quo* against
whatever is new and potential.

Spain: The Act of Choice

BUT IT STILL SEEMS to me that there is a region where it is proper to consider events, actions and the consequences of actions; another region where
it is proper to consider motivations; and yet another where we must consider
the interconnection between the two. Not only Mr. Amis, but scores of others,
right, left, and centre, are continually sliding—without giving warning, and
probably without knowing it themselves—between these regions. This results
not only in confusion; it leads on to denial or distrust of the validity of intellectual motivations, to the obliteration of the boundary between rational choice
on the one hand, and psychological or economic determinism on the other. If
men went to Spain, believing that certain events were taking place and that certain consequences would flow from their actions, it seems to me that we are less
than just, and we diminish the human stature, if we ignore the conscious act
of choice. Plenty of other men in the Thirties revolted against authority, had a
taste for violence or adventure, and so on; they did not go to Spain, but became
speed-way riders, or acrobats, or secret service men. Such speculation may take
us some way towards understanding the temperamental predisposition to take
certain choices; nothing about the act of choice itself. Goodness knows the
human reason and conscience are imperfect instruments enough; they glow fitfully amongst the bric-a-brac piled all around, which threaten at any moment
to topple over and extinguish their light—self-interest and self-esteem, indiges-
tion, guilt, class conditioning, memories of the woodshed, old superstition, the
lot. But we continue our intellectual work because we believe that, in the last
analysis, *ideas matter*; it is man's business, if he is not to be the mere victim of
involuntary reflexes or of a predetermined historical flux, to strive to understand
himself and his times and to make reasonable and right choices. This gives to all
our imaginative work a significance at once terrible and hopeful.

But Mr. Amis leaves us floundering in a miasma of involuntary motivation.
"Loving what is established and customary pulls you to the right: hating it pulls
you to the left." Fair enough. But reason, will, moral passion do not enter; it is
a matter of involuntary responses to external stimuli; love and hate are questions of "temperament only." "And behind that again lies perhaps your relations
with your parents." Intellectuals went to Spain because they quarrelled with their

daddies; now their own children are quarrelling with *them*. And so to our defi-nition of political romanticism: "an irrational capacity to become inflamed by interests and causes that are not one's own, that are outside oneself." Oh, hell. It's time we opened some windows. The fug "inside oneself" is becoming thick enough to cut.

The Intellectuals Disengaged

I DON'T KNOW WHY I am quarrelling with Mr. Amis—he is neither a relative nor an old housemaster of mine. There are other places in his pamphlet where, with a sort of apologetic honesty, he defends old humanist positions. But in the passages which I have cited it seems to me that he closely reflects the dilemma of many British intellectuals. On the one hand, they are united upon one article of faith: the defence of intellectual liberty. On the other, there is a general lack of conviction as to the power of ideas to influence political events or social develop-ment. Through half the world the intellectual is seen as an explosive, seditious, unstable element. In Britain the intellectual feels himself to be impotent. No one bothers whether his thoughts are dangerous or not.

Today it seems to me that the circuit by which ideas are transformed into effective social energies has been broken, by the withdrawal of the intellectu-als on one side, and the bureaucratic structure of the labour movement on the other. To justify the view that it is the working class which holds the master-key which can unlock the doors of human change (I would say "progress" if the word were not in disgrace) would involve arguing the case for socialism from first principles. But if this is granted, then we have a clue to the understanding of why intellectuals in Britain today feel themselves to be impotent, treasuring intellectual liberty but in a social void.

In the Thirties (despite follies and illusions) this circuit was *open*. Points of contact existed in the Left Book Clubs, the Communist Party, the Unity The-atres, the International Brigade, journals like *New Writing* and *Left Review,* which made possible an invigorating two-way flow of ideas and experience between a significant group of intellectuals and the most politically alert section of the labour movement.

Today increasing numbers of young intellectuals feel themselves to be rebels against "the Establishment": the slavery of the human soul to material trivia, the hypocrisy and tedium of political life, the debasement of standards by monstrous, sprawling, impersonal money-making media, the acceptance of mass-slaughter which retches in the speeches of "statesmen" and which helps to underpin our economy, the futile extinction of generous or dignified aspirations in the morass of expediences, competing self-interests, bureaucratic power-blocks. But since they can see no social force capable of making headway against this flux, their "revolt" consists in imagining themselves to be "outside" this thing, posturing and grimacing through the window. In fact, they are outside nothing but the humanist tradition.

Why, asked Engels over a hundred years ago, do workers strike against reductions, even when the uselessness of the strike is evident? "Simply because they *must* protest against every reduction, even if dictated by necessity; because they feel bound to proclaim that they, as human beings, shall not be made to bow to social circumstances, but social conditions ought to yield to them as human beings."

It seems to me that some of our younger intellectuals are beginning to strike, but as yet they are only striking *attitudes*. To do more than this, they must leap the gap which divides ideas from social energies. And this means, in the last analysis, opening new circuits between the "intellectual" and the people, in particular working-class people.

Neither Casuists nor Trimmers

HOW, THEN, ARE WE to leap the gap? I no longer believe that this is accomplished by joining anything. I have gained enormously from the friendships I have made in the Communist Party, and the experiences of active political life. But I think that a final point of crisis has come when Communist intellectuals, if they wish to continue with creative intellectual work, must leave the party; in this country certainly, if the forthcoming Congress fails to effect major changes; in other countries the choice will present itself differently. They must do this not simply because the Party is sectarian and so isolated from people that their effect is neutralised; nor because it is unpopular to be a Communist (we have put up with that for a good many years); but for two more cogent reasons. First, so long as the Party persists in its official blanket endorsement of the Soviet leadership, and all public expressions of dissent are regarded as offences against discipline, they are guilty of a breach of solidarity with those who are fighting for intellectual liberty in the Soviet Union and Eastern Europe. True, this is not a new problem, but it is presented with a new urgency: Communist intellectuals *above all* should make their voices heard in protest against the exile of Lukacs and the arrest of Harich. Second, in a period of such significance for socialist theory as this, they can no longer waste time and energy in the toils of a bureaucracy which demands everything from them, from stamp licking to *Daily Worker* selling, *except* honest intellectual work; which hedges ideas around with dogmatic anathemas, and inhibits their expression with disciplinary measures.

Nor do I think that the problem is necessarily brought nearer to solution by joining the Labour Party. Too many intellectuals who join the Labour Party seem to get swallowed up in seas of expediency. They concern themselves not with what is potential but with what is, in the short term, politically practicable. Will the voters wear it? Will it get proscribed? The logic of such "realism" is that they commence "re-thinking," which too often means thinking about ways of patching up capitalist society, making it work more efficiently and with less pain to the people. They cease to think as socialists and neglect a great part of the work of socialist intellectuals, which I take to be that of helping people to become aware of the vast human potentialities—economic, intellectual, spiritual—denied or frustrated by capitalist society, helping people to change their ideas and values *within* capitalist society until they see and feel it to be the intolerable and wasteful system which despite the precarious modifications of the present decade it still remains. But unless this understanding of the aggressive character of imperialism, the self-destructive forces within capitalist society, is continually awakened; unless this sense of antagonism to the capitalist ethos is continually aroused; then it seems to me that past gains and future potentialities of the labour movement are always in danger of perishing in the sands.

The real and substantial gains of the Labour Government of 1945–47 were the product, not of the present "late-capitalist-society-is-all-right-don't-rock-the-boat" mentality, but of the understanding and spirit of antagonism which in great part was nourished by that movement of ideas in the Thirties which it is now fashionable to dismiss as "romantic." I am not suggesting that it is *inevitable* that the intellectual who works actively in the Labour Party will forget what he is doing it for, will cease to be a socialist intellectual and become a social worker, or a log-roller, or one of the boys. Perhaps there are new currents stirring which will change the position. I don't want to encourage precious attitudes towards politics; we all have political responsibilities and the experience of rank-and-file political activity enriches us and keeps our ideas on the ground, I am suggesting that our responsibilities as socialist *intellectuals* are not solved by joining organisations; and that at this particular moment neither the Communist Party nor the Labour Party provide a congenial atmosphere for setting on foot a principled movement of socialist ideas. We cannot serve the working class or anyone else honestly as *intellectuals* contrary, socialism would emerge from its iron and into its human age.

I do not know whether these processes will work themselves out in five years or fifty years, but I still think that this is a bad time of the human day for intellectual loss of nerve or for speculations on the rate of Swedish suicide.

I understand that George Lukacs—the outstanding Hungarian scholar, survivor of Bela Kun's government, a commander of the International, minister in Nagy's government—has commenced in his Rumanian exile to write a work on socialist ethics. It seems to me that this old man has something to teach us of intellectual courage.

As long as the Communist tradition includes men like this, I want to remain associated with it. I am not going to spend years crippled by remorse because I was duped by the Rajk and Rostov trials, because I was a casuist here and perhaps an accomplice there. We were Communists because we had faith in the fundamental humanist content of Communism, and during the darkest years of the Cold War it was our duty to speak for this. I do not regret this, although I wish we had spoken more wisely and therefore to more effect. Now that the conflict within world Communism has come into the open, it is our duty to take sides.

And do not let us pretend there has been some easy solution to the political and moral conflicts of our time. The conflict between "liberal" and "humanist" values was not invented by social-democratic or Marxist theorists. It was an historical actuality. It existed on the map of the world, and within society on both sides of the line of division. Not only the world, but man himself was riven apart. Just as the denial of intellectual liberty brought down its revenge upon the Communist movement, so the denial of Communism, and of its humanist potential, has brought its own sickness into our political and cultural life. Hopes have been corroded away or have turned into sour dogmas mechanically upheld despite the evidence. Generous impulses have been denied as "romanticism"; just aspirations as "illusions." Intellectuals have lost confidence in the potentialities of the working class, and the working class has lost sight of its wider cultural perspectives. On every side, human horizons have closed in.

That is why I think that this is a moment, not only for "re-thinking," but above all for *re-affirmation*. We *must* call a halt to this retreat from humanism. We must open out the horizons once more. We must affirm that politics is concerned with more than oiling and servicing an economic machine—adjusting and neutralising competing self-interest here or there—which no one can control. We must affirm the thought which is central to Socialism—and which, above all, must unite intellectuals and the working class in a common cause—that man is capable not only of changing his conditions, but also of transforming himself; that there is a real sense in which it is true that men can master their own history.

Socialist Humanism

THE EMERGENCE OF SOCIALIST humanism as an effective intellectual and political force in the Communist world seems to me to create the conditions for the rekindling of moral and intellectual passion in our labour movement also. This movement may, in the main, first find expression among intellectuals. But the labour movement will not be slow to welcome a movement of ideas which deals not only with credit manipulations and death duties, but which summons the people's own initiatives and energies in the transformation of their environment and of themselves.

A friend, who describes himself as a "left social-democrat," tells me that all this is visionary stuff. I am, he thinks, the victim still of the messianic folly of Marxism, the illusion of the perfectibility of man. The strength of organised labour, improved economic techniques, have between them assured a fair prospect of stability to "late capitalist" society. By and by the socialist sector of the economy may be extended. Meanwhile, there are "no shortcuts." Socialists should be "realists," and get on with the work which lies about on every side: improving this and that, and above all restraining imperialism, whether Cyprus or Suez, and working to prevent world war.

Granted certain premises this is a reasonable position and it is certainly a humanist position. But it is not the position of *socialist* humanism. It stems from the realism of the sociologist but not the realism of the poet, and socialist humanism seeks to unite the two.

Whatever Hegelian hangovers persisted in their thought, neither Marx nor Engels fell into the old, Utopian trap of faith in human perfectibility. Belief in the original virtue of man is as incompatible with mature socialist theory as is belief in original sin. What they both affirmed, and what we must re-affirm, is the *revolutionary* potentialities of man. We must regain this understanding, for, unless we have it, we can never summon the courage to make the potential actual.

When we look backward through the bars of our own time, to Assyrian man, Athenian man, Aztec man, we gain a sense, not of human tedium but of human unexpectedness. Society can stagnate for centuries; it can assume monstrous shapes in the pattern of mental myths; but men can and do, almost without warning, take "shortcuts." Can we be sure that 20th-Century-television-man is here to stay?

I hold fast to the view that men are on the margin where pre-history ends and conscious history begins. We will need all our nerve if we are to cross that threshold. I do not think that this implies Utopian myths of human perfectibility. A society without opposed classes will not be a society without social friction of many sorts; every vice, as well as every virtue known to Shakespeare will still trouble the human soul. It will not lift from men's shoulders the responsibility, collectively and as individuals, to take actions and make choices in pursuit of the "good life." But it will free the act of choice from the dictation of necessity, from the history-old inheritance of blind, involuntary oppression and wasteful contests of economic self-interest within which all choices have been made. If men then choose wisely, they will open new vistas of communal enrichment, devising social arrangements which will foster the influence of "virtue" and limit the havoc which "vice" can do. And if the weight of evidence today seems to deny this hope, then we can still protest, refusing to be victims either of circumstances or of ourselves; for it is in this rebellion against fact that our humanity consists.

PUBLISHED IN THE *UNIVERSITIES AND LEFT REVIEW* 6 (Spring 1959), Thompson here identifies a critique of that journal, for example, the jibe that the younger generation is "angrier about ugly architecture than they are about the poverty of old-age pensioners," or more problematically that "they are anti-working class," an accusation he calls unfair. Still, he finds "an ambiguity" in the *ULR*, including "a tendency to underestimate the tensions and conflicts of working-class life, and the creative potential—not in the remote future but here and now—of working people: a tendency to assert the absolute autonomy of cultural phenomena without reference to the context of class power: and a shame-faced evasion of that impolite historical concept—the class struggle."

Commitment in Politics

Intelligence enough to conceive, courage enough to will, power enough
to compel. If our ideas of a new Society are anything more than a dream,
these three qualities must animate the due effective majority of the work-
ing-people; and then, I say, the thing will be done.

—WILLIAM MORRIS

By "politics" I do not of course refer to that annex to the Hall of Fame,
filled with self-important TV personalities and Inside People, which Mr.
R. H. S. Crossman finds so "charming." Nor do I mean the heady atmosphere of closet-factions which has bedeviled the British Left for so long. The
distaste which we feel for all that is a measure of our maturity before the responsibilities which "that old bitch gone in the teeth, a botched civilisation" has seen
fit to dump upon our shoulders. If restraining the life-negating and lunatic propensities of capitalist society is a necessary responsibility, it is still an infuriating dispersal of human energies. It is because we still live within the anarchy of
"pre-history" that we are obliged to commit ourselves to the barbaric rituals and
inefficient acts of social war which make up capitalist "politics."

But any man who can find "charm" in the politics of twenty-five years of
blood-letting and bewildered defensive actions stands self-condemned as a
philistine. I suppose it is this tone of enthralled gossip about political trivia—
this balancing of corrupt expediencies and this patter about the behaviour of
rogues—which sometimes makes one want to take a half-brick down to Great
Turn-stile. "Politics," for many of my friends, has meant some years of agonised
impotence in the face of European Fascism and approaching war; six years of war,
whose triumphant conclusion and liberating aftermath were blighted by betrayals; and ten years of makeshift defensive campaigns in face of the Cold War and
the fatty degeneration of the Labour Movement. There has been little charm,
much disenchantment: more spectacular quarrels than enduring friendships:
neglect of personal interests, impoverishment of personal relations, leading in
some to spiritual *ennui* or to self-righteous sectarian pride. The very texture of
political life has been oppressive—the endless committee work, ineffectual campaigns under mendacious national leadership, electoral contests with unworthy

candidates. Those who, after fifteen or twenty years of this, are still "committed" to politics, are often committed with glassy-eyed submission. They look to those first manifestations of a new generation in revolt, the N.D. Campaign and *ULR* with a mixture of suspicion and stifled hope.

The suspicion resolves itself into the jibe which I have taken as the title to this article. These *ULR* types (the jibe runs) are passionate advocates of commitment in the arts, but they evade commitment on the central issues of class power and political allegiance. They are angrier about ugly architecture than they are about the ugly poverty of old-age pensioners, angrier about the "materialism" of the Labour Movement than about the rapacity of financiers. They wear upon their sleeves a tender sensibility; but probe that tenderness, and one finds a complex of responses which the veteran recognises as "anti-working-class." They are more at ease discussing alienation than exploitation. If they mention Marx, it is the Marx of the 1844 manuscripts, not the Marx of *Capital* or the *Eighteenth Brumaire;* they are interested in the diagnostician but not in the revolutionary surgeon of the human condition. Like the anarchists of the 1880s, the fringe of the working class which fascinates them is the criminal *lumpen-proletariat.* They see the authentic expression of the younger generation in a squalid street-fight in Notting Hill, but the thousands of young men and women who flock every night into the Technical Colleges at Batley, Stoke-on-Trent, or Darlington, do not come into the picture at all, except as exemplars of the ethos of *Room at the Top.* If this Partisan generation (the jibe continues) cannot be dismissed as neo-Fabians, this is only because Fabianism is too dowdy and too exacting in its practical demands. They have replaced the authority of Bentham and Mill with that of Arnold and F. R. Leavis, and if they distrust manipulative social engineering in the utilitarian tradition, they offer only educational and cultural therapy in its place. In both cases the initiative for enlightened change must still come from the intelligentsia above, even though the statistician is replaced by the sociologist and the administrator by the literary critic. They are too pure-at-heart to immerse themselves in political action which makes sustained demands upon tact or organisational stamina; but respond lyrically to individualist or sensational protests, no matter how ineffectual or divisive in conception. And so (to bring the commination service to a conclusion) the whole lot may be dismissed by the committed socialist as the last intellectual waifs and strays in the long romantic grouse against industrialism, striking in Soho the final futile attitudes of protest in the face of the inexorable approach of the nuclear age.

Place of the Working Class

THERE ARE TWO REASONS why these jibes demand examination. First, because they *are* circulating, even among keen readers of *ULR*. It would be strange if this were not so. The active rank-and-file socialist has seen some pretty strange birds of passage through the movement in the past quarter-century. It is only to be expected that when a new movement of socialist intellectuals appears, it should be met with the questions: How long are they likely to stick? Are they in it with us?

Second, because the jibes are not altogether without foundation. If I thought them wholly false I would not bother to submit this article. If I thought them true in any essential point I would submit it elsewhere. The question is complex. I do indeed find in *ULR* one of the most healthy and constructive growing-points for revolutionary socialism in this country; I do not doubt for a moment the integrity and commitment to the socialist cause of its editors. And yet this movement of ideas has emerged at a time when (for many reasons) the political consciousness of our working people is dulled and their creative political initiatives are at their most sluggish for many years. The younger generation which has matured within this context has, inevitably, generalised from this experience. But these generalisations—unless they are held *in* perspective by a sense of history—can lead on to attitudes which are both precious and self-isolating; and which, if unchecked, could be as corrosive in the socialist movement as those opportunist and philistine attitudes against which *ULR* is in recoil. These attitudes seem to me to stem from an ambiguity as to the place of the working class in the struggle to create a socialist society: a tendency to view working people as the *subjects* of history, as pliant *recipients* of the imprint of the mass media, as *victims* of alienation, as *data* for sociological enquiry: a tendency to underestimate the tensions and conflicts of working-class life, and the creative potential —not in the remote future but here and now—of working people: a tendency to assert the absolute autonomy of cultural phenomena without reference to the context of class power: and a shame-faced evasion of that impolite historical concept— the class struggle.

Evasion of Class Struggle?

THESE ATTITUDES ARE NEVER dominant in *ULR*; but they are obvious enough elsewhere, and are incipient in certain contributions to *ULR* 5. It is a matter of tone, emphases, omissions, which appear side by side with challenging analysis. Taken singly these instances may be unimportant; taken together, a certain impression is given; an impression which is unfairly precipitated early in the number by Gordon Redfern's boisterous passage of historical impressionism, *The Real Outrage.* Here the working class is seen as the passive object of social transformations which take place with geological inevitability. "The industrial conurbation grew quickly. Masses of the population drawn from the countryside became meaningless as human beings, but important as cogs in the means of production." Meaningless to whom? Surely not to themselves? Are working people to be allowed no consciousness of themselves, no power of moral reflection, no agency in shaping industrial society? The period to which (I take it) Gordon Redfern refers was meaningful enough in working-class history; it is the period of Luddism and Peterloo, trade union experiments and Owenism, the 10 Hour Movement and Chartism, and the proliferation of popular religious, educational and co-operative societies.

But Gordon Redfern's impressions leap over the agitator, the Chartist journalist, the union organiser, and come to rest on the dupe and the turncoat. Discussing the appeal of middle-class "snob culture," he writes: "Dim and without the faculty to interpret, to these heights the workers raised their eyes, this became their goal. (How else can we explain the anachronism of the knighted trade union leader?)"

Which workers? Which trade union leaders? If we explain Sir Walter Citrine, must we not also explain Tom Mann? But the give-away phrase comes at the conclusion to his article, where he describes our people as "a population jaded almost beyond redemption."

It is worth looking at, this phrase. Gordon Redfern (and many others who *feel* in this way but who are too sly to say so) will no doubt believe that they owe some allegiance to the working-class movement, as the ultimate political force which will achieve socialism. But it is a very abstract allegiance. Real working people fill them with nausea: "They know no more than the material standards of the television and washing machine which they have gained." On every actual count they turn aside with condescension or disgust: the workers are materialist, self-interested, philistine, television-addicts, corrupted by prosperity, and so on. (The fact that some of these attitudes are akin to those held by Tory ladies in Bournemouth does not prevent them from being embraced by quite a number of working-class "scholarship boys" who have supped on a diet of T. S. Eliot.) Above all, working-class people are seen in terms of the papers that most of them read and the films and programmes that most of them watch. Since many of the attitudes embodied in the mass media are contemptible, and since the architectural environment of the industrial working class is ugly and anarchic, it is not difficult for the intellectual to effect an emotional transference from the media and the environment to the *people*. Whatever he thinks of individual working people, the idea of the working class evokes a response of contempt, dislike or fear. "A population jaded almost beyond redemption."

If this is true, then there is little left for the enlightened minority to do in politics except to strike attitudes. It is theoretically possible to hold to a "revolutionary" hatred of "industrialism" or "the Establishment" or the mass media, but, since the working class is seen as the great philistine force whose gullibility and taste for trivial sensation and material advantage underpins the whole thing, practical socialist politics appear as hopeless; and, in extreme cases, the hatred may be directed against the working class itself. In every effective sense, such attitudes *are* "anti-working class."

Having made this point, it would be far too easy to rush for consolation and security back into the arms of old Auntie Dogma. Whatever the working class approves is right: it is the only true revolutionary force in society, because of its very situation: the intellectual must distrust his own responses, and submit his will to the will of the people. But we have had enough of all that; to romanticise the working class and its organisations is not only futile, it is also a flat betrayal of socialist responsibility. A realistic recognition of the forces at work which are corrupting the working-class movement is one of the points from which any socialist analysis must commence. Thousands of rank-and-file members of the Labour Movement are as anxious about these corrupting influences as are Mr. John Osborne and Mr. John Braine. Listen to the ageing Labour councillors, the W.E.A. committee, the veteran trade unionist, lamenting the lack of support for their activities: "they're all out for themselves," "it's the television," "the move-ment has lost its moral dynamic," "only a slump will wake them up"—this is the small change of discussion. To romanticise the working class, or to abstract from it a doctrinaire emblem of evergreen militancy, is as much a betrayal of living working people as are the attitudes which I have termed "anti-working class."

Sense of History

I THINK WE ARE LACKING, chiefly, in a sense of history; we might discuss the uses of literacy a little less, and the uses of history rather more.

The following assumptions appear in several articles in *ULR* 5: first, that "materialism" is an unworthy social motivation; second, that in contemporary "consumer capitalism" there has been some qualitative (even "revolutionary") alteration in the material drives of working people. "Capitalism as a social system is now based upon consumption," writes Stuart Hall (*A Sense of Classlessness*, *ULR* 5); and "not only has the working class been built into the market itself but commodities—things-in-themselves—have accumulated *a social value* as well. They have become insignias of class and status." He offers as evidence for this a number of most perceptive insights into the degree to which the capitalist ethos has today penetrated into the centres of working-class life; but he offers no seri-ous *historical framework* for this judgment whatsoever. When has the working class *not* been "built into the market"? Who on earth consumed the products of the early industrial revolution, if the working people had no serious share? When have commodities *not* had a social, as well as strictly utilitarian, value? The upright piano preceded the television set into the skilled worker's home;

the china plaque with a biblical inscription preceded the plastic nymph; sanded floors gave way to rough carpeting and have now given way to imitation Axminsters. At every stage there has been a striving for status within the working class; and if we are now concerned with a change in quality, and not merely in degree, we must be offered more serious evidence.

Competing Moralities

THE LAMENT ABOUT the "materialism" of the workers has, after all, appeared several times before in our history. It was heard on all sides among Chartist veterans in the prosperity which followed the Great Exhibition. In 1859 a Yorkshire Chartist was writing that his fellows were "thoroughly disgusted at the indifference and utter in-attention of the multitude to their best interests" and regretting the "foolish integrity and zeal" of Ernest Jones in seeking "to bring about the enfranchisement of the un-thinking and ungrateful multitude." Ten years later the former Chartist, Thomas Cooper, revisited Lancashire and summed up his impressions in a passage which has become a *locus classicus* of working-class history:

> In our old Chartist time . . . Lancashire working men were in rags by thousands; and many of them lacked food. But their intelligence was demonstrated wherever you went. You would see them in groups discussing the great doctrine of political justice . . . or they were in earnest dispute respecting the teachings of Socialism. *Now*, you will see no such groups in Lancashire. But you will hear well-dressed working men talking of cooperative stores, and their shares in them, or in building societies.

Twenty years later again, and at the commencement of the Dock Strike, Engels was lamenting England's "bourgeois proletariat." And this period, from 1850 to 1880 and beyond, saw a striving for status within the working class as sharp as any to be found today: self-made man against skilled worker, the skilled unionist against the labourer, the butty system in the pits. Exploitation has never been something done *at* a cohesive working class by employers above them; it has also been part of the very conditions of life and work of the whole people. The ethos which Stuart Hall describes so perceptively, and terms "the status ladder," went by the name, in Victorian England, of "self-help." Self-help was equally divisive, it entered as deeply into the organisations of the working people.

I am making two points. First, working-class history is not the record of a coherent "way of life"; it has always been a *way of struggle*, between competing moralities. At any given point a whole complex of objective and active, subjective factors determine which morality is dominant. The objective factors are most obvious: in times of relative prosperity and social flexibility, when it is possible for individuals or groups to "better themselves," the acquisitive ethic and the status-striving assert themselves. Conversely, in times of hardship, when it is most clear that the working class (or groups within it) can only defend themselves or advance by collective action, the communal ethic flowers.

This way of struggle, against class rule above, and between competing moralities within the working class, has never been a blind, spontaneous reflex to objective economic conditions. It has been a conscious struggle of ideas and values all the way. It has been possible for working-class organisations to hold fast to the vision of collective good, in the face of the acquisitive surge in times of prosperity. It has been possible for treacherous leadership (as at the time of the General Strike) to shatter that vision for a decade. And, the more closely we study it, the more we are forced to a recognition of the role of the politically active minority. In times of brutalisation and degradation, working people have asserted their humanity only by revolt against these conditions; and the most conscious, morally engaged form of revolt has been in political organisation. For 150 years the political minority has been the carrier of the aspirations of the majority; it has been the point at which the diffuse ideal of community has come to effective expression. For working people above all, the road to human fulfilment in capitalist society has been bound up, in one way or another, with political organisation. It is through conscious action against exploitation and class oppression that they have ceased to be victims of their environment, and have achieved the dignity of actors in the making of their own history.

Grounds for Hope

TO DESCRIBE THE EVOLUTION of "industrialism" in sociological terms which belittle the organisation, influence, and ideas of the political minority, is to deprive us, not only of honourable traditions, but also of our grounds for hope in the present. It is not the "materialism" so much as the *politics* of the working class today which is at fault.

The two of course are related. And this brings me to my second point, which is that some of us are being a great deal too precious about the "materialism" of working people. The myth of the Great Prosperity is, after all, Macmillan's. Millions do not know it; millions more live at a distance of two or three wage-packets from poverty, and need only an accident, a separation from the husband, a sickness or death in the family, to be pushed into extreme hardship. The millions who *do* live in greater security, who do bring in the bonuses and overtime, who do go after the bedroom suites and the homemaking gimmicks, certainly are subject to most of the commercially induced pressures towards a "middle-class style of life" which Stuart Hall anatomises; but *why* do he and others dwell so exclusively on the negative features of the situation? Why does Gordon Redfern couple sneeringly the television and the washing machine? The first is a problem of a special order; the second is not a symbol of "status" but a machine to wash clothes with. I do not know what moral and cultural values are attached to the kitchen sink, a washboard, and the week's wash for a family of five. But if we are getting more washing machines, we should recognise in that fact at least the *potential* of greater emancipation for working women.

I am asking not only for a sense of history, but for a sense of the dialectics of social change. It may be true that the dominant ethic today is a blend of Joe Lampton and the Labour electoral glossy, but that does not tell us what to expect tomorrow. Less than a year after Engels had complained of our "bourgeois proletariat" he was standing on a van at London's first May Day, rejoicing at the sight of "the grandchildren of the old Chartists re-entering the line of battle." But these men were not the same as their grandfathers, and they were not entering the same battle. The Lancashire followers of Blatchford made fuller and more complex claims upon life than their grandfathers in the Plug Riots had done. Where the Bradford Chartists had fought against the Bastille and against starvation, the Bradford I.L.P. fought against infant mortality, for nursery schools, council houses, and free school meals. What do we want the present generation of working people to fight *for*? We do not want to push them back into the old, cramped, claustrophobic community which was based on the grim equality of hardship. The aspiration towards community, if it arises in the present generation, will be far richer and more complex, with far more insistence upon variety, freedom of movement, and freedom of choice, than in the old-style community.

Misuse of Hoggart

I MUST CONFESS to some impatience with this nostalgia for the "whole way of life" of the old working-class community. Stuart Hall tells us that a skilled maintenance operative remarked: " 'I wanted a house and a bit of space around it: after all, that's what we came for. People are too close to you—breathing down your necks ... ' And we thought of Bethnal Green."

What did Stuart Hall think of Bethnal Green? It is one thing to recognise the positive values created in the slums in the teeth of squalor, overcrowding and hardship, so long as we recall the human cost and the many casualties on the way. But it is another matter if we exalt these positives to the point where we see the slum-dweller's desire for a house "with a bit of space" only as a melancholy falling-away from a noble "way of life." Are family privacy and the sense of community *necessarily* opposed? Is it not possible that we should look forward to a more complex interaction between self-cultivating and civic values? Are there not new positives and potentialities in the new way of life, which are the strengths upon which we must build, in countering the self-regarding and acquisitive features?

I suspect that the current tendency to sentimentalise the old working-class community may in part be traced to a *misuse* of Richard Hoggart's *The Uses of Literacy*. I shared in the general acclaim for this book upon its appearance: it is splendidly evocative in its opening chapters, splendidly perceptive in its local criticisms. But as the book is put to uses which its author cannot have foreseen, one's criticisms tend to grow more harsh. From the standpoint of the historian of the working class it is a valuable, but highly misleading, document. I do not refer only to the absence of conflict in the early chapters, the absence of many adult preoccupations (especially at the place of work), the neglect of the role of the minority, the omission or underestimation of most of those influences which combine to create the labour movement in this century. Nor am I concerned at the moment with the persistent suggestion, in the later chapters, that the readers can be identified in an over-simplified way with the attitudes in the papers which they read—the failure of Hoggart seriously to examine the tensions which exist between the actual experience and relationships of the readers, and the false consciousness of the mass media. My central criticism is of the misleading and anti-historical framework of the book. In the first part, subjective impressions, largely based on childhood memories, and unchecked by historical referents; the whole combining in a picture of the old way of life. In the second part, impressions drawn from reading matter alone, combining in a picture of the new. The further the reader is from the book, the more it simmers in his memory, the more he forgets the peculiar technique employed. And the more it appears to him as an historical analysis of the currents of working-class cultural change in our time. But this is precisely what the book is *not*. If it were so, the evidence of *Reveille* and the *Daily Mirror* would have to be balanced against Northcliffe's *Daily Mail* at the time of the "Hang the Kaiser" election and Horatio Bottomley's *John Bull*; or the family of Hoggart's recollections would have to be weighed beside equally close empirical insights into the family on the new Leeds housing-estates.

Culture Not Peripheral

I AM NOT UNDERESTIMATING the gravity of the situation which Hoggart illuminates. But his case is presented in such a way as to emphasise the passivity of the present-day working-class reader, and so induces a sense of hopelessness. But the working-class reader has been besieged before, if not so seductively, then at least as relentlessly. He has survived the propaganda of church and squire, the Steam Intellect Tracts, the sentimental mush of the Sunday School and the orthodox Methodist pulpit, as debilitating and degrading in their way as anything offered today. Survival has not always been easy; at times, the course of social change has been diverted, or temporarily reversed, and the active political minority has been almost totally submerged. I agree that the problem of the mass media today, with their vast power, centralised control, and suggestive influence upon the very "springs of action," is of crucial importance. Questions of "culture" today are not peripheral to the "real political issues" of class power; they are central to the whole way of struggle. What is at issue is the mind of the working class: its consciousness of itself, its knowledge of its own potential strength. I ask only that we see these problems within some historical frame of reference, and in the context of struggle. The resistance to the mass media comes not only from old strengths and traditions derived from the old working-class community, it is generated daily in the experience of working people, and nourished by the active minority. If we see the working class as the passive recipients of the mass media, then we may disarm ourselves in the face of them. Worse than this, we may not bring to the minority the support which they so urgently need. The suggestive forces of the mass media cannot be resisted by the fostering of a negative current of critical resistance alone. They must be met by other, positive forces which can only come from a vigorous socialist movement in which the political minority and the intellectuals make common cause. The constructive aspirations towards a full socialist community will be nourished from a hundred sources; and the socialist intellectuals, the architects who project the new cities, the scientists who can explain the hazards and the opportunities, the writers, the historians, even—perhaps— the sociologists (if they will break their Family-fixation and breathe some fresh air) must provide much of the nourishment. And in the process I hope we may become a little less self-conscious ourselves about status and class, and cease to play the game of the Establishment by drawing an abstract line between the "real working class" of heavy industry, and the teachers, the technicians, the draughtsmen, the white-coated workers and the rest. We do not want the jealous neighbourhood community which erects barriers; we want the socialist community which includes all.

Whole Way of Struggle

I HOPE THE TENOR of my criticisms has now become clear. If placed within an historical perspective, recent sociological writings can greatly add to our understanding of the very texture of life, the tissue of social and personal relationships, the cultural norms. But without this sense of history the record of our working class can appear as an instinctual, almost vegetable, evolution, in which the active role of the minority, as the agent of social change, is belittled, as well as the moral and intellectual resources which have been called forth in a whole way of struggle. Our society today—our democratic liberties and our social services— is in great part the product of this struggle, and of the adjustments to it on the part of capitalist interests. If Campaigners can meet in Trafalgar Square today, it is because of the great struggles for freedom of speech and assembly waged by radical and socialist working men in the 1880s and 1890s. And unless we have this sense of history, we will not see the potential within living working people. Commitment in politics *must* mean commitment to living people.

This does not mean uncritical allegiance to the existing social attitudes, or political institutions, of the working class. (*Which* institutions, anyway? And in what sense can certain bureaucratic organisations today be said to be the true expression of the needs of the existing working people?) Most certainly the acquisitive ethos and the politics of glossyism have got to be challenged in every centre of working-class life. But the challenge must come *from within*, not from a righteous minority outside. The movement today is blighted by flattery; everyone flatters working people, from the intimate fireside tele-politician, with his appeal to the "moderate right-thinking" elector, to the self-appointed vanguardist exalting the effortless, instinctive judgment of the "true proletarian." The great pioneers never built on flattery: they denounced, they challenged, they offered the hardships of organisation, self-education, the difficult mastery of political understanding, the painful awakening of richer social aspirations: "Now, young chaps, what are *you* going to live for?" demanded Tom Mann. We have to make this challenge again, and we can offer a complexity of fulfilment unattainable sixty years ago. But we shall be listened to—we shall have the right to expect attention—only if our commitment to the living generation is beyond question.

All this is given added point in the aftermath of the Aldermaston demonstration. The presence of some thousands of young "middle-class" people was a great feature of the march. Who could have supposed, from an aloof analysis of the reading matter of the intelligentsia three years ago—*Waiting for Godot* and *1984*, the back end of the *New Statesman* and the front end of *Encounter, The Outsider* and Mr. Khruschev's secret speech—that out of such despair and contempt for common people, this swift maturity of protest could arise? The individualists are marching, because they know that peace is the very pre-condition of individualism; and as they march, they discover within themselves unsuspected aspirations—new social bonds, a new sense of potential community, an intuition into the nature of class power.

Let us hope that the splendid spirit of antagonism to the expediencies and moral myopia of the orthodox politicians, which was so evident in the nuclear disarmament campaign, will not overbalance into the anti-political moral purism of the sect. Commitment to principle need not be a different thing from political commitment. In the last analysis, commitment in politics entails the assumption of the fullest human responsibility available to men in class society—a responsibility entailed by the tissue of human relationships into which we are committed by the very fact of birth—the purposive and sustained action, in association with others, to bring class society itself to an end. It is from this central human commitment that commitment in every other field must flow. And this *political* question is central to our whole discussion of both *community* and *culture*. It is *in the socialist movement itself* that the aspiration towards community should find its most conscious expression.

There is a long and honourable tradition of such total human commitment within our working-class movement. For several generations, thousands of men and women have come forward whose lives have been enclosed within this whole way of struggle. They have officered organisations for twenty, thirty and more years, defining the meaning of their lives in terms of the wider movement, looking forward to little more than a vote of thanks, and a declining standard of living in their old age. They have lived through as many defeats as victories, and have spent much of their energy in challenging their own leaders, or in repairing their defections. They have seen their colleagues fall away, and the clever politicians find the rooms at the top. They have been the poor bloody infantry of the movement, who have been sent in to hold the positions which the dashing cavalrymen have entered. For decades at a time they have been deserted, not only by most of the intellectuals, but also by a great part of their own class. Never far from the realities of class power, they have felt the full shock of every setback in their own lives. They have been accustomed to fighting defensive battles, and "politics" for them has meant, more often than not, dealing with contingencies as they have arisen. Confined to one community and to a few places of work, they have made their own choice between the values of community and the acquisitive ethic. It is easy enough to forget at what cost:

What is the price of Experience? Do men buy it for a song?
Or wisdom for a dance in the street? No, it is bought with the price
Of all that a man hath, his house, his wife, his children.
Wisdom is sold in the desolate market where none come to buy,
And in the wither'd field where the farmer plows for bread in vain.

Such total commitment may generate vices which are complementary to its virtues: a suspicion of the individualist, a tendency to exalt the need for organisational unity, and to fall into defensive political routines, a narrow pragmatic "realism." Today the vices may be more apparent than the virtues; and the minority, where it is still to be found, in the Labour Party, the trade unions, or the Communist Party, is often disheartened and has lost its sense of direction. I am not suggesting that our Labour Movement today is staffed at the rank-and-file level wholly by men of such single-minded purpose. But I am insisting that it is from this honourable tradition that all of us—and most especially the new Aldermaston generation—have most to learn. We must learn from the steady attention to organisation, and from the true moral realism which has enabled men, year in and year out, to meet each situation as it has arisen—each industrial or political challenge, each threat to peace—and to act in relation to it without the least regard for personal gain. If I describe this total commitment as being, in the last analysis, commitment in the class struggle, I do not mean that its truest expression is to be found in revolutionary posturing or bull-at-a-gate industrial militancy. Intelligence, resourcefulness, a sense of the needs of the wider movement, humanity, and—in the common human struggle to prevent nuclear war— restraint and a capacity for compromise; all these qualities may, at one time or another, be demanded by the logic of events, and signify a truer revolutionary maturity than the posturings of those enthusiasts who (in Shaw's phrase), "mistake their own emotions for public movements." But, however various its forms of expression, we must see this total commitment as the ultimate value from which the aspiration for community is constantly renewed. And intellectuals, above all, should strive to associate themselves with this tradition, as a corrective to those many influences which enable them to come to terms with the Establishment without loss of self-esteem, and which tolerate and even reward the radical providing that he does not touch the sensitive points of class-power. We need (finally) this corrective to the extravagances of utopianism. Political action consists in influencing and changing living people. The region of political choice is limited by the stubborn nature of the stuff with which we must work. And the value of utopianism is to be found, not in raising banners in the wilderness, but in confronting living people with an image of their own potential life, in summoning up their aspirations so that they challenge the old forms of life, and in influencing such social choices as there are in the direction that is desired. Utopianism and realism should not form into rival contingents; they should quarrel in a constructive way in the heart of the same movement.

I am not stating this case for political commitment in any narrow, organisationally limited way. I do not think that there is any one single organisational solution for socialists today. Nor am I asking people to "root themselves in the labour movement" by conducting parasitic factional activities within organisations which are dying through bureaucratic paralysis and lack of an influx of youth. People *are* looking for new ways, new forms of political expression; there must be direct channels opened up to the minds of younger working people, as well as actions in the old organisations. Next year the banners of Trades Councils must move from Aldermaston to Trafalgar Square: but the skiffle groups and the jeans-and-ponytails must still be there. It is because *ULR* has broken free of old dogmas and organisational routines; because its contributors voice richer aspirations than are found in the sterile formulations of Old Dogma or the seedy solicitations of New Glossy; because they bring with them a generosity of spirit without which the most "correct" political theory is impotent; because they understand that, as the old battles for bread are won, new tensions and needs are arising; because they start from the need to change people and not resolution-jobbing or institutional manipulation; because they understand that the great battle today is for the mind of the working people, and the greatest need is for the vision of community to be reborn; because—above all—their vision of socialism entails, not a succession of electoral rat-races, but the revolutionary transformation of the whole life of man—for all these reasons the jibes at the opening of this article may be dismissed with contempt. But let us keep steadily in view the realities of class power in our time; the community to which we look forward is potential only within our working-class movement. The "power to compel" must always remain with the organised workers, but the intellectuals may bring to them hope, a sense of their own strength and potential life. And the facts of class power in our time will not allow us the luxury of self-isolation. We are committed, with a total commitment, to meet each contingency as it arises, knowing that it is our fate and our responsibility in capitalist society to see many of our hopes and energies ploughed into "the wither'd field," but knowing also that there is no force which can change this society except within ourselves. We have no choice in this. And if we evade this choice, we degrade our own humanity.

APPEARING IN *THE NEW REASONER* 9 (SUMMER 1959), THIS article offers a view of Thompson's politics and perspectives in these years, though by no means reflects the views of all in the movement. Thompson sees the New Left as "laboratory work," a work in progress, its task still one of breaking "anti-humanism"—with the "authoritarianism and anti-intellectualism" of Stalinism, on the one hand, and "the idiocies of the Cold War and the facts of power within Western 'over-developed societies,'" on the other. He sees as yet no unified theory, no prescribed "road to socialism," but nevertheless sees a context full of new openings and possibilities. Its arenas will be "cafes, communes, workshops, and trade union meetings," above all the CND and the trade union movement. But here "the New Left does not propose itself as an alternative organization to those already in the field; rather, it offers two things to those within and without existing organizations—a specific propaganda of ideas, and certain practical services (journals, clubs, schools, etc.). What will distinguish the New Left will be its rupture with the tradition of inner-party factionalism, and its renewal of the tradition of open association, socialist education, and activity directed towards the people as a whole. It will stop fooling people that international or internal problems are going to be solved by the existing Parliamentary Labour Party, or by a series of electoral contests, with slightly more 'left' candidates. It will break with the administrative fetishes of the Fabian tradition, and insist that socialism can only be built from below, by calling, to the full, upon the initiatives of the people."

The New Left

"I am really sorry to see my countrymen trouble themselves about politics," wrote William Blake in 1810. "House of Commons and Houses of Lords appear to me to be Fools; they seem to me to be something Else besides Human Life." And yet on the next page of his notebook he was denouncing "the wretched State of Political Science, which is the Science of Sciences."

We share his dilemma today. Against the vast back-cloth of nuclear promise and nuclear threat, the old political routines have lost their meaning. Mr. Macmillan's business with the fur hat: Mr. Gaitskell, sharing the platform on NATO Day (the day after London's May Day), with M. Spaak and Mr. Selwyn Lloyd— these things no longer arouse scorn, or indignation, or partisanship of any kind. They are tedious. They are "something Else besides Human Life." Strontium-90 is a merciless critic; it penetrates alike the specious rhetoric about a " free community of nations," the romantic *longueurs* of imperialism in retreat, the flatulent composure of the Fabian "social engineer," the bluff incompetence and moral atrophy of the "political realists."

And yet it is these men who hold within their control the very course of human life. And so the business of controlling *them* is indeed the "Science of Sciences."

It is in recognition of this fact that some members of the younger generation are beginning to take up political activity. They are doing this, not because they have clearly formulated political objectives, but because they think it necessary to watch the politicians.

It is a difficult generation for the Old Left to understand. It is, to begin with, the first in the history of mankind to experience adolescence within a culture where the possibility of human annihilation has become an after-dinner platitude. Tommy Steele anticipated Mr. Godfrey Liam by several years, in writing the appropriate hymn for NATO:

> The first day there'll be lightning
> The second there'll be hail
> The third daybreak there'll be a big earthquake
> So, brother, forward my mail.

Rock 'n roll you sinners,
Sing to save your soul—
There ain't no room for beginners
When the world is Rock 'n Roll.

It is a generation which never looked upon the Soviet Union as a weak but
heroic Workers' State; but, rather, as the nation of the Great Purges and of Stalin-
grad, of Stalin's Byzantine Birthday and of Krushchev's Secret Speech, as the vast
military and industrial power which repressed the Hungarian rising and threw
the first sputniks into space.

A generation which learned of Belsen and Hiroshima when still at elementary school; and which formed their impressions of Western Christian conduct
from the examples of Kenya and Cyprus, Suez and Algeria.

A generation nourished on *1984* and *Animal Farm*, which enters politics at
the extreme point of disillusion where the middle-aged begin to get out. The
young people, who marched from Aldermaston, and who are beginning, in
many ways, to associate themselves with the socialist movement, are enthusiastic enough. But their enthusiasm is not for the Party, or the Movement, or the
established Political Leaders. They do not mean to give their enthusiasm cheaply
away to any routine machine. They expect the politicians to do their best to trick
or betray them. At meetings they listen attentively, watching for insincerities,
more ready with ironic applause than with cheers of acclaim. They prefer the
amateur organisation and the amateurish platforms of the Nuclear Disarmament Campaign to the method and manner of the left-wing professional. They
are acutely sensitive to the least falsity or histrionic gesture, the "party-political"
debating point, the tortuous evasions of "expediency." They judge with the critical eyes of the first generation of the Nuclear Age.

Established sources who want to see the young people got hold of and who
are alarmed at the first symptoms of a self-activating socialist youth movement,
have sounded the alarm. The Labour Party Executive has even appointed a committee to sit on the question of Youth. But Youth has been making its own inqui-
ries; and the Labour Party Executive has not come out of them too well.

Various remedies are proposed. Young people are ungrateful, spoiled by the
Welfare State. They should be educated in the moral and spiritual values of the
pioneers of the movement or perhaps the Labour Party should compete with
the Young Conservatives in providing a slap-up "social" life? Or perhaps (thinks
Fabian Chairman, Mrs. Eirene White), the "more effervescent type of political
youth," who circulates round the U.L.R. Club and the nuclear campaign, will
grow out of it in time:

Fabians in general have their political emotions well under control and consequently the Society will never be . . . a mass organisation. . . . But there are other organisations in the field which may be more successful in attracting younger members. How far should this concern us? Not very much, I think, provided that by the time they are 25 or so, we can attract the kind of persons who are concerned with serious politics. (*Fabian News,* January 1959)

What they fail, all of them, to recognise, is that the young people who are entering political activity today are indeed "concerned with serious politics." Serious politics today, in any worthwhile scale of human values, commences with nuclear disarmament. Those who do not understand this are either stupid (in which case they may yet be convinced); or they have become so mesmerised with political trivia, or have pushed their emotions so far down under, that they mistake the machinery of politics for the thing itself (in which case they are no longer on the Left, but are on the other side).

The young marchers of Aldermaston, despite all immaturities and individualistic attitudes, are at root more mature than their critics on the Old Left. They have understood that "politics" have become too serious to be left to the routines of politicians. As for "moral and spiritual values," what can Old Left or Old Right offer, after all?

The fourth day there'll be darkness
The last time the sun has shone,
The fifth day you'll wake up and say
The world's real gone . . .
(Tommy Steele, *Doomsday Rock*)

In terms of traditional "politics," we have been living through the decade of the Great Apathy. And this has been a phenomenon common to all the highly industrialised nations, irrespective of differences in ideology and social structure. It can be traced, in part, to economic and social causes operative in East and West—the drive for "normality" and security in the aftermath of war, growing economic affluence (in a few favoured industrial countries), an affluence which has been coincident with the supreme international immoralities of the Cold War and of colonial repression. Above all, it can be traced to the Cold War itself, and to its military, political, economic and ideological consequences.

But the most characteristic form of expression of this "apathy" has been in the sense of impotence, on the part of the individual, in face of the apparatus of the State. This has arisen, in different countries, from quite different causes; American "Power Elite," Russian "Bureaucracy," British "Establishment," all draw their strength from greatly different social contexts, and the attempt to press superficial resemblances too far will lead to specious conclusions. Nevertheless, if we are concerned with the formative cultural influences upon the post-war generations, then the similarities acquire significance. It is important to assess how these similarities appear to the post-war consciousness:

1. *The Establishment of Power.* The increasing size, complexity, and expertise required in industrial concerns have contributed to the sense of "anonymity" of the large-scale enterprise, to the power of the managers, and to the sense of insignificance of the individual producer. World War, followed by Cold War, and reinforced in the Soviet Union by the highly centralised economic planning of the Stalin era, further intensified these changes and helped on the process of the consolidation of immense resources at the disposal of the State. In Britain this brought into being an unholy coming-together of the Federation of British Industries, the Trades Union Congress and Government to form a super-Establishment, which has invested its own procedures with an air of "official" sanctity so that the non-conformists or minority group ("unofficial" strikers, "proscribed" organisations, etc.), are presented as offenders against Decency, Law and Order—a process most clearly seen at work in the treatment of the "blue" union in the docks, the events at Briggs Motors, and the "official" Court of Inquiry into B.O.A.C.

2. *The Establishment of Orthodoxy.* Two factors have combined to generate a climate of intellectual conformity: first, the centralised control, either by great commercial interests or by the State itself, of the mass media of communication, propaganda, and entertainment, and the consequent elimination from them of minority opinions: second, the ideological orthodoxies and heresy hunting which have been a byproduct of the Cold War. In Russia this orthodoxy has been enforced by the authority of the State; but in the U.S.A. and Britain, where the forms of democracy have been preserved, the major political parties, Republican and Democrat, Conservative and Labour, endorse officially the Cold War orthodoxies of anti-Communism, NATO strategy, nuclear arms manufacture and the rest, so that on the crucial issues of human survival, the electorate are presented with no effective choice.

3. *The Establishment of Institutions.* Here the post-war generation encounters institutions which had already become "set" in their leadership, bureaucracy, procedures and policies, in the war or immediate post-war years. These institutions enshrine and perpetuate attitudes which have their origin in a prewar context; they appear, to the post-war generation, as institutions set apart from and above them.

This is notably the case with the British Labour Party, which, while it may still hold the electoral support of great numbers in the post-war generation, has failed to win the loyalty or participation of the younger electors. The younger generation have no memories of Labour as a movement of storm and protest, a movement of men struggling and sacrificing to lift themselves and their fellows out of cramping and dehumanising conditions. They were born, rather, into the world of the block vote; it is the trade union that tells them what they can do and what they can't do. They see restriction where their fathers saw mutual support. And the young socialist today is not only concerned with changing the direction of Labour Party policy; he is hostile to its integration with the rest of the Establishment, hostile to the party bureaucracy, hostile to the "game political," hostile to the machine itself.

These are some of the ingredients of the Great Apathy. But "apathy" is a misleading term, confusing contradictory phenomena. On the one hand we have seen the blatant salesmanship of acquisitive materialism, and the conformists in State and Party and industry—in the U.S.A. the gaudy showcase of conspicuous consumption and the great rat-race, in the U.S.S.R. the time-serving conformity of the *apparatchiks*, in Britain Mr. Gaitskell's Glossy and Mr. Macmillan's Opportunity State and the ethic of "Room at the Top." And as a concomitant of all these, a profound moral inertia, retreat from political commitment, failure to engage the idealism of youth, and a slowing down of the dynamic of social change. On the other hand, there have been the scarcely concealed injustices and inequalities, the increase in criminality, the social neurosis and inarticulate frustrations—dope addicts and "Beats," *stilyagi*, gang conflicts and race riots. Perhaps only a minority react in this way, but the possibility of harnessing this latent aggression on a much wider scale is always there. Notting Hill is a warning. Sometimes the protest is just *against*; against nothing, as in the rock 'n roll riots. Sometimes we catch a glimpse of the immense potential of human energy and sympathy draining away for lack of channels of expression; the unutilised yearnings for something positive with which to identify oneself that find expression in gang-belongingness, or the desires to find a meaning in life which went to inflate the mass emotionality of Billy Graham's tours.

For a multitude, East and West, "apathy" has not been the expression of content, so much as the function of impotence. And impotence is generating its own forms of revolt, in which utter political disillusion combines with the anarchistic posturing of the isolated individual. On occasion it spills over into the frenzy of the impotent verbal assassin:

> I want to run into the street,
> Shouting, "Remember Vanzetti!"
> I want to pour gasoline down your chimneys.
> I want to blow up your galleries.

I want to burn down your editorial offices.
I want to slit the bellies of your frigid women.
I want to sink your sailboats and launches.
I want to strangle your children at their finger paintings.
I want to poison your Afghans and poodles.
(Kenneth Rexroth, *Thou Shalt Not Kill*)

The note is found among the "beat" writers; whenever the crust breaks it can be found in Eastern Europe as well—in the cult of Hemingway, the eager acceptance of *1984*, in the stories of Hlasko; it is present in the shriller passages of John Osborne. And, in less articulate or less histrionic forms, it is found at every level of society. It is present as a mood of anti-political nausea; a nausea which extends to the very language and routines of the orthodox, whether the rituals of Marxist-Leninist ideologues or the fireside insincerities of Western tele-politicians. It is found in the obstinate resistance to the canvasser: "There's not much to choose between 'em, they're all in it for themselves, what's the use?" It is expressed in the derisory vote of the A.E.U. membership, when confronted with the choice of Carron or Birch. The old routines have ceased to bring the old results. Such results as they do bring are rarely a cause for socialist congratulation.

WE PLACE THE PROBLEM in this context, not because we think that such hasty impressionism is a substitute for the hard work of close political analysis; not because we incline towards the attitudes of Rexroth or of Hlasko; not because we believe that advanced industrialism itself has given rise to a "mass society" in which the antagonism between the power elite, or state bureaucracy, and the alienated individual has superseded, in importance, class antagonisms. The watershed of the October Revolution cannot be argued away; and we believe that, in an atmosphere of relaxed international tension, the Soviet Union and Eastern Europe will prove to be the area of expanding liberty and human fulfilment, whereas the West, unless transformed by a strong democratic and revolutionary socialist movement, will prove to be the area of enroaching authoritarianism. Moreover—and the reservation is of great importance—whereas in the capitalist powers, and especially U.S.A., great private interests find the maintenance of tension and arms production profitable, in the East no comparable vested interests in the Cold War are to be found. While at the rubbing edges of the "Two Camps"—Jordan or Tibet, Albania or Turkey—the actions of military strategists and politicians, East and West, can be equally fraught with danger, nevertheless it remains true that the "natural" economic and social pressures in the East lead towards a detente, whereas in the West we are faced with the inertia of the "permanent war economy."

But the assertion of democracy in the Communist area cannot take place without a hundred contests with the entrenched bureaucracy, its institutions and ideology. And, equally, the regeneration of the Western socialist movement cannot take place without a fundamental break with the policies and orthodoxies of the past decade. And this two-pronged offensive is (it becomes increasingly clear) carrying the left Socialist in the West, and the dissident Communist in the East, towards a common objective. There is a rediscovery of common aims and principles, obscured during the violent era of the Third International. This does not constitute a conversion of sections of the Western labour movement to Communist orthodoxy, nor of disillusioned Communists to liberal social-democracy. It represents, rather, a rejection of both orthodoxies; and the emergence of a New Left which, while it draws much from both traditions, stands apart from the sterile antagonisms of the past, and speaks for what is immanent within both societies. It champions a new internationalism, which is not that of the triumph of one camp over the other, but the dissolution of the camps and the triumph of the common people.

It is the bankruptcy of the orthodoxies of the Old Left, and particularly their imprisonment within the framework of Cold War ideology and strategy, which has contributed to the characteristic political consciousness of the post-war generation—the sense of impotence in the face of the Establishment. Because there has been during the past decade no determined and effective grouping, with a clear internationalist perspective, challenging these orthodoxies, frustration has given way to disillusion, and disillusion to apathy. Now that such groupings are appearing, in different forms, in a dozen different countries, East and West, the Establishment immediately appears less firmly based; apathy appears as a less formidable phenomenon; and a certain identity of aim is discovered.

First, these groupings find a common enemy not only in the tensions of the Cold War, but also in the strategic postulates and partisan ideology of the war. The neutralist position is expressed in the diplomacy of the uncommitted Afro-Asian nations, Yugoslavia, etc., it is also a spreading heresy in the communist and Western world. It is the first sin of "revisionism" to come under attack; it was the supreme crime of Nagy and of Harich. It is the neutralist implication, of the Nuclear Disarmament Campaign which provokes the hostility of the Establishment (Mr. Gaitskell, Mr. Bevan, and all) in Britain. As the pressure grows greater in one "camp," so the response will grow greater in the other.

It must be the first task for any New Left in Britain to propagate and to deepen, in the labour movement and in the nuclear disarmament campaign, not the mere sentiment of neutralism, but the internationalist outlook of active neutrality. We must seek to bring our people to an awareness of their key position in world affairs by fostering a far wider understanding, not only of the outlook of the colonial and Asian peoples, but also of the potential strength of "revisionist" and democratic forces within the Communist world.

Second, these groupings find a common problem in gaining access to channels of communication to people, despite control over the cultural apparatus by the State, the Party, or commercial interests; and over the organizations of the labour movement by the party bureaucracies. This tends to keep the new groupings isolated and to emphasize their "intellectual" character. But their importance as growing points should not be underestimated. The problem differs greatly from one country to another. In France our comrades contest with an erratic and vicious censorship. There they present themselves as a distinct party (the Left Socialist Union) with little electoral influence but with widely influential journals (notably *France-Observateur*). In Italy, the "New Left" tendency is to be found among elements within both the Socialist and Communist Parties, and is expressed in more than one serious theoretical journal. In Russia and in much of Eastern Europe our comrades press against the barriers of editorial inertia, and contest with State orthodoxy in a hundred tortuous ways; in China and in Viet-Nam they are being "re-educated" in the communes and on the dams—a process which may not prove as one-sided as their educators hope. In Britain, the democratic forms are unimpaired, but access to the means of communication becomes increasingly difficult—when the media of television and press are largely tuned by the Establishment and are closed to the sustained propagation of minority opinions. Channels of communication within the traditional labour movement are sluggish and obstructed by the bureaucracy. The problem presents itself as one of constructing (however painfully slow the process may seem, though steady progress is being made) an *alternative* "cultural apparatus," firmly in the hands of the New Left, a cultural apparatus which bypasses the mass media and the party machinery, and which opens up direct channels between significant socialist groupings inside and outside the labour movement.

Third, there is taking place within these groupings a renaissance of socialist theory. It would be premature to attempt to define a unified and consistent body of ideas by which the New Left can be identified in any country. The laboratory work is still continuing, in journals, clubs and splinter parties, in sociological theses and in novels, in discussions in cafes, communes, workshops, trades union meetings. It would be possible to trace a recurring pattern in Communist post-1956 "revisionism"—the humanist revolt, the rejection of dogmatic in favour of empirical methods of analysis, opposition to authoritarian and paternalist forms of organisation, the critique of determinism, etc. But this would tell us more about the shedding of old illusions and the revaluation of old traditions, than about the affirmation of the enduring and the discovery of the new. It would tell us nothing about the crucial question: the confluence of the dissident Communist impulse with the left socialist tradition of the West and with the post-war generation. It is at this point of confluence that the New Left can be found.

1956 marks the watershed. In the first place, since 1956, there has been a worldwide and continuing movement of Communist dissidence which (if we overlook—as we should—Mr. Howard Fast) has not entered into the worn paths of traumatic anti-Communism, God-That-Failedism, Encounterism, and the rest; but which has, on the contrary, sought to affirm and develop the humane and libertarian features of the Communist tradition. The resilience and maturity of this heresy, which—excluded from the Communist Parties—has refused to lie down and die, or to cross to the "other camp," but which has instead struck independent roots in the labour movement, interposing itself between the orthodox Communist apparatus and the non-Communist Left—this has aroused the particular fury of the ideologues of *World Marxist Review.* Indeed, in certain countries it would be possible to identify the New Left by saying that it stands aside from the traditional contest between Social-Democratic and Communist orthodoxy; and looks forward to socialist reunification, not through some formal alliance of incompatibles, but as a result of the displacement of the ruling bureaucracies in both.

But we should go further. If there is, as yet, no unified theory of the New Left, there are many common preoccupations. There is no prescribed "road to Socialism"; but Socialism remains an international theory, with an international language. Confronted by the authoritarianism and anti-intellectualism of the Stalinist deviant of Marxism, Communist dissidence has broken with its scholastic framework and is subjecting the entire catechism to an empirical critique. But at the same time, confronted by the idiocies of the Cold War and the facts of power within Western "overdeveloped societies," a taut radical temper is arising among the post-war generation of socialists and intellectuals in the West. In the exchange between the two a common language is being discovered, and the same problems are being thrust forward for examination: the problem of political power and of bureaucratic degeneration: the problem of economic power and of workers' control: the problems of decentralisation and of popular participation in social control. There is the same rediscovery of the notion of a socialist community; in Britain the Fabian prescription of a competitive Equality of Opportunity is giving way, among socialists, before the rediscovery of William Morris's vision of a Society of Equals; in the Communist world the false community of the authoritative collective is under pressure from the voluntary, organic community of individuals, which, despite all the inhumanities of the past two decades, has grown up within it. There is, East and West, the same renewal of interest in the "young Marx"; the same concern with humanist propositions; the same reassertion of moral agency, and of individual responsibility within the flow of historical events. The New Left has little confidence in the infallibility, either of institutions or of historical processes. A true socialist community will not be brought into being by legislative manipulation and top-level economic planning alone. Socialism must commence with existing people; it must be built by men and women in voluntary association. The work of changing people's values and attitudes and the summoning up of aspirations to further change by means of Utopian critiques of existing society, remains as much a duty of social- ists as the conquest and maintenance of working-class power. At every stage, before, during, and after the conquest of power, the voluntary participation of the people must be enlisted, and the centres of power must themselves, wher- ever possible, be broken up. The New Left is made up of revolutionary socialists; but the revolution to which they look forward must entail not only the conquest but also the dismantling of State power. They are socialist theorists who distrust the seductive symmetry of socialist theory, and revolutionaries who are on their guard against the dogmatic excesses and the power-drives of the professional revolutionary.

THE NEW LEFT IN BRITAIN is, as yet, scarcely identifiable in terms of organ- isation—a few publications and journals, several successful Left Clubs, a grow- ing programme of conference and educational work initiated by this journal in association with *Universities and Left Review*. It is significant, however, for three reasons. First, it is giving political expression to a mood which is very widely diffused, both within the traditional labour movement and outside it; which has already precipitated in the nuclear disarmament campaign and which may soon precipitate in more specifically socialist form. Second, it is meeting with a response from younger people, and is giving expression to their frustrations and needs in a way that alarms the older bureaucratic organisations. Third, it is oper- ating within a context—in Britain—which is more favourable, and more preg- nant with possibilities, than is, perhaps, the case of any other Western country. In Britain the 1956 dissidence within the Communist movement coincided with Mr. Bevin's accommodation with Mr. Gaitskell and the disorientation of the tra- ditional Labour left. In both quarters the "cult of personality" gave way to the search for principled socialist policy. This re-examination of theory and of policy among elements on the Old Left coincided with the breakthrough, in *U.L.R.*, of an authentic voice from the critical post-war generation. The confluence of these three tendencies, which is now taking place, offers a unique combination of real contacts with the older and younger socialist generations. While the intel- lectual resources and political experience of our comrades in France and Italy are undoubtedly greater, we have the advantage of operating within a country where Communist/Social-Democratic antagonisms have never worked such havoc in the traditional labour movement; a country, moreover, whose critical position in the entire Cold War complex is becoming more and more evident.

The New Left is sometimes identified by observers by its concern with "cultural" questions, as opposed to the basic bread-and-butter preoccupations of the Old Left. But this is true only if it is understood that these "cultural" questions are questions about life. For the New Left wants political and economic changes *for* something, so that people can themselves do something with their lives as a whole. We have seen enough of a socialism perverted into the worship of poods of grains and tons of steel, with men identified as producers of material values and little else, where "consumption" has always to wait, and where "culture" is a means of social control directed by the Establishments. These "cultural" questions are not only questions of value; they are also, in the strictest sense, questions of political power. As even the Giants of publishing vanish from the scene, as Hultons and Newnes give way to Odhams, it becomes ever more clear that the fight to control and break up the mass media, and to preserve and extend the minority media, is as central in political significance as, for example, the fight against the Taxes on Knowledge in the 1830s; it is the latest phase of the long contest for democratic rights—a struggle not only for the right of the minority to be heard, but for the right of the majority *not* to be subject to massive influences of misinformation and human depreciation.

The true distinction between New and Old Left may perhaps be seen in their differing responses to the problem of political "apathy." To this problem there are two traditional responses on the Old Left: demonism and economism: and one organisational remedy which is proposed: fervent parasitic factionalism.

1. *Demonism.* This consists in attributing the "apathy" of the labour movement exclusively to the machinations of the bureaucracy (Transport House or King Street, or both, according to preference), and to the treachery of the existing leaderships. This convenient excuse enables the Old Left to fall back upon the old repertoire of militant slogans, and to evade the labour of analysing the actual social forces which have contributed to the rise of bureaucracy and which enable the leadership to maintain its power. It also enables the Old Left to hypostatise and idealise a mythical militant working class, which is bound down by the oppression of its own false leaders but which is at any moment about to break out into revolutionary actions—a working-class which is far more a construct from passages of Lenin and/or Trotsky than a derivation from actual observation of the real tensions and conflicts of contemporary working-class life.

The New Left has embarked upon the less comforting business of analysing the actual situation; notably in the analysis of Ralph Miliband in the *New Reasoner* ("The Politics of Contemporary Capitalism," "The Transition to the Transition," *New Reasoner* 6 and 7); and in the analysis of the cultural influences at work by Raymond Williams, Richard Hoggart, Stuart Hall, and other contributors to *U.L.R.* The contributors to *Conviction* have pursued an analysis on parallel lines. It is no longer possible (and it is still less "Marxist"!) to explain away Glossyism as the result of a crooked deal by Mr. Gaitskell; it is the authentic expression of certain features of contemporary society, and reflects the permeation of the acquisitive ethic into the centres of working-class life, and the enfeeblement of the ethic of community. The evident corruption of the traditional institutions of the labour movement has been possible only within a context of social mobility, of a "Room at the Top" educational ladder, and of a tacit accommodation to imperialism which has compromised the working-class movement as a whole. This is not the whole story; but if we are to find remedies, we must commence with an honest diagnosis.

2. *Economism.* This doctrine of economic man is supposed to be the original sin of Marxism. As a matter of fact, it is most evident in the blatant appeal to the acquisitive and self-regarding appetites in the policies of the Labour and Tory Right. On the Old Left it is notably found in the rank-and-file of the Labour Party, in the argument that what is "wrong" with the working people is the prosperity of full employment (usually attributed to armaments expenditure), and that we cannot hope for further socialist advance until "the next slump."

   This pernicious argument, which is an insult to working people (can they only think with their stomachs?), an insult to Socialism (will people only be driven to it by starvation?) and a contributory cause of apathy, is based upon a complete misreading of history. Slump does not necessarily engender socialist militancy (it did not do so in the 1930s): it may equally provide the breeding ground for authoritarianism. Some of the periods of greatest advance in our movement have been in a context of economic recovery (1889 and the new unionism), or have been the product of an enhanced political consciousness arising from non-economic causes (the anti-fascist war and 1945).

   The New Left is concerned, not to wait hopefully for the old disasters and repressions to engender the old defensive responses, but to discover the new frustrations and potentials within contemporary life, the new growing points. The way forward to Socialism lies not in frightening the children of the 1950s with the Ogre of the 1930s (although, true enough, he may still be lurking around), but in pointing the way to the great enrichment of social life potential within our society today. Enduring militancy is built, not upon negative anxieties, but upon positive aspirations; *Merrie England* and *News from Nowhere* helped to engender the enthusiasm and will which carried the younger generation of the 1890s away from the impoverished life of their fathers. And as certain of the basic material hardships of working people are diminishing, so fuller demands—which in the past may have appeared as "marginal"—come to the centre of the stage; for the humanisation of the social services and of conditions of labour, for democracy in industry, for old Smoke and Squalor to be rebuilt as new Community, for the cultural enrichment of leisure. It is always the business of the Left to foster the utmost aspiration compatible with existing reality—and then some more beyond. But if the New Left fosters these new aspirations, it certainly does not do so in the reformist spirit of Fabian gradualism; the tactics of reform must be developed within a revolutionary Strategy. And if the people move towards objectives which prove unattainable within the framework of capitalist society, their experience will complete their political education.

3. *Parasitic Factionalism.* Demonism and economism have led the Old Left to a common organisational solution. The conquest of socialist power is equated with the capture of the machinery of the established labour movement. The organised left faction, rooted in (or parasitic upon) the institutions of the labour movement will engage in mortal struggle with the established bureaucracy. When certain key positions of power are gained, the Slump will follow; and the faction, vanguard or elite will ride on the tide of militancy to power.

This combination of demonism, economism ("The tempo of the class struggle is quickening. The tide is turning.") and factionalism reach their apotheosis in the newest offspring of the Old Left, the Trotskyist Socialist Labour League. We read in our contemporary, *Labour Review,* this editorial opinion:

> Our journal has an indispensable part to play. Our allotted share of the task is enormous: no less than the education of a generation of working-class fighters and leaders, to whom it will be given to seize and hold State power, to accomplish the British Revolution.[1]

We have no such confidence in the intentions of history. Nor are we confident that the British Revolution will be such a classic and cataclysmic event. The last British Revolution was a ragged and mixed-up affair; and, after two hundred years of working-class organisation, and the evolution within the capitalist framework of a hundred forms of social association and democratic control, the next Revolution is likely to appear equally messy and eccentric in the eyes of the doctrinaire historian. While the ultimate explanation of the diverse forms of social and political conflict is to be found in the class-struggle, this does not mean that the Revolution must inevitably be preceded by the total disengagement of the working class from the capitalist State machinery, and the naked confrontation of antagonistic classes. The flash-point, which enflames the political consciousness of the people and illuminates them across the watershed of history, might be reached in some unexpected way: for example, in response to international crisis.

But we are more worried by the tactics and organizational forms (democratic centralism), adopted by the S.L.L. than by their objectives, which, if unrealistic, are consistent with traditional socialist idealism. These forms are those of vanguardism, in full Leninist purity; and after this quarter century it is difficult to look forward with elation to the seizure of State power by any vanguard, however dedicated its members. We do not want the conquest of power by the vanguard, but the distribution of power among the people. We must certainly assist in the education of a new generation of dedicated socialist leaders in the trade union and labour movements; but they must be dedicated to the enlistment of the people, in the participation, at every level, in the exercise of power.

Such vanguard theories are only the extreme expression of parasitic factionalism. It is the tragedy of the Old Left that it has, for over a decade, allowed the energies of so many active socialists to be dispersed in inner-party factional struggles. Socialists have thought too loosely of the Labour Movement, as if it were a faceless non-human *thing*, like the Rock of Ages, standing amidst the stream of British life, and growing each year larger from the accretions of trade union membership like limestone deposit. So long as one is "rooted in the Labour Movement," one can be certain to be on the winning, side in the long run. Hence it has become customary for left groupings to form organisations which are, in essence, parasitic upon the larger institutions of the movement. Such organisations are geared, not to the general public, but to the rhythms of electoral contests and of annual conferences; they address themselves to the ageing ward party and the emptying trade union meeting; they seek to change constitutions but not to change people; their master objective is the passing of certain resolutions, not the preparation of social revolution. Meanwhile, the Labour Movement has itself been losing its roots, not only in socialist theory, but also in the younger generation of working people. And the Old Left has become trapped inside the machinery. It has become enmeshed in factional struggles which acquire an intensity of hatred, directed not against the capitalist system or war preparations but against the immediate antagonists in Party or trade union. It has emerged from a decade of struggle to discover, not only that it has lost most of its battles, but that the battlefield itself is shrinking. It has emerged without any clear policy; without any fresh analysis of changing society; without any organised socialist base. The parasite is in danger of dying with the host.

The New Left in Britain does not offer an alternative faction, party, or leadership to those now holding the field; and, during the present period of transition, it must continue to resist any temptation to do so. Once launched on the course of factionalism, it would contribute, not the reunification of the socialist movement, but to its further fragmentation; it would contribute further to the alienation of the post-war generation from the movement; and the established bureaucracies, in any case, cannot be effectively challenged by their own methods—they have, on their side, all the resources of propaganda and devious influence, and they will neutralise or smash all serious contendants to their power.

But the New Left must not stand aside from the Labour Movement, and from its immediate preoccupations and struggles, in righteous anti-political purism. The majority of those actively associated with the New Left will, as a matter of course, be active members of the Labour Party and trade union movement. There exist already many valuable organisations and pressure groups within, or on the fringe of, the Labour Movement—the Campaign and Victory for Socialism, the Movement for Colonial Freedom, the Africa Bureau, and many others—which will command the support of socialists. The New Left does not propose itself as an alternative organisation to those already in the field; rather, it offers two things to those within and without the existing organisations—a specific propaganda of ideas, and certain practical services (journals, clubs, schools, etc.). What will distinguish the New Left will be its rupture with the tradition of inner-party factionalism, and its renewal of the tradition of open association, socialist education, and activity, directed towards the people as a whole. It will stop fooling people that international or internal problems are going to be solved by the existing Parliamentary Labour Party, or by a series of electoral contests, with slightly more "left" candidates. It will break with the administrative fetishes of the Fabian tradition, and insist that socialism can only be built from below, by calling, to the full upon the initiatives of the people. It will insist that the Labour Movement is not a thing, but an association of men and women; that working people are not the passive recipients of economic and cultural conditioning, but are intellectual and moral beings. In the teeth of the Establishments of Power, of Orthodoxy and of Institutions, it will appeal to people by rational argument and moral challenge. It will counter the philistine materialism and anti-intellectualism of the Old Left by appealing to the totality of human interests and potentialities, and by constructing new channels of communication between industrial workers and experts in the sciences and arts. It will cease to postpone the satisfactions of Socialism to an hypothetic period "after the Revolution," but will seek to promote in the present, and in particular in the great centres of working-class life, a richer sense of community—a socialist youth movement (semi-autonomous, if need be), rank-and-file international contacts, and social activities.

In organisational forms the New Left will draw upon the experience of the Left Book Club movement. Publications, Left Clubs, and more sustained educational and conference programmes: propaganda, carried forward independently or in association with existing organisations. These activities will generate enthusiasm and provide a sense of common direction and purpose for socialists active within the Labour Movement; but, at the same time, the Clubs and discussion centres will be places beyond the reach of the interference of the bureaucracy, where the intiative remains in the hands of the rank-and-file. If the bureaucracy reacts by anathemas and proscriptions, the Clubs and publications will continue, staffed by socialists who are members of no party, but who intend to provide a service for the whole movement. Since they will not be geared to the manoeuvres of parliamentary politics, they need not be inhibited by politic considerations and cautious secrecy. Since they provide no positions in the power apparatus, they will not attract the attention of the factionalist sects. Since their organisers will be without political ambitions, they will not be subject to the usual means of party discipline. Their influence will pervade the Labour Movement, as the Campaign is coming to pervade it; but because this influence derives from ideas it will elude administrative control. The bureaucracy will hold the machine; but the New Left will hold the passes between it and the younger generation.

But, in all this, we speculate. All still depends upon the context of Cold War. If this is long prolonged, into a state of permanent tension, then all optimistic perspectives will be closed, and Old Left and New Left, "revisionism" and "democratisation," will perish beneath the encroaching authoritarianism. But if the Campaign should succeed, if Britain should step aside from the power complex, then far more splendid perspectives will open up—of internationalism reborn and of renewed social advance. The orthodoxies of established politics will appear as irrelevant as the squabbles of the contractors who built the Great Pyramid, and the Old Left will give place to the New.

WITH THIS ARTICLE, THOMPSON INTRODUCES THE VOLUME *Out of Apathy*, published in 1960 by New Left Books. He begins with the "apathetic decade" and, defining apathy, suggests "it is an expression of the impotence of the individual in the face of contemporary institutions—the small man in the vast corporate enterprise, the single citizen confronted by the state, the individual trade unionist within the union 'machine.'" Against this, Thompson poses "a way out of apathy": in this "our allegiance lies with the rank-and-file of the Labour Movement and with the young people who are acting already against the imbecilities of our society but who are not satisfied with the traditional routines of Labour."

At the Point of Decay

It is often said that the original "dynamic" of the socialist movement derived from the "politics of hunger." Now that extreme want and mass unemployment are things of the past, socialists should dilute their policies in an effort to adjust to the mood of the electorate; or they should look around for another dynamic.

It is true that absolute standards of welfare have risen (making the politics of absolute hunger irrelevant). What is false is the suggestion that the elimination of extreme want has ever been, for socialists, a sufficient end in itself. Rather, this end has been shared with the radical and with the liberal traditions. The Chartist movement was shaped by the politics of hunger, but it was not socialist. It was Lord Beveridge who wrote the Preamble to the welfare state.

The socialist end has been the creation—*not* of equality of opportunity within an acquisitive society—but of a society of equals, a co-operative community. The prerequisite for this is the replacement of production for profit by production for use. A socialist society might be underdeveloped or overdeveloped, poor or affluent. The distinction between socialist and capitalist society is to be found, not in the level of productivity, but in the characteristic relations of production, in the ordering of social priorities, and in its whole way of life.

When seen from this point of view, contemporary British society gives as much reason for outrage as the society of the 1880s or 1930s. A decade which sat for its own portrait in *Room at the Top*, which adopted the motto "Opportunity State," and which allowed the priorities of the salesman, the general and the speculator to override all other needs, was in a fair way to fulfilling the slogan of the old capitalist Adam: "To each according to his greed."

But why, if this is true, has the sense of outrage found so little direct expression? Why has the Labour Party sailed ever closer to the wind of accommodation, and, at the same time, lost electoral favour among the people? Why do the traditional institutions of the Labour Movement suffer from the problems of ageing and of bureaucratisation?

"Apathy." The answer, only too often, serves to close the inquiry. But since it is evident that apathy is a symptom as much as it is a cause, it seemed to us that it was at this point that our analysis must begin. To start at the other end, to debate the merits of rival policies, is as foolish as to argue the merits of rival courses of medical treatment before a diagnosis has been made.

If he is to follow our argument, the reader will need one or two guidelines. We have, in part, discounted the two most common explanations of apathy. The first is that people are apathetic about public affairs because their prosperity leaves no room for discontent. The truth in this explanation readers can document from their own experience without putting themselves to the trouble of reading this book. But they can also gather, out of their own experience, all the evidence that is needed to show how inadequate this explanation is. Most British working people and many professional people are far from content with their standard of living. Once we have crossed the threshold of absolute deprivation (of food, clothing, medicine) the high-powered salesmanship of an acquisitive society tends to *aggravate*, not to diminish, material discontents. It is the business of the copy-writers to ensure that we are under constant solicitations to keep up with the Joneses. We need only scratch the surface of social life to find, not contentment, but envy, frustration and on occasion violence not far below. We can probe deeper, as Richard Hoggart has done, and discover more ugly propensities which are exploited by the commercial media.

What is peculiar to the apathetic decade is that people have, increasingly, looked to *private* solutions to *public* evils. Private ambitions have displaced social aspirations. And people have come to feel their grievances as personal to themselves, and, similarly, the grievances of other people are felt to be the affair of other people. If a connection between the two is made, people tend to feel—in the prevailing apathy—that they are impotent to effect any change.

Here we are brought to the second most common explanation of apathy: it is an expression of the impotence of the individual in the face of contemporary institutions—the small man in the vast corporate enterprise, the single citizen confronted by the state, the individual trade unionist within the union "machine." We are very far from discounting this important feature of an "overdeveloped society"; people are, in fact, apathetic because society *looks* like this, from below, and especially to the post-war generation which finds itself confronted by institutions which originated in a pre-war context, set in their routines and ideas, and officered by older men. But these facts must also be put into their context, and important qualifications must be made. The isolated individual has *always* felt himself to be impotent to change his social environment, except when in association with other individuals. British society is warrened with democratic processes—committees, voluntary organisations, councils, electoral procedures—but in recent years fewer and fewer people have felt it worthwhile to work their way through these passages. The important words here are "worthwhile"—"it's not worth the racket," "I'm not bothered," "let it drop," "what can you do?" "they're all the same." And behind these phrases there is the unspoken assumption that any results which may accrue from public action are bound to be disproportionate to the effort involved. The institutions themselves have become so deeply involved in the maintenance of the *status quo* that the energies of dissent become dispersed within them long before they touch the centre of power.

But, alongside this, the increasing complexity of industrial organisation, and the size of the modern private or public corporation, bring with them a new vulnerability. As *The Times* complained in a leading editorial ("The Disruptors," January 27, 1960):

> A strike of 200 Birmingham crane drivers and slingers threw some 6,000 others out of work . . . a stoppage of about 300 door assemblers made nearly 9,300 other workers idle. . . . The [motor] industry has become so interlocked that a strike by a handful of men in one factory can affect thousands of others in the same and other factories.

Colliery engine-winders can halt the pits: bus or tube drivers can disorganise the metropolis: a few score electricians can cut off power supplies to a whole industrial region. Nor is there any *inherent* constitutional or institutional reason why the status quo might not be challenged, from the top as from the bottom. The T.U.C might call a General Strike tomorrow—if it were not for the apathy of its members. A breakaway socialist group might contest a by-election—if it were not that the electorate accept the conventions of the game.

So that the apparent immobility of "the Establishment" conceals points of extreme sensitivity; and, equally, the bureaucratisation of public life (most noticeable in the Labour Movement) is as much a product of apathy as a cause. And where a part of the public has agitated for some important change, it has not found itself to be wholly impotent. So far from an imperturbable Establishment brushing off all attacks with a bored Edwardian gesture, we find that it is only necessary for a shop steward to ring a handbell in Briggs Motors, or for several score Direct Action demonstrators to go outside the conventions of "the game political," to send it into a dither. So long as discontent expresses itself within the authorised institutional channels, and participates in what Ralph Miliband has called "a B.B.C. world of minor disagreements," it appears to encounter immovable forces. When discontent expresses itself *outside* these channels—not anywhere outside, but at the right point with the right lever—the Establishment appears to rest upon an equilibrium of forces so delicate that it is forced to respond to determined pressure. In twelve months of consistent agitation a few thousand members of the Campaign for Nuclear Disarmament failed to attain their objectives; but they brought the Labour Party to the verge of crisis, sent its leaders hurrying to emergency meetings, created a furor in a million-strong union whose name had become a byword for bureaucratic centralism, modified the tone of our intellectual life, expedited the ending of nuclear tests, and contributed a new stock of wary, peace-loving platitudes to the politicians' vocabulary. For the politicians can only keep the public apathetic by pretending to want very much the same things as the public wants, and by pretending that they, in turn, are prevented from achieving these aims by their own impotence in the face of overwhelming circumstances—Russian intransigence or the inflationary spiral—which hem them in.

So impotence turns out to be only a rephrasing of the question; the individual's sense of impotence consists, at least in part, in the apathy of other individuals. And people are apathetic today because they do not *want* to act; they may not be contented as they are, but they do not believe that there is any workable alternative, or they very much dislike any alternative (such as Communism) which is proposed. This being so, they will make their own lives in their own way. And they are indifferent to politics because—if there are no real alternatives—it does not matter very much which lot gets in. The politicians have proclaimed for so long that they are at the mercy of circumstances that circumstances might just as well pick the next Cabinet.

But perhaps the apathetic are right? Perhaps there *is* no viable alternative to the present uneasy equilibrium of forces within a class-divided acquisitive society? Or perhaps it is in the interests of ruling powers to induce the *belief* that there is no alternative, and since these powers control the media which form public opinion, the dissident individual is indeed impotent in the face of an apathy mass-produced from above?

So long as we conduct the argument in conventional terms, both propositions are true. The present equilibrium of forces *is* precarious, and any sudden shift of power could precipitate crisis. A necessary part of that equilibrium is that political energies shall be confined within the authorised conventions of public life. And the media controlled by the Establishment (including the orthodox Labour Establishment) exert a continual persuasive influence to assert the conventions of the game, and to ridicule or isolate or ignore all those who step outside them: in brief, to induce public apathy. But, if we conduct the argument in different terms, we discover that neither proposition need remain true, and at the same time we find a way out of apathy.

This is what is attempted in this book. What is proposed here is that Britain is *over*-ripe for socialism. *Over*-ripe, not ripe. "Ripe" might suggest only that the objective preconditions for forms of socialist ownership and social organisation had matured, and that we might effect a transition to socialism whenever public opinion concurs. But by "over-ripe" something else is intended—we have passed the point of maturity and processes of decay have set in. Apathy is the form which this decay takes in our public life. Any vigorous initiative which probes beyond the conventional limits of party controversy calls in question the continuance of the capitalist system. If we nationalise engineering and the motor industry as well as steel, we may tip the balance against the private sector. If we tax the rich more severely and divert resources to the non-profit-making public services, we may slow down the metabolism of a capitalist economy. If we contract out of NATO, we would run the risk of complete economic and political disorientation. At each point the initiative might provoke repercussions which would necessitate a total transformation of relations of production, forms of power, alliances and trade agreements, and institutions: that is, a socialist revolution. But for such a transformation public opinion is unprepared; and least prepared of all is the orthodox Labour Movement which (despite the debates on Clause 4) has for years undertaken no serious thinking about the practicability of an immediate transition to socialism.

The reasons why capitalism has been left to rot on the bough are complex. First, in the context of dominant imperialism it was possible for liberal reformism (sometimes mistaking itself for "socialism") to continue to win substantial benefits for the people. Second, the experience of the Russian Revolution made the concept of a revolutionary transition—*any* transition—to socialism appear to be synonymous with bloodshed, civil war, censorship, purges and the rest— a confusion which the apologetics of indigenous Communists did a good deal to perpetuate. Third, this experience hardened the doctrines of reformism into dogma, to the point where the British Labour Movement has become largely parasitic upon the capitalist economy, with deep vested interests in its continuance, since all local reforms (whether for more wages or more welfare) are seen as dependent upon its continued health and growth. Finally, the capitalist economy was given a fresh lease on life in war, post-war recovery, and next-war preparations, while the flagrant corruptions of post-war Communism diminished still further within Britain the desire to consider any revolutionary alternative. So that British people find themselves today, with the assent of orthodox Labour, within the grand defensive alliance of international capitalism, and exposed on every side to the ideology of apathy.

Perhaps we should now find a different analogy for the over-ripe apple, since we are dealing not with one organism but with two—the declining capitalist and the immanent socialist. "Last-stage" capitalism is not a healthy growth; rather, it is like a cramped apple tree, starved of sun and air, which has begun to "shoot" at the top. And the immanent community of socialism, which is expressed in the powerful institutions of the Labour Movement and in a hundred forms of democratic association and control, is like a man whose psychic and physical energies are exhausted because they are exerted in a struggle *against* himself, in an effort to bring the demons of rebellion within him under control. Throughout

the movement there are inhibitions, checks, taboos, constitutional impedi-
ments, designed to prevent the democratic organisations of the people from fulfilling active democratic functions; restraining or turning back upon themselves
energies which might otherwise flow rebelliously outwards into public life. The
impulse is divided from the function; Labour constituency workers are headed
off from any action outside the conventions; the industrial power of the people
must be salted down into reserves; the nationalised industries instead of being
pace-setters must service the private sector. And, since there are prohibitions
thrown across all the natural lines of growth, the movement itself is in danger of
dying at the root.

Of all this the public is more or less aware. Certainly, people are more aware
of prohibitions and of inhibitions than of opportunities. When the Conservative
Minister of Defence informs them that Britain's "minimum insurance" against
war is £1,500 million (on war preparations), people recall that the same pro-
hibition was implicit in Mr. Gaitskell's and Mr. Bevan's rejection of unilateral
nuclear disarmament. The Tory electoral jibe that Labour was offering more
than the nation could "afford" stuck because people were aware that *this* system
will cease to work if profits are taxed beyond a certain point—and no alternative
was offered. Striking crane drivers and oxygen workers are aware of their own
power; but since this power is not felt to be part of any overall strategy of social
advance, and since the employers, the state, the Press and the T.U.C. unite in telling them that the use of their power is unfair, indisciplined, or criminal, they feel
their own power to be anti-social.

Among these prohibitions and inhibitions apathy sets in. But, in the absence
of an alert public conscience and democratic participation in social life, active
decay may spread to the point where the very conventions of the "game" are
themselves eaten away. Capitalist society can then become atomised, and a cock-
pit for rival groups of *ultras* who seek to hold the community to ransom in their
own private interests. The *ultras* may be Kenya settlers, price-fixing monopolies, takeover-bid financiers, irresponsible Press magnates, or even key industrial
workers deprived of any overall socialist strategy and striking blindly in their
own interests. When this point is reached (and we may be close to it now) apathy
could lead on by rapid stages to the authoritarian state.

The alternative is a reorientation of British democratic thinking, and of the
institutions of the Labour Movement, towards the attainment of a democratic
socialist revolution. By this we mean not the iron dictatorship of the proletariat
and the rest. No socialist revolution is conceivable in Britain unless we can fashion a new and humanised image of a socialist society within our reach, which is
clearly distinguished from both the Communist experience and the experience
of over-centralised bureaucratic state monopoly. But *this* is the "image" for which
we should be looking. It is necessary to follow through each line of thought to

the point where it breaks through the conventions within which our life is confined. What *will* happen if we go naked into the conference chamber? What *will* happen if we cease to pay insurance and opt out of the alliances of the "Free World"? What *will* happen if trade unionists begin to *use* their strength within an overall strategy of advance? What *will* happen if the economic equilibrium is disturbed? And then each line must be brought together in the knot of revolution.

If our argument is valid, then this is not a distant but an immediate problem. It is no longer possible to accept the Fabian prescription of gradual evolution "towards" socialism by means of episodic reforms stretching over the horizon into some never-never land in the twenty-first century. We must draw a firm line beneath the Fabian era. If the alternative appears "Utopian," it is less Utopian than the attempt of socialists to pull themselves up by the bootlaces of capitalism, and more realistic than the strategy of nuclear stagnation within which the present folly of politicians and apathy of the public are contained.

While there are points at which we disagree (especially Alasdair MacIntyre, who as a Trotskyite differs in some ways from all the other contributors), we have attempted a real collaboration. In, the first section, we examine the "foreground"; the private and public face of the Business Society. In the second section, we examine the international and ideological "background"; the diplomatic and intellectual dogmas which restrain us. In the final section we examine more directly the question of the "transition" to socialism.

Some readers may complain that our argument is remote from the hard facts of contemporary political life. Why no detailed discussion of political means, no declaration of allegiance with this or that group within the councils of the Labour Party? There are two answers. First, this discussion will be the subject matter for future books and is a continual theme of the *New Left Review*. Second, our allegiance lies with the "rank-and-file" of the Labour Movement and with those young people who are acting already against the imbecilities of our society but who are not satisfied with the traditional routines of Labour. The former have, by their stubborn defensive "holding actions" over the past fifteen years, made it possible for us to consider the strategy for a renewed offensive. The latter, by bringing back into public life the unconditional temper of the Aldermaston marches, have given us hope that this strategy will be successful.

We are not (as no doubt we may be represented) aloof and academic critics. We have been in there in the defensive battles; we have all done our envelopes, canvassed, served on committees, marched and the rest. And we may ask questions in our turn. How much longer can the Labour Movement hold to its defensive positions and still maintain morale? Is the aim of socialism to recede for ever in the trivia of circumstances? Are we to remain for ever as exploited, acquisitive men? It is because the majority of Labour politicians have ceased to hold any real belief in an alternative to capitalism that their kind of politics has become irrelevant. And it is because we have taken our share in the chores of the movement that we have a right to question their credentials. Who are they? Where are they going? Are they leading us anywhere at all? Or are they just apathetic bailiffs, waiting for the old master to die and the new to inherit the estates?

"REVOLUTION," THE CONCLUDING CHAPTER OF *OUT OF APATHY*, begins: "At every point the way out of apathy leads us outside the conventions within which our life is confined." It proceeds to revolution, and here Thompson begins not with Lenin but with William Morris and his insistence "upon the necessity for critical conflict in every area of life at the point of transition." Thompson dismisses the inevitability of violence and argues that there is more than one kind of revolution. "It is not the violence of revolution which decides its extent and consequences, but the maturity and activity of the people." But neither is "the point of breakthrough" just "one more shuffle along the evolutionary path." Thompson does not see revolution as envisaged by Morris and Marx. "Our coming revolution could be a 'consummation' of some things, a 'beginning' of others. Nor is there only one kind of revolution which can be made in any given context. A revolution does not 'happen': it must be made by men's actions and choices."

Revolution

A t every point the way out of apathy leads us outside the conventions within which our life is confined.

It is because the conventions themselves are being called in question, and not the tactical manoeuvring which takes place within them, that the gulf which is opening between the young socialist generation and traditional Labour politicians is so deep.

It is a gulf as deep as that which opened in the 1880s between the Lib-Lab politicians and the new unionists and socialists. "Mr. Gaitskell, if he read it, would certainly not obtain a clear idea of what, in detail, he was supposed to do"—this is Mr. Crosland's comment, when reviewing *The Glittering Coffin* in the *Spectator.* Mr. Howell or Mr. Broadhurst, if they had picked up a copy of *Commonweal,* would have been faced with similar difficulties.

Of course it is generally agreed (as Mr. Crosland remarks) that "the Labour Party badly needs a dose of iconoclasm at the present moment." Even psephologists can see that the Party requires "an influx of youth" if it is "to present itself to the electorate in a mid-twentieth-century guise." And Transport House Grundies, who have won past battle honours by decimating youth, are now prepared to encourage angry radical noises in coffee bars on the periphery of the movement.

But the icons which the Aldermaston generation is breaking are the very ones before which Mr. Gaitskell and Mr. Crosland bow down: the permanent Cold War; the permanent dependence of Labour upon "affluent" capitalism; the permanent defensive ideology of defeatism and piecemeal reform.

What lies beyond these conventions? Where is the point of breakthrough? Break through into what?

Semantics and Clause 4

IF THE IMAGE OF POWER must be remade at the base, it must also be remade at the top. The Clause 4 debate within the Labour Party provides every day fresh examples of the way in which concepts of power are concealed within the cloudy metaphors of rhetoric, which attempt verbal reconciliations between traditional socialist loyalties and actual accommodation to capitalism. "A clear statement that the party remains committed to capturing . . . the 'commanding heights of the economy' "—the *New Statesman* editorialises (March 5, 1960)—"is the formula on which Mr. Gaitskell could surely reunite the National Executive."

We cannot pretend to prescribe a "formula" which will "unite" the National Executive. But it should be noted that the image of the "commanding heights" offers more than it defines. To some, it may indicate the power of a Labour Chancellor to influence the Bank Rate; to others, the power to introduce a Five-Year Plan covering output of Icelandic cod, Somerset cider-apples and Scunthorpe steel. Are the "heights" those of Monte Cassino or of Hampstead Heath—the one required a certain effort to storm, and its storming was the turning point of a campaign, the other can be reached by tube from Westminster. And are we, by some sudden forced march (the nationalisation of steel and chemicals?) to find ourselves occupying the commanding heights of the economy, while at the same time leaving the Monte Cassino of the mass media of communication in the hands of irresponsible oligarchs?

Mr. Gaitskell's and Mr. Crosland's play with the terms "means" and "ends" is more obviously specious. It is true, of course, that the replacement of production for profit by production for use is (from one standpoint) only a means to the attainment of a Society of Equals. True also that it is only one means among many. But what is obscured in this argument is that *without* the displacement of the dynamic of the profit motive all other means will prove ineffectual, and it is the definition of this as an *essential* means which distinguishes the socialist tradition.

This does not mean that nationalisation by state monopoly is the *only* alternative to private ownership: the debate on other forms (municipal and cooperative) is fruitful. Nor does it mean that there is some *automatic* relationship between social ownership and socialist institutions or moral disposition: that the superstructure of a "good society" *must* grow in a certain way once the basis has been established. The Society of Equals cannot be made without a revolution in moral attitudes and social practices too far-reaching to be reduced by any National Executive to a "formula."

But here also we must guard against the *specious* appeal to morality, the posing of "values" outside the context of power. "Socialism," Mr. Crosland tells us,

> denotes a belief in the preeminence of certain values, such as equality or cooperation or collective welfare or internationalism. But such values are not absolute. They cannot be held rigidly and uncompromisingly, any more than can the opposite conservative values of hierarchy or competition or individualism or patriotism. ("The Future of the Left," *Encounter,* March 1960)

We are back at the game of Happy Families: we can pair off opposite "values" (which are not "absolute"), and look for the good society somewhere in the marital blur in the middle. If, however, we were to pair off exploitation and mutual aid, the business man's expense account and the railwayman's wage, advertising and education, nuclear disarmament and Blue Streak, we could reach a different result. For the contradiction which *expresses* itself in opposed values is grounded in the private ownership of the social means of production. The profit motive remains at the core of our social order, engendering conflicts which by their nature may be controlled or mitigated but cannot be resolved. Nor is this the most important thing. A controlled antagonism may be endurable: they exist even within Happy Families. We might put up with the Opportunity State, knowing that welfare services provide a set of rooms at the bottom for those who don't go up. But controlled antagonisms are constantly breaking out in new, uncontrolled ways: the compensation received by coal-owners burgeons into profits in light industry; the housing schemes of well-intentioned municipalities sink under the earth beneath accumulated interest repayments; money searches continually for new ways to breed money. And, at the end of it all, we have a society grounded on antagonism. We remain for ever removed from a Society of Equals.

Accommodations and Antagonisms

WHEN MR. CROSLAND, in the same essay, quotes with approval, "it may be better simply to say with William Morris that socialism is fellowship," it becomes difficult to know at what point a serious discussion may be entered. Morris was a revolutionary socialist. In his last years he agreed that the final conquest of power might take place by parliamentary means; but he still feared that the transition would be accompanied by violence of some kind:

We are living in an epoch where there is combat between commercialism, or the system of reckless waste, and communism, or the system of neighbourly common sense. Can that combat be fought out . . . without loss and suffering? Plainly speaking I *know* that it cannot.

Morris was not writing in ignorance of the Fabian alternative expressed in the *Essays* of 1889. It is worth recalling the terms of his dissent. Shaw proposed that there might be "a gradual transition to Social Democracy"; "the gradual extension of the franchise; and the transfer of rent and interest to the state, not in one lump sum, but by instalments." Morris objected that this ignored the essential antagonism at the heart of capitalist society:

The barrier which they will not be able to pass ... [is] the *acknowledgment of the class war*. The "Socialists" of this kind are blind as to the essence of modern society. They hope for a revolution, which is not *the* Revolution, but a revolution which is to ignore the facts that have led up to it and will bring it about. (W. M.'s italics).

It was not the necessity of a *violent* revolution upon which Morris was insisting, but upon the necessity for a critical conflict in every area of life at the point of transition. Transition from the system of "reckless waste" to that of "neighbourly common sense." could not be effected by some administrative or fiscal *coup d'état*. A merely parliamentary socialist party might "fall into the error of moving earth and sea to fill the ballot boxes with socialist votes which will not represent socialist *men.*" If the evolutionary road were followed, he repeatedly asked "how far the betterment of the working people might go and yet stop short at last without having made any progress on the *direct* road to Communism?"

Whether ... the tremendous organisation of civilised commercial society is not playing the cat and mouse game with us socialists. Whether the Society of Inequality might not accept the quasi-socialist machinery ... and work it for the purpose of upholding that society in a somewhat shorn condition maybe, but a safe one. ... The workers better treated, better organised, helping to govern themselves, but with no more pretence to equality with the rich ... than they have now.

With the foundation of the Labour Party it seemed that the Fabians had won the argument. The Webbs, G. D. H. Cole commented in 1913, "were able so completely ... to impose their conception of society on the Labour movement that it seemed unnecessary, for anyone to do any further thinking." Fabian theories (Mr. Strachey added in 1938), "not merely false, but almost absurdly inadequate ... to cover the complex, stormy, dynamic social phenomena of the twentieth century," were "allowed to become the theory of the British working-class movement." On the credit side, the advance in the strength of organised Labour, the encroachments of the welfare state; on the debit side, the division of Africa, the slump, two world wars. By 1930 the debate raged once more. "It is not so certain today as it seemed in the eighties that Morris was not right," commented Shaw in his preface to the 1931 edition of *Fabian Essays*. Throughout the next fifteen years the two outstanding non-Communist theoreticians of British Socialism—Harold Laski and G. D. H. Cole—were discussing constructively the nature of the "transition" in Britain, and the ways to circumvent capitalist resistance. But, after 1945, it was not capitalist opposition which was circumvented:

People who talk too much soon find themselves up against it. Harold Laski, for instance. A brilliant chap . . . but he started making speeches at weekends. I had to get rid of him. . . . G. D. H. Cole was another brilliant chap. A very clear mind. But he used to have a new idea every year, irrespective of whether the ordinary man was interested in it or not.

Thus Lord Attlee on "What Sort of Man Gets to the Top?" (*Observer,* February 7, 1960). With *that* sort of man at the top the system of neighbourly common sense might well seem unattainable.

To present the argument in this way is to foreshorten it, and, in the later stages, to caricature it. We have omitted, among other matters of substance, the constructive additions of syndicalists and Guild Socialists; the injection of the Russian example and of Leninism into the whole debate; the more sophisticated elaborations of post-Keynesian evolutionary theory; and the bedevilment of the whole argument by the ugly practices of the "dictatorship of the proletariat" on the Stalinist model.

But what we mean to direct attention to is the extraordinary hiatus in contemporary Labour thinking on this most crucial point of all—how, and by what means, is a transition to socialist society to take place. For Mr. Gaitskell the problem may be irrelevant. The political seesaw is its own justification. "The British prefer the two-party system," he informed a conference of the Congress for Cultural Freedom in 1958. "They understand team games and they know it gives them stable, strong government." For Mr. Gordon Walker (it may be) the goal is clear:

In the antechamber outside the Cabinet room where Ministers gather before meeting, there is a row of coat-pegs. Under each peg is the name of a great office of state. . . . Only Cabinet Ministers hang their hats and coats here—and only in the prescribed order—

or so he informs the open-mouthed readers of *Encounter* (April 1956), and we have no special reason to disbelieve him. But there remains a subtle difference between speculation as to *which peg* you may hang your coat on and *which point* will disclose the moment of revolutionary transition. Mr. Denis Healey and Mr. Crosland are anxious to disabuse us of this belief: *power* (they tell us) is all: when the coats are on the pegs, we may leave it to them:

There is much talk (though rather more in Chelsea and Oxford than in Stepney or Nyasaland) of the dangers of sacrificing principle; what is forgotten is the sacrifice of Socialist objectives, not to mention human freedom and welfare, involved in a long period of impotent opposition. (Crosland in *Encounter* again)

It is not clear which specifically *socialist* objectives (other than "values" which are not "absolute") Mr. Crosland has in mind. Nor do other potential peg-hangers offer us much more enlightenment. "The Liberal and Labour movements of the West," Mr. R. H. S. Crossman assures us, "have triumphantly falsified the predictions of Karl Marx":

They have used the institutions of democracy to begin the job of resolving the inherent contradictions of capitalism, evening out the gross inequalities, and transforming the privileges of the bourgeoisie into rights of *every* citizen. (also *Encounter,* June 1956)

But how does one "resolve" an "inherent contradiction"? And if the job has been *begun* at what point does it *end?* And if the contradiction ends in a *socialist* "resolution," which predictions of Marx will this triumphantly falsify?

And yet the only sustained approach to this inquiry is in Mr. Strachey's *Contemporary Capitalism.* "Last-stage capitalism" (he tells us): "will be succeeded not by still a third version of the system, but by something which it would be manifestly an abuse of language to call capitalism at all." (p. 41)

We should certainly be reluctant to abuse language. But meanwhile "last-stage capitalism" abuses our lives, and it would be of interest to learn when the "succession" is due to take place. "Democracy" (he tells us) "can hope to bit and bridle last stage capitalism, and then to transform it, ultimately to the degree that [it] is no longer capitalism" (p. 281). It seems that we must await a further volume before we may learn what underlies the terms "transform," "ultimately" and "degree." Perhaps Mr. Strachey is inhibited by echoes from the past?

It is . . . impossible for the working and capitalist classes to share the power of the State over a whole prolonged period of social evolution. . . . It is an illusion, in particular, to suppose that the capitalist class will passively allow the political power of the workers to grow and grow, while the Labour movement pursues a steady policy of socialisation and other encroachments upon capitalism (John Strachey, *What Are We To Do?,* 1938).

The absence of any theory of the transition to socialism is the consequence of capitulation to the conventions of capitalist politics. And the political accommodation is complemented by a social and moral accommodation which spreads out into every region of life. Ursula, in *The Rainbow,* regarded with horror the mining town of Wiggiston where her Uncle Tom was colliery manager, with its rows of houses "each with its small activity made sordid by barren cohesion with the rest of the small activities":

There was no meeting place, no centre, no artery, no organic formation. There it lay, like the new foundations of a red-brick confusion rapidly spreading, like a skin disease.

"Why are the men so sad?" she asked her Uncle Tom.

"I don't think they are that. They just take it for granted. . . ."

"Why don't they alter it?" she passionately protested.

"They believe that they must alter themselves to fit the pits and the place, rather than alter the pits and the place to fit themselves. It is easier," he said.

The dialogue reminds us of Mr. Crosland's incomprehension before *The Glittering Coffin:* "Smashing Things " was the title of his review. True, the miners *have* altered their environment, to a greater degree than most other workers. True, the smoke-stained squalor of red brick gives way before the garish squalor of neon and white tile. But the accommodation continues, there is no more "organic formation" or active, liberating social cohesion than before. The point is not that we assent to all of Ursula's emotional Luddism ("we could easily do without the pits"), but that conventional Labour politics have narrowed to a region of legislative manipulation where Ursula's protest is met with blank incomprehension. However the offices were distributed in the last Labour Cabinet, one feels that Uncle Tom's coat hung from every peg. Mr. Gaitskell has written "brother-hood" and "fellowship" into Labour's Constitution. But the Utopian protest, the vision of new human possibilities constrained within old forms, which is an essential part of the socialist dynamic, has become extinguished in the weary self-important philistinism and the myopic "realism" of the capitalist parliamentarian. Between television appearances, "brotherhood" and "fellowship" can scarcely be thought to have their incarnation in the Parliamentary Labour Party or the T.U.C.

Models of Revolution

TWO MODELS OF the transition (if we may simplify) are commonly on offer. The first, the evolutionary model, is of gradual piecemeal reform in an institutional continuum, until *at some undefined point* some measure will be taken (A bit more nationalisation? More state controls over the private sector?), when the balance will tip slightly in favour of the socialist "resolution," and we shall acclaim this moment with a change in our terminology. The main participation demanded of the people is to cross the ballot paper thirteen or fourteen million times. This model must be rejected if the evidence and arguments presented in the first part of this book are valid.

It should not be assumed, however, that the model of revolution as presented by some Labour fundamentalists is therefore acceptable. It is not only that its very terms carry an aroma of barricades and naval mutinies in an age of flame-throwers. It is also that the antagonisms of capitalist society are presented in a falsely antithetical manner—without any sense of the contradictory processes of change. An imaginary line is drawn through society, dividing the workers in "basic" industries from the rest. The class struggle tends to be thought of as a series of brutal, head-on encounters (which it *sometimes* is); not as a conflict of force, interests, values, priorities, ideas, taking place ceaselessly in every area of life. Its culmination is seen as being a moment when the opposed classes stand wholly *disengaged* from each other, confronting each other in naked antago-nism; not as the climax to ever closer *engagement* within existing institutions, demanding the most constructive deployment of skills as well as of force. It is " their" state versus "our" (imaginary) state; "their" institutions which must be "smashed" before ours can be built; "their" society which must be "overthrown" before the new society can be made. Communists and Labour fundamental-ists of the "statist" variety place emphasis upon an hypothetical parliamentary majority which, in a dramatic period of breaking-and-making, will legislate a new state into existence from above. Trotskyists place emphasis upon industrial militancy overthrowing existing institutions from below.

This cataclysmic model of revolution is derived from the Marxist tradition, although it owes more to Lenin, Trotsky and Stalin than to Marx. Two points only can be noted here. First, Marx's concession that Britain and America might effect a peaceful transition to socialism was negatived by Lenin in 1917 on the grounds that "in the epoch of the first great imperialist war" Anglo-Saxon "lib-erty" had become submerged in the "filthy, bloody morass of military-bureau-cratic institutions to which everything is subordinated." Hence, the necessary preliminary for "every real people's revolution is the smashing, the *destruction* of the ready-made state machine." This dictum Stalin ossified (in 1924) into the "inevitable law of violent proletarian revolution."

From this follows a wholly undiscriminating assimilation of *all* institutions to the "military-bureaucratic." Certainly, no approach to socialism today is conceiv-able without breaking up the Cold War institutions "to which everything is sub-ordinated"—NATO, the Aldermaston Weapons Research Establishment, and their multiform ramifications. But the point here is that we must discriminate. There is substance in Mr. Strachey's thesis of countervailing powers, provided that we are willing to take up the argument at the point where he fuddles it over. Since 1848, 1917, and notably since 1945, many of our institutions have been actively shaped by popular pressures and by adjustment to these pressures on the part of capitalist interests. But it is at this point that we encounter the second crippling fallacy of the fundamentalist. Since all advances of the past century have been contained within the capitalist system, the fundamentalist argues that in fact no "real" advance has taken place. The conceptual barrier derives in this case from a false distinction in Leninist doctrine between the bourgeois and the proletarian revolution. The bourgeois revolution (according to this legend) begins when "more or less finished forms of the capitalist order" already exist "within the womb of feudal society." Capitalism was able to grow up *within* feudalism, and to coexist with it—on uneasy terms—until prepared for the seizure of political power. But the proletarian revolution "begins when finished forms of the socialist order are either absent, or almost completely absent." Because it was supposed that forms of social ownership or democratic control over the means of production were incompatible with capitalist state power: "The bourgeois revolution is usually *consummated* with the seizure of power, whereas in the proletarian revolution the seizure of power is only the beginning."[1]

From this conceptual inhibition, many consequences flow. From this, the caricaturing of social advances as "bribes" to buy off revolution, and the attribution of supreme cunning to the capitalist system, which by a superb Marxist logic is able to anticipate and deflect every assault by the working class. From this also, the hypocritical attitude which concedes the need to struggle for reforms, not for the sake of the reform but for the educative value of the struggle. Hence, finally, the alienation of many humane people, who detect in the doctrinaire revolutionary an absence of warm response to the needs of living people and a disposition to anticipate the coming of depression or hardship with impatience.

But if we discard this dogma (the fundamentalists might meditate on the "interpenetration of opposites") we can read the evidence another way. It is not a case of *either* this or that. We must, at every point, *see both*—the surge forward *and* the containment, the public sector *and* its subordination to the private, the strength of trade unions *and* their parasitism upon capitalist growth, the welfare services *and* their poor-relation status. The countervailing powers are there, and the equilibrium (which is an equilibrium *within capitalism*) is precarious. It could be tipped back towards authoritarianism. But it could also be heaved *forward,* by popular pressures of great intensity, to the point where the powers of democracy cease to be countervailing and become the active dynamic of society in their own right. This is revolution.

There is not one abstract revolution which would have assumed the same form in 1889, 1919 and 1964. The *kind* of revolution which we can make today is different from any envisaged by Marx or Morris. Our coming revolution could be a "consummation" of some things, a "beginning" of others. Nor is there only *one* kind of revolution which can be made in any given context. A revolution does not "happen": it must be *made* by men's actions and choices.

It is not the violence of a revolution which decides its extent and consequences, but the maturity and activity of the people. Violence does not make anything more "real." 1789 was not more secure because it was cataclysmic, and 1917 was not more socialist because socialists seized power by force. It is possible to look forward to a peaceful revolution in Britain, with far greater continuity in social life and in institutional forms than would have seemed likely even twenty years ago, not because it will be a semi-revolution, nor because capitalism is "evolving" into socialism; but because the advances of 1942–48 *were* real, because the socialist *potential* has been enlarged, and socialist forms, however imperfect, have grown up "within" capitalism.

The point of breakthrough is not one more shuffle along the evolutionary path, which suddenly sinks the scales on the socialist side (51 percent, in the public sector instead of 49). An historical transition between two ways of life cannot be effected by an entry in a ledger. Nor, on the other hand, will it be effected by the intrusion into the Commons of a new species of anti-political politician—till at length Ursula's duffle-coat, stained with Partisan coffee, hangs from every peg. But can we be satisfied with the formula of a "conquest of class power"? Which power? Vested in whom? The cataclysmic model offered dramatic symbols—the storming of Bastille or Winter Palace. But what are we to storm? The Institute of Directors? The National Coal Board?

Certainly, the transition can be defined, in the widest historical sense, as a transfer of class power: the dislodgment of the power of capital from the "commanding heights" and the assertion of the power of socialist democracy. This is the historical watershed, between "last stage" capitalism and dynamic socialism—the point at which the socialist potential is liberated, the public sector assumes the dominant role, subordinating the private to its command, and over a very great area of life the priorities of need overrule those of profit. But this point cannot be defined in narrow political (least of all parliamentary) terms; nor can we be certain, in advance, in what context the breakthrough will be made. What it is more important to insist upon is that it is necessary to *find out* the breaking point, not by theoretical speculation alone, but *in practice* by unrelenting reforming pressures in many fields, which are designed to reach a revolutionary culmination. And this will entail a confrontation, throughout society, between two systems, two ways of life. In this confrontation, political consciousness will become heightened; every direct and devious influence will be brought to the defence of property rights; the people will be forced by events to exert their whole political and industrial strength. A confrontation of this order is not to be confined within the pages of *Hansard*; it involves the making of revolution simultaneously in many fields of life. It involves the breaking up of some institutions (and the House of Lords, Sandhurst, Aldermaston, the Stock Exchange, the Press monopolies and the National Debt are among those which suggest themselves), the transformation and modification of others (including the House of Commons and the nationalised boards), and the transfer of new functions to yet others (town councils, consumers' councils, trades councils, shop stewards' committees, and the rest).

As the kind of revolution which is possible has changed, so has the kind of potential revolutionary situation. We need no longer think of disaster as the prelude to advance. In one sense, we are now constantly living on the edge of a revolutionary situation. It is because we dare not break through the conventions between us and that situation that the political decay of apathy prevails. But such a revolution demands the maximum enlargement of *positive* demands, the deployment of constructive skills within a conscious revolutionary strategy, the assertion of the values of the common good—or, in William Morris's words, the "making of Socialists." It cannot, and must not, rely exclusively upon the explosive negatives of class antagonism. And this is the more easy to envisage if we cease to draw that imaginary line between the industrial workers and the rest. The number of people who are wholly and unambiguously interested in the defence of the *status quo* is small, despite Ralph Samuel's warnings of the growing retinue of the corporations. Alongside the industrial workers, we should see the teachers who want better schools, scientists who wish to advance research, welfare workers who want hospitals, actors who want a National Theatre, technicians impatient to improve industrial organisation. Such people do not want these things only and always, any more than all industrial workers are always "class conscious" and loyal to their great community values. But these affirmatives coexist, fitfully and incompletely, with the ethos of the Opportunity State. It is the business of socialists to draw the line, not between a staunch but diminishing minority and an unredeemable majority, but between the monopolists and the people—to foster the "societal instincts" and inhibit the acquisitive. Upon these positives, and not upon the débris of a smashed society, the socialist community must be built.

How the New Model Might Work

AND *HOW* IS THIS to be done? At this point a new volume should begin.

The elaboration of a democratic revolutionary strategy, which draws into a common strand wage demands and ethical demands, the attack on capitalist finance and the attack on the mass media, is the immediate task. It demands research and discussion: journals, books, Left Clubs. It demands organisation for education and propaganda. It demands the exchange of ideas between specialists and those whose experience—in nationalised industry or in local government—enables them to see more clearly than the theorist the limits of the old system, the growing-points of the new.

It demands also a break with the parliamentary fetishism which supposes that all advance must wait upon legislative change. Most popular gains have been won, in the first place, by direct action: direct action to increase wages, improve working conditions, shorten hours, build co-ops, found nursery schools. We do not need even a " formula " from the N.E.C. of the Labour Party, before we can form tenants' associations or socialist youth clubs, write plays or force upon the Coal Board new forms of workers' control.

Nor should this be seen as an *alternative* to the work of the existing institutions of the Labour movement. The defenders of Clause 4 are, in one sense, holding firm to the concept of socialist revolution. Too often the concept is defended out of *religious* loyalty. What is required is a new sense of immediacy. Socialists should be fighting not a defensive battle for an ambiguous clause, but an offensive campaign to place the transition to the new society at the head of the agenda. In this, the protest of the Aldermaston generation, and the traditional loyalties of the Labour rank-and-file could—although they will not automatically do so—come together in a common agitation.

In the end, we must return to the focus of political power: Parliament. It is here that the prospect appears most hopeless, the conventions strongest, the accommodation most absolute. But we need not despair. It is the greatest illusion of the ideology of apathy that politicians make events. In fact, they customarily legislate to take account of events which have already occurred. (Did *Lord Attlee* really free India? Did *Lord Morrison of Lambeth* wrest the pits from the coal owners?) Of course, more socialists must be sent into Parliament. But, in the last analysis, the context will dictate to the politicians, and not the reverse. And socialists must make the context.

Meanwhile, our local problems are contained within the larger context of nuclear diplomacy and imperial retreat. From this, an opportunity and a challenge. The opportunity for a revolutionary breakthrough might as possibly arise from international as from local causes. Should the protest in Britain gain sufficient strength to force our country out of NATO, consequences will follow in rapid succession. The Americans might reply with economic sanctions. Britain would be faced with the alternatives of compliance or of a far-reaching reorientation of trade. The dilemma would agitate the consciousness of the whole people, not as an abstract theory of revolution but as an actual and immediate political choice, debated in factories, offices and streets. People would become aware of the historic choice presented to our country, as they became aware during the Second World War. Ideological and political antagonisms would sharpen. Non-compliance with America would entail winning the active, informed support of the majority of the people for policies which might bring with them dislocation and hardship. One choice would disclose another, and with each decision a revolutionary conclusion might become more inescapable. Events themselves would disclose to people the possibility of the socialist alternative; and if events were seconded by the agitation and initiatives of thousands of organised socialists in every area of life, the socialist revolution would be carried through.

Of all Western countries, Britain is perhaps the best placed to effect such a transition. The equilibrium here is most precarious, the Labour movement least divided, the democratic socialist tradition most strong. And it is *this* event which could at one blow break up the log-jam of the Cold War and initiate a new wave of world advance. Advance in Western Europe, and further democratisation in the East, may wait upon us.

Is it useless to wait? Will Iceland or Italy break through first? Will Britain founder under old habits, rotting institutions, its hull encrusted with nostalgia, drifting half-waterlogged into the twenty-second century, a bourgeois Spain among the socialist nations? It would be foolish to be sanguine. But foolish also to underestimate the long and tenacious revolutionary tradition of the British commoner.

It is a dogged, good-humoured, responsible tradition, yet a revolutionary tradition all the same. From the Leveller corporals ridden down by Cromwell's men at Burford to the weavers massed behind their banners at Peterloo, the struggle for democratic and for social rights has always been intertwined. From the Chartist camp meeting to the dockers' picket line it has expressed itself most naturally in the language of moral revolt. Its weaknesses, its carelessness of theory, we know too well; its strengths, its resilience and steady humanity, we too easily forget. It is a tradition which could leaven the socialist world.

PUBLISHED IN *NEW LEFT REVIEW* I/6 (NOVEMBER–DECEMBER
1960), Thompson returns here to the subject of revolution. Always
willing to engage with others, Thompson responds to critics both
right and left, as well as to fellow New Leftists, offering this suggestion: "I have gone a long way round to suggest three simple things.
First, that we should cease chucking round the terms 'Marxism' and
'working class' in an indiscriminate and rhetorical manner. Second,
that in the New Left those who reject and those who are committed
to the Marxist tradition must cease to regard it as if it were a loyalty
test or the demarcation-line of a foot-and-mouth-disease area and
(accepting the good faith of fellow socialists) bring their respective
insights and disciplines to the examination of a particular practical
and theoretical fresh look at the whole problem of working-class
'consciousness' today, resisting the inclination to cry 'treason' if in
the process we find that deep-rooted prejudices and assumptions
come under criticism."

Revolution Again! or Shut Your Ears and Run

"Under which King Besonian?"

"My God!" cried Gudrun. "But wouldn't it be wonderful, if all England *did* suddenly go off like a display of fireworks."

"It couldn't," said Ursula. "They are all too damp, the powder is damp in them."

"I'm not so sure of that," said Gerald.

"Nor I," said Birkin. "When the English really begin to go off, *en masse*, it'll be time to shut your ears and run."

"They never will," said Ursula. "We'll see," he replied.

—*WOMEN IN LOVE*

The word "revolution" is like a bell which makes some salivate approval or disapproval according to the conditioned response. After looking at the title of the last chapter of *Out of Apathy* some said: "Revolution: Apocalyptic, Marxist pipedream, opiate of the intellectuals, nostalgia for Chartism, utopian rhetoric, etc." Others said: "Revolution? I go for that—down with the lot, Bomb, Establishment, mass media, Shell building and all—roll on the day!"

In the published discussion (as well as in readers' letters and Club meetings) many interesting lines have been followed up. But for most readers it is clear that this concept suggests (at best) a very remote contingency, (at worst) an exercise in scholasticism. My suggestion that "in one sense, we are now constantly living on the edge of a revolutionary situation" was either shrugged or laughed off.

And yet this seems to me to be the crux of the argument. I don't mean that we are living on the edge of a situation which will suddenly disclose itself in some dramatic manner so that everyone will recognise it to be revolutionary. Nor do I mean that we are *bound* to enter an early crisis which will only admit of a revolutionary solution—Hanson's "Judgment Day" argument, while relevant to Grossman's present position seems to me to be irrelevant to the theme of *Out of Apathy*. We might easily miss "our" revolution just as we missed it in 1945.

I accept Charles Taylor's criticism that at the end of the essay I sketched in the possible con sequences of a British withdrawal from NATO with such brevity that it gave rise to the notion of cataclysmic crisis in a new form. Yet I did not intend to suggest that if we succeed in disentangling Britain from NATO we will thereby trick the British people into an unforeseen situation with an inescapable revolutionary outcome. It is because the Cold War is the greatest effective cause of apathy, inhibiting or distorting all forms of social growth, and because NATO is the fulcrum of Western capitalist power, that the British people will be unable to extricate themselves from this context without developing a popular struggle which will at the same time generate pressures in a hundred other directions, and awaken the political conscious-ness of the nation.

The first stage of this struggle commenced at Aldermaston and culminated in the Scarborough victory. The second stage has now commenced, and as I write delegates are returning to their constituencies and mobilising support, as the members of the Long Parliament went back to the provinces to raise their troops of horse. The struggle this year is going to be far sharper than anything we have seen for fifteen years.

As Stuart Hall shows, we are embarking on a struggle, not to "win" the Labour Movement, but to transform it. And at the end of this? May we not still find the Tories in power, the Labour Party "fragmented" (terrifying word—what is it now?), and the "electorate" dismayed and confused? Perhaps this will be the short-term outcome. But if this were all, how are we to explain the profound anxiety with which the Establishment views the failure of Mr. Gaitskell to con-tain the rebellion within the Labour Party? Behind the talk, in Liberal and Con-servative journals, of the "threat" to our "two-party system," there is surely the fear that energies are being released which have for fifteen years been safely con-tained within certain bipartisan limits and conventions, and that these energies may in the longer term endanger the system itself? Labour is ceasing to offer an alternative way of governing existing society, and is beginning to look for an alter native society. Mr. Macmillan no longer sits comfortably in a chair which Mr. Gaitskell has kindly provided. He sits in the same chair as was used by ex-Premier Kishi of Japan.

This is only one point where the conventions of our political life are now being threatened, and one reason why I cannot agree that the discussion of the concept of revolution is academic. Indeed, it seems to me of immediate contemporary relevance, in the sense that it is in the light of this concept—the kind of transition to socialist society which we envisage to be possible—that we must make many other judgments this year: it affects the kind of Labour Party we want to see, the emphasis in trade union activity, the role of Left Clubs. The fact that few readers have felt this relevance suggests either that I am wrong; or that I presented the argument so badly that it failed to come across. I prefer to accept the second criticism, which means that I must go back and try to do it again.

First, in self-defence. *Out of Apathy* was conceived as a book about apathy. This was where we came in; the New Left first appeared as a revolt *against* apathy within a particular social and political context. We wished to show the inter-connections between certain phenomena of "apathy" in economic, social, intellectual, and political life: their common ground in an "affluent" capitalist society in the context of Cold War: and to suggest that tensions and positive tendencies were present which might—but need not necessarily—lead people out of apathy and towards a socialist resolution.

I think that *Out of Apathy* does in fact do this. But at this stage our space was overrun, and it was only by stretching the good temper of the publisher that we were able to beg a further 5,000 words for a conclusion. All the contributors felt that the book would be left hanging in the air unless at least an attempt was made to tie up the ends by raising the question of the transition to a socialist society—what lay beyond the conventions of our bipartisan foreign policy and "mixed economy," how do we get from an irresponsible to an humane and responsible society, from a dominative, acquisitive ethic to communal self-activity? This is what *Revolution* attempted to do, and the faults in execution are my own responsibility.

Second, we underestimated the degree to which readers (and reviewers) would be led, by their own expectations as well as by publicity, to expect a quite different kind of book. Outsiders, who had a vague notion of the New Left as yet one more pressure-group contesting for power within the Labour Party, expected from the first of our books a "definitive" statement of our "position," something in the nature of a grand manifesto together with an immediate twelve-point pro gramme for the Labour Movement, CND, and world socialism. Insiders—readers of *NLR* and members of Left Clubs—were no less impatient to find a standard around which to rally—a crisp statement of aims—something to join, something to fight for, something to *do.*

And hence that cloudburst of frustration which descended on our heads.

For the first error, an apology. This article is a penance. For the second, not so much apology—especially to members of Left Clubs. If we had attempted a grand synthesis and programme it would have been a shoddy short-term job, and would now be blowing around in the post-Scarborough winds along with a dozen other "left" programmes of the past five years.

The New Left is not the kind of movement that should be comforted by a fake Book of Answers; nor should it be the kind where the rank-and-file down below wait for "them" up top to hand down the only correct "line." One part of our approach can never be broken down finally into any ten-point programme—how much of the values of sex equality or of community, or of the aspiration for a common culture, can be captured inside a set of specific proposals? But the part which can wants to be done well, and not scratched into shape for an emergency con ference resolution. It *is* being done all the time (for example, the articles of John Hughes Raymond Williams and Duncan Macbeth in *NLR* 4), and it will be one of the functions of future New Left Books to elaborate these policies.

A Scent of Honey

HOWEVER, THE ELABORATION of particular policies implies a general critique of society—and when we replace the passive term "critique" by the notion of a nexus of radical changes in many interconnected fields, then we are back once again at the problem of revolution. It is exactly this crucial point in the outlook of the New Left which has come under increasing attack this summer—an attack which has developed in such similar form in so many different places that one is almost tempted to look for a conspiratorial co ordinating hand. There is at least the indefatigable hand of Mr. Julius Gould who— foiled in his attempt to kill *Out of Apathy* at birth in the *Observer*—has pursued it into the correspondence columns of the *Times Literary Supplement*, where he denounces its "crude and vociferous Marxism": "Responsibility for this rests with the small group of ex-communists who have attained such power over the New Left and have skilfully used it as a vehicle for reviving and publicising their Marxist faith." (16 Sept. 1960)

The same conspiracy theory of New Left history (as well as the same bullying, pejorative employment of the term "Marxist") is offered by Mr. Bernard Crick in the *Political Quarterly* (July–September 1960): the "fund of inchoate idealism" of *Universities and Left Review* "has been taken for a ride by a few old Marxists who know what they want"; and it is embroidered in *Socialist Commentary* (September 1960) by Mr. John Gillard Watson, who finds that the "old Marxists" are "distorting" the history of the New Left, "trying to dominate" the movement, and "know how to exploit political innocence and the enthusiasm of ULR and its readers." (In the same article I am likened to Zhdanov and accused of the "peculiarly dishonest" use of quotations from D. H. Lawrence—O.K., I am still using them). But such abuse apart—and these critics cannot be argued with since they offer, not arguments, but a display of spleen—more scrupulous critics concentrate upon the same supposed incompatibility of the "Marxist" and "idealist" tendencies in the New Left. Professor J. M. Cameron has warned Third Programme listeners against the "vestigial Bolshevism" of the New Left, which he attributes largely to the Marxist "opiates" smuggled in by the *New Reasoner* group. And Ken Coates has written to the *Listener* (6 October 1960) eagerly confirming the Professor's thesis (although he would draw from it an opposite conclusion), finding the New Left to be poised in a struggle for mastery between Prometheus and Adam—or (perhaps less prosaically) Alasdair MacIntyre and Charles Taylor.

There are two problems here—one of long-term philosophical and theoretical clarification, one of immediate political significance. The first problem—of the difference in origin, emphasis, and assumption of particular writers on the Editorial Board of this journal—demands exact and discriminating discussion and I can only refer to it in passing here. No doubt there are differences in emphasis, and as time goes on they may become more apparent and *fruitfully* so. We have always been confident that the confluence of several traditions in our movement is a source of strength, not of division; and we have no hankering after some enforced ideological conformity—that "rigid external formality" beloved of all sects from Milton's time to our own, which leads (in his words) "into a gross conforming stupidity, a stark and dead congealment of wood and hay and stubble, forced and frozen together." (*Labour Review, Marxism Today* and *Socialist Commentary*). We prefer to discuss theoretical differences openly in these pages; and I must disappoint our critics by telling them that when it comes to Board discussion on NATO, Mr. Gaitskell, or even Mr. Julius Gould, the Prometheans and Adamists find they are in complete accord.

But the second problem—as to why this particular attack should have been mounted against the New Left at this moment—must be taken up at once. The burden of the criticism in the respectable press is that two years ago there was a splendid "radical" idealism growing up among young people around *ULR* which has now become tainted with Marxism—the old men of the *New Reasoner* are the spoonful of Victorian tar which is spoiling the abundant barrel of Partisan honey. Moreover, the scent of that honey has provoked much licking of lips in many quarters; many a hard and opportunist eye was seen to water enviously as the Aldermaston marchers went by last Easter. It is true that two years ago, when *ULR* was struggling with deficits, and its voluntary production team was on the point of breakdown, neither *Political Quarterly* nor *Socialist Commentary* nor the Third Programme noticed the splendid "inchoate idealism" that was being displayed. But today all the opportunist politicians of the "left"—Messrs. Gaitskell, Grimond and Gollan (not to mention Messer Gerryhealy)—would like to make a takeover bid for the "idealism of youth." "Here is a set of attitudes ready to be taken up, made use of and assisted," declares Mr. Crick, regarding enviously "the actual rank-and-file of the New Left": "There is no lack of a sense of service which could be invoked, even if not directly for politics. Let there be no doubt about it, *Out of Apathy* does not represent these people . . ."

And more recently Mr. Crosland has made a guarded gesture in the direction of—

questions of education, of leisure, of culture and aesthetics, and the general backcloth and fittings of the society. It is the function of contemporary parties of the Left to nurture and articulate these more imaginative, idealistic aspirations. (*Encounter*, October 1960)

"Attitudes ready to be taken up, made use of," "even if not directly for politics," "backcloth and fittings"—these are surely the give-away phrases? I am suggesting that it is not the "Marxism" of any particular members of the New Left which gives such offence, but *the politics* which informs our whole critique and which unites each separate part of it. It is the knot which ties together the parts which our critics would like to cut—the *connections* between Raymond Williams' critique of advertising and John Hughes' exposure of the subordination of the public to the private sector, between our analysis of "questions of education, of leisure, of culture" and our analysis of the Business Society, and between our polemic against Cold War strategy and our critique of the intellectual components of apathy. A concern about the Bomb or *apartheid*, an emphasis on cultural "fittings," a propensity to rush around with banners and discuss the Good Life in coffee-houses—any one of these things, taken by itself, might be absorbed with advantage into the existing political setup. What is proving indigestible is our insistence that none of these things *can* be taken separately: that socialists must confront the capitalist *system*, where the Bomb is endorsed by the media, which are upheld by advertisements, which stem from private concentrations of power, which exploit people both as producers and as consumers, by creating a mental environment which fosters acquisitive and impoverishes community values in such a way that traditional working-class consciousness appears to be eroding with the assistance of Mr. Gaitskell's capitulation to the Bomb and to the psephological arguments of adaptation. This (when we have got our breath back) is the House which the Irresponsible Society is building for Jack; and we have declared it to be all *wrong*, from foundation to roof. Mr. Crick and Mr. Crosland would prefer us to take the House as given, and to concern ourselves with the furnishings and decoration. It is because we insist upon the connections between the structure and the fittings, between the architect and builder and the people who live within it, that our critique is revolutionary, and therefore is proving intractable to all attempts to "take it up" as a youthful contemporary veneer to the politics of piecemeal reform.

"Stand and Deliver, Comrade!"

I DON'T THINK that the attempt to nobble the "rank-and-file of the New Left" ever had much chance of success. The Clubs are growing in numbers, organisation, and maturity—and it is their *politics* which is making them grow. But it reminds me that there were (self-styled) "Marxist" eyes which watered as well. When Ken Coates criticises the "ambivalence" of the New Left it is because he does not consider us "Marxist" enough. This criticism deserves serious discussion, the more specific and the less scholastic the better, just as the opposite criticism—that some of us are held back by "Victorian" Marxist notions which no longer have validity—is one which I don't wish to side-step. But I am getting bored with some of the members of "Marxist" sects who pop up at Left Club meetings around the country to demand in a your-money-or-your-life tone of voice whether the speaker is a Marxist, whether he "believes in" the class struggle, and whether he is willing to give instant adhesion to this or that version of the Creed. What I take issue with is not the earnestness with which the sectarians advocate their doctrines but the readiness which they display to denounce all those who disagree as traitors to the socialist cause. The passage from comradely criticism to wholesale anathema is alarmingly swift. Michael Kidron, an editor of *International Socialism*, concludes a review of *Out of Apathy* which contains valuable and pertinent criticism with the judgment: "It has ideas, but unless these ideas become working-class ideas aimed at working-class power they will remain irrelevant to the socialist movement and powerless to advance it." (Autumn 1960)

The tone is unmistakeable, and it is scarcely less bullying than that of Mr. Gould. I am not now concerned with the distinction made between an "idea" and a "working-class idea"—a distinction which, although I have worked for some years as an historian in the Marxist tradition, I still find difficult. But I suspect that Michael Kidron, in this passage, is not concerned with this kind of discrimination either. What he means to imply is that he has an anathema ready to deliver at the whole of the New Left, as a set of phoneys and dilettante *litterateurs*, but that he is graciously holding his hand for a few minutes in the hope that one or two of us may, at this late hour, decide to side with the "working class." By "working class" he means *his* side and *his* doctrines, since it is the delusion of all Marxist sectaries that their group or journal is the ark in which the true Marxist Covenant is preserved. He would have got much the same effect if he had simply cribbed the lines of Ancient Pistol: "Under which king, Besonian? speak, or die."

The word "working class" is about the most dangerous word in the rhetoric of the labour movement. We all employ it, and with its extraordinarily rich associations it has power to move us all. For this reason most of the bad ideas which gain acceptance in the labour movement are loudly acclaimed by their advocates as being "in the interests of the working class" (watch out next time you see Mr. Sam Watson or Mr. John Gollan using the word!). But a bad idea is not any better for being "working class," and if one cares about the advancement of the working-class movement it is a great deal more harmful. In fact, the Right-wing usually employ the term descriptively, to commend those *capitalist* attitudes and values which some working people assent to when they are reading the *Daily Mirror*; whereas the sectaries employ it Platonically to indicate not ideas actually held by significant numbers of working people but ideas which they *ought* to hold, or which it would be in their *interests* to hold, if they conformed to an approved doctrinal system. In this case, a "working-class idea" is an idea of which Michael Kidron approves.

I am sorry to seem to pick upon contributors to *International Socialism*, which seems to me the most constructive journal with a Trotskyist tendency in this country, most of the editorial board of which are active (and very welcome) members of the Left Club movement. But these are additional reasons for making these criticisms: first, because a socialist dialogue is very difficult when it is conducted with people who, in one part of themselves, *want* to be able to "write off" the New Left as an intellectual diversion; second, because this tone can become damaging to the Club movement and can discredit whatever is creative in the Marxist tradition. I cannot forget an appalling meeting of the London Club (to discuss *Out of Apathy*) at which half-a-dozen Covenanting sects were present, each reaching by means of their "Marxist science" diametrically opposed conclusions. The vibrant self-consuming hatred displayed by one sect for another can have left no emotional energy over for concern with the capitalist system or nuclear war; and the air was thick with the sniff-sniff-sniff of "theorists" who confused the search for clarity with the search for heresy. The word "comrade" was employed, in six-foot-high quotation marks, like deadly barbs on the polished shaft of Leninist irony—embellishing devastating witticisms of the order of "perhaps *Comrade* Thompson will tell us if he supposes that socialism will come at the behest of the Virgin Mary?"

The Hectoring Prophets

WE ARE ALL ONLY too familiar with these attitudes and with this tone—most Clubs have suffered from one or more of the hectoring prophets, heterodox or orthodox, of Diabolical and Hysterical Mysterialism. The *connections* are seen, but they are seen to be everything; and everything can be reduced to a few basic texts. When someone discusses NATO, he is belaboured for not mentioning a building workers' strike; and when he is discussing the mining industry he is attacked for not bringing in a full analysis of Soviet bureaucracy. Where criticism is forceful and valid—as for example, of the failure of the New Left to develop its work in the trade union and industrial field—it is not offered constructively—how can we best improve this together?—but as an item of denunciation, a proof of the dilettante character of our movement. Marxism is conceived of, not as a living tradition, but as a self-enclosed doctrine, a means of flattening and simplifying whatever phenomena are under investigation so that certain plausible facts may be selected (and all others discounted) in order to ornament or "prove" preexisting assumptions. A great deal of what is today most stridently acclaimed as "Marxism" is no more than thinking of this order, whether it commences with the assumption that Soviet leaders are all-sinning or all-knowing. This accounts for the scholastic style in which so many "Marxist" statements are couched—theses and counter-theses so neatly sewn at every seam that reality cannot break in at any point. When I hear someone announce that he intends to "apply Marxism *to*" a problem, I cannot help calling up a mental picture of a Victorian headmaster with a cane: what he *means* is that he is going to make the facts dance to his tune whether they like it or not. At the worst, such people (and I am not thinking here of our comrades of *International Socialism*) can be an active nuisance within the Socialist movement, with their jargon, their conspiratorial hocus-pocus, their discussion-hogging, their dissemination of suspicion, and their willingness— from whatever motive—to wreck any organisation which they cannot hobble. But for the most part they are guilty only of a self-isolating political immaturity, which enables them to see the connections but not the people who must be connected; and which constantly drives them towards an élitist outlook and strategy since, if all existing left groupings are suspect except their own, they must look for support to an hypothetical uncontaminated working class which in some hypothetical eventuality will loom up from the docks and the mills and follow their lead.

I have gone a long way round to suggest three simple things. First, that we should cease chucking round the terms "Marxism" and "working class" in an indiscriminate and rhetorical manner. Second, that in the New Left those who reject and those who are committed to the Marxist tradition must cease to regard it as if it were a loyalty test or the demarcation line of a foot-and-mouth-disease area and (accepting the good faith of fellow socialists) bring their respective insights and disciplines to the examination of particular practical and theoretical problems. Third, that we accept the advice of C. Wright Mills, and take a long and fresh look at the whole problem of working-class "consciousness" today, resisting the inclination to cry "treason" if in the process we find that deep-rooted prejudices and assumptions come under criticism.

THE OLD CONSCIOUSNESS AND THE NEW

THE CROSS-FIRE from all sides converges on this point. How can we assume anything so ridiculous as a revolutionary working-class consciousness within an affluent society? "What," asks Sol Encel (*NLR* 4) "is to provide the dynamic for the breakthrough?" How am I to convince "not the habitués of the Partisan, but the young Coventry motor worker," asks Peter Marris, who sees working people as status-seekers caught up "in an endless search for reassurance against the fear of being looked down upon." Michael Kidron criticises me because, in writing of a revolutionary confrontation between two systems, two ways of life, I give no precise definition of the social context:

> Confrontation between whom? . . . The tiny fuzz that surrounds this question spreads rapidly: the moment Thompson directs the working class off-stage in his social confrontation, the state of that class's political and social consciousness becomes of no immediate concern to him. It then becomes easy to Thompson to *fix* that consciousness: to *give* it goals, to . . . ignore the material factors in its development . . .

Mr. Crosland (*passim*) and Harry Hanson (*NLR* 5, "Socialism and Affluence") found their positions upon assumptions—and some evidence—about contemporary working-class consciousness, although their conclusions are very different, Mr. Crosland taking an optimistic view of encroaching classlessness, Harry Hanson taking a pessimistic view of the corrupting influence of "affluence." And Professor Wright Mills asks us to get outside this argument altogether:

> What I do not quite understand about some new-left writers is why they cling so mightily to "the working class" of the advanced capitalist societies as *the* historic agency, or even as the most important agency, in the face of the really impressive historical evidence that now stands against this expectation. Such a labour metaphysic, I think, is a legacy from Victorian Marxism that is now quite unrealistic.

And he offers as an alternative "the cultural apparatus, the intellectuals— as a possible, immediate, radical agency of change."

We should note the way in which a kind of economic *reductionism* disables the discussion of class, both among anti-Marxists and Marxist sectaries. In truth, the prevailing ideologies of both East and West are dominated by a debased caricature of Marxism; although, in the first case, we have a picture of the means of production spontaneously generating revolutionary activity and consciousness, with the working class seen not as the agency but intermediary of objective laws; whereas in the second place the picture is much the same, but the motor of change has been removed, and we see all men (except the "intellectuals") as prisoners of their economic interests, social "structure," and status-conditioning.

Both Crosland and Hanson seem to me to be victims of this fallacy: both argue from a static notion of the working class and of its characteristic consciousness which is derived from some Victorian phenomena and some from the nineteen-thirties. Both argue that "affluent" capitalism is mopping up some class grievances and is eroding traditional forms of working-class consciousness. Both conclude that therefore the "basis" for the socialist movement has been weakened. Neither of them can shake sufficiently free of traditional ways of thinking to conceive of new forms of class consciousness arising which are both more consonant with changed reality and more revolutionary in implication. But why *should* such a notion appear to be "utopian"?

Static Concept of Class

IT CAN ONLY APPEAR utopian if we have a static concept of class: if we assume that the working class is a given entity with a "fixed" characteristic consciousness which may wax or wane but remains essentially the same thing—a working class which emerged as a social force somewhere around 1780, with steam and the factory system, and which has thereafter grown in size and organisation but has not changed significantly in form or in relationship to other classes.

In fact, "it" has never existed; what is misleading is the use of one term, "working class," to describe so many greatly differing manifestations of class conflict in greatly differing contexts. Certainly, some continuing traditions may be observed; but when we employ a term, like *bourgeoisie* or "working class" which covers a whole historical epoch, we should not expect the specific forms of class consciousness in any particular segment of this epoch to have any immediate relationship to those in another segment. In this epochal sense, forms of "working-class consciousness" may be found to differ as much from each other as the consciousness of Roundheads differed from Lancashire cotton masters.

The definition of social class is notoriously difficult; and it is commonplace knowledge that Marx himself never offered any extended definition. But this presents less difficulty to an historian than to a sociologist or philosopher, since to an historian a class is that which *defines itself as such* by its historical agency. For Marx, a class defined itself in historical terms, not because it was made up of people with common relationship to the means of production and a common life-experience, but because these people *became conscious of* their common interest, and developed appropriate forms of common organisation and action. Discussing the French peasantry, Marx wrote (in *The Eighteenth Brumaire*):

> The small peasants form a vast mass, the members of which live in similar conditions, but without entering into manifold relations with one another. Their mode of production isolates them from one another, instead of bringing them into mutual intercourse. . . . In so far as millions of families live under economic conditions of existence that divide their mode of life, their interests and their culture from those of other classes, and put them into hostile contrast to the latter, they form a class. In so far as there is merely local interconnection among these small peasants, and the identity of their interests begets no unity, no national union, and no political organisation, they do not form a class.

Thus the Marxist concept of class (to which I am personally committed) is an *historical* concept, which bears in mind the interaction of objective and subjective determinants.

Interaction of Classes

MOREOVER, WE MUST BEAR in mind that the historical concept of class entails the notion of a *relationship* with another class or classes; what becomes apparent are not only common interests as *within* one class but common interests as *against* another class. And this process of definition is not just a series of spontaneous explosions at the point of production (though this is an important part of it); it is a complex, contradictory, ever-changing and never-static process in our political and cultural life in which human agency is entailed at every level.

Perhaps this would seem less abstract if we took some examples from our own history. The 1830s and 1840s are often thought of as the "classic" period of early working-class consciousness—the confrontation of the "two nations." In 1808 a magistrate was writing: "The instant we get near the borders of the manufacturing parts of Lancashire we meet a fresh race of beings, both in point of manners, employments and subordination." It seemed, to conservative and radical alike, as if the new instruments of production had *created* a new people with a revolutionary potential. The notion is repeatedly found in Engels' early *Condition of the Working Class* where he refers to the proletariat as having been *engendered by* the new manufacture and speaks of the "factory hands" as "the eldest children of the industrial revolution," who "have from the beginning to the present day formed the nucleus of the Labour Movement." Hence one fixed notion of the working class entered the socialist tradition which is still influential today—the notion that the origin and growth of working-class consciousness was a function of the growth of large-scale factory production whose inevitable tendency must be to engender a revolutionary consciousness.

But if we look inside the portmanteau phrase, "working class," it falls into a great number of constituent parts. We find not only a factory proletariat (itself subdivided among overlookers, skilled workers, women and juveniles) but a far greater number of artisans and outworkers; as well as miners, agricultural labourers, seamen, migrant Irish workers, and so on. Moreover we often find (notably in Chartist times) that the most revolutionary "shock troops" of the working class were not factory proletarians at all but were the depressed handworkers; while in many towns, including large industrial towns, the actual nucleus of the labour movement was made up largely of artisans—shoemakers, saddlers and harnessmakers, building workers, booksellers, small tradesmen, and the like. Further, so far from being vacillating "petit-bourgeois" elements, these were often (as George Rudé finds them to be in his study of *The Crowd in the French Revolution*) among the most consistent and self-sacrificing participants in the working-class movement. The vast area of radical London in the mid-nineteenth century drew its strength from no major heavy industries (the dockers and engineers only made their impact later in the century) but from the host of smaller trades and occupations—coachmen and coach-builders, bakers, servants, streetsellers, carters, brewers, paper-workers, glue-boilers, watchmakers, hatters, brush-makers, printing-trades . . .

Factories Do Not Explain Peterloo

WHAT I AM INSISTING upon is that the emergence of the factory system by itself does not explain working-class consciousness in Britain in the period between Peterloo and the end of Chartism. The people who created this consciousness were not "new-minted"—many of the traditions of the "Journeymen and Labourers" whom Cobbett addressed went far back into the eighteenth century. There were abundant causes for *division* between different members of this class—as between old skilled groups like the croppers or the woolcombers and the new factory workers or the unskilled Irish immigrants, and so on. And the most numerous groups of working people (notably the handloom weavers and many of the artisans) were actively and bitterly hostile to the new factory system, so that many features of working-class politics between 1780 and 1850 can be understood, not as a revolt *for* anything approaching socialism, but as a revolt *against* industrialism. The cry which arises from repeated agitations is not "to each according to his needs" but "in the sweat of thy own brow." When all this is borne in mind it is all the more remarkable that the Chartist period exhibits the "classic" features of working-class consciousness. Why? Unless we are to fall in with the fashionable (and ignorant) academic game of relating it all to the trade-cycle, we must surely find that, while the movement was fueled by economic grievances, the form and the direction of the movement was decided by political and cultural influences. Chief among these, the aristocracy and middle-class, by the settlement of 1832, defined without any possibility of error *their* notion of class: at the crucial point of class *relationship* an unambiguous line was drawn, defining their common interest in preserving a monopoly of the rights of political citizenship as against the majority of the nation. It remained to the Chartists to define their common interests around the demand for the vote, which became the symbol of the dignity and worth of every man, and this they did with extraordinary skill. But this consciousness—and its appropriate forms of organisation—were *made*, not "generated": and it is only necessary to glance at the *Northern Star* to see that it was the constant day-to-day work of the Chartist leader and organiser to weld together the most disparate elements—weaver and factory worker, artisan and Irish—and to discount divisive sectional interests in the common interest of the class. Moreover, material factors did not *dictate* that Charist consciousness *must* be such—the conditions might equally well have facilitated other class alignments, and partial suffragists, educational and temperance reformers, and Anti-Corn Law Leaguers were constantly seeking to detach sections of the workers from Chartism and attach them to the Radical, free-trading, middle-class.

The Affluent Society: 1848–88

THUS THIS FIRST GREAT phase of "working-class consciousness" was a creation out of diverse and seemingly contradictory elements; and it happens to have been based less upon the factory proletariat than upon miners, weavers and artisans. In the forty years after 1848 this consciousness appears to dissolve and then to take a new form; and we seem to encounter all Crosland's and Hanson's problems of the "erosion of affluence." Although during these years we see little alteration in the objective relationship of working people to the ownership of the means of production, and although the factory proletariat increases both absolutely and in ratio to the rest, we find no corresponding strengthening of the subjective components of class, while the 1832 definition of relationship *between* classes becomes blurred in many ways. What happened was that a combination of political defeat and of economic recovery led to the disintegration of Chartist consciousness into all the disparate elements which had been contained with such skill within it. The hand-workers were too depressed, dispirited, and ageing to continue to fight: skilled workers found means to advance themselves within the existing setup: unskilled workers relapsed into "apathy." Those factory workers who succeeded in improving their conditions directly by organisation found, ironically, that it turned them away from the dispersal of energy in grandiose class agitation and towards the politics of adaptation and class collaboration. Their very success in "militant" action (combined with their reconciliation to a capitalist work morality and work discipline, the desire to "get on" and the desire for security) gave them an increasing stake in the continuation of the "system." Not only the politics of revolution, but also the politics of piecemeal reform, find their origin in the "dark, Satanic mills."

But this is only one part of the story, since beneath the dominant political consciousness of collaboration or "Lib-Labism," processes were at work in the industrial communities which were laying the basis for a new kind of "working-class consciousness." This above all was the period of the creation of the values of working-class community around the mines, the factories and docks—the independence of "Labour" found expression in scores of class organisations (trade union, religious, social, educational, co-operative, etc.) which preceded the actual emergence of the Independent Labour Party and the New Unionism. Working people talked, dressed, worked, shopped, worshipped, and thought differently from people of other classes. For this reason Marx and Engels tended to discount the political consciousness of "Lib-Labism" as a temporary phase of "bourgeoisification" (their word for the "corruption" of the skilled workers by "affluence") which would end when the specially favoured position of Britain in the world market came to an end. Engels lived to see, in the dock strike of 1889 and the first successes of the I.L.P., a new potentially more revolutionary political consciousness which (he thought) confirmed their predictions.

Affluence and Adaptation

I AM CONCERNED to stress that the problems of "affluence" are by no means new; and that divisive, sectional and adaptive pressures have *always* been found in working-class experience, asserting themselves in different contexts according to the economic and social conditions, the skill or blunders of Labour leaders and organisers, and the way in which capitalist politicians have "handled" the grievances of working people.

These pressures towards adaptation appear to have been greatly strengthened in the past fifteen years, for reasons which are familiar to us all: the
diminution of primary poverty and unemployment: the provision of educational and other "ladders": the strength of organised Labour in its "countervailing" roles: the influence of the mass media and the prevalence of the ideology
of "opportunity"; new methods of manipulating the worker in his consumer
role, and so on. Moreover, Crosland and others have laid great stress upon factors which appear to be making for an actual "shrinking" in the "working-
class" itself—the changing ratio of the numbers of people employed in
industry and in the services, technological changes within industry itself
which alter the ratio of "primary" and "secondary" productive workers, and
the growth of the ideology of "classlessness" whereby according to subjective
criteria a growing number of people (especially young people) do not regard or
do not wish to regard themselves as "working class."

Changing Form?

I THINK IT IS FOOLISH to dispute the *general* weight of this evidence. But what
is at issue is whether we are really living through a period in which working-
class consciousness as such is disintegrating, or whether it is changing its *form*—
whether certain traditional values and forms of organisation are dying, so that
we are—just as in 1848—at the end of a particular phase of working-class history; and whether a new kind of consciousness may not be arising which it is
our business to define and give new form. If the characteristic workingman of
the 1830s was the handloom weaver or artisan, so the characteristic Labour man
of the 1930s may be thought to have been the miner or the worker in heavy
industry—and we may have come to identify all working-class traditions with
his traditions, and see cause for dismay in the decline of his influence. But there
is nothing *inherently* socialist in the production of coal or machine-tools as
opposed to services or cultural values, apart from the rich traditions of struggle
which the workers in the former industries inherit. As automation advances we
should expect to find that the ratio of primary to secondary productive workers will change, and socialists should only welcome this change if it leads to
more and more people being involved in the exchange of valuable human services (welfare, education, entertainment and the like) and not (as at present)
in salesmanship, packaging, and bureaucratic administration. What this change
will shatter (and is already beginning to shatter) is not "the working class" but
traditional notions of the working class as a fixed, unchanging category with a
fixed consciousness and unchanging forms of expression. It is certainly true that
the conditions out of which the characteristic Labour movement of the first half

of this century was formed have changed. The dominant ideology of this move-ment has consisted *not* in the expression of revolutionary class consciousness, but in harnessing class grievances to a liberal-radical programme. The character-istic appeal of Labour has been not for a new system but for a "fair share" within the existing system, a "fair deal" and "equality of opportunity." The definition of class relationship fell less along the line of ownership than upon the line of class privilege: it was Tory exclusiveness, heartlessness, and social advantage which aroused the most bitter attack. But this line of relationship has become blurred by recent adjustments of capitalist class consciousness to the experience of the war and of defeat in 1945. The modified Tory "image," with its accent on humane industrial relations, sound public administration, and the "Opportunity State," has robbed the traditional Labour appeal of its traditional foil. The cry of "equal-ity of opportunity," while an effective challenge to the old Tory privilege, is today met half-way by the new ideology of "classlessness" propagated by the media of the Business Society: "Get on, get ahead, get up!" Labour, so far from opposing, finds itself deeply implicated in "the system"; as the ladders of educational and technical opportunity are let down, so some of the traditional fuel of class griev-ance is used up.

Moreover, the traditional Labour politician who hawks over the grievances of the Thirties begins to appear increasingly hollow and insincere; and can be presented, as the trade unions are presented in the mass media, as speaking not for "all," or for the "common man," but for selfish vested interests. And the tradi-tional appeal even loses its force for the real underprivileged—if Labour speaks on behalf of "opportunity" then it has *less* to say for the millions who "fail" the intitiative tests or the eleven-plus and who don't "get on." The cry for "equality of opportunity" merges with the myth of classlessness and provides—as did "Self-Help" before—an ethical legitimisation of the system.

All this is apart from the *actual* corruption of institutions of the Labour movement—and of people within it—which all socialists know a great deal about but which we rarely speak of frankly. I am suggesting that we should be grateful to Crosland for forcing us to look at certain facts in contemporary work-ing-class consciousness, even if we read the facts differently and draw opposite conclusions. There is a real—and perhaps growing—danger of "the working class" (in its epochal connotation) splitting down the middle. On the one hand we will have the "old" working class, grouped round the pits and heavy industries of the North and of Scotland, which holds to its traditional values and forms of organisation. On the other hand, the "new" working population—with which most younger workers will identify themselves—which accepts the ideology of "classlessness" and is uninterested in or hostile to the traditional Labour move-ment. It is perfectly true that the traditional class appeal of the "old" not only has virtues which deeply move us but also has narrow, impoverishing features—a defensiveness and exclusiveness which many young working people resent. It is true also that if fewer people think or affirm that they are working-class, this expresses a cultural reality which cannot be argued away by dragging in the term "false consciousness"; it indicates an important *fact* about the consciousness of people who—so far as objective determinants are concerned—remain working people. Socialists may argue that the common interests which unite the "old" and "new" are vastly more important than those which divide them; but the fact will remain that many working people are scarcely conscious of their class identity and very conscious of their desire to escape the narrowing features of class. And if these tendencies continue, we could see a hardening of attitudes in the "old," coupling the defence of sectional interests with a truly Luddite obstinacy; while among the "new" the ideology of classlessness will provide a powerful reinforcement to the acquisitive society.

Making a New Consciousness

IT IS NOT "GIVEN" that the disparate elements must take this form. The fact that they have begun to do so indicates the failure of the traditional Labour movement to adjust to social change and to fight in new ways for the common good. It has been unable to challenge the acquisitive society because it has for so long adapted itself to it and its ideology has mirrored it. An important part of the struggle now going on in the Labour movement is in fact for the creation of a *new* class-consciousness, consonant with contemporary reality, with the line of relationship with the enemy redefined, with a new definition of the identity of popular interests, with a new language of politics and a new moral temper, and with new organisations and the transformation of old ones. Can we succeed, as the Chartists for a time succeeded, in binding together old and new into a movement of the overwhelming majority of the people?

It seems to me that a great deal of the work of the New Left over the past three years has been directed towards the definition and creation of this "new" consciousness. One part (for example, in *The Insiders, The Controllers*, and in Titmuss' *Irresponsible Society*) has been in disclosing the real centres of economic and political power in the Sixties, and in indicating where we must seek to effect a cleavage in consciousness, between the great business oligarchies and the people. It is this definition of class relationship which the Labour right-wing (with their demogogic tilts at "privilege" and "snobbery" and their actual enjoyment of Parliament as a Top Person's Club), and the Old Left (with their cloth cap nostalgia and their general air of suspicion towards the salariat, professional workers and all who are not actually employed in basic industries) have so lamentably failed to establish. But as yet our definition of the enemy (and of the common interests of the people *as against* the business oligarchs) has scarcely broken into public consciousness. We have got to find far more vivid ways of impressing these facts upon people, taking up example after example of the undemocratic power and the irresponsible behaviour of those who now occupy the central stronghold of capitalist authority. Rent-racking, car crises, Clore-Cotton mergers, Cunard loans, *Chronicle* assassinations—we must ensure that each one is seen, not as an isolated outrage, but as an expression of class power.

Another part has been in our redefinition of the common good in terms of a society of equals, rather than of equality of opportunity, with a renewed emphasis upon the values of community. And with this has gone an emphasis upon those common interests around which the social democracy ("old" and "new" working class, technicians and professional workers) can be united as against the unsocial oligarchy—demands for peace, welfare, social priorities, education, cultural values, control over irresponsible power. With this, also, has gone an attempt to feel our way towards a new language of socialist politics embodying an ethic and attitudes to labour consonant with a society of equals. Insofar as we have got on with this work we have been very much concerned with "working-class ideas, aimed at working-class power"—such notions of the common good have repeatedly found expression in working-class history. But the new "working-class consciousness" which is forming is likely to be broader and more generous than that which was dominant in the Thirties; less "class-bound" in the old sense, speaking more in the name of the whole people. To attempt to force it back into older forms might well be only to isolate sections of the working-class and to lead them into defeat. And yet, at the same time, this consciousness could well become a *revolutionary* consciousness, since the notion of the common good (unlike the notion of opportunity) implies a revolutionary critique of the entire capitalist *system.* The demands which will be made—for common ownership, or town planning, or welfare, or democratic access to control of industry or mass media—cannot be met by a wage-increase here and a ladder there. And in struggling for these demands people will learn through experience the incompatibility between capitalist irresponsibility and the common welfare, and the need for revolutionary change. It is true (as Kidron suggests) that I am arguing that we can *fix* this new working-class consciousness and give it its goals. More than that, I am saying that it is the constant business of socialists to endeavour to fix this consciousness, since—if we do not do it—the capitalist media will "fix" it for us. Political consciousness is not a spontaneous generation, it is the product of political action and skill. But of course this "fixing" cannot be done on paper. It is above all the function of the party of Labour to present, every day and in every field of life, this vision of the common good; to define, again and again, the line of demarcation with the enemy; to mobilise people in the struggle for particular objectives, and to relate each contest—for wages or for nursery schools or for decent cities—to each other and to the larger conflict. This is what the present struggle to transform the Labour movement is about.

Collective Power of the People

TOM MANN ONCE had a vision of the Labour movement as the constructive expression of the social powers of millions of individuals, so that every worker should feel its organisations as a multiplication of himself, as the embodiment of the collective power of common people. Few workers today see the organisations of the Labour movement as the active projection, in terms of power, of their own aspirations; only too often they see them as separated from, and sometimes hostile to, their interests—a Party they vote *for*, a union they have to join, endless channels in which their energies are dispersed, diverted, opposed, or translated into committee-politics and bumf. If the new class consciousness is to be embodied in the existing institutions of the Labour movement, then this sense of the intimate identity between people's needs and their organisations must be re-created; and this will entail a transformation of the leadership, policies and structure of these organisations at least as far-reaching as that which the older unions underwent in 1890–1910. Whether this is possible we shall begin to find out in the coming year. If it is not possible, then new organisations will have to be created. If it is possible—if this vast organised power can be seen to speak, act and organise in the furtherance of a new vision of the common good, then we will swiftly realise that we are living "on the edge of a revolutionary situation."

A NEW KIND OF POLITICS

I PREFER THE HISTORICAL concept of "revolution" to that of "a transition to socialism." The second phrase too often implies that the objective is fixed— that there is a "given" society which can be attained by a "seizure" of power which implies, not so much a change in the system, as a change in who runs the system, not a change in ownership but a change of owners. Moreover, the sociologist's term, which Wright Mills employs—"a major structural change"— seems to me inadequate since it suggests certain administrative *measures* which effect changes in institutions rather than continuing *processes* which arise fiom popular activity and participation.

I suspect that it may be because of this static sociological terminology that he is able to ask whether "the cultural apparatus" may not be able to displace the working class as the agency of change. The danger is, not that

the "cultural apparatus" or the "intellectuals" will be ineffectual in bringing
certain changes about, but that these changes, if effected, will be scarcely
worth having. Although this may be far from his intention, it would be only
too easy in Britain for people to deduce from his words a Fabian or manipulative tactic which would result (at best) in a socialism "for" the people but
not *by* the people themselves. It is possible that when Wright Mills offers the
intellectuals "as a possible, immediate, radical agency of change" he is thinking
of them, not as the leading agents of revolution, but as the force which
may *precipitate* a new consciousness and initiate much broader processes. In
this case I am much closer to agreement with him, since it seems to me to
be a crucial role of socialist intellectuals to do exactly this; and this in fact
is what is happening all round the world today. But while socialist intellectuals
may "trigger off " these processes, they will only defeat and isolate themselves if they assume the hubris of "main agents," since the kind of socialism
which we want is one which is impossible without the participation of the whole
people at every level.

Moreover, certain of Wright Mills' emphases (and the prevalence today of
a kind of intellectual isolationism) seem to me to be the product of particular
experiences of the past ten years, which have resulted from causes (of which
Wright Mills has himself offered a brilliant analysis) which may be ephemeral;
and one of which has been the failure of most intellectuals in America and Britain to act as anything but the agents of the status quo. A generation of younger
radical intellectuals is now coming up whose experience of this period of quiescence leads them to underrate the "slumbering energies" of working people,
the extra-ordinary diversity of skill and creative ability denied expression and
seeking for outlets; the way in which the daily exposure of working people to
exploitation contradicts the solicitations of the mass media; the way in which
community values and notions of the common good survive tenaciously in
industry, in social life and in working-class organisations; the way in which even
"apathy" is often an active, ironic negative opposed to the celebration of "affluence." What I think socialist intellectuals in Britain tend, above all, to forget, is
what it has meant for our people to have been for so long without real political leadership. I do not mean peripatetic politicians, but the kind of leadership
which is in there with the people, in the factories, the streets, the offices, taking
up their grievances, articulating their aspirations, knitting together one agitation
with another in a general popular strategy. The only nationwide leadership of
this kind on offer during the past ten years—that of the Communist Party—has
disqualified itself in so many ways that it can scarcely be used as an example;
but even so, any experience of this kind of vigorous Communist leadership, in
a mining village or a Sheffield engineering works or among St. Pancras tenants,
reveals the richness of response awaiting to be aroused. If only the Labour Party

were to be transformed into a party capable of giving this kind of direct leadership, without the élitist manipulation or the suspect strategy of the Communist
Party, then the problem of agency would be solved.

The historical concept of revolution, then, is not one of this change in "structure" or that moment of "transition," nor need it be one of cataclysmic crisis and
violence. It is a concept of historical process, whereby democratic pressures can
no longer be contained within the capitalist system; at some point a crisis is
precipitated which leads on to a chain of interrelated crises which result in profound changes in class and social relationships and in institutions—"transition"
of power in the epochal sense. Since it is a process whose very nature is derived
from heightened political consciousness and popular participation its outcome
cannot be predicted with certainty; it is a process not only of making but also
of *choosing*, which makes it all the more important that socialists should know
where they want to go before they start. Moreover, we cannot possibly prescribe
in advance the exact conditions under which this "breakthrough" will come—
around what issue, in what context, with the aid of what "external" crises. Nor
can we prescribe with and certainty the institutional changes that will be necessary—although here I think that the criticism of my article is entirely justified,
that I and other New Left writers have failed to discuss sufficiently the "theory of
the State," and that we need not only to think in detail about the kinds of institutional change and democratic transformation of the machinery of State which
are desirable, but also to begin to press for these changes now.

But I repeat the argument of "Revolution": in the end, we can only *find out in
practice* the breaking-point of the capitalist system, by un relenting constructive
pressures within the general strategy of the common good. I think the objection
of the sectaries to this—that it is merely "reformism"—is just fatuous; it is on a
level with the arguments of the anarchist zanies of the 1880s who denounced the
new unionism as a "palliative." The Socialist Labour Leaguers and the rest who
try to attach "down with the boss" slogans to CND demonstrations are on a level
of immaturity with those who denounced Tom Mann and John Burns for not
carrying a red flag at the head of the dockers' demonstrations of 1889. Although
they rant about the "class struggle," they are just about beginning to lisp the first
letters of its alphabet. But, on the other hand, I think that those who scoff at the
possibility of our people moving *forward* into a revolutionary situation in pursuit
of "ideal" demands instead of being whipped into it by economic disaster are
victims of a similar impoverished economic reductionism. I just do not know
where this notion of working people as unresponsive to anything except direct
economic motivations came from; it certainly does not come out of the history
of the British working class. The very notion of class-consciousness entails the
recognition by the individual of greater values than personal self-interest; and
the values and the very language of our movement reveal this time and again.

Enlargement of Demands

MOREOVER, IT IS JUST not true that our working-class history shows a series of struggles around bread-and-butter demands. This history is, in fact, far more to be understood as a continual *enlargement* of popular demands, a broadening concept of the common good. From bread riots to agitations for the vote, for the humane treatment of the poor, for working conditions and living conditions, for the education, health and amenities of the people. There seems to me no grounds for the psephological assumption that—somewhere around 1950—all this tradition ended, and the British working class (considered in the mass) became a dessicated calculating machine. Perhaps, by a paradoxical dialectic, it is *in the myth of classlessness itself* that a new and revolutionary class consciousness may be maturing? The Business Society may be fostering attitudes which it is in our power to give new forms of expression incompatible with the continuance of the acquisitive society. The young workers who seem to be turning away from the traditions of their fathers are at the same time turning away from the notion of belonging to an exploited class and are asserting (in the first place, perhaps, only as "consumers," but implicitly as citizens) the claim to full social equality. The man who does not wish to wear a working-class cap, drink in a dreary Victorian workingman's institute, and shop at a working- class shop, may see these as insignia of class segregation. It is difficult for the socialist to regard him without a sense of nostalgia for the values of his father which he has lost; but at the same time he may be more open to an appeal to the common good than to the "interests of the working class," more responsive to a critique of the system as such and less concerned to defend a sectional interest within it. Moreover, in particular ways the force of this general critique of the system is becoming daily more apparent, in the false and irresponsible priorities, the transport muddle, the decay of our cities, the inadequacy of social services and the rest. And in his life-experience there will be much which will impell him to question—not cultural "backcloth and fittings" and optional luxuries—but the immorality of social life and the boredom of work, and the credentials of a society which offers him a lifetime of fifty-week years of labour in a confined environment for other people's profit and tells him he has never "had it so good." Finally, he will be led to this critique (and is already moving in this direction) because he is living at a time of greater danger and opportunity than men have ever lived in before; one must have a curiously eccentric and debased view of human nature to suppose that the defence of peace is beyond the comprehension of—and is something separate from the interests of—the working class. If we are to arouse this common democratic consciousness, of the people as against the oligarchs and (eventually) the *system*, we cannot (as

Kidron warns) "ignore" the material factors in existing consciousness. On the contrary, we must study far more closely these factors, and look for every occasion—whether in theory or in action—to emphasise points of common interest between miner and white-collar worker, technician and textile worker. That is why we should reject Harry Hanson's pessimistic advice—to surrender to an inevitable split between the "affluent" and the "traditional"—but should instead work actively to splice together the strengths of the old and the strengths of the new, so that if the split comes (as now seems likely) it comes on *our* terms, and not on Mr. Gaitskell's. Instead of sneering rather self-righteously at the Old Left (as some New Lefters have given the impression) we should be working hard—especially in Left Clubs—to build bridges of understanding. We should be helping the CND youth to understand the great traditions of Labour, its power and capacity for self-renewal. And by bringing the "Old Left" into contact with a younger socialist tradition we will bring encouragement which—far more than self-righteous criticism—will help it to shed some outmoded attitudes. In fashioning this new popular consciousness, which could develop so swiftly that it would leave Mr. Gaitskell and his Parliamentary caucus flapping about like fish on dry land, it may be that the Left Club movement has a crucial part to play this winter.

What we need now, to give body and practical definition to the approach of the New Left, are some examples of socialist actions which go beyond the barren resolution-mongering and parliamentary idiocy in which so much of the Labour movement is caught up. There were plenty of programmes about improving the lot of "outcast London" in the early 1880s; but it was only when the gasworkers and dockers began to *do* it that a realistic movement emerged. It was the force of example of determined socialist groups—Jowett at Bradford, Lansbury and Crooks at Poplar—which gave point and force to new national policies in social welfare. A thousand examples could be given. And today we can only find out how to break through our present political conventions, and help people to think of socialism as something done *by* people and not *for* or *to* people, by pressing in new ways *on the ground*. One socialist youth club of a quite new kind, in East London or Liverpool or Leeds; one determined municipal council, probing the possibility of new kinds of municipal ownership in the face of Government opposition; one tenant's association with a new dynamic, pioneering on its own account new patterns of social welfare—play-centres, nursery facilities, community services for and by the women—involving people in the discussion and solution of problems of town planning, racial intercourse, leisure facilities; one pit, factory, or sector of nationalised industry where new forms of workers' control can actually be forced upon management; one experimental "Quality Centre" on the lines which Raymond Williams has proposed—a breakthrough at any one of these points would immediately help in precipitating a diffuse aspiration into a positive movement which would have far more hope of commanding wide public support than any movement of journals and books can ever hope to do.

To mention such possibilities is to call up an army corps of difficult objections. How? Where? What kind of a club? Which municipal council? How much could it get away with? People wouldn't support it! How could it be financed? There are long answers to all these questions.

But the short answer is that the difficulties are essentially the kind of difficulties which socialists have encountered before, and have sometimes overcome. Moreover, they are exactly these difficulties which we *must* overcome if we are to advance towards the kind of society—the socialism of democratic self-activity—which we say we want. "Apathy," like "affluence," has a long history in relation to our working-class movement. The problem is not one of "seizing power" in order to create a society in which self- activity is possible, but one of generating this activity now within a manipulative society.

THOMPSON REVIEWED RAYMOND WILLIAMS' 1961 BOOK, THE instant classic, *The Long Revolution*, in two parts in the New Left Review: I/9 (May–June 1961) and I/10 (July–August 1961). Williams' would become a founder and outstanding practitioner of Cultural Studies in Britain. Thompson later wrote in the *New York Review of Books* that the "British New Left . . . [arose from] the communist crisis of 1956; the campaign for Nuclear Disarmament, which enlisted onto the margins of British political life a new generation of activists; and the far-reaching cultural criticism of contemporary society identified with the names of Richard Hoggart and Raymond Williams . . . [and] of the two Williams was the more searching theoretician" (February 6, 1975). Here Thompson offers his own views on culture, including a critique of Williams' concept of "a whole way of life," offering in its place "a way of conflict" and a deeper emphasis on class. "I cannot help seeing Mr. Williams sometimes as the inheritor of Jude. The gates of Christminster have opened and let him in. He maintains to the full his loyalties to his own people—and passage after passage of *The Long Revolution* show he is alert to all the specious social pretensions and class values associated with the place. But, in the end, he is still possessed by Jude's central illusion."

The Long Revolution

Raymond Williams' new book, *The Long Revolution* (Chatto & Windus), develops the important themes of *Culture and Society*—the study of the theory of culture, and an analysis of the stage reached in the development of a "common culture."

Within two months of the publication of *The Long Revolution* the reception of the book is so well assured that I am released from the usual inhibitions upon a socialist reviewer—the need to repair the hostility of the general press. I have no need to insist upon the importance of Raymond Williams' achievement. Even a brief passage of his writing has something about it which demands attention—a sense of stubborn, unfashionable integrity, a combination of distinction and force. His work, over the past ten years, carries an authority which commands the respect of his opponents; and the positions which he has occupied must be negotiated by critics and by historians, by educational theorists, by sociologists and by political theorists.

This is to say that his work is very important indeed, and that—so far as we can speak of a New Left—he is our best man. But, paradoxically, his influence as a socialist critic has been accompanied by—and has, to a certain degree, been the consequence of—his own partial disengagement from the socialist intellectual tradition. It is this problem which I wish to discuss. The greater I may start by mentioning that I have a real difficulty with Raymond Williams' *tone*. At times, in *Culture and Society*, I felt that I was being offered a procession of disembodied voices—Burke, Carlyle, Mill, Arnold—their meanings wrested out of their whole social context (that French Revolution—is its full shock and recoil really *felt* behind Mr. Williams' treatment of the late romantic tradition?), the whole transmitted through a disinterested spiritual medium. I sometimes imagine this medium (and it is the churchgoing solemnity of the procession which provokes me to irreverence) as an elderly gentlewoman and near relative of Mr. Eliot, so distinguished as to have become an institution: The Tradition. There she sits, with that white starched affair on her head, knitting definitions without thought of recognition or reward (some of them will be parceled up and sent to the Victims of Industry)—and in her presence *how one must watch one's*

LANGUAGE! The first brash word, the least suspicion of laughter or polemic in her presence, and The Tradition might drop a stitch and have to start knitting all those definitions over again.

The Tradition

THE TONE IN WHICH one must speak in the presence of The Tradition has recently been indicated by Mr. Williams (during the course of a review in the *Guardian*) in a comment upon the nature of "genuine communication": "You can feel the pause and effort: the necessary openness and honesty of a man listening to another, in good faith, and then replying."

The point, as Mr. Williams would say, is taken: genuine communication can be like this, and this also tells us much about the strength of his own style. But The Tradition has not been like this at all: Burke abused, Cobbett inveighed, Arnold was capable of malicious insinuation, Carlyle, Ruskin and D. H. Lawrence, in their middle years, listened to no one. This may be regrettable; but I cannot see that the communication of anger, indignation, or even malice, is any less *genuine*. What is evident here is a concealed preference—in the name of "genuine communication"—for the language of the academy. And it is easy for the notion of "good faith" to refer, not only to the essential conventions of intellectual discourse, but also to carry overtones—through Newman and Arnold to the formal addresses of most Vice Chancellors today—which are actively offensive.

I am suggesting three things. First, through a great part of the history covered by Mr. Williams' "tradition," the tone of the academy has seemed less than disinterested to those millions who have inhabited the "shabby purlieus" of the centres of learning. When Jude and Sue finally came to rest at Christminster, Hardy offers us a view of at least one part of "the tradition" through their eyes;

> At some distance opposite, the outer walls of Sarcophagus College— silent, black and windowless—threw their four centuries of gloom, bigotry, and decay into the little room she occupied, shutting out the moonlight by night and the sun by day.... Even now (Jude) did not distinctly hear the freezing negative that those scholared walls had echoed to his desire.

It may seem strange for me—and I was born and bred at Christminster—to remind the author of *Border Country* of the "freezing negative" which has become associated with the academic tone, but I think that the reminder is needed. My second point is that men communicate affirmations as well as definitions, and in certain situations one may feel that indignation is a more appropriate response than discrimination. Third—and this is a more substantial objection—I am very doubtful as to whether The Tradition is a helpful notion at all; indeed, I am of the opinion that there is not one but two major traditions under review in *Culture and Society*, with sub-traditions within both, and that the extraordinarily fine local criticism from which this book is made up becomes blurred just at those points where this notion of The Tradition obtrudes.

I will return to these points. Indeed, *The Long Revolution* forces one to do so. If there is a revolution going on, then it is fair to suppose that it is a revolution *against* something (classes, institutions, people, ideas) as well as *for* something. Mr. Williams' answer would appear to be that it has been against "a familiar inertia of old social forms," "the pressures and restrictions of older forms of society," "non-democratic patterns of decision," "older human systems," "authoritarian patterns" and "the dominative mode." What he has to say about all these is always important and sometimes outstandingly so. But a sense of extreme fastidiousness enters whenever logic prompts us to identify these "patterns," "systems" and "forms" with precise social forces and particular thinkers. If we are against these institutions and forms (but Mr. Williams does not use "we" in this sense), then we can scarcely fail to notice that Mr. Eliot (for example) has defended them. It might follow that the long revolution is, at this point, a revolution against Mr. Eliot's ideas; and it is difficult to see in what sense William Morris or D. H. Lawrence belong to the same tradition as Mr. Eliot, unless we are using "tradition" in the sense in which we can describe both Calvin and Ignatius Loyola as belonging to a common "Christian tradition." But once we include both Reformation and Counter-Reformation within one common tradition, we must recognise that we are in danger of becoming so aloof that the energies of the disputants cannot be seen through the haze.

This is not the only tone which Williams employs. There is another, emergent, tone, most evident in the final sections of both books, which conveys the stubborn democratic passion, the sense of human worth and dignity, of Jude himself. Characteristically, it is a passion so well controlled that it is most often expressed in negative clauses: "there are in fact no masses," "it is difficult to assent even in passing to . . .," "this does not even sound like democracy," "but the actual men and women, under permanent kinds of difficulty, will observe and learn, and I do not think that in the long run they will be anybody's windfall." What a sense of the tenacity of the common people is conveyed in that last (negative) clause! And yet, in *The Long Revolution*, I find altogether too many constructions of this order:

The 19th-century achievement . . . shows the re-organisation of learning by a radically changed society, in which the growth of industry and of

democracy were the leading elements, and in terms of change both in the
dominant social character and in types of adult work. (140)

... a society which had changed its economy, which under pressure was
changing its institutions, but which, at the centres of power, was refusing
to change its ways of thinking. (143)

It seems obvious that industrial democracy is deeply related to questions
of ownership; the argument against the political vote was always that the
new people voting, "the masses," had no stake in the country. The development of new forms of ownership then seemed an essential part of any
democratic advance, although in fact, the political suffrage broke ahead
of this. (313)

Abstract Social Forces?

WHAT IS EVIDENT in all these passages is that certain difficulties in Mr. Williams' style (that "density" of which some reviewers have complained) arise
from his determination to de-personalise social forces and at the same time to
avoid certain terms and formulations which might associate him with a simplified version of the class struggle which he rightly believes to be discredited.
But I think that he has evaded, and not circumvented, the problem. The first
example says a great deal less than might be supposed upon a rapid reading—in
the 19th century society changed, and so did education, and there is some correlation between them. The phrase "the growth of industry and of democracy"
conceals more than it reveals about the crucial social conflicts. The second
example is a contortion, almost like mirror-writing, which avoids identifying
the points of conflict: if Dame Society was changing all these garments, who
or what bewhiskered agent was standing outside the boudoir and forcing her
to this exercise? And in the third example I am simply lost. Whose argument
against the political vote? To whom did the question of ownership seem bound
up with that of political democracy? In answer to the arguments of Ireton,
Burke, and Bagehot, those who represent the majority tradition in the fight
for the franchise until 1884, were at pains to separate the questions of political
democracy and of social ownership. The political suffrage had already "broken,"
in 1867 and 1884, before British socialism emerged as a significant force. But
why "broke"? Is it not another example of a term chosen according to some
principle of selection which prefers the impersonal to the personal and the passive to the active construction? If he had said, "the political suffrage was won,"
it would have implied the questions *by whom* and *against whom*, and this would

have entailed rewriting the entire passage. Nor do I think this to be a quibble. Behind the words "broke" and "won" one might detect two very different statements about history: "history happened like that" and "men have made history in this way."

The Collective "We"

I DO NOT THINK that Mr. Williams makes either statement in *The Long Revolution*: this is the central ambiguity which the book, despite all its great merits, does not finally resolve. The tone of Mr. Eliot and Mr. Williams' own constructive sense of democracy are at odds to the very end. To make his meaning finally clear I think he must remake his style. He must resist the temptation to take his readers and himself into the collective "we" of an established culture, even when he uses this device to challenge assumptions which "we" are supposed to hold (and yet which have been under challenge from a minority for over 100 years). And I must plead with him to erase such sentences as this:

Few would now regard [Chartism] as dangerous and wicked, as it was widely regarded at the time: too many of its principles have been subsequently built into the "British way of life" for it to be easy openly to agree with Macaulay, for example, that universal suffrage is "incompatible with the very existence of civilization." (58)

Oh, the sunlit quadrangle, the clinking of glasses of port, the quiet converse of enlightened men! And Jude and Sue in their lodgings across the way, which have now been "built into" our way of life. And what about *their* way of life, the way of the common people? Is it not relevant that they also had opinions, and regarded Macaulay as dangerous and wicked in their turn? And how wide (or narrow) must an opinion be to be handled with this deference—does it become a part of The Tradition only when it can be washed down with port?

Conditioned by Context

BUT I HAVE STOPPED listening "in good faith." And this reminds me that Mr. Williams is no more of a disembodied voice than those voices he has interpreted to us. His problems were set, and his tone has been conditioned by, a particular social context: and it is in relation to this context that we can appreciate the size of his achievement. Mr. Williams tells us that he set himself ten years ago the body of work which is brought to its completion in *The Long Revolution*. Ten years takes us back to the aftermath of Zhdanovism; the onset of the Cold War; the enfeeblement of the energies which had brought Labour to power in 1945; the rapid dispersal of the Leftist intellectual climate of the war years, and the equally rapid assertion over a wide field of the authority of Mr. Eliot.

Eliot—Raymond Williams was to write in *Culture and Society*—"raised questions which those who differ from him politically must answer, or else retire from the field." I do not myself think that it was Eliot who asked these questions: I still think that *Notes Towards the Definition of Culture* is a mediocre book. It was the context which insisted that the questions be asked, and it now seems inevitable that Eliot should have come forward as the questioner. But a part of his book is made up of assertions which are so little supported in the text that they could not possibly have carried influence unless there had been a general pressure of experience forcing assent:

> We can assert with some confidence that our own period is one of decline; that the standards of culture are lower than they were 50 years ago; and that the evidences of this decline are visible in every department of human activity.

It is the "confidence," supported by nothing more than a footnote citing a work by Mr. Victor Gollancz, which was new. And the confidence was not misplaced. By the end of the decade the intellectual Left was in evident rout: "progress," "liberalism," "humanism" and (unless in the ritual armoury of cold war) "democracy" became suspect terms: and all those old banners which the Thirties had too easily assumed to be stowed away in ancestral trunks were raised in the wind again.

Raymond Williams stayed in the field. I find it difficult to convey the sheer intellectual endurance which this must have entailed. Looking back, I can see the point at which I simply disengaged from the contest; and I can recall friends who were actually broken (as many of their analogues in the Labour movement were broken) by the experience of this period. There were so many ways to retire— into mere apathy, into erudite specialisms, into the defensive rhetoric of Communist dogma, into Parliament or antique shops or academic careerism. Some insight into the stress of this time—and also, perhaps, into Williams' own sense of isolation—may be found in the conclusion to his essay on Orwell:

> We have . . . to understand . . . how the instincts of humanity can break down under pressure into an inhuman paradox; how a great and humane tradition can seem at times, to all of us, to disintegrate into a caustic dust.

And—at the end of the essay on Eliot—"The next step, in thinking of these matters, must be in a different direction, for Eliot has closed almost all of the existing roads."

Again, he gives too much credit to Eliot: the roads forward had been closed by the general *impasse* of the international socialist movement, and Eliot was ready to point this out. Worse, the major intellectual socialist tradition in this country was so contaminated that Williams could not hope to contest with reaction at all unless he dissociated himself from it: the follies of *proletcult*, the stridency and crude class reductionism which passed for Marxist criticism in some circles, the mixture of quantitative rhetoric and guilty casuism which accompanied apologetics for Zhdanovism—all these seemed to have corroded even the vocabulary of socialism. With a compromised tradition at his back, and with a broken vocabulary in his hands, he did the only thing that was left to him: he took over the vocabulary of his opponents, followed them into the heart of their own arguments, and fought them to a standstill in their own terms. He held the roads open for the young, and now they are moving down them once again. And when, in '56, he saw some of his socialist contemporaries coming back to his side, his smile must have had a wry edge.

As one of these contemporaries I wish to salute his courage. It is an achievement of the order which reminds us that in intellectual contest it is not numbers but sheer quality which wins in the end. Raymond Williams is one of the very few intellectuals in this country who was not broken in some degree during that decade; and who maintained his independence from the attractive poles of cold war ideology. The first part of this achievement was defensive: in *Culture and Society* he contained the intellectual counterrevolution at crucial points, confronted the force of obscuranticism and social pessimism and in doing so reasserted the values of the democratic tradition. The second part, in *The Long Revolution*, is to offer new directions and "creative definitions"; and to develop a theory of culture "as a theory of relations between elements in a whole way of life." There can be no doubt that many of his definitions clarify problems and point towards their solution. But I must record my view that he has not yet succeeded in developing an adequate *general* theory of culture.

Pressures of a Decade

FOR MR. WILLIAMS DID NOT emerge unmarked from the pressures of that decade. I am reminded of George Orwell's comment upon a certain type of Labour leader: "not merely while but *by* fighting the bourgeoisie he becomes a bourgeois himself." I do not only mean that tone and those mannerisms of style which are derived from Eliot. It is also that Mr. Williams has accepted to some degree his opponent's way of seeing the problem, and has followed them into their own areas of concern, while at the same time neglecting other problems and approaches which have been the particular concern of the socialist tradition.

I will take two examples of the way in which the pressures of the past decade can be seen as a limitation upon *The Long Revolution*. In his chapter on "The Growth of the Popular Press" Williams is at pains to demolish the 1870 Education Act=*Titbits*=*Daily Mail* myth. This he does effectively—so much so that the business of demolition can be seen as the active principle according to which his evidence is selected. But as a consequence a number of questions highly relevant to the historian of the working-class movement are never asked at all—questions of quality, of the relation of the press to popular movements, and of the relation of ownership to political power. While the struggle to establish an alternative popular press is mentioned, it is done so in an annexe [appendix] apart from the main narrative—it is not seen as a continuing part of the same story, where power, the pursuit of profit, and the response of democracy interlock. The *Northern Star*—the most impressive 19th-century working-class newspaper—is not mentioned here, nor in the analysis of culture in the 1840s, although it offers substantial evidence on the other side of the story. The collapse of this press— and the decline in quality when contrasted with *Reynold's* or *Lloyds* two decades later remain unexplained. As the story proceeds into this century, the quantitative narrative passes by all those points at which power intervened or at which choices were involved which might have led to a different outcome. We are left with an impression of a great "expansion" and of a concentration of ownership, and if this was the story then it had to be so. This must lead on—as it does in the final section of the book—to the conclusion that if there is to be a remedy it must come through far-reaching administrative measures which will ensure a newly independent press. But I hold this to be utopian. We shall never develop an opinion strong enough in this country to force such measures, which oppose at a critical point the interests of the capitalist class, unless we are strong enough to found an independent socialist press which can voice and organise this opinion. It is one of the paradoxes of the critical younger generation, that one may hear on every side voices deploring the effects of advertising and of the centralised media, but scarcely a voice which goes on to say: we must combine to produce, finance, and sell an independent paper. Sooner or later the attempt must be made once more; and if it should be made I have no doubt that Mr. Williams would give it immediate support. But my point is that his analysis does not lead people towards this kind of active confrontation, because he has given a record of impersonal forces at work and not a record of struggle.

In this case I think he has asked the wrong questions. In his analysis of culture in the 1840s, and of the growth of the reading public, I think he has excluded a whole area of relevant evidence. Both studies abound in new insights, and it would be ungrateful to quarrel with them if this is all that is being claimed. But Mr. Williams makes a greater claim: "Cultural history must be more than the sum of the particular histories, for it is with the relations between them, the particular forms of the whole organisation, that it is especially concerned."

And the analysis of the 1840s is offered as a paradigm in application of "the theory of culture as the study of relationships between elements in a whole way of life." (46) I have spent a good deal of time in the 1840s, and his 1840s are not mine. He deals splendidly with the popular novel and reveals unsuspected connections: with the Chartist press and the teeming political theory of the time he deals scarcely at all. The seven "factors" which he offers as dominating "the general political and social history" of the period are an arbitrary selection; and to abstract factors in this way is the first step towards muddling problems of relationship and causation. Points of conflict are blurred: defeats and failures are minimised: the dominant social character is tricked up in its Sunday best, and the charges against the middle-class (brought by Dickens or Oastler or Fielden or any Chartist branch) of hypocrisy, dual standards, and self-interest, go unexamined—there are no good or bad men in Mr. Williams' history, only dominant and subordinate "structures of feeling." In the result, we are left with a general euphoria of "progress"; whatever has happened the emphasis lingers upon "growth," "expansion," "new patterns." All three social characters (he tells us): "contribute to the growth of society: the aristocratic ideals tempering the harshness of middle-class ideals at their worst; working-class ideals entering into a fruitful and decisive combination with middle-class ideals at their best." (63)

This is indeed a complacent judgment upon a decade which saw the Duke of Wellington (aristocratic ideals?) commanding a mob of middle-class specials against a Chartist demonstration; and which ended (to mention some of the negative evidence which is not considered) with scores of gifted working-men in jail, transported, or emigrating from tyranny—with tens of thousands of hand-loom weavers starved out of their "whole way of life" at home and with millions starved out of theirs in Ireland—and with the first great working-class party in Europe in total defeat. For such a decade as this (and I do not mean to deny the positive evidence) "growth" can be a misleading term. Suffering is not just a wastage in the margin of growth: for those who suffer it is absolute.

Reading Publics

THE "READING PUBLIC" is another misleading term. Given this simple undifferentiated notion we become committed to a simple quantitative narrative. But in fact there have always been a number of reading publics, differentiated not only according to educational and social levels, but, crucially, in their manner of production and distribution of the product and in the relation between the writer and his audience. It is not enough for Mr. Williams to note a rise in the number of pamphlets, etc., during the Civil War which can be correlated with "a rise in social and especially political interests." We miss the understanding of a new *kind* of reading public, hinted at by one Puritan divine:

> When I came to the Army, among Cromwell's soldiers, I found a new face of things which I never dreamed of. I heard the plotting heads very hot upon that which intimated their intention to subvert both Church and State. . . . A few fiery, self-conceited men among them kindled the rest and made all the noise and bustle, and carried about the Army as they pleased. . . . A great part of the mischief they did among the soldiers was by pamphlets which they abundantly dispersed. . . . And soldiers being usually dispersed in their quarters, they had such books to read when they had none to contradict them.

And the same inadequacy is even more marked in Williams' treatment of the 1790s, where he notes the extraordinary sale of Paine's *Rights of Man*, and adds as his only comment: "It seems clear that the extension of political interest considerably broadened the reading public by collecting a new class of readers, from groups hardly touched by the earlier expansion." (163)

Notice once again the impersonal construction: it is the "extension" of interest which "broadens" the public and "collects" a new class of readers. This enables us to side-step the fact that we are considering an *alternative* reading public and an *alternative* press, created by the initiative of a "few fiery, self-conceited men" in the face of Church, Commerce, and State. Everything is different. So far from being rewarded or held in esteem for their work, the writers—Lilburne or Paine—were jailed or driven into exile; their work was circulated by illegal, voluntary means in the face of many hazards; and the very *manner* of reading was different—in the London Corresponding Society and among Sheffield cutlers it was the common procedure that a chapter of Paine's work would be "set" and then it would be read aloud and discussed at the next week's meeting. Perhaps there are over-dramatic examples: but the "few fiery, self-conceited men" have been at their work of kindling an alternative public for several centuries now, and they constitute a tradition which is not sufficiently taken into Mr. Williams' survey of the evidence.

I would not make so much of these criticisms if I did not think them pertinent to Mr. Williams' main claim—to have offered a new general theory of culture. These criticisms might be merely local, and indicate some deficiency, at these points, in Mr. Williams' equipment.

A comparison between the inadequacy of his treatment of the popular press and the superb chapter on "The Social History of Dramatic Forms" is instructive;

in the latter there is a sense of conflict, paradox, of cultural "lag" and contradiction, which his own expert knowledge and sense of the medium has brought into the very texture of his style, and which is so signally absent from the former. And yet I am convinced that these deficiencies are not only local, but are symptomatic of general limitations in Mr. Williams' method.

We may start by noting the limitations of the tradition out of which Mr. Williams' work arises. The Tradition (if there is one) is a very English phenomenon: it is comprised in the main of publicists, writers, critics and philosophers (of an English variety); throughout *Culture and Society* there is no frontal encounter with an historian, an anthropologist, a sociologist of major stature. If Williams had allowed himself to look beyond this island, he might have found a very different eleven of Players fielding against him, from Vico through Marx to Weber and Mannheim, beside whom his own team might look, on occasion, like gentlemen amateurs. Even within this island there are other traditions which he might have consulted: I think of the life-long engagement with the problem of culture of Professor Gordon Childe. And the omission is significant: the archaeologist, or the student of primitive society, in his consideration of the idea of culture, must be governed by peculiarly stubborn material which resists the tendency towards idealist speculation—or, frankly, talking "out of the top of one's head"—which is the vice of the amateur gentleman tradition. Moreover, in common with the conceptual historian, he must be aware that definitions alone are sterile. False definitions will certainly lead on to bad history, bad sociology, bad archaeology; and Raymond Williams' patient work of clarification has cleared away a great deal of litter of the past two decades. But to adumbrate a theory of culture it is necessary to proceed from definitions to evidence and back from the evidence to definitions once again; if the anthropological and historical evidence is not fully consulted, then we may not know what it is that we should ask, nor what it is that we must define. And for an adequate theory of human culture, the evidence to be consulted is very wide: we must be able to think of a Mesolithic or an Aztec culture, and of feudal and capitalist culture in their epochal (not their pejorative) sense.

Is There a Tradition?

WHEN THE PROBLEM is seen in this perspective it is self-evident that its solution is beyond the reach of any one man: this must be the work of many men, contributing to a tradition. But such traditions exist, and notably that tradition which originates in Marx. It is here that I find a curious ambiguity in all of Mr. Williams' work. In one sense, a great part of both books can be seen as an oblique running argument with Marxism: in another sense Marx is never confronted at all. In *Culture and Society* there is a chapter in which the confusions of certain English Marxist critics are exposed: as one of those pilloried I may take the opportunity of saying that I found the criticism wholly constructive and helpful. But by abstracting some Marxist criticism from the main tradition ("the validity of his [Marx's] economic and political theory cannot here be discussed") Williams evaded the point that what Marx offered was not a theory of art and a theory of politics and another theory of economics but *a theory of history*, of the processes of historical change as (in Williams' own notion of "culture") "the study of relationships between elements in a whole way of life." Now the point here is not whether Marx's theory was essentially *right*: it is evident that Mr. Williams is critical of its tendency towards economic and technological reductionism (although it is not always clear whether he is arguing here with Marx or with his vulgarisers), and that he holds—as I do—that the imagery of basis and superstructure is far too mechanical to describe the logic of change. The point is, rather, is there a tradition there to which—despite all that has happened, all that must be revalued, and all the new evidence that must be taken in—we can return? Or must we start at the beginning again?

It is this tendency to "write off" the socialist tradition which is so disturbing in *The Long Revolution*. It can be noted in a dozen ways, and it is evident throughout the four conceptual chapters with which the book opens. For a socialist thinker Mr. Williams is extraordinarily curt with the socialist tradition—and indeed in his reference to *any* minority radical tradition. One might never suppose that socialism, in the 19th and 20th centuries, is a major direction of European thought. The Labour movement is credited from time to time with the creation of new *institutions*, but it is never credited with a *mind*. On the one side the "older human systems," on the other side "expansion," "growth," and new institutions, and in the middle The Tradition, savouring the complexities dispassionately and trying to think out the right thing to do in response to "industry" and "democracy." At times Mr. Williams seems to lean over backwards in the attempt to evade making an obvious connection with Marx; for example, his enlightening discussion of exiles, vagrants and rebels (90–94) demands but does not receive some correlation with Marx's notion of alienation: and in his attempts to break down the subject/object antithesis (23, 99) one feels impelled to scribble *Theses on Feuerbach* in the margin. At other times Mr. Williams' self-isolation from any tradition leads to statements so portentous as to appear arrogant, as in his initial discussion of creativity where (as it seems to me) he is not upsetting our whole received outlook but is bringing important new evidence to support a way of looking at the problem which has already been reached independently by some anthropologists and historians: "To take account of human creativity the whole received basis of social thinking, its conception of what man in society is, must be deeply revised." (115)

Yes, but Marx wrote something of this sort, in relation to Promethean man, back in the 1840s; and the renewed interest—in Poland, France and this country—in the 1844 MSS indicates that Mr. Williams is not as isolated at this point as his claim implies.

New and Old Vocabularies

THE EVASION OF THIS confrontation involves him at times in thinking which I would almost describe as shoddy: as, for example, his reference to "socialists such as Marx" who related "the system of decision (politics) to the system of maintenance (economics)" but who excluded from their thinking "the system of learning and communication" and relationships based on "the generation and nurture of life." (114) This is a strange accusation against the authors of *The German Ideology* and *The Origin of the Family*. The point, once again, is not whether Marx and Engels saw these "systems" in the right relationship—nor whether, in the state of knowledge then available to them, it was possible for them to do so. There is room for argument here, but Williams refuses to retrace the argument. It seems evident to him that in the later Marxist tradition "art is degraded as a mere reflection of the basic economic and political process, on which it is thought to be parasitic. . . . But the creative element in man is the root both of his personality and his society; it can neither be confined to art nor excluded from the systems of decision and maintenance." (115) Amen to this: an amen which found dramatic expression in the squares of Warsaw and Budapest in 1956. But we do not owe this insight to the discoveries of Professor J. Z. Young, however valuable his supporting evidence may be. It is also explicit in Marx's view of *homo faber*:

We presuppose labour in a form that stamps it as exclusively human. A spider conducts operations that resemble those of a weaver, and a bee puts to shame many an architect in the construction of her cells. But what distinguishes the worst architect from the best of bees is this, that the architect raises his structure in imagination before he erects it in reality. (*Capital*, I, iii, VII)

Oh, *that* book! Do we really have to go over all that old nineteenth-century stuff again? We have all felt this response: Marx has become not only an embarrassment but a bore. But *The Long Revolution* has convinced me, finally, that go over it again we must. If Mr. Williams had done so—if he had had any frontal encounter with historical materialism—I cannot believe that he could have left his chapter on "Images of Society" unrevised, nor that he could have discussed "the crucial question of the nature and origin of change" in the space of four pages (118–21), without stumbling upon the crucial arguments of agency and determinism. His conclusion (if it is a conclusion)—"people change and are changed"—is of course the beginning of the problem: and it is exactly here, in 1844, that Marx began. I can understand only too well the temptation to avoid a discussion in a field so confused and so highly charged with irrelevant emotion. But the fact is that we need a book as good as *Culture and Society* discussing the Marxist and *marxisant* tradition in the same definitive way. The alternative for which Williams has opted demands no less than the creation of a new vocabulary; and the danger here is that Williams is making a dialogue between himself and (among other) historians and economists extraordinarily difficult. I think that his terms for "politics" and "economics"—the "system of decision" and the "system of maintenance"—are misleading in a number of ways, and contribute to a fragmented view of the social process which makes more difficult his own avowed intention of synthesising "an adequate sense of general human organisation"; they make it more difficult, for example, to conceive of relationships of power, property and exploitation as co-existing simultaneously within all the "systems." Further, if we segregate these four activities as co-equal "systems" (politics, economics, communications, and the family) then we must look to some other discipline to examine the manner according to which the systems are related to each other; and this synthesising discipline will very soon make imperialist claims. These claims are commonly made today by sociology, and Williams has now staked a counter-claim in the name of "cultural history": "I see this cultural history as more than a department, a special area of change. In this creative area the changes and conflicts of the whole way of life are necessarily involved." (122)

I must dispute this claim. Now if Williams by "the whole way of life" really means the *whole* way of life he is making a claim, not for cultural history, but for history. The fact that this claim can now be made, with some colour, against history by both critics and sociologists is a devastating comment upon the relegation of history to an inferior status in this country. I can only speculate here upon the reasons for this: one part may be found in the failure of Marxist historians to take into account whole areas of concern disclosed by sociologists and critics (although there is a sturdy minority tradition associated with Dona Torr, Mr. Christopher Hill, and contributors to *Past and Present* which may assume greater importance in the future). Another part is analysed in Mr. E. H. Carr's splendid Trevelyan Lectures, whose quality serves to emphasise the absence of conceptual historical thinking of this order in this country for some years. A further part lies in the eagerness with which academics in the empirical tradition have taken upon themselves the role of narrative drudges, making whole history schools into a kind of piece-meal baggage train serving more ambitious departments.

And yet another, I suspect, can be attributed to a mere shift in fashion and a recrudescence of the amateur gentleman tradition (you have to slog at economics or philosophy but anyone's opinion about "culture" or "society" is as good as anyone else's).

I do not dispute, then, that Mr. Williams may have been provoked into making his claim by the eagerness with which historians, under the chiding of Sir Lewis Namier and Professor Popper, have abandoned theirs. The place has been widely advertised as being "To Let." But before we accept the new occupant we must first look at the references of a "whole way of life." This is Mr. Williams' talisman. It is being suggested that society is constituted of elements (or activities or systems) which, when taken together in their mutual interaction, constitute "a whole way of life." At this point we become involved in abstractions which teeter again and again on the cliffs of tautology. If way of life equals culture then what is society apart from way of life: does society equal culture also? We are dragged from the edge by the word "organisation": "The "pattern of culture" is a selection and configuration of interests and activities, and a particular valuation of them, producing a distinct organisation, a 'way of life.'" (47)

The point, then, is that culture is more than the elements or activities in inter-relation: it is the way in which, in a given society, these elements are related, giving rise to a distinct organisation or meaningful form to the whole society. "The analysis of culture is the attempt to discover the nature of the organisation which is the complex of these relationships." (46) But we are now surrounded with cliffs: I find it difficult to conceive of a society apart from the complex of its relationships or apart from its organisation, and I had supposed that historians, sociologists, anthropologists, in their different ways, were—or ought to be—concerned with exactly these questions of relationship between elements and principles of organisation. If Mr. Williams wishes to colonise all this in the name of culture, we need not argue about the name. And yet it is obvious that something more than this is being claimed, both in Mr. Williams' own practice and in the manner in which the claim is phrased—". . . is the attempt to discover the nature of . . ."—this surely suggests a process so delicate, a responsiveness to "social character" and "structures of feeling," for which the discipline of the critic will be more appropriate than the blundering discipline of the historian? What then is the "cultural historian" who (we must remember) is specially concerned with the "creative area" where "changes and conflicts . . . are necessarily involved"? He cannot be a whole-way-of-life historian or we are back in a tautological teeter. He must have the equipment of a critic with that kind of literary-sociological flair which is so interesting (and so refreshing) a phenomenon of contemporary American and British writing. Good: I am ready to root for Richard Hoggart as King and David Riesman as President USA. But there is a simple assertion: in all those coils of abstraction nothing has been proved.

202   E. P. Thompson and the Making of the New Left

A Principle of Selection

RAYMOND WILLIAMS IS OFFERING creative definitions, and I am asking questions, and mine is the easier and less worthy task. But I think he has tried to take in too much, over-reached himself, and is in danger of losing some of the ground he has really gained. If he had argued that the social "sciences" had neglected a crucial area of culture which cannot be evaluated or interpreted without the equipment of the critic, I would have fought by his side. But this "whole way of life" is suspect for several reasons. It derives from Eliot: and in its first assertion is associated with religion: "There is an aspect in which we can see a religion as the *whole way of life* of a people, from birth to the grave, from morning to night and even in sleep, and that way of life is also its culture."

Mr. Williams noted of this, in *Culture and Society*, that in this sense of "culture"—"Eliot, like the rest of us, has been at least casually influenced" by anthopology and sociology. One might wish that the acquaintance had been less "casual." For Eliot went on, in a well-known passage, to argue that the term "culture"

> includes all the characteristic activities and interests of a people: Derby Day, Henley Regatta, Cowes, the 12th of August, a cup final, the dog races, the pin table, the dart board, Wensleydale cheese, boiled cabbage cut into sections, beetroot in vinegar, 19th-century Gothic churches and the music of Elgar. The reader can make his own list.

The point, of course, is that while "the reader" may make his own list the serious student of society may *not*. To decide which activities are characteristic implies some principle of selection and some theory of social process. Mr. Williams, in his essay on Eliot, notes that he has here selected examples of "sport, food and a little art"; and suggests that characteristic activities should "also include steelmaking, touring in motor-cars, mixed farming, the Stock Exchange, coalmining, and London Transport." And this is the only serious qualification which he offers to Eliot's piece of sloppy and amateurish thinking. The reader can still make his own list: but it ought to take in rather more.

There are a lot of points here. To begin with, despite the qualification, Eliot's ghost haunts Mr. Williams—and other *NLR* writers—whenever they mention the "whole way of life." Whatever is claimed, the predominant associations are with leisure activities, the arts and the media of communication. "Whole" is forgotten (unless in the sense of the integrating *ethos*) and we slide from "way of life" into "style of life." When we speak of an individual's way of life, we usually mean to indicate his style of living, personal habits, moral conduct, and the rest, rather than his position, work, power, ideas and beliefs—and the same range of associations has become attached to the term in the literary-sociological tradition. But if Mr. Williams is serious about including steelmaking, coal mining and the Stock Exchange in his list, then we are back at the beginning again (culture equals society) or still searching for a principle of selection. The way of life associated with coal mining cannot be considered apart from the "elements": we must know a lot about technological conditions (are women chained to tubs or is there an automated coalface?), about who owns the pits, and whether the miners are tied in conditions of servitude or have the vote and a strong trade union. I am sorry to be so obvious, but we are concerned with definitions, and this phrase must be cross-examined in its turn.

But we must be more obvious still. Why must the list stop here? Why not also include, as "characteristic activities," strikes, Gallipoli, the bombing of Hiroshima, corrupt trade union elections, crime, the massive distortion of news, and Aldermaston marches? Why not indeed? The "whole way of life" of European culture in this century (as the Eichmann trial reminds us) has included many things which may make future generations surprised at our "characteristics." But not one example is included in Eliot's nor in Mr. Williams' list which forces to the front the problems of power and of conflict. If such examples had been there we might have been impelled to go on and question the word "life." I am not being flippant—"life" is a "good" word, with associations of unconscious vitalism: life "flows," it is "ever-changing," in "flux," and so on—and so indeed it is. But I think it has flowed through chinks in Mr. Williams' reasoning into a pervasive euphoria of "expansion" and "new patterns." It is perhaps the mindless force which has built the institutions of the Labour movement and which is there behind his impersonal constructions. I wish that he had remembered of "life," as (Mr. Carr has just now reminded us) Marx insisted of "history": "*History* does nothing, it possesses no immense wealth, fights no battles. It is rather *man*, real living *man* who does everything, who possesses and fights."

We might note a tentative definition from the archaeologist, Professor Grahame Clark: "Culture . . . may be defined as the measure of man's control over nature, a control exercised through experience among social groups and accumulated through the ages."

I do not offer this as a final definition: it is formulated in reply to different questions. But it seems to me to have two merits which are not to be found in the amateur tradition. First, it is a definition in terms of *function:* it raises the question of what culture *does* (or fails to do). Second, it introduces the notion of culture as experience which has been "handled" in specifically human ways, and so avoids the life equals way-of-life tautology. Any theory of culture must include the concept of the dialectical interaction between culture and something that is *not* culture. We must suppose the raw material of life experience to be at one pole, and all the infinitely complex human disciplines and systems, articulate and inarticulate, formalised in institutions or dispersed in the least formal ways, which "handle," transmit, or distort this raw material to be at the other. It is the active *pro-cess*—which is at the same time *the process through which men make their history*— that I am insisting upon: I would not dare, in this time of linguistic hypertension, to offer a new definition. What matters, in the end, is that the definition will help us to understand the processes of social change. And if we were to alter one word in Mr. Williams' definition, from "way of life" to "way of *growth*," we move from a definition whose associations are passive and impersonal to one which raises questions of activity and agency. And if we change the word again, to delete the associations of "progress" which are implied in "growth," we might get: "the study of relationships between elements in a whole way of *conflict*." And a way of conflict is a way of *struggle*. And we are back with Marx.

To pass from a "way of conflict" to a "way of life" is to pass out of the main line of the socialist intellectual tradition. I don't mean that Raymond Williams has "broken" with socialism: at many points he has a more constructive insight into the possibilities of socialism in this country than anyone living. But in his first conceptual chapters he has cast loose his moorings; and some of his insights in the last section, "Britain in the 1960s," do not arise so much from his stated conceptual framework as from unstated allegiances or traditional assumptions— derived from Marx or Morris or evoked in *Border Country*. Indeed, they often contradict what has gone before. At the end of his interesting discussion of prob-lems in the field of publishing he comments: "We should be much clearer about these cultural questions if we saw them as a consequence of a basically capitalist organization, and I at least know a better reason for capitalism to be ended." (33)

But "culture" is being used here in a different— and more limited—meaning from the one which we have been discussing; and "capitalism" carries implica-tions which might conflict with a "system of maintenance." Again and again in these pages unsuspected connections are revealed which throw light upon con-temporary capitalism as a social system, or "way of conflict," which call in ques-tion his own unsatisfactory definition of capitalism as "a particular and tempo-rary system of organising the industrial process" (by whom? for whom?).

It may be that Mr. Williams' originality demands free play outside a tradition within which so much is now confused. But if others accept his vocabulary and his conceptual framework, without sharing his allegiances, they may come up with very different results. For between these "systems" and that "way of life" I fear that they may forget that at the centre there are men in relation with one another: that "organising the industrial process" involves ownership, that owner-ship involves power, and that both perpetually feed property-relationships and dominative attitudes in every field of life. And that, between this system and a human system there lies, not just a further long episode of "expansion" and "growth," but a problem of power.

Power, indeed, does not seem to find an easy [way into this discussion]. Lawrence "was very much more rich and exciting than the usual accounts infer." But their inference still stops short at the inference of socialism—Edward Carpenter at Milthorpe and his many working-class disciples do not enter the picture, and we scarcely see that group of ILP activists who were among young Lawrence's closest friends and of whom one witness told Mr. Harry Moore: "England was almost remade by groups such as ours in that Midland town." And this process of remaking was a way of struggle *against*, or in spite of, the bourgeois tradition. And so we come back to "Miriam":

> In the drawing-room Violet Hunt said she thought she had seen my handwriting—hadn't I sent some poems of Lawrence's to the *English Review*? I said I had, and how delighted we were to have Mr. Hueffer's reply. Then she exclaimed: "But you *discovered* him." To which I replied that we had been acquainted with one another ever since we were hardly more than children.

The two traditions are there, in a moment of poignant contrast: for Miriam it is the final loss of Paul, and her own return to the other tradition, ending—Mr. Moore accusingly throws out—in the "pilgrimage to Russia." In Lawrence the traditions continued to argue within him all his life. But—this is surely Miriam's point?—*her* tradition had *discovered itself.*

Problems of Ideology

I HOPE IT IS CLEAR that I am not arguing for some crude reductionism. I am arguing that Mr. Williams has lost the sense of the *whole* way of conflict in which the two traditions are involved. I cannot help seeing Mr. Williams sometimes as the inheritor of Jude. The gates of Christminster have opened at last and have let him in. He maintains to the full his loyalties to his own people—and as passage after passage of *The Long Revolution* show—he is alert to all the specious social pretensions and class values associated with the place. But, in the end, he is still possessed by Jude's central illusion:

> "Of course"—Sue is speaking—"Christminster is a sort of fixed vision with him, which I suppose he'll never be cured of believing in. He still thinks it a great centre of high and fearless thought, instead of what it is, a nest of commonplace schoolmasters whose characteristic is timid obsequiousness to tradition."

I know well enough the difficulties. To see "bourgeois culture" in this way is to encourage a cheap intellectual sectarianism, which alienates the uncommitted, and which leads on to exactly that kind of intellectual disengagement and retreat into dogma which left Mr. Williams to fight it out on his own in the last decade. But what Mr. Williams has never come to terms with is the problem of *ideology*. We cannot be satisfied with his definition of man as "essentially a learning, creating and communicating being" (100), together with the insistence that the "central fact" of the social process "is a process of learning and communication" (99). This is taken so far that "communication" becomes a new reductionism: "the process of communication is in fact the process of community" (38), "sexual relationship . . . is our fundamental communicating process" (34), and—"Everything we see and do, the whole structure of our relationships and institutions, depends, finally, on an effort of learning, description and communication." (37)

If this is left here, then the central problem of society today is not one of power but of communication: we must simply overcome barriers of élites, status-groups, language, and divisive cultural patterns, and expand into a common culture. And this is, indeed, exactly where sections of the *NLR* evidence to the Pilkington Committee (*NLR* 7) left it:

> We are not simply concerned with the rights and aspirations of minorities and dissenters (though these rights are crucial) but with the idea of cultural growth through universal participation which, being universal, would cut across and help to dismantle the barriers of class, work activities and the rest of the apparatus of the divided society.

Raymond Williams may not be responsible for the confusion of such passages as this. But since he is cited in the text at this point as the authority on a "common culture" it is reasonable to suppose that the confusion in his notion of "communication" is a contributory cause. The objection is not only that this is the only place in the *NLR* evidence where the rights of minorities are discussed. It is also that the role of minorities *is* crucial if "the idea of cultural growth through universal participation" (can 50 million people gain access to TV?) is not to be mere wishful rhetoric. Cultural or social "growth" is a far more strenuous process, fraught with far more conflict and tension, than such formulations allow; ideas and values are not made by the "full democratic process" but by individual minds at work within this process. Whether we start from Marx or from Mill, from Arnold or from Morris, we must see that procedures appropriate to democratic institutions cannot be taken over wholesale into the republic of ideas. Questions of truth and value will *never* be settled through some kind of majority vote in a condition of intellectual universal suffrage, any more than they can be settled by decree or patronage of Party or State.

This should be clear enough in a capitalist society, where the rights of minorities are "crucial" not only to socialists but also to any minority, in ideas or the arts, which is an irritant to the *status quo*. But it is not clear to me how "universal participation" or a "common culture" can "dismantle the barriers of class" which are also barriers of *interest:* if improved communication enabled working people to understand better the way of life of the corporate rich they would like it less, and feel the barriers of class more. Only Dr. Buchman would disagree. The *aspiration* for a common culture in Raymond Williams' sense ("common meanings, common values") is admirable; but the more this aspiration is nourished, the more outrageous the real divisions of interest and power in our society will appear. The attempt to create a common culture, like that to effect common ownership and to build a co-operative community, must be content with only fragmentary success so long as it is contained within capitalist society.

Active and Diverse

BUT IT DOES NOT FOLLOW that in a socialist society intellectual and cultural conflict will become any less strenuous or less diverse. In a co-operative society one might suppose a wide area of shared values and meanings; and another, expanding, area of fruitful conflict—diversity of experience and of artistic modes, diversity in relationships and in the organisation of factories and of different kinds of community. If we reject (as we should) the equation socialist "base" = a given cultural "superstructure," then the culture will be (within certain limits) the whole way of life which *people make for themselves;* and unless we insist upon the role of minorities and of conflict in the process of making we might get an unpleasantly conformist answer. In allowing this suggestion, of organic uniformity, to gain currency, Mr. Williams has exposed the New Left to the pamphlemic of Mr. Richard Wollheim, under the sustained mediocrity of whose assault I am still reeling. (Richard Wollheim, *Socialism and Culture,* Fabian Society: 4s. 6d.). I was repeatedly reminded, when reading it, that the Fabians too can draw upon a long heritage of literary criticism, and that the original utilitarian reformist, Jeremy Bentham, once tried his hand at the art, coming up with the following result: "Prose is when all the lines except the last go on to the end. Poetry is when some of them fall short of it."

Mr. Wollheim's prose does indeed go on, right to the end of the amateur gentleman tradition; and he proves himself to be a veritable Sidney Webb of cultural theory, offering educational gradualism, the mild permeation of the working class with middle-class values, and piecemeal artistic reform. "The historical mission of Socialism," we learn from Mr. Wollheim: "is to introduce to the world a form of society where the individual may realise himself by drawing at will upon the whole range of human culture which is offered up for his choice freely and in its full profusion."

The world will thank Mr. Wollheim for being introduced to something so nice: the imagery is that of the prospectus of a new self-service store. Mr. Wollheim will draw Proust and Mr. Jones will draw *Seventy Splendid Nudes* and Mr. Brown will draw the Book of Revelation and I will draw the *Niebelungenlied* and what the hell shall we all *do* with what we draw? How shall we live? Will we be there at all, or some other kind of person with different values and tastes? And what shall we *add* to the store of our own? This facile vision of the eclectic consumer in an "affluent" culture evades the point at which the real discussion starts—that a culture is *lived* and not passively *consumed*. We are concerned with the *whole* way of life of a socialist society, and that area of shared values and meanings which might distinguish a socialist from a bourgeois culture.

Is it worth going on? Does anyone listen? After all that has been written by Hoggart and Williams in the effort to engage in a serious discussion of culture, Mr. Wollheim comes up with his homilies and the *New Statesman* gives him a four-barreled salute. I fear that we may continue to wade knee-deep in these commonplaces until Mr. Williams does three things. He must meet Mr. Wollheim's objection that "common meanings, common-values" express "two quite different ideals." He must make clear the distinction between communication and human relations. And he must bring closer together the notions of a common culture and of the common good.

The questions are not easy. But what has been left out of Mr. Williams' notion of "communication" is (from one point of view) *power* and (from another) *love*—or hate. To say that sexual relationship is "our fundamental communicating process" is to say something and nothing, unless we go on to consider that vast spectrum, from aggression to all the notations of love, of what is being communicated. The partner in this communication may be no more than the instrument of the others' satisfaction: or, reduced still further, we may say that the copulation of animals is also a fundamental act of communication. What makes the difference (although advertisers may forget this) is human culture on the one hand and the attitude of the partners to each other—of love, or spite, or boredom—as mediated by their culture, on the other. While attitudes may only find expression through a system of communication, the two things are not the same: and to assimilate all this to the term "communication" is in fact to smudge many of the distinctions which our culture has made available. And we may be instruments or things, consumers or users, exploited or valued, in other forms of communication too. I would add to Mr. Williams' list of the "essential" attributes of man that he is a creator of moral values. And one might go on to claim that "the whole structure of our relationships and institutions depends, finally, on an effort" not only of communication but of *love*. Mr. Williams (and he is not alone

in this) again and again attempts to annex the sense of value-making to the customary sense of communication: "our descriptions of our experience come to
compose a network of relationships," "our way of seeing things is literally our way
of living" (38). But he has no warrant to do this, and I find in this not so much a
central cause for dispute as a central confusion.

It is this confusion which enables him to lose sight of power; and it is only
when the systems of communication are replaced in the context of power-rela-
tionships that we can see the problem as it is. And it is the problem of ideology.
I think this is the crucial question which those who think like Mr. Williams and
those in the Marxist tradition must find ways of discussing together. Mr. Williams gives glimpses of the problem; but he never considers how far a dominant
social character plus a structure of feeling plus the direct intervention of power
plus market forces and systems of promotion and reward plus institutions can
make and constitute together a *system* of ideas and beliefs, a constellation of
received ideas and orthodox attitudes, a "false consciousness" or a class ideology
which is more than the sum of its parts and which has a logic of its own. He
does not consider how, in a given cultural milieu, there may be an impression
of openness over a wide area and yet still at certain critical points quite other
factors—of power or of hysteria—come into play. Nor does he consider the
contrary problems of "utopia" (in Mannheim's sense); and of an intellectual
tradition associated with social groups opposed to established interests—which
must make its way without the benefit of institutions or cultural apparatus of its
own, and which is exposed to the dangers of sectarian aridity or of losing its best
men in the institutions of the "other side."

I hope that we can give this problem of ideology more thorough examination. Meanwhile I may offer a more personal suggestion. It may be that the
"scholarship boy" who comes to Christminster undergoes quite different intellectual experiences from the middle-class intellectual who enters the socialist
movement. In the first, there is a sense of growth *into* the institutions of learning,
with less of a crisis of allegiance than is sometimes suggested: the sense is that
of Jude entering into his inheritance on behalf of his own people. The dangers
besetting the middle-class socialist intellectual are well enough known. But he
may, nevertheless, in joining the socialist movement experience more sense of
intellectual crisis, of breaking with a pattern of values: there is still a rivulet of fire
to be crossed. For this reason his tendency is towards intellectual sectarianism,
or—as Hardy noted in Sue—the sudden relapse into former patterns of
response. But the working-class scholar may tend to persist in the illusion of
Jude: the function of bourgeois culture is not questioned in its entirety, and the
surreptitious lines of class interest and power have never been crossed.

Queries and Assent

MY COPY OF *The Long Revolution* is marked at many points, with queries and with marks of admiration or assent. In developing a critique I have followed the line of the queries: I might have written another and very different article along the line of assent. I have developed the critique because I hope it may throw light on a certain confusion of traditions in the New Left. Too much of our thinking has been simply a flux of ideas and attitudes: year by year names come forward, are cheered, are dropped, and are replaced by new names; themes are taken up and drop from our hands while half-understood and while still not broken down into policy and into programmatic form. The flux of ideas is good; but there is also the suspicion of the jargon of a *coterie*, and at a certain point the desire for "openness" can become an excuse for unprincipled thinking.

In this flux there have been two consistent themes: the writing of Raymond Williams (and of those most close to him) and the attempt to revalue the Marxist tradition. If these themes are to come together, and the New Left is to gain in intellectual coherence, then there must be a dialogue—about power, communication, class, and ideology—of the kind which I have tried to open. Mr. Williams is a thinker of such force and principle that he has made it inevitable that the argument should be taken up.

He is in command of the field and deserves to be so. But I am concerned at the fact that in the past few years so much stimulating writing has burgeoned in the field of criticism and of literary sociology: so little in the sciences and in traditional social studies; and so very little in the field of political theory. Concern with the "popular arts" and with status is great; concern with wages and with welfare more slight; while "technology" and "politics" are bad names. Mr. Williams and others have greatly enlarged our whole view of socialist politics: they have diagnosed a manifest crisis in social consciousness which many traditional theorists had neither the equipment nor the language nor—one feels—the sensibility to analyse. It would be unfair to criticise him for leaving undone work which other specialists should do.

But a problem of synthesis remains: these new areas of concern must be related in new ways with other areas of experience which are part of the working people's daily "way of conflict." Wages, after all, are for the millions very much a matter affecting the "whole way of life," but for some time *New Left Review* has overlooked the point. Moreover, certain of Raymond Williams' ambiguities in this book seem to me to offer sustenance to the weaknesses, rather than the strengths, of our movement. The sociological pluralism by which priority is given to none of the "elements" in society, together with the emphasis on impersonal "growth" and the underplaying of minorities,—all these seem to lead on to a pluralistic—even an anarchistic—attitude to problems of political organisation and leadership. We need only work for health in our own way in whatever bit of the cultural or political milieu we happen to find ourselves, and life itself—or Labour institutions—will knit all our efforts together without the hard drudgery, the propaganda, the creative organisation, at which the New Left, with honourable exceptions, is so bad.

And yet are we really so far from a synthesis as my critique suggests? For when we come to the final section of *The Long Revolution*, time and again my own criticisms appear to be answered. Eliot is no longer in evidence, and Raymond Williams comes through in a more authentic and more committed tone, "for and with the people who in many different ways are keeping the revolution going." There is much splendid—and splendidly constructive—writing, teaching throughout an understanding of the processes of social change, and with successive insights into tensions in contemporary consciousness. It is also splendidly compressed: old muddles are cut through and new approaches summarised—whether in the distinction drawn between "consumers" and "users," or the proposals in the field of publishing, or in the earlier discussion of education (153–54) where in the course of two pages proposals are offered so bold and condensed that one can see in them new institutions in embryo and opportunities a generation ahead.

How can I disagree so radically with his conceptual system, and assent so warmly to so many of his conclusions? It seems to me that Mr. Williams, in this final section, is drawing less upon his own system than upon an understanding of the dialectics of the social process—of the *logic* of change—which is loosely derived from the Marxist tradition, but which he has so much made his own that he is scarcely aware of the derivation. And since so much of this critique has been negative I wish here to offer a suggestion as to the ground upon which a parley might take place. I believe that George Lichtheim's *Marxism* and Wright Mills' forthcoming study of *The Marxians* provide the basis for a complete revaluation of the Marxist tradition. Meanwhile, if Mr. Williams will abandon his vocabulary of "systems" and "elements" and his diffuse pluralism, and if the Marxists will abandon the mechanical metaphor of base/superstructure and the determinist notion of "law," then both might look once more at a phrase of Alasdair MacIntyre: "What . . . the mode of production does is to provide . . . a kernel of human relationship from which all else grows." ("Notes from the Moral Wilderness"— *New Reasoner* 7.) Both might then accept that the mode of production and productive relationships determine cultural processes in an *epochal* sense; that when we speak of the capitalist mode of production for profit we are indicating at the same time a "kernel" of characteristic human relationships—of exploitation, domination, and acquisitiveness—which are inseparable from this mode, and which find simultaneous expression in all of Mr. Williams' "systems." Within the limits of the epoch there are characteristic tensions and contradictions, which cannot be transcended unless we transcend the epoch itself; there is an economic logic *and* a moral logic and it is futile to argue as to which we give priority since they are different expressions of the same "kernel of human relationship." We may then rehabilitate the notion of capitalist or bourgeois culture in a way that owes much to Marx but also much to Weber, Morris, Veblen, Tawney and others who have studied its characteristic patterns of acquisitiveness, competitiveness, and individualism. We might then go on to rehabilitate the notion of a *socialist* culture, again in the epochal sense, growing from (and being sustained by) a co-operative mode of production for use and a corresponding kernel of co-operative productive relationships. This is more than a "common culture" since it insists (what Mr. Williams stresses too little) that we cannot have such a culture—unless as an aspiration pitted against the private evil of capitalism—unless we achieve at the same time the common good: only in this way can common meanings and common values come together. Once again, this socialist culture will not *make itself* any more than socialist communities or political institutions can safely be left to make themselves: the making will be strenuous and will offer many choices. But we have reason to hope— and some grounds for this in working-class life and institutions—that from the kernel of human relationships characteristic of the socialist mode of production, a co-operative ethic and new patterns of communal values will grow. And if Mr. Williams could accept some such adjustment in his system, then the way would be open for him to bring back into his thinking a rich heritage of speculation, from More and Winstanley, from the Owenite socialists and the "Utopians," as well as from Morris and Marx, as to possible socialist ways of life.

History of Human Culture

THIS MIGHT ALSO enable us to clear up a crucial point of ambiguity. The two poles, of "culture" and "*not* culture," to which I have referred, were described by Marx as "social consciousness" and "social being" (or existence). While the two are seen in dialectical interrelation, it was Marx's view that *in class society* "social being determines social consciousness." Not the "pattern of culture" but class relationships have been the final determinant of that "distinct organisation" which Mr. Williams calls a "way of life"; and for this reason we must see history as a way of conflict. It is this condition which socialists are working to end. Only in a free and classless society will history become the history of human culture because only then will social consciousness in the end determine social being.

I know the world of argument contained in "determine," "free," and "class-less." But I am suggesting that Mr. Williams, in his claim for the primacy of "cultural history," is making a contrary proposition: "culture" determines "social being." And I would claim, with Marx and against Mr. Williams, that this is not, in the final analysis, the "creative area"—*yet*. For this reason I am held back from final assent to "Britain in the 1960s," and the obstacle is in the title of the book. My own view of revolution (I am often assured) is too "apocalyptic," but Mr. Williams is perhaps too bland. His three revolutions—democratic, cultural, industrial—are by his own admission all parts of *one*. And can one revolution go on—and for how long—without either giving way to counter-revolution or coming to a point of crisis between the human system of socialism and capitalist state power?

The crisis, as Mr. Williams insists, is a crisis of consciousness and of human relationships. The human system of socialism is manifest on all sides, in our means of social production, in new patterns of feeling, in fragmentary institutional forms, so that it seems necessary and inevitable that we shall grow into it any day now. But for societies, as well as individuals, there may be a "river of fire": an epochal transition in which men become aware that they are making history and in which institutions are broken and remade. "Revolution" and "growth" become incompatible terms at this point. Which term will Mr. Williams choose?

It is his greatest service that he has, more than anyone, made articulate the potential of the common good, as a general aspiration and in particular constructive ways. It is because this good is the *common* good that he avoids polemic and the language of class-power. I think of such passages as this:

If socialism accepts the distinction of "work" from "life," which has then to be written off as "leisure" and "personal interests"; if it sees politics as "government," rather than as the process of common decision and administration; if it continues to see education as training for a system, and art as grace after meals (while perhaps proposing more training and a rather longer grace); if it is limited in these ways, it is simply a late form of capitalist politics, or just the more efficient organization of human beings around a system of industrial production. The moral decline of socialism is in exact relation to its series of compromises with older images of society and to its failure to sustain and clarify the sense of an alternative human order.

This is what we are working for; and this, in a sense, is what makes all of us, from different traditions, distinctively New Left. At points like this I have felt, again and again, that the gap between the two notions of "revolution" is narrow indeed. Can a junction be effected between the two? Or will it continue to be a dialogue along the way?

"WHERE ARE WE NOW?" WAS NEVER PUBLISHED. IT WAS written in April 1963 as a memo to the new Editorial Board of the *New Left Review*. In it, Thompson defends the New Left, or what came to be known as the "first" New Left, in a criticism of the editor, Perry Anderson, and the new board, which he refers to as the "Team." Much of it is in response to what Thompson sees as the adoption of a "Third Worldism," with reference in particular to an *NLR* article, "The Third World" (I/18, January–February 1963) by Keith Buchanan, but also with reference to Sartre and Fanon. This shift seems to include, he suggests, abandoning both the revolutionary traditions in the "West" as well as any commitment to present practice. "Where Are We Now?" also includes a brief discussion of Marxism as interpreted by the Team and a defense of "socialist humanism." This is just one of what would become a number of exchanges between Thompson and Anderson. Thompson would return with the "Peculiarities of the English" (*Socialist Register*, 1965), Anderson with "The Left in the Fifties" (*NLR* I/29, January–February 1965) as well as *Arguments within English Marxism* (London: Verso, 1980).

Where Are We Now?

At the last Board I made a number of criticisms of the tone, etc., of the review. In subsequent discussion it has seemed possible that a more general theoretical critique might be of some value. Since the differences between the Team and some members of the old Board now appear to be substantial—and might indeed result in the disengagement of some of the latter from the review—it would falsify the spirit of our last seven years of work if no attempt at a theoretical confrontation was made. But while I have discussed many of the points below with Dorothy, and borrowed a number of them from her, this is a personal statement rather than a statement of any "group" viewpoint.

I am afraid that it has been written at great speed, in order to send it round in advance of the Board, which accounts for its looseness, prolixity, and for the relapse into the shorthand of metaphorical rhetoric in the last sections.

I commence at a disadvantage. The points at issue are by no means clear. There is an evident disposition on the part of the Team to turn aside from certain of their former preoccupations, as well as contributors and to address themselves to new themes. Much of this is admirable, and indicates a desire for variety and for the remedying of past failures. But it is also evident that principles of selection are at work which flow from ulterior assumptions. Although these assumptions have not been made explicit, and editorial policies are justified in seemingly a-theoretical terms—the pursuit of certain "standards," "rigour," etc.—it is clear that not only the standards but also the *positions* of the past are being called in question.

One part of this is simply the shift in emphasis, interests, and even group-jargon familiar in all intellectual change. Most of the Team shared the same intellectual life, at Oxford and around the "New University"; and it is clear that they also shared an impatience with some of our work. I don't think that such a shift is a serious matter, but I do think that the Team ought to take stock of their position and ascertain how much of this shift is a mere shift of attitude, or indeed of *fashion*, of a kind familiar in student circles, and how much of it is based upon the thorough examination of the rejected positions. It is my impression that Team members are often ignorant of the problems and context of our past work; that they exaggerate our errors, on a most cursory view of the evidence; and tend too often to retreat into certain attitudes, sanctified by ritual phases, in which our positions are caricatured. Among these phrases are "intellectual work" (as opposed to our supposed engagement in adventurist tactics); "internationalism" (as opposed to "insularity," etc.); and "Marxism" (as opposed to "empiricism," Fabianism, Englishness, impressionism, and other named varieties of vice.)

However, this is not a question of a shift in fashion *only*. It is too early, perhaps, to expect that any member of the Team should attempt a precise theoretical formulation of their positions. But it seems to me to be possible to place together an outline of this position from various clues: conversations, correspondence, the evidence of nearly a year's editorial policy, the primacy given to "third world" emphases," and so on. I propose to proceed as follows. First, I shall look briefly at the terms "intellectual work" and "internationalism." Second, I shall ask some questions about "third world" orientation. Third, about Marxism. Fourth, about socialist humanism. Finally, about the position of Britain within the context of the Cold War.

Intellectual Work

IT IS PROPOSED that the review is now engaged in this kind of work, and that this is a sufficient reply to any criticisms on the score of political disengagement, etc.

It is difficult to know what it is that we have been engaged in over the past seven years if it has not been intellectual work.

The work was, however, first undertaken in a peculiarly difficult and engaged context. It was shaped by peremptory pressures, of audience and context, at a time when the "new left" was not only a tendency but also a national presence and fleetingly, a movement.

There was thus a continual tension between the need to consolidate our theoretical work and the demands of context. I think the tension was on the whole fruitful, and much more might be said both about the errors and the achievements of this period. But the question of priorities (as between theoretical and programmatic work, etc.) was often debated by the Board. It was an effect decided for us, by the disintegration of the "movement" during 1961, and the related crisis in our own organization. It became evident that a phase of intellectual consolidation was not only desirable but inevitable.

Thus there is no reason to suppose a central disagreement as to the requirements of "intellectual work" between the old Board and the new Team. It was essential to change the emphasis from one *kind* of intellectual work to another kind; and this entailed some disengagement from real political context, some disregard of immediate political pressures and responsibilities, and perhaps the alienation of a part of our readership. It involved also a more academic manner, the more careful planning of research, etc.

What was by no means necessary was a sharp break in continuity: a polemical rejection of the past: a disregard for the existing audience: or an abrupt shift to new themes and preoccupations. This is not consolidation: it is rejection. The new review is not cultivating more carefully ground which was broken over-hastily in the past. It is simply evacuating old territory and pitching its tent elsewhere.

Internationalism

WHERE? THERE IS THE recurrent suggestion that the Editor and Team are pitching upon new internationalist ground. The former new left was insular, parochial, etc. The Team will now enlighten the island-bound natives. Indeed, the editorial of the current *NLR* reproves us all.

I am unwilling to accept these strictures. Both *ULR* and the *New Reasoner* were, in different ways, part of an international discourse. If I were to document this with reference to the past six years, it is the Team (I believe) which would be enlightened.

Of course there is always room for discussion of the record, and there is always a problem of editorial priorities. Certainly, there have been omissions and "sensitive areas of silence." But the charge which is raised against the old review (at least in implication) is more general. I suggest it flows from certain ulterior assumptions:

1. That there is one crucially important area of concern—the Third World—which the old review neglected. I shall examine this below.
2. Second, a marked disposition on the part of the Team to favour one particular idiom of international theory, to the neglect of other idioms. I will identify this idiom as "sophisticated French Marxism," but will attempt a more serious definition in the discussion of Marxism below.
3. Third, certain assumptions about the nature of socialist internationalism, which I may challenge briefly by stating certain counter-propositions:
   i. There are repeated examples in history of the dangers of allowing admiration for the example of other peoples to become intellectual abasement before them. I hope we are not to exchange the Workers' State for the Third World.
   ii. Internationalism should imply, not a translating agency working one way, but a discourse in which we participate.

iii. Since internationalism is not an attachment but a relationship, it is of little value unless one can bring it to a just sense of the strengths and potential of one's own people. Like any other relationship, it must be based upon self-respect.

iv. It involves not only analysis but reciprocal *action*. (In this sense, most CND branches can claim to be as "internationalist" as *NLR*.)

v. Internationalism is not, by itself and alone, an adequate basis for general political orientation: i.e. because the situation of the Soviet Union, or Cuba, or the Third World is such and such, *therefore* British socialists must orient themselves in this or that way. Only at times of exceptional crisis can this be so. More commonly, we must orient ourselves at least as much upon an estimate of the needs and possibilities of our own people as upon the claims of others: the orientation arises at the place where competing claims intersect. This is not to say that at times we may be deeply impressed with the sense that the predicament of other peoples overrides our "parochial" concerns. But even as we shall be powerless unless we are able to convey this sense of urgency to our own people and we can't do this unless we understand their problems and their idiom, and have some right to claim their attention. However difficult this point may be in practice, I am sure that it is important. If we allow the intellectual left here to become so transfixed by the overwhelming problems of the Third World that it ceases to be responsive to British realities, then we may glide into a pharisaical self-isolation, which defeats our own intentions.

Third World

THIS IS AT THE center of the Editor's preoccupations. The outstanding articles in recent numbers have been his own articles on Angola. The expertise of the Team is weighted in this direction. The last of projected articles announced to the last Board mortgaged perhaps one half of the space of the journal (so far as major articles are concerned) for a year ahead to third world studies. The blue number of the review offers an editorial, and Buchanan's article, as points of general theoretical orientation.

Questions of editorial priorities can be raised, but no one will wish to dispute the great importance of this area of concern. The knowledge which several members of the Team bring to this, and the stimulating manner of their approach, is—taken by itself—a most positive accession to our work.

It is not of great value to discuss how far *NLR* neglected this theme in the past. There was some lag. But "third world consciousness" is of very recent development. Ghana gained its independence only in 1957. Most of the important milestones in its development (the Algerian struggles: the Accra conferences: the Cuban revolution) belong to the past six years. None of these events went unnoticed in the old review, although we often had great difficulty in finding authoritative contributions. If the old *NLR* can be criticized for inadequacy (as it can), so also can the existing review. I have myself criticized our failure to carry analytic material on Cuba in 1962, despite the urgency of events, the polemic opened by Draper upon *NLR*, and the fact that Robin had access to information on the Cuban situation of a kind which makes others of us envious. The same criticism might be made of our failure to carry material on the Central African Federation, an issue with which our readers are particularly concerned. There is an uncomfortable suggestion of pharisaism in a review which, on the one hand, editorially rebukes the British labour movement for its insularity and its complicity with colonial repression, and on the other hand neglects its primary duty to provide information and analysis upon those areas where we are most directly implicated.

But this is not the central issue. And this issue appears to me in this form: is "third world consciousness" not only important (as we must all accept), but does it also offer a general orientation for our review, and for British socialists in the 1960s?

What would such an orientation consist in? I will attempt to state it, offering a montage of the *NLR* editorial, Buchanan's article, Fanon's *Les Damnées de la Terre*, and Sartre's preface to Fanon.

"THREE GREAT ZONES structure the contemporary world." One is the Communist world (although China is annexed by Buchanan to the Third World). Another is the late-capitalist world. The Third World is, in terms of the categories of the other two worlds, in no important sense either capitalist or socialist. It is comprised of "proletarian nations." These nations are those in Africa, Asia, and Latin America, recently liberated from direct imperialist oppression, but remaining subject to "infamous exploitation" as primary producing countries which suffer from the "scissors" defined by Myrdal and others in the operation of the world market ("To them that hath," etc.). "The Third World is a universe of radical scarcity": its overriding problems are those of bread and land, "aggravated" (soto voce) "by the demographic leap in those countries." The gulf dividing the Third World from the affluent world of neo-capitalism (and perhaps of the near-affluent Soviet Union?) is far deeper than the gap dividing workers and capitalists in the West; and perhaps deeper than that between capitalism and communism. "The West" is, indeed, directly responsible for the conditions of the Third World: when it is not engaged in shoring up bestial regimes, imperialist or puppet—Angola, South Vietnam, South Korea—the difficulties of the Third

World may be attributed to the legacy of imperialism, indirect exploitation, the propping up of effete ruling classes, etc. If it were not for "the West" there would be great grounds for optimism as to the third world nations Their hunger, and their bitter memories of imperialism, have given to their peoples an anti-capitalist disposition; their insoluble agrarian problems will urge their peasantry into revolutionary courses; a strong indigenous bourgeoisie does not exist; where industrialization can be undertaken only by foreign capital, national sentiment will place this under stringent controls; while in other countries, industry will be fostered directly as a "public sector" of the economy. Nationalist consciousness can lead by a direct road to socialist consciousness; indeed, from Cambodia to Guinea and Algeria this is already happening. In the "third world consciousness" the Cold War is first irrelevant, and second an infamous squandering of human resources. The entire Third World could be industrialized and poverty abolished for the cost of two (or three or five) years of the nuclear arms race. If it were not for this, certain Third World ideologues would rather see the "old rich ones"— the white Europeans—fighting each other; instead, the Lebanese delegate at the United Nations was quite unmoved at the repression of the Hungarian revolution, as was most of Asia. (The excitement aroused by this in the Western socialist and communist movements is yet one more example of European "narcissism".) It is not quite clear where the Soviet Union (still less China) stands in relation to the Third World, but the position of "the West" is unambiguous. The entire West, including its working-class movements and its liberal and Hellenist intellectual traditions, stand impeached by the Third World's existence. (The Algerian war was the occasion for a "striptease" which revealed the ugly realities of Western ideology beneath the liberal and humanist garments.) Indeed, "the efforts of Western workers to raise their standards of living have contributed more to the deterioration of the position of the underdeveloped countries than has the profit motive of industrial or commercial leaders." (*NLR, sic*). In Britain, whose society is especially myopic, parochial, etc., "the narrowess of our society has marked its opposition," and the Left "has far too long simply affirmed its internationalism," while effectively participating in the general guilt. Above all, "the West" can no longer be considered as offering any growing-points towards a fully human society, a society of socialist humanism. (The hope indicated by Sartre is that the dialectic of violence will eventually return to Europe. As the peoples of the Third World discover their humanity when firing a rifle at a white face, so there may a sanguinary consummation of the logic in Europe, by which Europeans rediscover humanity by destroying the colons in their own midst, and the cultural colon in the heart of each one of us.) It is in the Third World that the energies of change are to be found. Short of some Sartreian sanguinary crisis, or some miraculous change of heart and repudiation of "materialism," "the West" has nothing to offer. It has been bypassed by "history." As capitalism is pressed back to its "homelands" on the North Atlantic shores, we may expect an increasingly introverted ("narcissistic") political and cultural economy, until affluence itself is undermined by the repudiation by the Third World of the terms of Western exploitation. (Or perhaps the "proletarian nations" will "rise" and "overthrow" the West, in some more physical manner?) Essentially, "internationalist" socialist intellectuals must put their roots, not into polluted Western soil, but into that of the Third World. We must see ourselves through their eyes, and adopt the modes of "third world consciousness."

This is montage, at points it verges on caricature (although it is scarcely possible to caricature the mystique of violence and purgative barbarism in Sartre's preface to Fanon). I put it together to indicate a *drift* of ideas and attitudes, not a firm position held by the Team. And there is a great deal in this general drift which is immensely challenging and stimulating. A great deal, equally, appears to me to be rhetoric of an enthusiastic and innocent kind—in the case of Sartre, not so innocent. Among scores of questions which come to mind, I will indicate a few.

In what sense—rhetorical or exact—are we to accept the notion of a "third world"? What is the line of demarcation? Does Ireland belong? Outer Mongolia? Sicily? In what sense do Brazil and Angola, India and Guinea, exhibit identical phenomena? If capitalism is retreating to its North Atlantic homelands, what are we to make of the vigorous indigenous capitalisms in South America and Asia? If the Third World is definable not as a politico-economic but as an ideological formation—the mode of consciousness characteristic of the "proletarian nations"—then in what sense is it a *zone* which *structures* the contemporary world? On what grounds can we suppose that so recent an ideological phenomenon will propagate itself, endure in this form, and resist annexation by e.g. Maoism? How soundly based is the argument of the "scissors"? Is it seriously proposed that the "affluence" of the West (and the impending "affluence" of the Soviet Union), *plus* the main cost of the Cold War, is being borne by the peasantry of the Third World, as a result of the tribute exacted on the world market? Is this an economic or a moral proposition? If economic, then it is surely urgently in need of theoretical exposition—one had supposed that direct and indirect exploitation of the Third World was only *one* factor (and in economic terms a subsidiary factor) to be set alongside other factors, such as the increase in productivity per man hour in the advanced industrialized nations. If the economic proposition is largely invalid, then we should say so; however understandable the "third world consciousness" in historical terms, we are surely not in business to propagate illusions? Even if we agree that some "Western" pundits use the "population explosion" as a let-out, does this mean that we are justified in evading the problem—a problem which (incidentally) we also experienced during the Industrial Revolution, and not as a result of external oppression. Can we justify the moralistic use of pejorative statistics,

such as the suggestion that the enormously complex problems of industrialization could be accomplished by such and such a lump sum extracted from the
Western arms budgets? In what sense is it useful to argue that the gulf between
the Third World and East and West alike is deeper than that between capitalism
and communism, when a) the latter conflict threatens to blow the world apart,
and b) the Third World cannot solve its problems unless it makes some choice
between capitalist and socialist solutions?

These are some of the questions which come to mind, and no doubt the
Team are aware of many of them. They mitigate in no degree the appalling problems and poverty of the Third World. But facts are stubborn things, and I wonder
whether these "third world" categories may not be examples of macroscopic and
"global" thinking which overlooks the detailed "inscape" of phenomena, and
ends up by flattening and blurring what it should illuminate?

If what is under consideration is an ideological phenomenon, arising from
multiple convergent experiences of imperialism, national struggle, and hunger
(in situations where agrarian problems are primary), then should we not distinguish between the roles of interpreter and analyst, and that of apologists? I was
uneasy at a confusion between the two in Mills' *Listen Yankee*. It is one thing to
respond with deep sympathy to the writings of Fanon, Touré, Sengher or Che
Guevara. More: we have a clear duty to publish these views, and to measure
our preoccupations against their force. It is another thing to ape these views, or
to propagate them uncritically because they are moving and authentic in their
own context.

This is more the case, since the rhetoric of every social and national revolution, nourished and protracted beyond its due context, can become a source
of mystification and chauvinism. One may point to the rhetoric of revolution
employed by bourgeois politicians in 19th- and 20th-century France; of Irish
nationalism in the past thirty years; and even the curious twist by which Israel
became the ally of Eden and Mollet.

The clothes of revolution only too easily become the habit of pious scoun-
drels. The rhetoric is used to evoke a national consensus, and to distract attention from intractable problems. Of course it is premature to suggest any similar
phenomenon in "third world consciousness" today. Nevertheless, the language
of the "proletarian nations" against the "old rich ones" contains it within these
dangers. (To take a simple example: one can easily find it in the mouth of an
ardent Moslem militarist, of feudal stock, who at the same time is locking up
trade unionists and peasant agitators, and suppressing birth-control propaganda.) Every great liberating impulse is in danger of reproducing, out of the
very conditions of its struggle, the vices of its antagonist in inverted form. We
have seen this in Stalinism, and something of the sort is happening in Maoism
also. Thus, out of the racialism of imperialist oppression there can spring the

opposite, an anti-white nationalist chauvinism. The latter is morally far more comprehensible and venial than the former. And yet in its turn it could serve as the rhetoric of indigenous politicians, interested in diverting attention from internal contradictions. It is certainly true that in certain conditions nationalist consciousness might lead on directly to socialist consciousness. Many factors (some listed in my "montage") might lead in this direction: where one has a single-crop economy, under foreign (imperialist) ownership, there are obvious reasons why struggles for political and economic expropriation may tend to go forward together. But exactly at the point where socialism comes on the agenda, the theory of the "three zones" is called into question. As Cuba underlined, the struggle to effect a transition to socialism is likely to bring any "third world" nation within the tensions of the Cold War; to throw it into dependence upon the Soviet world; and to influence it deeply with Soviet or Maoist ideology and forms. Indeed, one wonders how far "third world consciousness" may prove to be an ephemeral phenomenon, and how far it may become increasingly divided between different and competing influences—Soviet, Maoist, American, etc. For a distinctive "third world consciousness" to become consolidated, which is clearly marked off from both capitalist and orthodox communist ideology, might well require also a breakthrough of one of the advanced nations in one of the other two "zones."

This is to state matters too baldly. It is evident that an interesting situation is arising in a number of "third world" countries, in which industrialization is being carried forward under the leadership of a party whose nationalist consciousness in a sense subsumes the consciousness of any single class or group; and that we may see the growth of a public sector of the economy (the most advanced sector at that) alongside petty capitalist and feudal forms of land ownership, tenure, and marketing. Here we have the state arising, perhaps fleetingly, "above" classes, as a mediator between classes, or as the dispenser of essentially humane services (medical, educational, etc.). This is a situation which certainly requires close, sympathetic attention; and analysis rather more precise than Buchanan's throwaway remarks about "new forms" of socialism. Equally, if this is regarded as a likely way of advance towards socialism it is not altogether compatible with the other model, of peasant-based revolutionary armies, who bring the revolution with guns to the laggard towns.

In short, I am both ignorant and confused, but I see grounds for suspicion as to some of this Third World rhetoric. I am far from convinced that this is a phenomenon distinct enough, or internally coherent enough, to demand analysis by means of a new set of categories. I am alarmed lest we should encourage a geographical fragmentation of socialist theory (even if this takes place under the slogan of "global" theory), which employs one set of categories (and standards) to examine the Soviet bloc, another for the "West," and yet another for the Third

World. This would result in a relativism which (I suspect) would lead ultimately to a detached accommodation with Communist ideology. The problem of orientation facing British socialists is certainly difficult, but its difficulties should not be ones for which we are unprepared. Having learned the consequences of confusing analysis and apologetics in the past, one hopes that we are not to forget this when we face the Third World. I assume that it is unnecessary to defend myself from the suggestion that I wish to impose abstract liberal criteria upon "third world" situations; none of us, I suppose, would wish a "two-party-parliamentary-system" upon Cuba or Indonesia. Nevertheless, the argument that Chinese austerity is unavoidable, that Cuban dependence upon the Soviet bloc is inevitable, and that the one-party state of Ghana &c is wholly comprehensible, shade off at a certain point into apologetics—that these things are both justifiable and admirable. But a distinctive characteristic of socialist humanism ought to be an extreme sensitivity towards this type of apologetics, and a stubborn resistance against gliding from the first kind of statement to the second.

We have a task which is difficult, easily misrepresented, and quite probably one that will not quickly be understood in the Third World itself. We have at one and the same time to see (and interpret) the great liberating impulses of the Soviet and Chinese revolutions, and of the emergent nationalisms of Asia and Africa; and to adopt a critical and at times uncompromising stand as to certain socialist principles and humanist values. It is the *critical* standpoint which is truly that of internationalism. The execution of Communist trade unionists in Iraq and of intellectuals (again, often Communist) in China is no prettier because these events happen in a third world: they happen also in our world, and the victims have the right to expect from us the duties of solidarity. Because one's heart has leapt at the Cuban revolution, and because one pukes at the libels upon Ghana in the *Daily Express*, this does not mean that one can pass over in silence offensive ideological or authoritarian tendencies in these countries. If the "third world consciousness" appears to us to be compounded of truth and of illusion, we do poor service, to them and to ourselves, if we propagate the illusion as well as the truth.

The simple derivation of all indigenous social problems in the "third world" from the past or present influence of the West appears to me to be such an illusion. So also is the view that there is *one* pattern of third world advance, based upon peasant revolution. I remain unconvinced that the emergent nations can bypass all the problems of class formation and political evolution on "Western" models, although some may do so. Latin America offers some evidence on the other side. And the Cuban revolution itself did not spring out of a peasant-hunger situation alone (of a kind easily translated into African terms) but also from long and complex political traditions. To the degree that Third World ideologists make the West the whipping-boy for indigenous problems, to that degree they will find their solution more difficult. In vast areas of this "world," the peasantry have the most difficult struggles to encounter with an indigenous feudality; and I see no a priori reasons why a really nasty indigenous bourgeoisie or military elite, with feudal associations, might not consolidate itself in certain Asian and African countries. Indeed, within the limits permitted by the Cold War, it is not impossible that one or other more or less predatory nationalism might not arise in Africa, under the banner of Pan-Africanism or Pan-Arabism.

It is not that I wish to be pessimistic. But if we exaggerate the differences in the Third World situations, we may neglect similarities; and we may also neglect the points at which we may make our internationalism effective, by clarifying what it is that socialist humanists in Moscow, London and Accra ought to be working for *together*. The notion that there is a deeper gulf between the Third World peoples and those rich nations then between capitalists and workers appears to me unhelpful, unless it is stated in precise terms, as a literal comparison (of diet, health, conditions, etc). The danger is that we shall be led by the analogy into a logical fallacy, and compare unlikes. Thus while the literal "gulf" is deeper it does not follow that the peoples of the West and the Third World are necessarily placed in antagonistic life situations, that a conflict of interests is inherent in these situations (as there is between the "capitalists and workers"). In the days of direct imperialist rule, it was the policy of revolutionary socialists to emphasise at every point the identity of interests of the working people of the imperial countries and of the subject peoples, in a common struggle against common oppressors. When whole peoples were repressed by the "English," "French" and "Germans," the theory of inherent antagonism would in fact have force: but why should the liberation of these peoples make the contradiction *more* acute? Surely it is more true that the *consciousness* of the gulf has become more acute, as these nations have attained identity and confidence? If this is not what is meant, then we must ask how far the imagery of the "proletarian nations" is to be taken? Does the metaphor imply an irreconcilable antagonism between the "old rich ones" and the "third world"—which will result in some ultimate conflict, in which our own loyalties must be with the oppressed? Such is the tone of Fanon and of Sartre. What then is the source of this antagonism? The tribute exacted by international finance and through the world market? But in whose interests is this exacted? Of all of us? And inevitably? Or of specific vested interests? And thereby indirectly of the capitalist economies? And if the latter, should not the "third world" see in socialist opposition to these interests a source of allies? And if the repression continues in pursuit of the strategic claims of the Cold War, then equally should not the "third world" find allies in those forces, east and west, which are working to dismantle this abnormal human condition?

The argument is pressed further. It is the entire "West," or white world, which stands impeached by its complicity with colonialism. Not only its economic and political structure, but its cultural traditions stand condemned as resting upon torture and genocide. Surely this is loose and unhistorical thinking? All hitherto-existing societies have had their foundations in some forms of exploitation and violence. Greek society was founded on slavery, and its modes of conscious-ness were thereby impaired, but we do not reject as vitiated its entire intellec-tual and cultural output. The commercial revolution—the essential precursor to the industrial revolution—was made possible by the gold looted by Spanish adventurers and cut-throats in Mexico and Peru. In this sense, all Western his-tory since 1600 rests on a basis of robbery, murder and bad faith. The techniques of advanced industrialism, which are now so much needed by the third world, are themselves on product of this process. Progress indeed is "double-edged, double-tongued." The global view which sees the West always in the perspective of Asian and African hunger contains an important part of the truth. But it is not the *whole* truth, and what is chiefly lacking is a sense of the dialectics of histori-cal change—of the interpenetration of opposites, of forms of exploitation in the third world and of liberating impulses in the West—of the identity of interests of peoples and unlike life-situations, and so on.

It is elementary that the standard of living may be defined in two quite dif-ferent ways: in purely statistical, absolute terms (dietary, housing, etc.) and in terms of social norms and potential fulfillment offered by a society at a given productive and social level. If we contrast standards in the statistical sense, we will come up with the "proletarian nations" versus the "old rich ones" antithesis. If however we take a dynamic view, we may get a different kind of answer. For the important problem then is not only what is the existing contrast between the two, but what is the most fruitful mutual relationship between them? And if we look for such a mutually beneficial relationship, then we become less transfixed by the immediate contrasts and more preoccupied with the problems of bring-ing together those social forces within both worlds which can be led by interest or by ideal motives to establish this new kind of relationship. In the first view, we appear to face a gulf which no voice can cross: there is extreme hunger, bitter-ness, pride on one side: fear and guilt on the other. In the second view, we must search for a genuinely internationalist and socialist resolution.

Buchanan offers simply an abstract and moralistic condemnation of "the West," with a peculiar (and unexplained) animus evinced against the western proletariat. I am sorry that such an undiscriminating notion as "the West" should gain currency in our review. One had supposed that the best traditions of intel-lectual work and of socialist theory belonged not to the West or the Third World, but were international—and a good deal has been said and suffered to uphold this belief. I have an uncomfortable feeling that the Editor follows Fanon-Sartre in dismissing this as pseudo-liberal rhetoric. But there is some history relevant to this also.

The Third World emerged in different ways. On the one hand, it emerged through the throes of the bitterest colonial war, accomplished by genocide, torture, and vicious repression. (I don't know if we can draw comfort from the fact that these amenities of Western civilization have not been reserved for colonial peoples, as Fanon's tone implies. Jews and anti-fascists were suffering all these things less than twenty years ago within the "homelands" of capitalism itself.) The "schema" of Fanon (although these appear to me as a complex of related attitudes rather than as scientific schema) are derived almost wholly from data of this kind. So also is Perry's admirable account of Angola. On the other hand, we have those peaceful transitions to independence, and notably the record of India, Ceylon, Burma, and hence forward to Ghana. It is not too much to say that the transfer of powers in India (for Asia) and Ghana (for Africa) were events of equal importance for the emergence of a Third World as any examples in the first group. The presence of the two nations has been of profound continental and international influence.

Now Perry makes the valid point that any adequate analysis of a colonial situation demands an examination of the balance of forces within the metropolitan country. Hence India and Ghana present a particular challenge to British socialists, in that the analysis of their liberation entails also an analysis of our own society. It is of interest to recall the orthodox Marxist standpoint, as formerly expressed by the British CP and by its most able exponent, Palme Dutt. Throughout the Thirties and early Forties, while actions on behalf of India had a high priority in the work of the British CP, it was almost an article of faith that India must ultimately gain independence through a bloody conflict of force. (Gandhi—and civil disobedience in general—were criticized as failing in revolutionary realism.) Hence when the transfer of powers in fact took place after the war the first response of orthodoxy was to proclaim that no "real" transfer had taken place, that India's economy and political life were still controlled by British diplomacy and capital. And in confirmation much was made of the continued presence of British agents and officers, as well as of the role of the princelings and of Pakistan as agencies of the continued British presence. When this line of argument was falsified by events, apologetics retreated behind a second line of defence: which was that in 1945 the British power was so weak and war-exhausted and the Indian masses so militant that to hold power by force was a sheer impossibility. Britain had in fact been expelled by force, even if only metaphysical force. This was supplemented by the standard last-ditch defence of doctrinaire British Marxists—wise references to the extreme cunning and flexibility of the British ruling class.

Of course the overwhelming factor involved was the organization and militancy of the Indian people. On the other hand, the arguments of British war-exhaustion are thin. At no time in the 20th century did the British have larger forces and greater stocks of advanced war equipment than in 1945, very much of this in the East. And in fact, the Dutch and the French fought colonial wars, while on this important occasion the British did not. What I think has been very much left out of account is the degree to which a consensus favoring Indian independence had developed within Britain itself, making it politically unfeasible to fight a colonial war upon the sub-continent. What had led to this consensus? There were a number of factors; and the assessment of their respective force would demand a fuller analysis than I could attempt. But we may note, first, the rhetoric of constitutionalism, which was always a specific form of advanced British imperialism ("fair" paternalist administration, the rule of law, the gradualist promotion of areas of "self-government"). Second, the middle-class humanitarian and Christian-missionary conscience, which, while assuming most hypocritical and nauseous forms in the 19th century, nevertheless contained within itself a logic inimical to direct repression, as well as a more humane and radical minority tradition. Third, there was the traditionally anti-imperialist stance of the labour movement, reinforced by the particular dedication of the Communist and ultra-left groups. Finally, there was the fact that while direct imperialist tribute from India was still important, it no longer played the fantastically large part in the British economy that it did in the age of railway-construction and the floatation on the London exchange of the Indian Debt.

I wish to draw attention to the second and third factors. For one thing they point to some history which I believe the Team may have missed. The history of British-Indian relations has not been a simple series of Amritsars. And if we are to cite Amritsar, we must also cite the repercussions of Amritsar—the outcry, the disgrace of General Dyer, etc. Of course, the traditional concern with some aspect of Indian rights (if only the Lockeian concern for the rule of law, the property-rights of princes, etc.) reaches back to the Whig opposition (the impeachment of Hastings) in the 18th century. The first breakthrough of a plebian radical candidate at the polls (Paull at Westminster, 1806) came with a candidate fighting on the platform of the impeachment of Wellesley for breaking faith with Oudh. James Mill's preoccupations were more limited and strictly utilitarian (sound administration and finance), but the taut humanity of his son went very much further. The socialist movement took up J. S. Mill's tradition and emerged with a markedly anti-imperialist stance (notably William Morris). From the 1880s onwards India can be seen as litmus paper, distinguishing the authentic from the false internationalist. Thus Hyndman's submerged jingoism was revealed in his earliest writings on India; the Fabians were notoriously ambiguous (or plainly compromised) on colonial issues; while there was no Labour leader whose attitude to India was more paternalist than MacDonald. By contrast, from Hardie to the left the resistance to imperialist rule was consistent. Around E. D. Morel, Blunt, Leonard Woolf, C. P. Trevelyan and others a strong middle-class anti-imperialist tradition also developed. In the Twenties and Thirties we find an interesting situation. So far from our Left having no internationalist traditions, I would say that next to "Spain" and anti-fascism itself, there was no issue which so seized the imagination and claimed the attention of British socialists as India. Lenin's *Imperialism* was perhaps the most widely studied of all Marxist texts in the Thirties, while Dutt's *India Today* was the most thorough and influential political work by any English Communist leader. (The first Communist elected to Parliament—in Battersea, I think—was an Indian.) The left Liberal and socialist press carried regular material on the Indian struggle by Brailsford, Shelvankar, Sorensen, my father, and many others. One of the four or five outstanding Congress leaders—Krishna Menon—was permanently in England, directing the agitation of the Indian League. Moreover, there was a marked interpenetration of ideas between the Indian nationalist movement and British Left. The student movement, notably at Oxford and Cambridge, always had a large Asiatic element, whose members were active and prominent. (Some of us received our first tuition in Marxism from Indian comrades, and vice versa.) Already in the Twenties, British agitators (the Meerut prisoners) had assisted the Indian CP into being; and if one follows the reports of Congress, or of Communist and Trotskyist movements in India, Ceylon and Burma, many intellectuals who returned from this British milieu will be found in leading roles. By the end of the Thirties this interpenetration, and this long anti-imperialist agitation, had become of historical importance. Despite the rearguard action of the MacDonaldite old guard in the Labour Party, the British labour movement had come to assume its duty towards the Indian people as a first responsibility. Even in the worst war years, it was automatic that the biggest annual meetings of the socialist clubs at Oxford and Cambridge (whose attendances resembled the best CND meetings of recent years) were those addressed (very angrily) by Krishna Menon. As political consciousness rose during the war, so anti-fascist and anti-imperialist feeling became identified. As we fought Hitler's oppression of Europe, as it was assumed that India would be "given" her freedom at the end of the war. The decision taken by Congress (after a sharp internal struggle) to support the anti-fascist war taken at least in part upon an estimate of the reality of this changing consensus within Britain. Even in the war itself a minority of British troops in India and Burma (notably CP members) engaged in organized politicial work with the Indian movement (see, e.g. Clive Branson's letters or consult Harry Hanson or John Saville).

Hence in 1945 it was politically impracticable for a Labour Government to have fought a colonial war in India, even supposing it had "wished" to do so, which is a large supposition. (It was after all a major election promise that India should be free.) And I want to stress this for two reasons. Ignorance of history usually brings some revenge into contemporary analysis. And, first, to ignore this record is to ignore important differences existing today in the Third World. By and large, the emergence of those areas under Anglo-Saxon domination has been less marked with the extreme bitterness, torture and dehumanization seen in Algeria or Angola. Hence also the interpenetration of cultures, and of socialist theory, has been more important. Second, to be ignorant of these facts may lead also to the underestimation of a continuing tradition within Britain. And after all, this is "our" tradition—for some of us, in a very direct and personal sense, a tradition scored with our own memories and enriched by our own comradeship with Asian socialists. Is there any special reason why we should always offend our own people, overlook our better traditions; and berate the British for an insularity which is, in some part, a Parisian myth? Surely this tradition must be valued, if one is to have the insight to understand why and in what ways it is breaking down, and how it can be given fresh life?

This tradition extends beyond the Indian connection. When I describe the younger CND folk (and indeed the Team) as big-headed in some ways, I moan that there is a continual proclamation of principles, values, ideas, which in fact have long been actively endorsed by a minority tradition in Britain, and in which most younger people are (one feels) *willfully* ignorant. (There is a parallel here between Team modes and *Look Back in Anger* which I direct to the attention of the literary editor.) It is true that this anti-imperialist tradition has not yet found its historian. Ralph Miliband's valuable book nevertheless obscures the tradition of places, because, by concentrating attention on the accommodations of the leadership, it neglects to describe the continual pressure of articulate minorities. (The word India is not to be found in the index.) The tradition is also obscured because it was often associated with the initiatives of the Communist Party. This is one reason why I am unwilling to engage in any indiscriminate repudiation of the Communist tradition, because a large part of the internationalist and anti-imperialist conscience of Britain in the Thirties and Forties can be seen at work there. I was startled recently to learn that no member of the Team had read *India Today*. Of course, we can all be faulted on our reading; but I think caution should be shown in generalising as to British failings when such crucial evidence as this book symbolizes is left out of account.

What also is unknown? Hobson? Brailsford's *War of Steel and Gold*? Brockway? The point is that this is a deep and authentic tradition in the British labour movement: one need only note the almost ritualistic fervour with which Jennie Lee's annual speech on colonialism at the Labour Conference is received. Where then has it broken down? Exactly in the labour movement, one feels—indeed, John Rex and others tell me that in the late Fifties it was easier to get response on African affairs from Christian or United Nations circles than (beyond resolution-mongering) from trade union branches. (But even so, we assume that despite all their affluence the organized trade unionists always will pass the right resolution—and usually do.) Now surely this breakdown requires analysis, rather than attitudinizing abuse? The old impulse, while still there in a formal sense has ceased to "bite." In my view it is over-hasty to assume some direct correlation between this lethargy and British "affluence" (as to whose meaning I am perplexed). I think the breakdown results far more from the general crisis of socialist theory and the loss of direction contingent upon the Cold War. Once again, one may note that with the exception of the colon situation in Kenya, the only places where Britain has been engaged in actual situations of colonial warfare have been ones in which the ostensible legitimation has been found in the strategic demands of the Cold War—notably Cyprus and Malaya. And from this, several points may be suggested.

So far from being peculiarly insular, the British labour movement has always been fairly sensitive to international pressures. In every major crisis within the movement from the Twenties to the present day, the "left" has been identified with certain internationalist policies—the response to the Soviet revolution, Spain, the anti-fascist struggle, the Second Front, Greece, Israel, the Marshall Plan, the Cold War, Korea, CND. The internationalist tradition was seriously weakened in the late Forties by the efforts of the last manic phase of Stalinism, on the one hand, and Bevin's capitulation to American policies on the other. To see exactly how the old élan was broken up would require some very close discussion of issues and even of the fate of individuals: it is difficult to recall those crazy years when Zilliacus and Basil Davidson were fingered as Western "spies," when men like Claud Cockburn (if anyone is like him!) were driven out of the left, Brockway cold-shouldered as a "Trotskyist," while people like Pritt and Platts Mills became so much identified with the Communist apparatus that they lost much of their wider influence. This made it easier for the Right, personified in Bevin (one remembers Abadan) to draw upon the ugliest and most philistine sentiments of loyalty. The point is that the Cold War was deeply divisive, and from the standpoint of the socialist rank-and-file it was difficult to find any sense of direction. Thus where imperialist actions were closely associated with Cold War issues, the movement was riven, dismayed, confused. The nadir of the tradition (which I would put at 1949–1956—Korea, Kenya, Malaya, Cyprus, Suez) came when Cold War propaganda had reached its height; and when those who maintained the anti-imperialist tradition most staunchly were in many cases Communists or fellow-travelers, whose influence was diluted by their complicity with Stalinism. Equally, there is some indication that this phase came to an end, and a new anti-imperialist impulse can be felt, from the time of Suez, with CND, the new left, and the campaign against apartheid.

During the worst phase the Communist strand of anti-imperialism, as still active in the unions, etc., did probably become more formal and ritualistic. For an important reason. To the Communist ideologue much of the general internationalist tradition became subsumed in the single duty of complying with Soviet strategy, World Peace Council campaigns, etc. While resolutions continued to be passed about Malaya or Kenya, really active efforts were concentrated upon paper-chasing for a "Five Power Peace Pact" and so on. Hence the tradition among many working people became enfeebled. And what happened here was far far worse in France. An analysis of the tragedy of Algeria would require not an anatomizing of the "affluence" of the French workers but of the false internationalism of the leadership of the PCF.

Team members became politically conscious at a time when these traditions were at their nadir, and it is natural that they should have little regard for them. But "our" tradition has been there nevertheless. It has existed not only as a moment of conscience, a protest: it has also been historically *effective*. And this we must surely seek to continue, *as* an effective tradition, and not only as one of contemplation? (Hence my feeling that a truly internationalist review would feel the duty to carry urgent material on Cuba, the Federation, Katanga, &c which can be of some immediate service to our ill-informed labour movement.)

Moreover there are aspects of this contemplative bias which elude my comprehension. Two years ago John Hughes and Michael Barratt Brown contributed in programmatic form an alternative policy to the Common Market, which stressed the importance to Britain of increasing economic and political contacts with the Third World. The policies of positive neutrality and of general economic realignment where seen as running together. Both emphasized the common intersections of interest between the peoples of the "proletarian nations" and of Britain. Perhaps the programme required criticism and much development; and the authors were ready to attend to this. But this is one of several parts of the new left outlook which the Team has dropped without explanation; or with more explanation than in-group gossip implying that this kind of writing lacked "precision," "rigour," or academic reputability. Intellectual work, yes: but to what purpose? How bloody precious can you get? With the collapse of the Common Market negotiations, one would have thought that the new left was poised to enter the national discussion, with the basis for a programmatic alternative which would offer perspectives of long-term aid in the industrialization of Asia and Africa, and consequent major reorientation of British industry in ways impossible without socialist planning and controls? But here, as so often nowadays, I am simply left with a feeling of impotence . . . Why?

I fear that the preoccupation of the Team with the Third World is not only academic. It also contains a déracinée element, analogous to the ouvrierism current in some left intellectual circles in the Thirties, some of whose consequences were lampooned by Orwell. Third worldism of the Fanon type, psychologically comprehensible in Algeria and Angola, can be in London or Paris an emotional stance, an orientation which actually performs a disservice to that world itself.

Instead of aping "working class" manners and adopting "proletcult," it seems the fashion now will be to attach ourselves to peasant-revolutionary movements: adopt their dismissal of "the west": tolerate a mystique of violence, virility and simplicity, in which men can *only* find their humanity with a rifle in their hands aimed at a white face . . . and leave it to our insular, ill-informed, pragmatic comrades in the labour movement or CND to do what they can to carry on the effective, *active* internationalist tradition, on their own.

Marxism

THE THIRD WORLD orientation of the Team appears to me to be comprehensible but to be naïve and to be a new form of revolutionary romanticism. By contrast, there appears to be an attitude to socialist theory which is highly sophisticated, even scholastic. I have been told on several occasions that there is "no Marxist tradition" in England, which is patently untrue. At the same time, it is by no means clear what the Team (or the Editor) mean by Marxism. On one hand, we are led to suppose that Marxism exists, as a sophisticated, flexible, but ascertainable *system*, to which the review owes allegiance. This is suggested, e.g., in the note appended to Perry's third article on Angola. On the other hand, it is policy that many former contributors to the review (who consider themselves to be working within the Marxist tradition) should be replaced in favour of reputable academic writers, from without the Marxist tradition. The latter (it seems) can be assimilated with extraordinary ease to "Marxist" theory. Indeed, all that is "best" in bourgeois academic thought can be "taken over" by Marxists, just as if one took a brick out of one wall and put it in another. The only bricks which must be discarded are a) those of the old *NLR*, b) the "English empiricism."

For the record, there is a long and fairly vigorous Marxist tradition in England. It goes back at least to the 1880s and thereafter is unbroken. A few names apart, it does not become a powerful intellectual influence until the late Twenties. There is also a vigorous working-class tradition, from the SDF to various minority groups, and thence to the CP, NCLC, much trade union education, etc. It is impossible to teach a WEA class or attend a trades council or labour party without becoming aware of this continuing tradition. What is absent is not so much this tradition (I believe a good miners' school in Scotland, Yorkshire or South Wales could more than hold its own with its opposite numbers in France or Italy) as a certain kind of articulate tradition in Marxist journalism.

But for various reasons, and at several levels, the indirect influence of Marxism has been more powerful than the direct; and in this way it has saturated much supposedly "empirical" thinking. Both the SDF and the CP have served as transmission-belts, with an exceptionally high turnover of membership. Tens of thousands of people (literally) have had a Marxist schooling in these bodies, or in the Left Book Club and student societies, but have for one reason or another passed out dissatisfied at the other side. Many graduated in Marxism, and then became dissatisfied with the narrowness of political outlook, the inappropriateness of Leninist schema to Britain, and so on. (The same process has been going on in the past seven years, especially in the student socialist movement, where many have undergone intense attachments and disillusioning experiences with the Trotskyist sects.) Hence this is an important *pattern* in English (and Scottish) intellectual life; and the outcome is not only (as perhaps the Marxists of the Team suppose) a jejeune acquaintance with Marxism, followed by an abject relapse into "empiricism," "Fabianism," and other sins. (This of course is true in some cases.) It has also given rise to a Marxist-influenced eclecticism, in which many hundreds of individuals have retained certain Marxist notions, rejected others, and attempted to come to terms in their own way with the English empirical idiom. At a distinguished level you will find an eclectic variant of Marxist-plus-empiricist thinking (with a dash of this or that extraneous ingredient) in most disciplines: Cole, Laski, Titmuss, Briggs, Joan Robinson, Carr, Balogh, and many others come to mind. I have argued that Raymond offers an original variant of this eclecticism.

Several points follow. So far from our living in an island culture blissfully unaware of Marxism, our culture is sensitized to Marxist concepts in a hundred ways. (Examine, for example, the part played in the development of the ideas of either Keynes or Leavis by their encounter with Marxism: both what was rejected and what was not.) Some of the most formidable positions of established reaction are ones thrown up in polemics with Marxism. Hence it really is no good to suppose that Marxism is a banner with a strange and novel device, which will carry all before it. As a result of this long pattern of attraction and repudiation, Marxism is a position English intellectuals are wary of, and not only because the Congress for Cultural Freedom has sought to make it so. If the Team wishes to rescue Marxism from its disreputable associations with various forms of schematic or pejorative thinking, apologetics, etc., then to proclaim "Marxism" is not enough. It is necessary to be aware of, and to engage in polemic with, the various brands of "authentic Marxism" already on offer.

The position in the New Left has hitherto been fluid. We have included Marxisants, Marxist-influenced eclectics, Raymondists, and Marxists tout court. For the Team to proclaim *NLR* as a "Marxist" journal certainly indicates a change of tendency, and insofar as this may hasten definitions this may be welcome. If the Team has any desire, however, to carry the old Board with it, there must be a recognition that important differences of emphasis exist, which are based on something rather more than English muddle. In my view the coexistence of tendencies in *NLR* in the past was fruitful; and the various variants of English empiricism which have assimilated more or less of the Marxist tradition are of great interest—and possible points of growth. I would be sorry to see a magical invocation of Marxism in the pages of *NLR* if it is not accompanied by critical and controversial discussion of a number of Marxist theories—of class, ideology, basis and superstructure, historical agency, etc.

I also suspect the tendency to locate the Main Enemy in a thing called empiricism (which is three times worse if Fabian and unspeakable if English). When Tom Nairn describes empiricism as the "English Ideology" I think he is committing the error of confusing an idiom with an ideology. Quite different ideological tendencies will be found in England, now and in the past, which are all expressed in the empirical idiom; and equally analogous ideological positions will be found in England and in France, but expressed in very different idioms. I doubt whether Bacon, Adam Smith, Samuel Johnson, Hazlitt, William Morris, and Orwell, all of whom adopt this idiom, can be said to belong to one recognizable ideological tendency. But I can see very well how one can speak of utilitarianism and Fabianism as an ideological tendency; and this helps one at once to locate its leading ideas and their characteristic class bias. It is true that an idiom may have a disposition to favour certain ideological traits. Thus the French passion for global generalization encourages the déracinée, cosmopolitan character of its theory; while the empirical idiom favours theoretical evasiveness and insular resistances. I wonder, however, how far the Team is aware of empiricism's strengths? Granted that the idiom may cover up commonplace philistinism, torpor or idiocy; it may also conceal acute intelligence and theoretical toughness, of a kind which Teutonic and Parisian intellectuals commonly underestimate, but which Marx certainly noted with respect. And this leads to three further points:

i. I wish we were less obsessed with empiricism and more concerned with *bourgeois ideology*.

ii. While it is true that there has been a powerful attempt in the past 20 years to erect empiricism *into* an ideology (or an end-of-ideology)—an attempt largely furthered by disenchanted Central European intellectuals who have lodged in academic posts in Oxford, LSE etc, from which they have tried to annex our idiom and offer it as a *system*, discovered by the practical ingenuity of the obtuse Anglo-Saxons but requiring Hungarian or Teutonic genius to make articulate—I see no bloody reason why we should cede this idiom to them. I regard the Poppers, Berlins et al., as systematic bourgeois ideologists masquerading as empiricists (under the supposed "neutrality" this brings); and as a confirmed Englishman I don't see why we shouldn't blast them in our own national idiom of we choose to

iii. The attempt to reject altogether this idiom, and substitute for it another imported from France or Italy, will, I fear, be self-isolating.

When it is said that there is "no Marxist tradition" here, what is really implied is that we do not have a certain kind of highly sophisticated and subtle tradition of Marxist exegesis. To the degree that this is to be found in Europe, many of us must plead guilty to some intellectual insularity. And we can readily agree that it is admirable if windows are opened, and if many different idioms and accents are heard. But I must also offer some reservations, which will undoubtedly consign me everlastingly to the category of "English parochialism":

i.   I hope selection will be made according to the cogency and availability of the ideas and not according to some abracadabra. That is, I hope we do not find a new kind of intellectual in-group, which has its private passwords, comprising references not to specific ideas but to authors and texts available only to an elite of readers.

ii. I am interested in the principles of selection. That is, I hope that sublimity of Hegelian paradox will not take precedence over concreteness and relevance. Perry has said on more than one occasion that the review must find room for a confluence of influences and has instanced the old legend that Marxism, like some turnip-mutation, had three roots—English economics, German philosophy, and French socialism. There is now a disposition to look for a new Trinity—perhaps in Italian Marxism, French existentialism, and American academic sociology. I can't see why. I am as interested in the unsystematic humanism of Tiber Dary as in the impressive systematizing of Lukacs, in the humanist revisionism of Kolakowski as in the "premature" revisionism of Gramsci. One might equally well offer some other Trinity, or even Quadrinity—why not Polish humanism, Italian Marxism, Viennese psychology, and . . . dare one say it? . . . English historical-empiricism. I am *not* arguing for the exclusion of anything: I am simply saying that we should not overlook the fact that *some* selective principles will be operative.

iii. Here goes. While most of us owe something to Sartre, and will be well advised to learn more, I hope most emphatically that we shall not be asked to ape the *déracinée* marxistentialism of certain Sartian extravaganzas. If we are going to borrow ideas from these circles, I hope *NLR* will also carry a sharply critical, indeed polemical, view of the historical role of the Sartre circle. I write while still infuriated by Sartre's foreword to Fanon's book. Where Sartre writes so elegantly about European narcissism, his own circle would appear to be the ultimate in this: if Paris is the city which talks incessantly about itself, what are we to say of this circle? Of its introverted intellectual life? Of its profound political irresponsibility, in initiating this or that impulse or movement for which it takes no responsibility, and which (very likely) it will subject to bitter attack the next year? Of its *grandiose mondiale* pronouncements? Of its failure to support the real left movements in France?

Of its emotional parasitism upon the drama of revolution, its refurbishing of neo-Sorelian mystiques of violence? Of its preoccupation with mammoth intellectual apologies? Of its continual tendency towards the *intellectualiza-tion* of issues—that is, the neurosis of the intellectually déracinée, who sees each issue in the real world not as a challenge to understanding (and through understanding to action and control) but as an occasion for literary efferves-cence, pirouettes of intellectual agility? Who finds even in torture material for Hegelian antitheses? Who must answer to no movement, no collective, for what is said, but only to the sublime right of French intelligentsia to speak for *la conscience mondiale*? And who now (judging by Sartre and Fanon) are performing the ultimate *trahison des clercs*, acting as the elegiac prophets of a new mystique, in which humanism can be regained only through colonial and civil wars, and in which the last duty of western intellectuals is to cel-ebrate the effeteness of their torture-vitiated culture and announce its super-session by the culture of the Third World—the more bitter, tormented, virile or barbaric the better? Or perhaps I exaggerate: for this surely will not be the last duty undertaken by Sartre? When civilization is finally annihilated in nuclear war, he will surely be spared at least long enough to write 40,000 words on the ultimate paradox of alienation?

I don't suppose that this is all that can be said of Sartre. We all admire some part of him. But I put it down, because I can detect the same tendencies to derac-ination and intellectualization, in the name of a higher socialist theory, in our own circles. Higher it may be. Socialist it is not.

I also hope for some clarification of the assumption that, while the review is not "Marxist," the most diverse colloquy of academic writers in non-Marxist and anti-Marxist traditions should be encouraged: and that their contributions can be simply slotted into its pages, so that thereby the "best" of bourgeois thought can be appropriated to Marxism. The policy of openness I accept. Equally, it seems to me that the assimilation of ideas which emerge in one tradition into another tradition requires arduous and discriminating work. To pursue this fur-ther would lead on to an enquiry as to the Team's attitude to some academic sociology. I am of course aware that one test of the vitality of the Marxist tradi-tion will be found in its response to much contemporary sociology. The point is—how critical will this response be? I hope it will not consist in maintaining a patina of Marxist terminology (or neo-Hegelian terminology) while falling spell-bound before some current academic notations of class, social conflict and structure. This enquiry I am not competent to pursue, al though I am confident that the enquiry must soon be made. I am ready myself to argue it only in rela-tion to the theory of class, and in particular in relation to Dahrendorf, which I consider to be a profoundly anti-historical, and thereby anti-Marxist, work.

I will conclude this section with a more personal note. I belong to an intellectual grouping, which gave its political allegiance to the CP in the late Thirties or early Forties, but which was nonetheless repelled by the alien and schematic manner and matter of its thinking. Since the conditions of CP intellectual life discouraged controversy, the form which our "premature revisionism" took was to accentuate the "Englishness" of our preoccupations. One reason why some of us turned to the field of English history, sociology and economics was in an effort to connect Marxist ideas with British contexts and to humanize and make concrete the abstract schema of Communist orthodoxy. (I suspect that Raymond's return to the tradition of "Culture and Society" and Hoggart's preoccupation with working-class mores stemmed from a related impulse: we were all, in different ways, reacting against the déracinée elements of the Thirties which Orwell lampooned.) It can be argued that not insularity but an excess of international preoccupation has been a vice of the English left intelligentsia. Given the world of the 20th century this is understandable. Spain, fascism in Europe, the European resistance, the Soviet Union (in allegiance or in disenchantment), Korea, Hungary, Cuba all these names indicate not only real events but the great inner crises and traumas of the English left. And for this reason some of us have accentuated "Englishness" (or Scottishness or Welshness) as a "brake," a corrective, a control. It is sad to find that our preoccupations are caricatured as mere parochialism; and especially so, when it seems that the old cycle of errors is to be repeated, albeit in more sophisticated forms.

For indeed it *always* seems that events are more "real," more critical, more urgent, outside of this stubborn, tradition-bound, equable island. (Even violence erupting in Notting Hill or fake fascists on the stump provokes a response of delight from our déracinée young Communists and Trotskyists—here at last is something "real," something that fits their "schema.") And yet the *difference*, the lack of violence—might this not matter too? Might it not (*sotto sotto voce*) even have some soupcon to offer to the discourse of international socialism? While we strain to catch the idioms of the Third World, of Paris, of Poland, of Milan, might there not be a growing discourse around us, pregnant with possibilities, not only for us but for other peoples? But this discourse is strange; we can scarcely interpret it; it is in an idiom, which we have ceased to understand. It comes from a philistine subculture. It is mere English. It has no articulate spokesmen—they are all kneeling in the presence of other, more sophisticated, voices.

Attention, internationalists and intellectual workers! The old mole, revolution, may still be at work in Battersea and Fife, in Tynesdde and Ebbw Vale. It may manifest itself in conflicts far removed from your schema; it peeps from the edges of TWTWTW [*This Was the Week That Was*]; it turns up in Parliament Square on successive days; it moves along the oh so contemptible and a-theoretical youngsters who despite all obituaries still vaguely inhabit CND. Alas, we have no colons to shoot (and thereby to attain to our humanity); no peasants to shoot us; no campesinos who can bring revolution to our towns. But the towns themselves? Perhaps something "real" could happen even in them, even in Britain? Perhaps if we turn away from our own people, this might be the worst way in which we could also betray the First, the Second and the Third World?

Socialist Humanism

FOR THERE IS ONLY one world. And socialist humanism is about the unity of socialist theory. It seeks, through all the diversities of context, of sociological and cultural determinants, to articulate the common voice of world socialism.

I doubt weather socialist humanism can be usefully defined, but the attempt must be made again and again. If reduced to a set of propositions it becomes at once abstract and utopian. If we abandon the effort for one moment we fall victims to the *realpolitik* of determinism. It reveals itself as much in the form of a fruitful quarrel between agency and determinism, aspiration and context, people as they are and as they might be, as in any systematic theory. It postulates the validity and importance of forms of perception and of moral growth which have not, hitherto, been successfully formulated in Marxist schema. As a position in the world today it is most evident as a critique of other alternatives. Indeed, it exists by virtue of a continuing polemic, on the one hand with Communist orthodoxy, and on the other hand with liberal and social-democratic ideology. It is distinguished by a particular sensitivity to the arguments of *realpolitik*, of determinism, and of scholastic mystification, which lead towards ideological complicity with either of the opposing ideologies.

I will seek to illustrate this by one example. I have suggested that Fanon, and more heinously Sartre, offer an apologia for a new mystique of violence, *Les Damnées de la Terre* is a book which commands the most sympathetic attention; when one recalls the context from which it has sprung, it appears not only comprehensible but inevitable. The damned can discover their own humanity only in absolute rebellion against the *colons*, the imperialist power, and in repudiating the ideology and culture of the West:

When the peasant takes a gun in his hands, the old myths grow dim and the prohibitions are one by one forgotten. The rebel's weapon is the proof of his humanity. For in the first days of the revolt you must kill: to shoot down a European is to kill two birds with one stone, to destroy an oppressor and the man he oppresses at the same time: there remain a dead man, and a free man ... (Sartre)

The notion here of course is not new. The outcast and the violent has always had its appeal to the intellectual. But the idea can be seen firmly in place, early in the Marxist tradition. When describing the unspeakable conditions of the British proletariat in 1844, Engels wrote:

> They can maintain their consciousness of manhood only by cherishing the most glowing hatred, the most unbroken inward rebellion against the bourgeoisie in power. They are men so long only as they burn with wrath against the reigning class. They become brutes the moment they bend in patience under the yoke.

In their elevation of the humanist values of revolutionary pride, Marx and Engels rarely glorify violence as such. It is true that they saw as a weakness in the English tradition the absence of the purgative experiences of an advanced bourgeois-democratic revolution ("One sees what a revolution is good for, after all!") They also assume (though this is implicit rather than explicit in Marx's passionate humanism) that the morality of the oppressed would prove superior to that of the oppressors. At some places they suggest a relativistic morality, at others they suggest ulterior criteria, a "fully human" morality.

The ambiguity of the Marxist tradition on this should be familiar. The socialist humanist must surely insist that the experiences of the 20th century demand something more than ambiguity? The revolutionary humanism of 1917, of the march of the Chinese 8th Route Army, and of the Yugoslav partisan movement—these were formative influences upon many of us. (I suspect that we were moved by Raid's *Seven Days* or Davidson's *Partisan Picture* in similar ways to those in which readers are moved by Fanon today.) I cannot see how anyone can be in any serious sense a socialist humanist who has not been profoundly moved by these experiences, and by the Cuban and Algerian revolutions. (It is exactly the myopia, the failure of response, and the complicity with imperialism which is one of our profoundest causes of disagreement with the Fabian tradition—some of whose exponents, ironically, the Team are now anxious to woo to the review in order to hasten the displacement of the old guard.)

But the point is that an admiring, committed response to revolutionary humanism is surely, in 1963, not enough? We cannot permit Sartre to mystify us with one part of Marxist revolutionary morality, wrested from context, and diluted from Sorelian solution. For the lesson of the 20th century is not only that humanism is discovered in revolutionary struggle; anti-humanism is discovered there also. Out of the logic of revolutionary struggle there arises that discipline, that embattled ideology, those quasi-military forms, which endanger the humanism of the revolution itself. All this is (or ought to be) too familiar to bear repetition. To accept the necessity for Algerians or Angolans of this revolutionary dedication is one thing; to glorify it is yet another; to fail to state what is known of its dangers and putative consequences is another again. If we accept (as indeed I do) that for the enslaved the moment of violent rebellion is also a moment of the attainment of richer human attributes, we are surely not tricked into believing that rebellion, gun in hand, is the *only* measure of the attainment of humanity? (After all, in important ways, Lawrence's novels or de Beauvoir's *Second Sex* are also about the attainment of humanity—and not only by means of the rebellion of the "oppressed" against the "oppressor"?)

The Sartre example may not be a good one, but it fell at hand. In this case, the critique of socialist humanism would appear to be directed both against the judgement of revolutionary violence by absolutist liberal criteria (which would effectively deliver the colonial peoples into the hands of their oppressors) and against the glorification of that necessity, which, while being humanly liberating within that context, is nevertheless a regrettable necessity, in the light of ulterior "fully human" criteria, not least because of the perpetuation of violent and authoritarian forms among the liberated peoples. Do we really—always and automatically—advocate agrarian-revolutionary solutions in Latin America? (One should surely remember the failures as well as the successes in this course: for example, the thousands of casualties in Luis Carlos Prestes' abortive Brazilian revolt of the 1920s?) Or, to turn the "schema" round, have the Indian people *not* attained "humanity" because they were not given the chance to discover it in armed rebellion? And (while I am irritated by some of the Direct Actionist hagiography about Ghandi) are we to dismiss the non-violent traditions of struggle *tout court*?

I have tried to indicate one example of the critique which stemmed from positions shared by most of us in the former New Left. I am conscious that our essays in definition were inadequate. This inadequacy is however no excuse for abandoning the work. If a younger, more brilliant generation was now emerging, which was addressing itself to this with better equipment, I would be happy to retire quietly from the scene. But since this is not the case, and our positions are simply being evacuated and forgotten, then it is necessary for a few of us to continue, with such clumsy equipment as we have. In my view, the work of definition can leave one with only a fragile sense of identification with any single "Marxist" tradition, since it involves discriminating between relativist and ulterior criteria in Marx's own thought; rejecting altogether the metaphor of basis and superstructure; maintaining a constant watchfulness against falling back into the cardinal sin of latter-day Marxism—reductionism, or historical and sociological determinism; walking a veritable tight-rope between notions of free agency and those of determinism; reconstructing an historical model in which greater autonomy is granted to "cultural" agencies (varying in degree from one context to another), while at the same time recalling that cultural agencies are themselves in some degree determined—i.e. maintaining and developing the Marxist concept of ideology. This and much more. We must have a House of Theory; but we must also be allowed to discuss the architect's plans.

Nor is this a purely speculative concern. Nor one whose consequences will only become apparent in many years time. It is a living concern, as the continuing conflict between post-Stalinist and humanist revisionism in the Communist world demonstrates month by month. And we ourselves are more than observers. Our ideas have found their way into that discourse in the past and they could do so again. Those who continue the contest (or are silenced) in the East are our direct allies. Potentially also, there appears to be much in the consciousness of the Third World which could give to socialist humanism new notations and great force. Socialist humanism has always entailed the belief that in totally different contexts, the humanists in the Communist world and the revolutionary or left socialists in the "west" are pursuing the common objective of a humane and democratic socialist society, in which, in one way or another, the paternalist and manipulative forms give way to the initiatives of "self-activity." The closer one gets to the real context of political life (for example, the conflict between neutralists and CP members in a CND branch; or the problems of forming a new kind of Left in the miners union or the ETU), the less abstract this talk of socialist humanism appears, the more urgent the work of definition, and the more difficult the work of definition and of programmatic relevance.

What I cannot accept is the notion that we of the tired and guilty "West" have nothing to offer, no right to engage in this international discourse. To be sure, one responds to Fanon: how else could such a man, in such a context, write?:

Leave this Europe where they are never done talking of Man, yet murder men everywhere they find them, at the corner of every one of their own streets, in all the corners of the globe. For centuries they have stifled almost the whole of humanity in the name of a so-called spiritual experience. Look at them today swaying between atomic and spiritual disintegration. [. . .] That same Europe where they were never done talking of Man, and where they never stopped proclaiming that they were only anxious for the welfare of Man: today we know with what sufferings humanity has paid for every one of their triumphs of the mind.

Come, then, comrades, the European game has finally ended; we must find something different. [. . .] Europe now lives at such a mad, reckless pace that she has shaken off all guidance and all reason, and she is running headlong into the abyss; we would do well to avoid it with all possible speed.

But I do not accept that we belong to this "West" of torturers and their accomplices. And for us, the "European game" can never be finished. We owe allegiance neither to the West of NATO nor to the East of Khruschev. If "our" tradition has failed (although it has not always and altogether failed—fascism was defeated, India did achieve freedom, the Poles and Yugoslavs have edged forwards), then it is for us to put it in repair. Our work may be exceptionally difficult and unrewarding; it may be easy to suppose ourselves bypassed by "history," that the humanist values discovered in the West are corrupted beyond recall, that they are doomed to perish with a "dying culture." And intellectuals are often tempted to surrender to the Established Fact, or to abdicate in favour of the barbaric vigour of a "lower" or simpler culture—the mystique of the national consensus ouvrierism and proletcult, the cult of the Third World, or the cult of the practical common sense of the Labourist workingman. As the culture of the "West" disintegrates, so the temptations of petty or grand intellectual treasons will multiply, and traditions must be defended, as they have been defended in Belsen and Siberia and Budapest in the past. They must be defended up to the last moment of their ultimate refutation: the refutation of humanism through nuclear war. And if we defect, that refutation moves closer to us. It takes hold of our elbows and begins to guide our pens.

We must continue to work, at the point where intellectual integrity and responsibility to the real movement intersect. That is to say: in the spirit of Marx.

Britain and Ourselves

AS IT HAPPENS I am not satisfied by this legend of the finished West. I think that it is not beyond possibility that an advanced capitalist nation might effect a transition to socialism; and to a socialist society of a very different type to any known hitherto. This is not, in the immediate future, *likely*. But it is *possible*. And our expectations of this score are much confused by irrelevant models of the nature of such a transition, none of which are adequate to our own context and possibilities.

Of West European nations, the two where this possibility seems most evident are Italy and Britain. The British situation is extraordinarily complex, and almost every factor which might make one sanguine might equally, with a slight shift in the balance of forces, militate against success. Paradoxically, the very things which make Britain hopeful are those which create the greatest perplexity when we attempt to analyse our situation by any existing Marxist "categories." There is the peculiar way in which the rhetoric of one era becomes the effective political consensus of the next, so that the very flexibility of ruling groups in retreating before mass pressure at the same time brings on its heels the conditions for their next withdrawal. (This is to phrase, in different terms, Raymond's emphasis upon the patterns of "growth" in our social life.) There is the fact that

244   *E. P. Thompson and the Making of the New Left*

the very" insularity" of the British experience between the wars left the Labour movement less bitterly divided than in Europe. There is the interesting strength of Marxist-influenced empiricism, which I have indicated. There is the imme- diate predicament of British capitalism, accentuated by the Common Market crisis. There is the way in which quasi-autonomous cultural influences (for example, through the educational system) are themselves changing the pattern of political expectations. There is the dialectic by which the rhetoric of "oppor- tunity" and classlessness might prefigure the emergence of a new type of "class consciousness," in which it is not inconceivable that salaried, professional and wage-earning strata might discover a common sense of identity as between "the people" and as against isolated centers of financial power and "vested interest": i.e. a "populist" or Jeffersonian radical consciousness, but on a higher level, and within a context in which a socialist resolution alone is possible. (I may suggest that this thesis of mine, in "Revolution Again," has perhaps been dismissed too summarily.) There is the importance of the whole CND-moralist revolt, which, it seems to me, the Editor and the Team very much undervalue—although, para- doxically, they are mutants of this same revolt.

These points are no more than shorthand, and one is more than aware of the negative evidence: in particular, the inadequacy of the existing labour move- ment as an instrument of change. The other great inadequacy, however, lies in the very field of theoretical and programmatic work which, it is supposed, offers our own *raison d'être*. And this is, finally, why I can no longer take much interest in *NLR* as it now stands. I wish it well, I hope it continues. But it is my experience that there is a lack of knowledge and concern with British problems, a lack of any real sense of the possibilities and growing-points within the British scene, com- bined with a lack of collective spirit of a kind which (by linking with the knowl- edge and approaches of the older Board) might remedy the former weaknesses. Indeed, there is a real resistance to many of those comrades who first built the New Left and who remain, in my opinion, the most responsible comrades, either as contributors or advisors, in certain fields. It is not sufficient to explain this as a conflict of generations. The socialist tradition should surely not be reduced to a three-generation novel, complete with Victorian Papas and Oedipal revolts? Until the last Board I think the older members of the Board were restrained in their interventions, and warm in their encouragements: perhaps too much so. I am not prepared to see advisors and contributors, who have fought repeated and difficult struggles both intellectually (yes: against Fabianism, imperialism, Stalinism *and* pseudo-empiricism) and in the real movement, displaced accord- ing to some haphazard and eclectic and undisclosed scale of preferences—and perhaps (if I understand the current drift) replaced by academics, Fabians and others, who have a greater reputability. I do not want the review surrounded by ideological barbed-wire, and I have long favoured more openness. But what appears to me to be happening is very different: a sophisticated accommodation with Communist orthodoxy in the international matters, an accommodation with Fabianism at home. I think that we have deserved better than this. We have never expected our positions to go unchallenged: we have been ready to face polemic: and ready to engage in collective work and discussion. It is not the Team but ourselves who may demand some explanations.

The defence of socialist humanist positions is so important in principle; and the development of the theoretical and programmatic writing on British problems is so important both in principle and in practice, that it might be well if those who think generally as I disengaged from the review. This would enable the Team to get ahead with its nine-headed work, whatever they think this to be. It would free the center of the review from tensions (perhaps)—we no longer have a socialist collaboration, and we may soon have nothing but a mutual frustration. It might, equally, free those of us who do not disengage from our frustrations, and so enable us to reconsider how our own work can best be continued.

If it is thought valuable for the two groups to maintain some loose contact—such as occasional theoretical discussions—I am certainly not opposed to this. But, in the end, if one thinks as I do, some way *must* be found for continuing our work. And this is now urgent. Internationalist and national concerns now intersect at so many points: the predicament of British capitalism and the needs of the Third World both intersect in a policy of trade realignment which is being forced upon the consideration even of orthodox bourgeois economists: such a policy of realignment intersects also with the CND thrust towards positive neutrality, and might underpin it; at the very least such a policy (with the accompanying problem of unemployment) will demand controls and planning of a character which, under a Labour Government, can be given an increasingly socialist complexion; the accompanying tensions and transitions are likely to make general political consciousness more alert. It is difficult for me to understand how far removed the Team must be from the real life-situations of millions of working people, that they reacted with surprise—even incomprehension—when several of us challenged Buchanan's talk of "affluence." Further, the standards of our people can only be properly assessed when we do this within the context of the *possibilities* of life within existing society, and the *denial* of these possibilities in a hundred ways: it is exactly at these points of denial that one can see the growing-points of the new movement. However unsystematic Stuart's NLR may have been, it never ceased to explore these frustrations and these growing-points. And exactly at this time, when the accredited party of the ruling-class faces a crisis of public confidence comparable to 1906, a number of unresolved problems are forcing themselves into public consciousness: unemployment: housing and social problems: wages and salary policy: educational problems: problems of the control of the media: of the rationalization of British industry, and of the humane priorities involved. All these will prove a forcing-house for social enquiry of a kind which was seen in the 1880s and 1930s.

What is surely required—and here I burn my last boat—is that socialists of our kind should now be somewhat more plain-spoken and less clever: more willing to break our demands down into programmes: more willing to defend our positions, and less willing to drop them at the first hint that they aren't respectable, or that something *far* more clever has been published in Paris or said in Balliol. In other words, we should be willing to put our boots into the British scene and walk around among British people, listen to them a bit more; have a touch of humility before their experience, without a precious fear that the least contact with programmes or slogans will soil our intellectual integrity.

It is a question of emphasis. I don't wish theoretical problems to be evaded—we have always needed at least two kinds of journal. But now we can surely see British people bumping up against facts: and we should surely be in there with them, helping to draw conclusions. Because if in our muddled way we were able to break or grow through to a new kind of socialist society, this would be an event of comparable importance for Europe with 1789. The logic of the Cold War would be broken at its most sensitive point—that there is Communism or Capitalism and Nothing Else. Indeed, I am ready to say again: it is this or nothing. There will be no way out of the Cold War, except through the consummation of fire, unless somewhere in the advanced capitalist world, one nation can move. From the very pervasity of historical development, that nation might be our own. If we fail to enlarge what slender possibilities there are, we fail ourselves *and* we fail the world. For whatever gulf there may be between the "proletarian nations" and the "old rich ones," both will burn in the same fires.

No, Jean Paul, we are not finished. True, we no longer have the least moral claim on hegemony. But, right or no right, the world is tied in a contradiction, one of whose knots lies across London, Paris, and Rome. And English Socialists! Insular, moralistic, empirical, affluent, compromised—nevertheless, three worlds might be waiting for us!

THOMPSON WOULD SAY THAT MORRIS "SEIZED" HIM; ONE result was his 900-page study, *William Morris: Romantic to Revolutionary*, 1955, revised in 1976. Morris remained with him; in the 1976 edition, looking back on the 1950s, Thompson wrote, "I found, perhaps, the will to go on arguing from the pressure of Morris behind me." In this lecture to the William Morris Society in 1959 at the Hall of the Art Workers Guild in London, Thompson said: "Morris was one of our greatest men, because he was a great revolutionary; a profoundly cultured and humane revolutionary, but not the less a revolutionary for this reason. Moreover, he was a man working for practical revolution. It is this which brings the whole man together."

The Communism of William Morris

When I received an invitation to lecture to this Society I thought that the occasion might provide me with an opportunity to do two things which will, I hope, be not only of personal interest. First, I wish *to* look back at my own book on Morris (*William Morris, Romantic to Revolutionary:* Lawrence & Wishart, 1955) and to comment on a few matters of detail arising since its publication. Second, to review—in a much wider sense—the assessment of Morris' Communism in that book.

One cannot live for seven years in William Morris' company without becoming intensely absorbed, not only in his work and ideas, but also in the problem of their presentation and interpretation in the contemporary world. And, sooner or later, we in the William Morris Society must pay more attention to some of these more technical problems. We must assist in the preparation of a scholarly bibliography of Morris' work. We should take due note of the fact that many of his lectures and essays remain unpublished. I do not think that we require a complete unabridged edition of every line William Morris wrote, every occasional piece, every Note in *Commonweal,* every lecture. These writings inevitably repeat one other; nor does it enchance the memory of a great man to reproduce ephemera. But, still, there are fine passages from his lectures which are available only in ms., and others available only in *William Morris, Artist, Writer, Socialist* or in my own book. A selection of socialist essays and writings, based on a thorough and scholarly perusal of all the sources, might meet with a most exciting response from the younger generation. Who more than Morris combined anger with maturity, who had a richer historical understanding of the devices and resources of the Establishment?

The question of the letters is more difficult. Mr Philip Henderson did a notable service in bringing forward his selection: it is a wise selection and well presented. But surely we shall need soon a more comprehensive collection— not a complete one (it would be foolish to publish all those scrappy notes dunning League branches to pay up their subs which are preserved in the files at Amsterdam, or the little notes arranging family arrivals and departures which are in the British Museum); but a more comprehensive collection, with rather more *apparatus scholasticus*, is still required. The question is: at what time should the work be commenced? New letters still appear from time to time; an edition prepared today could not hope to be definitive. And yet, if the work is not commenced soon, material may be lost. The most notable additions since Mr Henderson's selection are: (1) the letters to Glasse, published by the *Labour Monthly*; (2) the letters to the late Fred Henderson, published in an appendix to my book; (3) the important letter to Faulkner on sexual relations, preserved in the Bodleian, and also published in my book. I also draw upon some scores of unpublished letters in the Walthamstow and British Museum bequests, but these had been well sieved by Mr Henderson before me.

Since my book was published a few more have come to my knowledge. Some letters to Joseph Lane have now been released in the British Museum (from the Burns Collection), but they add nothing material to the story I have given. There are letters of Morris on the Eastern Question in the Bryce papers at Oxford, which I overlooked. Some new papers of the Socialist League have come into the possession of Mr Chimen Abramsky. I have turned up two or three new letters myself, in Labour periodicals of the time. The most interesting was published in the *Labour Leader* (18 April, 1903), and then lost to view.[1] It is written to the Rev. William Sharman, Unitarian Minister and member of the Socialist League, in 1886 or 1887:

My Dear Sharman,

I believe I shall be about on the 28th. I shall be pleased to see you at my house if you can come; but let me have notice.

As to the matter of education, it is after all a difficult one to settle, until people's idea of the family are much changed; but in the meantime here is the problem: How is it possible to protect the immature citizen from the whims of his parents? Are they to be left free to starve his body or warp his mind by all sorts of nonsense; if not, how are they to be restrained? You see that one supposes in a reasonable community that experience will have taught the community some wisdom in such matters; but the parents may, and probably will, lack this experience. Well, then, hasn't the young citizen a right to claim his share of the advantages which the community have evolved? Must he be under the tyranny of two accidental persons? At present the law says yes, which means that the young citizen is the property of the two accidental persons.

Putting myself in the position of the immature citizen, I protest against this unfairness. As for myself, being the child of rich persons, it did not weigh heavily on me, because my parents did as all right people do, shook off the responsibility of my education as soon as they could; handing me over first to nurses, then to grooms and gardeners, and then to a school—a boy farm, I should say. In one way or another I learned chiefly one thing from all these—rebellion, to wit. That was good; but, look you, if my parents had been poorer, and had had more character, they would have probably committed the fatal mistake of trying to educate me. I have seen the sad effects of this with the children of some of my friends.

On the whole, experience has shown me that the parents are the *unfit-test* persons to educate a child; and I entirely deny their right to do so, because that would interfere with the right of the child, as a member of the community from its birth, to enjoy all the advantages which the community can give it. Of course, so far as grown people are concerned, I quite agree with your view of complete freedom to teach anything that anyone will listen to. But for children, I feel that they have as much need for the revolution as the proletarians have. As to the woman matter, I do not think Bax puts it unreasonably in his article,[2] though I have heard him exaggerate that in talk, and have often fallen foul of him. Let me know what you think of it.

Mind you, I don't think this change in the family (or in religion) can be done by *force*. It is a matter of opinion, and must come of the opinion of people free economically. I rely on the stomach for bringing it about.

Yours fraternally,

—WILLIAM MORRIS

And there may yet be letters of greater interest to be found: notably, letters from earlier years may be in the papers of the Baldwin and Price families, to which Mr Henderson failed to gain access. In the socialist years, the two infuriating blanks are Bax and Faulkner. Morris wrote some of his most intimate and revealing letters to Faulkner. We know that these were preserved after the death of both men—they were shown to Mackail, jottings on them exist in Mackail's notebook at Walthamstow, and very brief extracts appear in his book. Then Mackail returned them—to whom? To Faulkner's sister? But how is it that the one letter now available—that on sexual relations—came to be preserved in the Bodleian? My enquiries as to the descendants of Faulkner met with no success. But here is a man who spans the whole arch of Morris' active life—from Oxford days, through the Firm, alongside Morris in Anti-Scrape and alongside him in the League. Perhaps some other enquirer—more persistent than I, closer to Oxford and to London—might still meet with success?

The case of Bax is not so important. We know that he preserved certain letters of Morris, for he quotes them in his autobiography. He is not likely to have excluded anything of major value—and yet we cannot be sure. With so many other sources to pursue, I never followed up this track. If a more comprehensive edition of the letters is to be prepared, then it must be done.

What other fresh information has come to light in the past five years? I will mention two matters, and then I have done with the first part of this "review." First, a little more has come out—from the Gladstone papers and from a manuscript at the Manchester Reference Library—about the business of the Poet Laureateship: the amusing enquiries and Gladstonian annotations which reveal why Morris, as a self-confessed Communist with undesirable associations, was deemed unsuitable as the Troubadour of the Empress Brown. Second, we now have available the Lafargue correspondence, between Engels and Paul and Laura Lafargue, published recently in Paris. This correspondence, which fills in Engels' running commentary on League affairs, adds very little to the picture which I have given of the movement in the 1880s: the most revealing passages concern the background to the formation of the Second International. They do, however, force me to say that—in my desire to pay tribute to two very great men—I was less than honest in my appraisal of the difference in outlook which divided them. As in several of the letters already known, Engels' tone towards Morris and the League is sharp: and the sharpness of tone is such that one cannot but accuse Engels of a failure to recognise the stature of the great socialist thinker in William Morris. Engels and Morris came from different traditions; but while Morris strained hard and successfully to understand and to absorb much of Engels' tradition, Engels made no comparable effort in Morris' direction. One cannot but feel that Marx, whose early ethical revolt was germane to the romantic tradition, and who retained his capacity for response (if highly critical response) to the romantic protest of Carlyle, would have sensed the greatness of William Morris in a way that Engels failed to do.

I am not trying to judge as between the two men. In matters of political strategy Engels was certainly Morris' master—his criticisms were often abundantly justified. But I am emphasising the degree of incompatibility between them: an incompatibility which, by various twists and turns of history, became perpetuated in the mainstream of the later Marxist tradition, and which made it incapable of absorbing the great enrichment of the ethical content of Communism which was Morris' unique contribution. Since it is this ethical tradition to which a younger generation of socialist revolutionaries are now returning, this should properly be our main concern.

I have in no way altered my opinion that—if we are to acknowledge William Morris as one of the greatest of Englishmen—it is not because he was, by fits and starts, a good poet; nor because of his influence upon typography; nor because of his high craftsmanship in the decorative arts; nor because he was a practical socialist pioneer; nor, indeed, because he was *all* these; but because of a quality which permeates all these activities and which gives to them a certain unity. I have tried to describe this quality by saying that Morris was a great moralist, a great moral teacher. It is in his moral criticism of society (and which of his actions in the decorative arts, or in Anti-Scrape, or the renewal of interest in Icelandic Saga, was not informed by a fundamental criticism of the way of life of his own time?)—and in the crucial position which this criticism occupies in our cultural history at the point of transition from an old tradition to a new[3]—that his greatness is to be found. And this greatness comes to its full maturity in the political writing and example of his later years. I have gained the feeling that— perhaps through fear of controversy and out of respect for admirers of William Morris who do not share his political convictions—this Society has tended to be reticent on this matter. But Morris was one of our greatest men, *because* he was a great revolutionary, a profoundly cultured and humane revolutionary, but not the less a revolutionary for this reason. Moreover, he was a man working for *practical* revolution. It is this which brings the whole man together. It is this which will make his reputation grow as the years advance.

English revolutionaries in the past 100 years have been men without a Revolution. At times they have convinced themselves of the Revolution's imminence. H. M. Hyndman, when he founded the Social Democratic Federation in 1882, looked forward to 1889 as the probable date of its commencement. For a time Morris (whose thinking was greatly influenced by the Paris Commune) shared this cataclysmic outlook. But when he founded the Socialist League in 1884 he had already grown more reticent: "Our immediate aim should be chiefly educational . . . with a view to dealing with the crisis if it should come in our day, or of handing on the tradition of our hope to others if we should die before it comes."

Five years later again, when writing *News from Nowhere*, Morris postponed the commencement of the Revolution to 1952. In the sixty years that would intervene he foresaw much "troublesome and wearisome action," leading to the triumph of "demi-semi-Socialism," which would improve the *condition* of the working class while leaving its *position* unchanged. At the end of this vista of reform he still saw an ultimate revolutionary confrontation; and in one of his last lectures—delivered in 1895, the year before his death—he avowed:

I have thought the matter up and down, and in and out, and I cannot for the life of me see how the great change which we long for can come otherwise than by disturbance and suffering of some kind. . . . We are living in an epoch where there is combat between commercialism, or the system of reckless waste, and communism, or the system of neighbourly common sense. Can that combat be fought out . . . without loss and suffering? Plainly speaking I *know* that it cannot.

He was a revolutionary without a Revolution; more than that, he *knew* that he did not live within a revolutionary context. He did not, like Cromwell, have Revolution thrust upon him; nor did he, like Lenin, build a dedicated party within a society whose revolutionary potential was apparent. In the eyes of his opponents he was the very type of the socialist "trouble-maker" or (as they would phrase it today) the maladjusted intellectual. He wanted to stir up revolt where no revolt was. He wanted to make contented men discontented, and discontented men into agitators of discontent: "It is to stir you up *not* to be content with a little that I am here tonight." And he spent his energy recklessly during the last fifteen years of his life, with the aim of creating a revolutionary tradition—both intellectual and practical—within a society unripe for Revolution.

This is, of course, the role for which the romantic poet is cast, and many have been content to dismiss Morris, the revolutionary, with this platitude. The late romantic poet, author of *The Earthly Paradise,* and the Utopian dreamer, author of *News from Nowhere,* are confused in the same sentimental—or irritable—portrait of baffled unpractical idealism.

The portrait is false. For one thing, the convention supposes an effervescent iconoclastic youth, succeeded by premature death or by a respectable and pedestrian middle-age. This was not the course of Morris' life. Certainly, he rebelled in his youth. It was a moral rebellion, stemming from the romantic tradition, nourished by Carlyle and Ruskin. The enemy was "bourgeoisdom and philistinism." The tilting-grounds in his "holy warfare against the age" were the visual arts. The battle was joined with fervour, but it had scarcely started when—as happened with more than one Victorian rebel—the enemy opened its ranks to receive him with acclaim. Morris, in his late thirties, seemed doomed to enter the family album of Victorian men of letters. That tedious poem, *The Earthly Paradise,* was taken into the bosom of that very "bourgeoisdom and philistinism" against which Morris had risen in revolt. So costly were the products of the Firm in the decorative arts that it was forced to depend upon the custom of the wealthy. And while the Morris fashions began to penetrate the drawing-rooms of the select, the Railway Age and the architects of Restoration continued to desecrate the outside world.

This was the first time that success spelt failure to Morris: he savoured the futility of his revolt like gall. "Am I doing nothing but make-belief then, something like Louis XVI's lock-making?" he asked. And—when supervising work in the house of the Northern iron-master, Sir Lowthian Bell—he turned suddenly upon his patron "like a wild animal" and declared: "I spend my life in ministering to the swinish luxury of the rich."

He repudiated success as other men repudiate calumny. He plunged into more intricate problems of craftsmanship at the Firm. He sustained his "hatred of modern civilization" by translating Icelandic Saga. He deliberately sat on his top hat. He launched his great campaign for the protection of ancient buildings. He opened his morning paper and was astonished to find that Britain was on the eve of a major war, on behalf of the Turkish Empire. His response was to become an agitator.

This agitation was to carry him, by way of an acute personal and intellectual crisis, into the embryonic socialist movement, which he joined in his fiftieth year. From this time forward he was to see war—whether overt, imperialist and bloody, or stealthy, respectable and bloodless—as the authentic expression of the Victorian ethos. It was from the circumstances of war that he was to draw one of his most evocative images of capitalist society:

Do not be deceived by the outside appearance of order in our plutocratic society. It fares with it as it does with the older forms of war, that there is an outside look of quite wonderful order about it; how neat and comforting the steady march of the regiment; how quiet and respectable the sergeants look; how clean the polished cannon . . . the looks of adjutant and sergeant as innocent-looking as may be; nay, the very orders for destruction and plunder are given with a quiet precision which seems the very token of a good conscience; this is the mask that lies before the ruined cornfield and the burning cottage, the mangled bodies, the untimely death of worthy men, the desolated home.

This second rebellion was at one and the same time the consummation of his youthful revolt and the genesis of a new revolutionary impulse within our culture. This time there was to be no reconciliation. The Victorian middle-class, which dearly loved an idealist reformer, was shocked not so much by his rebellion as by its practical form of expression. "Mr Morris . . . is not content to be heard merely as a voice crying in the wilderness," complained one aggrieved letter-writer, "he would disturb the foundations of society in order that a higher artistic value may be given to our carpets."

For Morris broke with the conventional picture of the rebellious romantic in another respect. In everything to which he turned his hand he demanded of himself *practical* mastery. As he turned to the dye-vat and to the loom, so he turned his hands to the work of making a Revolution. There is no work which he did not take upon himself. He spoke on open-air pitches, Sunday after Sunday, until his health broke down. He addressed demonstrations of miners and of the unemployed. He attended innumerable committee meetings. He edited *Commonweal*, and sold it in the streets. He appeared, as prisoner and as witness, in the police courts. "I can't help it," he answered a reproof from his closest friend, Georgie Burne-Jones. "The ideas which have taken hold of me will not let me rest. . . . One must turn to hope, and only in one direction do I see it—on the road to Revolution: everything else is gone."

And yet, for all this evidence of practical personal commitment cannot the charge of misguided romanticism still be sustained? While Morris accepted almost *in toto* the economic and historical analysis of Marx, he always avowed that his "special leading motive" in becoming a revolutionary socialist was "hatred of modern civilization." "It is a shoddy age," he roared at a *Clarion* reporter. "Shoddy is King. From the statesman to the shoemaker all is shoddy!" The reporter concealed his boots further beneath the table: "Then you do not admire the commonsense John Bull, Mr Morris?" "John Bull is a *stupid, unpractical oaf,*" was the reply. Nothing infuriated Morris more than the complacent philistinism of the "practical man," unless it was the complacent philistinism of the unpractical one. "That's an impossible dream of yours, Mr Morris," a clergyman once declared, "such a society would need God Almighty Himself to manage it." Morris shook his fist in reply: "Well, damn it, man, you catch your God Almighty—we'll have Him."

But as we draw further from his time, it is Morris, and not his critics, who appears as a realist. He was a healthy man, living in a neurotic society. I speak of *moral* realism, not the realism of the practical revolutionary. As leader of the Socialist League he made blunders enough—Engels had justification for his irritable characterisation of him, in private letters, as a "settled sentimental socialist." But Engels underestimated the vigour of that long tradition of moral criticism which was Morris' inheritance. With his rich historical experience, and his concrete response to social reality, Morris had astonishing insight into the lines of growth, the elements of decay, within his culture. In lectures, speeches, passing notes in *Commonweal,* he cast his eyes forward to our time. He foresaw (in 1887) that the opening up of Africa would lead to the ending of the Great Depression, followed by "a great European war, perhaps lengthened out into a regular epoch of war." He foresaw Fascism. He foresaw (and regretted) the Welfare State.

The enemy, as in his youth, was still "bourgeoisdom and philistinism." But now he stood appalled before the destructive urges which he sensed within the Victorian middle classes, whom—he said—"in spite of their individual good nature and banality, I look upon as a most terrible and implacable force": "The most refined and cultured people . . . have a sort of Manichean hatred of the world (I use the word in its proper sense, the home of man). Such people must be both the enemies of beauty and the slaves of necessity."

The utilitarian, competitive ethic he now saw as the ethic of Cain; he had always known that it murdered art, he had come to understand that it murdered man's dignity as a creator in his daily labour, he now discovered that it could murder mankind. He spoke in a lecture of "the strength of that tremendous organisation under which we live. . . . Rather than lose anything which really is its essence, it will pull the roof of the world down upon its head." He was consumed with the urgency of the socialist propaganda. If capitalism were not to be displaced by a clear-sighted constructive revolutionary movement, if it were to end in mere deadlock and blind insurrection, then "the end, the fall of Europe, may be long in coming, but when it does, it will be far more terrible, far more confused and full of suffering than the period of the fall of Rome."

In this tormented century such insights are worth more than a pedantic sneer. It is as if Morris had cast his eye over Gallipoli and Passchendaele, over purge and counter-purge, over concentration camps and scorched earth, over the tragedy of Africa and the other tragedies to come. At times one feels, indeed, that he deduced from the acquisitive ethic within class-divided society an Iron Law of Morality no less rigid than Lassalle's Iron Law of Wages. Into the maw of the Age of Commerce "honour, justice, beauty, pleasure, hope, all must be cast . . . to stave off the end awhile; and yet at last the end must come." He might have found the proof, the culminating logic, of such a Law in our own ingenious devices for annihilation.

Morris was sceptical—especially in his last years—as to the tendency towards the immiseration of the masses within capitalism. But he was convinced of the tendency towards the moral immiseration of the dominant classes. Whence was this terrible diagnosis derived? It came, by one road, from Carlyle's denunciation of a society where cash-payment is the sole nexus of man with man; by another road, from his own study of the conditions of nineteenth-century labour and productive relations; by yet another, from Marx's moral indignation, and its foundation in the manuscripts of the early 1840s. Morris did not use the term "alienation," which has regained currency today; but he was—and remains—our greatest diagnostician of alienation, in terms of the concrete perception of the moralist, and within the context of a particular English cultural tradition. From these economic and social relationships, this moral logic must ensue.

And this logic demanded that the ethic of atomised, acquisitive society be opposed by the ethic of community. As between these two there could be no shadow of compromise. It was this logic which drove Morris to the street-corners, to play the fool's part as revolutionary agitator in the complacent streets of Gladstone's England. And here we meet with the second great irony of Morris' career. For a second time his rebellion met with success; and for a second time success was flavoured with gall.

This is not to say that Morris' section of the movement—the Socialist League—was successful. It petered out into anarchist tomfoolery, leaving Morris stranded in his Hammersmith Socialist Society. But, indirectly, the propaganda helped to set a mass movement in motion: and, indeed, the direct political influence of Morris is often underrated. By the early 1890s men whom Morris had helped to convert were leading dynamic popular movements: Tom Mann and the new unions, Blatchford and *Clarion*, the Socialist Leaguers Jowett and Maguire, who were architects of the Yorkshire I.L.P. And yet this was not the success for which Morris had looked.

Here lies the dilemma of the revolutionary within a society unripe for revolution. If he stands aside from the main currents of social change, he becomes purist, sectarian, without influence. If he swims with the current, he is swept downward by the flow of reformism and compromise. In the 1880s Morris had hoped that the propaganda would "*make Socialists* . . . cover the country with a network of associations composed of men who feel their antagonism to the dominant classes, and have no temptation to waste their time in the thousand follies of party politics." At that time he was an uncompromising anti-parliamentarian. A parliamentary socialist party would, he thought, enter into a path of compromise and opportunism: it would "fall into the error of moving earth and sea to fill the ballot boxes with Socialist votes which will not represent Socialist *men*." The "rollicking opportunism" of the Fabians, and especially of Sidney Webb, met with his absolute opposition. Webb's mistake (declared Morris) was "to overestimate the importance of the *mechanism* of a system of society apart from the *end* towards which it may be used."

The *end* he himself always described as Communism. When, in the nineties, the whole movement set in the direction of piecemeal reform, eight-hour agitation and parliamentary action, he welcomed this as a necessary process in awakening the aspirations of the workers. But, in his last lectures, he asked repeatedly "how far the betterment of the working people might go and yet stop short at last without having made any progress on the *direct* road to Communism?":

> Whether . . . the tremendous organization of civilized commercial society is not playing the cat and mouse game with us socialists. Whether the Society of Inequality might not accept the quasi-socialist machinery . . . and work it for the purpose of upholding that society in a somewhat shorn condition, maybe, but a same one. . . . The workers better treated, better organized, helping to govern themselves, but with no more pretence to equality with the rich . . . than they have now.

Herein lies his realism, overleaping his own circumstances, and searching the dilemmas of our own time with a moral insight so intense that it can be mistaken as callous. When the prospect of "the capitalist public service . . . brought to perfection" was put before him, he remarked that he "would not walk across the street for the realisation of such an 'ideal.'"

The nub of the question lies in the concept of community. Webb and the Fabians looked forward to Equality of Opportunity, within a competitive society: Morris looked forward to a Society of Equals, a socialist community. It is not a small difference that divides these concepts. In one—however modified—the ethic of competition, the energies of war. In the other, the ethic of co-operation, the energies of love. These two ethics Morris contrasted again and again by the names of False and True Society; False Society, or Commercial War; and "that true society of loved and lover, parent and child, friend and friend . . . which exists by its own inherent right and reason, in spite of what is usually thought to be the cement of society, arbitrary authority."

It was the greatest achievement of Morris, in his full maturity, to bring this concept of community to the point of expression: to place it in the sharpest antagonism to his own society, and to embody it in imaginative terms and in the "exalted brotherhood and hope" of the socialist propaganda. To this he summoned all his resources—his knowledge of medieval and of Icelandic society, his craftsman's insight into the processes of labour, his robust historical imagination. He had no time for noble savages, and even less for the Fabian nostrum of State bureaucracy. No amount of mechanical manipulation from above could engender the ethic of community; "individual men" (he said) "cannot shuffle off the business of life onto the shoulders of an abstraction called the State." Contrary to the prevalent opinion, Morris welcomed all machinery which reduced the pain and drudgery of labour: but decentralisation both of production and of administration he believed essential. In True Society, the unit of administration must be small enough for every citizen to feel a personal responsibility. The community of Communism must be an organic growth of mutual obligations, of personal and social bonds, arising from a condition of practical equality. And between False and True Society there lay, like a "river of fire," the Revolution. It was the work of a realist to indicate where that river ran, and to hand down to us a "tradition of hope" as to the lands beyond those deadly waters.

In conclusion, if there is one part of my long study of Morris which—in the light of the political controversies of recent years—would seem to be a fruitful area of re-examination, it is in those passages where I seek to relate the basis of Morris' moral critique of society to the Marxist tradition. The question is complex, and leads into an intricate succession of definitions. I feel now—as I did then—that Morris' and Marx's critique of capitalism are complementary and reinforce each other. There can be no question of disassociating the two. Moreover, I would wish to retract nothing of what I have written of Morris' profound debt to the writings of Marx; these gave to his own criticisms much of their form and some of their force.

But I have tended at certain points to suggest that Morris' moral critique of society is *dependent upon* Marx's economic and historical analysis, that the morality is in some ways secondary, the analysis of power and productive relationships primary. That is not the way in which I look upon the question now. I see the two as inextricably bound together in the same context of social life. Economic relationships are at the same time moral relationships; relations of production are at the same time relations between people, of oppression or of co-operation; and there is a moral logic as well as an economic logic, which derives from these relationships. The history of the class struggle is at the same time the history of human morality. "As I strove to stir up people to this reform," William Morris wrote in his Preface to *Signs of Change*:

> I found that the causes of the vulgarities of civilization lay deeper than I had thought, and little by little I was driven to the conclusion that all these uglinesses are but the outward expression of the innate moral baseness into which we are forced by our present form of society.

This is the phrase—"innate moral baseness." And if capitalist society in Britain today displays fewer of the extreme hardships and oppressions of Morris' day, the innate moral baseness of the acquisitive ethic, and of exploitive rather than cooperative social relationships, gives rise to new inhumanities, to the atomisation of social life, and to the greater international idiocies.

There is nothing here which contradicts Marx's analysis. What I am insisting on is not only that Morris' discoveries are complementary to those of Marx, but also that they are a *necessary* complement; that without this historical understanding of the evolution of man's moral nature (to which Marx scarcely returned after the 1844 manuscripts) his essential concept of the "whole man" becomes lost, as it has so often been lost in the later Marxist tradition. A generation is now arising to whom the moral critique of society makes a more direct appeal than the traditional analysis of economic causes. For this generation, Morris' writings have lost, in the passage of years, none of their pungency and force. And as socialists see Marx's genius in transforming the traditions of English economic theory and of German philosophy, so they should see how Morris transformed a great tradition of liberal and humane criticism of society, and how he brought this into the common revolutionary stream. And if this achievement had been more widely recognised, perhaps fewer Marxists would have been found who could have supposed that the overthrow of capitalist class power and productive relationships could—by itself—lead on to the fruition of a Communist community: that, if the forms of economic ownership were right, the rest would follow. They would have realised—as Morris proclaimed in all his work—that the construction of a Communist community would require a moral revolution as profound as the revolution in economic and social power.

It is because William Morris, in imaginative and in day-to-day polemical writing alike, sought to body forth a vision of the actual social and personal relations, the values and attitudes consonant with a Society of Equals, that he remains the greatest moral initiator of Communism within our tradition. And I hope that this Society will foster an understanding of this central greatness.

THIS HOMAGE FIRST APPEARED IN 1960 IN *ESSAYS IN LABOUR History*, a collection of articles gathered in memory of the late G. D. H. Cole (1889–1969), edited by Asa Briggs and John Saville. Cole was a Fabian, a Guild Socialist, a supporter of the British "co-operative movement" and wrote, with Raymond Postgate, *The Common People, 1746–1946* (1946). Thompson's account of Tom Maguire, a young Leeds socialist of the 1890s, says a great deal about his own socialism. Maguire sided with William Morris; as a young man "he went through the whole gamut of experiences which made up the lives of the 'pioneers': the open-air work, the occasional big meetings for Morris or Annie Besant . . . the weekend outings when propaganda and pleasure were combined, the excitement when the first premises were opened, the songs and camaraderie of the fervent sect. A poet, a man of great intellectual vigour and curiosity, he was naturally drawn to William Morris's side of the movement."

Homage to Tom Maguire

As the writing of labour history becomes more professionalised, so the centre of interest shifts from front-line engagements to the disputes and strategical plans of GHQ. In the Colindale Library, the Public Record Office, the national archives of trade unions, the Place or Webb Collections, the techniques proper to a constitutional or economic historian can be employed. The dubious reminiscences of local worthies can be disregarded (unless required for "colour"), the regional skirmishes can be dismissed with an irritable footnote, and the historian can get down in earnest to national minute-books, Congress proceedings, intrigues among the leadership, and underhand political agreements.

And yet—how far are the techniques of the political or constitutional historian adequate to deal with the tensions and lines of growth in movements which (until the highly bureaucratised post-1945 era) have always been exceptionally responsive to problems of local social and industrial context—local splits and breakaways—groundswells of opinion at the rank-and-file level?

The national historian still tends to have a curiously distorted view of goings-on "in the provinces." Provincial events are seen as shadowy incidents or unaccountable spontaneous upheavals on the periphery of the national scene, which the London wire-pullers try to cope with and put into their correct historical pattern. And provincial leaders are commonly denied full historical citizenship; if mentioned at all, they are generally credited with various worthy second-class abilities, but rarely regarded as men with their own problems, their own capacity for initiative, and on occasions a particular genius without which national programmes and new political philosophies can never be wedded to movements of men. Hence labour historians tend to fall into a double-vision; on the one hand, there are the mass movements which grow blindly and spontaneously under economic and social pressures: on the other, the leaders and manipulators—the Places, the Chartist journalists, the Juntas and parliamentarians—who direct these elemental forces into political channels. And where this superficial national approach is beginning to give way to a more mature school of local history, employing sociological techniques, nevertheless we still find that the national and local pictures are rarely put together.

The early years of the ILP provide a striking example of this. The ILP grew from the bottom up: its birthplaces were in those shadowy parts known as "the provinces." It "was created by the fusing of local elements into one national whole. From the circumference its members came to establish the centre."[1] Its first council seat was won in the Colne Valley: its first authentic parliamentary challenges came in Bradford and Halifax: its first conference showed an overwhelming preponderance of strength in the North of England;[2] its early directories show this strength consolidated.[3] When the two-party political structure began to crack, and a third party with a distinctively socialist character emerged, this even occurred neither in Westminster nor in the offices of Champion's *Labour Elector* but amongst the mills, brickyards, and gasworks of the West Riding.

Unless we register this fact, it is futile to speculate on the true origins of the ILP. Certainly Hardie and Burgess and Blatchford were the foremost propagandists for an independent party of labour. Certainly Champion worked for it, and so did Mahon, the Avelings, and the Hoxton Labour League: so—for that matter—did Hyndman when he first founded the Democratic Federation, and Engels in his *Labour Standard* articles of 1881, and the pedigree is a great deal longer than that.[4] Indeed, there was no lack of prophets. The problem was to translate prophecy into stable organisation and mass enthusiasm. Moreover, local grievances, severe industrial disputes, mass disaffection amongst Liberal voters—these in themselves were not sufficient to bring the thing about. The 1880s saw more than one false dawn—the crofters' struggle, the socialist propaganda among the Northumberland miners during the strike of 1887, the municipal revolt at Bolton in 1887.[5] In every case the socialist pioneers threw their hats in the air; in every case they retired disappointed and puzzled, as the electorate swung back to old allegiances, the new organisations crumbled, the councillors were reabsorbed by the Great Liberal Party.

The customary national picture of the West Riding breakthrough attributes the emergence of the ILP to one event—the great strike at Manningham Mills, Bradford. Pressed forward blindly by economic hardship and the effect of President McKinley's tariffs, the good-hearted Nonconformist Yorkshire workers turned instinctively to the arms of "Nunquam" and Keir Hardie. But this will not do at all. It does not explain why a strike at one firm could have become the focus for the discontent of a whole Riding. It does not explain the nature of this discontent. It does not explain why the Yorkshire ILP was so deeply rooted, so stubborn in face of Liberal blandishments, so competently led. It passes over incidents of equal importance to the Manningham strike. It implies an appalling attitude of condescension towards these provincial folk who are credited with every virtue except the capital human virtue of conscious action in a conscious historical role.

If we must counterpose to this legend our own propositions, then they are these: the two-party system cracked in Yorkshire because a very large number of Yorkshire working men and women took a conscious decision to form a socialist party. The fertilisation of the masses with socialist ideas was not spontaneous but was the result of the work, over many years, of a group of exceptionally gifted propagandists and trade unionists. This work did not begin with street-corner oratory and end with the singing of the "Marseillaise" in a socialist clubroom, although both of these activities played their part; it required also tenacity and foresight, qualities of mass leadership and the rare ability to relate theory to practice without losing sight of theory in the press of events. And if we must have one man who played an outstanding role in opening the way for the ILP, that man was a semi-employed Leeds-Irish photographer in his late twenties—Tom Maguire.

i.

OF COURSE, AN INDIVIDUAL does not create a movement of thousands: this must be the product of a community. And the West Riding woollen district, in the 1880s, was a distinctive community, with common characteristics imposed by its staple industries, geographical isolation, and historical traditions. Although the population was rapidly swelling and absorbing immigrants,[6] Yorkshire traditions were vigorous, local dialect almanacs still thrived, the *Yorkshire Factory Times* made a feature of dialect stories and verses, and in the more isolated areas, like the Colne and Calder and Holme Valleys, memories were long. In such communities, an "alien agitator" from outside would make little headway; but once the local leaders moved, the whole community might follow. Leeds, on the western edge of the woollen district, was a more cosmopolitan city, with more diverse industry, a larger professional and clerical population, and a recent influx of Jewish workers into the ready-made clothing trade.[7] New ideas, new national movements, tended to extend their influence to the woollen districts, not directly from London but by way of Leeds; the textile workers' leaders learnt their socialism from the Leeds and Bradford Socialist Leagues; Ben Turner, the dialect poet from Huddersfield, was initiated into the movement when he "flitted" for two years to Leeds.[8]

It is important to recall how far "independent labour" was already, in the mid-1880s, part of the structure of this community. In one sense, the ILP gave political expression to the various forms of independent or semi-independent working-class organisation which had been built and consolidated in the West Riding in the previous thirty years—co-operatives, trade unions, friendly societies, various forms of chapel or educational or economic "self-help." Among these, the co-operative societies were strongest;[9] George Garside, who won the first ILP seat in the Colne Valley, was a prominent co-operator.[10] The trade unions were the weakest. In the late sixties or early seventies trades councils existed in Leeds, Bradford, Halifax, Huddersfield, and Dewsbury; but by the early eighties all had disappeared except for those at Leeds and Bradford, and these survived in attenuated form through the support of skilled and craft unions.[11] When the Bradford Trades Council invited the TUC to meet in their home town in 1888, one of the reasons given was "the fact that the work-people engaged in the staple industries of the district are in a very disorganised state";[12] a Bradford Congress would boost local morale—as indeed it did, although in unexpected directions. Ben Turner's history of the early years of the textile union is a record of erratic spurts of organising, followed by dissolution and apathy: "We were all poor folks with poor incomes and poor trade and hadn't the vision that we ought to have had."[13]

If the "independence of labor" found expression in some parts of the community's life, there was little evidence of this in the early eighties in the political complexion of the West Riding. It required a new generation, and the new militant unionism, to twist "self-help" into socialist campaigning. The prevalent tone of the earlier years is one of surfeited, self-satisfied Liberalism. Local papers were busy celebrating the improvements in standards of life since the hungry forties, and recalling for the hundredth time the wisdom of the repeal of the Corn Laws. Local historians, with genuine feeling, commended the passing of the sanded floors and cellar-dwellings and oatmeal diet of the days of the "poverty-knockers"; and some looked back, almost with nostalgia, to the fiery woolcombers and the Chartist weavers with their torchlight meetings.[14] In March 1885 a gathering of Chartist veterans took place in a Halifax temperance hotel; after an "excellent repast" and an address reviewing the progress of the people since 1844, the best thanks of the meeting were moved "to Mr Gladstone and his government for passing into law those principles which we have endeavoured during a long life to enjoy." The motion was seconded by George Webber, at one time the most intransigent of physical force leaders. "The majority of those attending the meeting," the report concludes, "have become men of business and in some cases employers of labor"; and the reporter could not pass over the opportunity for taking their lives as a text for a small piece on the rewards of "economy, industry, and temperance."[15] Even Ernest Jones's Chartist stalwarts had found their place in Smiles's Valhalla.

Indeed, it is difficult to recognise the Bradford of Jowett's recollections— squalid back-to-back, open privy middens, an infant mortality rate (in some districts) of over one in four[16]—in the complacent compilations of a committee originated by Sir Jacob Behrens to inquire into the Condition of the Industrial Classes in 1887.[17] Here the statistics are carefully compiled, the rise in the wages of the skilled workers abundantly proved, the abolition of some of the worst abuses of the forties noted. And yet, less than three years later, not only the *Yorkshire Factory Times,* but also local Liberal and Conservative papers carried exposures of decaying slums, insanitary conditions, appalling social evils.[18] What made the difference?

It is true that a new generation was arising which demanded more of life than had contented their parents. In the 1850s the cramped blocks of back-to-backs were at least a step forward from the cellars, and the warren-like "folds" of earlier days; in the nineties the ending of all back-to-back building was to be a leading point in ILP municipal campaigns.[19] But too much influence in this change of outlook should not be attributed to the Education Act of 1870. The ILP strongholds, Bradford and Halifax, were also the strongholds of half-time working; children went into the mills at the age of 10, on passing Standard III, and in Halifax, by a little-known local exemption clause, they could commence work when barely literate.[20] Moreover, in the previous twenty years the enforcement of the Factory Acts in the West Riding had been notorious for its laxity;[21] 12 per cent of those married at Bradford Parish Church in 1887 still signed their names with a cross.[22]

Nor should too much weight be placed upon the argument that the general improvement in trade in the later eighties emboldened the textile workers and placed them in a strong position for strike action and organisation. This was certainly a factor in the success of the Leeds unskilled agitation among the bricklayers' labourers and others. But the textile industry presents a very different picture. The West Riding woollen trade provides a notoriously dangerous field for generalisation, owing to its manifold subdivisions, local variants, and specialised markets; where American tariffs might create chaos in the fine worsted industry of Bradford they would leave Batley, the new "shoddyopolis," unaffected.[23] Nevertheless, certain common features may be indicated. (1) Yorkshire employers had been "spoiled" by the abnormal boom years, 1870–74, a boom to which they looked back, even in the nineties, with nostalgia; during this period there was a spate of mill-building, inflated valuations, and profits were admitted to be "inordinately large."[24] (2) In the ensuing ten years, tariffs (especially in Germany and USA), keener world competition, and the onset of the "great depression," led to a marked decline in profits, sharp local competition, and readjustments within the industry;[25] but despite a falling-off in overtime, and the onset of periods of short time, the volume of trade continued to expand and (as a Leeds observer noted) "in many trades the *sum of profits* has been to some extent kept up by the *increased volume* of trade."[26] Between 1886 and 1890 (the year of the McKinley tariff) problems of competition and readjustment were intensified. (3) Throughout these fifteen years (1875–90) we have nothing approaching a depression of the kind met by the cotton industry in the interwar years of this century. Vast fortunes continued to be amassed, and the brunt of the crisis was borne by the textile workers whose wages declined throughout the period.[27] This decline was effected through direct wage reductions; increased mechanisation and intensification of labour; and the increasing proportion of women to male workers in the industry. (4) Thus we have in the wool textile industry of the late eighties an extreme example of the gulf which opened between the labour aristocracy and the unskilled workers at this time in other industries. Despite a few pockets of organised male aristocrats—power-loom overlookers, card setters, warp dressers, and the like[28]—the bulk of the labour force endured a stationary or declining standard of living. The high proportion of women and juvenile workers, and the variations and jealousies between town and town, mill and mill, and even shed and shed, placed almost insuperable difficulties in the way of trade-union organisation.[29] Men's wages were continually forced down to the level of the women, and throughout the district the custom of the "family wage" prevailed. (5) In these conditions, general trade unionism could scarcely "get off the ground" unless backed by exceptional resources. The skilled trade unionists cannot be blamed for indifference; in 1876 the Bradford Trades Council made a sustained attempt to organise the dyers, but only ten workers attended a well-advertised meeting.[30] The Weavers' Union, consolidated after the Huddersfield strike of 1883, hung on for several years only by the skin of its teeth.[31] It was the enormous publicity provided by the Yorkshire Factory Times, founded in 1889, by the successful struggles of the unskilled workers in London and (above all) in Leeds, and the indefatigable activity of socialist and new unionist propagandists which provided the catalyst for the movement of 1890–93.

Even so, a paradox must be noted: it was not the success, but the partial failure—the impossibility of complete success—in the trade-union field, which turned the textile workers into the channels of independent political action. Had the Manningham Mills strike ended in victory, like the struggles of dockers, gasworkers, and building workers, then Bradford might not have been the birthplace of the ILP. Defeat at Manningham, and the precarious nature of the partial organisation achieved elsewhere, were a spur to political action—and for three leading reasons. First, the bitter indignation aroused by economic oppression and social injustice, against which industrial action appeared to provide no effective remedy, was bound to break out in the demand for an independent-class party opposed to the parties of the employers. Second, if the causes of poverty could not be removed, its effects could be tackled by resolute independent action in the field of local government: hence the great importance of the early campaigns of the ILP in the West Riding on unemployment, against the half-time system, for "fair contracts," school milk and medical services, on sanitary problems and artisan's dwellings, nursery schools and slum clearance.[32] Third, the complexity and subdivisions of the textile industry, and the preponderance of women and juvenile workers, together with the sub-contracting and "sweat-shops" in the Leeds tailoring industry—all these gave overwhelming point to the demand for the Legal Eight Hour Day. Political action was seen as the only effective remedy for industrial grievances.[33]

The appeal of the Legal Eight Hour Day had a massive simplicity; it appeared to offer at one blow results which trade-union action could only hope to achieve after many years of hazard and sacrifice; it might go some way towards relieving unemployment as well. Moreover, the demand was in the direct line of the strongest West Riding traditions: Oastler and the Ten Hours Movement; the more recent campaign of the Factory Acts Reform Association, whose efforts to win the nine-hours day resulted in the 56½ hour week in 1874. The experience of half a century had led Yorkshire workers to believe that arguments that a shorter working day would lead to lower wages and loss of trade to foreign competitors, were no more than employers' propaganda points.[34]

Here we have some of the ingredients from which the West Yorkshire ILP was made. A close-knit community, in which the independence of labour found social, economic, religious expression. An industry facing readjustment and competition. Declining wages and appalling social evils. Tremendous problems in the way of effective trade-union organisation. A strong tradition of campaigning for legal protection in industry and limitation of hours. And to this tradition, another must be added: the tradition of the *political* independence of labour. The Chartist organisation had survived in West Yorkshire as long as in any part of the country. Halifax was Ernest Jones's "constituency," and while Chartist sentiments were appeased by the adoption of Stansfeld, the friend of Mazzini, as one of the two members in 1859, the flame broke out afresh during the Reform League agitation. Jones stumped the West Riding, addressing enormous crowds; he was invited to stand both in Dewsbury and Halifax, and although he preferred Manchester, the Halifax men revolted against one of their sitting members, the local mill-owner Akroyd, and sponsored the independent candidature of E.O. Greening, the Co-operator, who achieved the very respectable poll of 2,802.[35] This was in 1868; lads in their teens at the time would be scarcely 40 years of age when the ILP was formed. When John Lister contested Halifax for the ILP in 1893 his election manifesto appealed to "Radical Halifax," and his supporters recalled the traditions of Greening, Jones, and (local veterans) Ben Rushton and John Snowden, and demanded indignantly whether a "Whig" should be allowed to sit for such a borough.[36]

All the same, we should not seek for an unbroken independent labour tradition, from Chartism into ILP. On its dissolution Greening's election committee handed on its funds to the Halifax Liberal Electoral Association; and were not those man-eating tigers, Geo. Webber and Ben Wilson, toasting Gladstone in lemonade in 1885? In 1884 19-year-old Tom Maguire was writing to the *Christian Socialist*, warning that land nationalisation might prove a diversion from the main assault on the bastions of capitalism, as Corn Law Repeal had proved before:

Do you not remember, good folk, the Bright and Cobden cry of "Free Trade and Corn Law Repeal," which along with capitalistic combination, annihilated Chartism, the only genuine political movement of modern times in favour of the people? . . . Ernest Jones and Bronterre O'Brien are forgotten, ridiculed, out of history. John Bright and Richard Cobden are household words.[37]

The surviving Chartists, and many of their sons, had come to terms with Liberal Radicalism; they were (as Engels said) the grandchildren of the old Chartists who were now "entering the line of battle,"[38] rediscovering Chartist traditions from family or local folk-lore or published reminiscences.[39] A quite remarkable proportion of the young men and women prominent in the early Yorkshire ILP claimed Chartist forebears or the influence of Chartist traditions in their childhood.[40] "Eh, love, you cannot understand now," one Chartist great grandfather said to a little girl who was to become a leader of the Bradford textile workers, "but when you get to be a big girl I want you always to think for the people, and live for the people, for it will be a long time before they can do it for themselves."[41]

One further ingredient must not be overlooked: Radical Nonconformity. We may leave on one side the futile and unhistorical argument that goes by the name, "Methodism or Marxism?" The attempt to suggest that the ILP was founded by a slate of Methodist parsons and local preachers is even more wildly inaccurate than the attempt to attribute it to the single-handed efforts of Engels and Aveling. Of those prominent in its formation in Yorkshire, Tom Maguire was an atheist with an Irish-Catholic background; Isabella Ford a Quaker; Ben Turner and Allan Gee (a late convert from Liberalism) were secularists;[42] Alf Mattison was a disciple of Edward Carpenter; John Lister a Catholic; Walt Wood, the gasworkers' leader, would appear to have been a happy pagan—as may have been Paul Bland and Tom Paylor;[43] only Jowett, W. H. Drew, and perhaps Balmforth of Huddersfield, among the initiators of the movement, suggest themselves as active Nonconformists. In truth, Radical Nonconformity had become a retarding social and political influence in the eighties, its face set in a perpetual grimace at the Established Church and the Anglican landed aristocracy; the face was, only too often, the face of a mill-owner, like Alfred Illingworth, the Nonconformist worsted-spinner, whom Tillett fought in West Bradford. The Bradford textile workers owed their socialism no more to the Methodist Church than the peasants of South Italy owe their communism to the Catholic; and if the socialists succeeded in sweeping whole chapel-fulls of the former into the movement, by their broad, unsectarian, ethical appeal, the credit is due to them and not to the Nonconformist "Establishment" which fought the ILP every inch of the way.

Once the breakthrough had been made, it is true that the movement gained a moral dimension; that Radical Christian tradition, which had been seen before on a Luddite scaffold and in Chartist chapels and camp meetings, swept the West Riding like a revivalist campaign; we meet again the full-toned moral periods, the Biblical echoes, the references to the Sermon on the Mount.[44] It is not a question of creed, belief, or church, but a question of language, a question of moral texture. It was as much a revolt *against* organised Christianity as a form of Christian expression. The Yorkshire ILP was a sturdy cross-bred. Its leaders owed much of their theory to Marxist propagandists; but they preferred the moral exhortations of William Morris to the doctrinaire tones of Hyndman, and they were happier with "Nunquam" than with Quelch. When they found out that Tillett was a Congregationalist, it made a fine propaganda point with the electorate.[45] But this was not among their reasons for their choice of him as candidate; he was selected as a prominent new unionist and a socialist.[46] Nonconformity—"Radical" Nonconformity—was outraged. The Bradford and District Nonconformist Association passed a unanimous resolution of confidence in Alfred Illingworth, MP, the "widely esteemed Nonconformist," and a correspondent to the *Bradford Observer* wrote of the ILP's intervention in terms that suggest they were guilty of sacrilege: "A humble but ardent supporter of a politician whom I regard as a constant and sagacious servant of God and the people, how could I see without sorrow, and I may say horror, the entrance of Mr Ben Tillett to fasten like a viper on his throat?"[47]

Mr Illingworth's throat now and, the implication runs, God's throat next. The Nonconformist Association called a public meeting in support of both, with a pride of reverends on the platform. Tillett's followers packed the meeting, and Drew and Pickles intercepted Jowett—on his way to a Co-operative meeting—with the cry: "You are just the man we want." At the public meeting, Briggs Priestley, MP, presided, fresh from an unpopular piece of parliamentary sabotage against a Factory Bill. One after the other, two reverends were shouted down; then the audience stormed the platform, pushing up Jowett, Minty, and Pickles (dubious "nonconformists," these last two), and remaining in uproar until Jowett was allowed to move an amendment. Impressively he warned the clergy: "If you persist in opposing the labour movement there will soon be more reason than ever to complain of the absence of working men from your chapels": "The labourers would establish a Labour Church (cheers and 'Bravo Jowett') and there they would cheer for Jesus Christ, the working man of Nazareth (cheers)."[48]

The Labour Churches in Bradford and Leeds, when they were established, were not only undenominational; it is also difficult to describe them as Christian or religious in any sense except that of the broad ethical appeal of the "religion of socialism" whose text was Morris's "Fellowship is Life." They retained sufficient ceremonial forms, and a sufficient admixture of Christian speakers, for the

Nonconformist members to feel at home; but the "hymn" might be Maguire's "Hey for the Day!" and the "sermon" might be by Edward Carpenter from a text from Whitman. Carpenter's friend and disciple, Alf Mattison, was first secretary of the Leeds Labour Church, while the "sermon" at the Bradford Labour Church, on the occasion of the foundation conference of the ILP, was preached by George Bernard Shaw—a tactful but uncompromising address which ended with the avowal that he was an atheist.[49] We must not underestimate the importance of the religious associations drawn upon in the speeches of Hardie or Tillett; these reverberated in the hearts of a generation who had picked up their little education in Sunday school or chapel. But these owed little to any doctrine of personal salvation or personal sin; the sin was the sin of the capitalist class, and salvation must come through the efforts of the working class itself, expressed through solidarity and brotherhood, and aspiring towards a co-operative commonwealth. Tom Mann, when he stumped Yorkshire, had little Christian charity to spare for non-union men or blacklegs, even though he was willing enough to employ the parable of the Good Samaritan as a scourge on the back of the Ossett Corporation which had let out its scavenging by contract.[50] The broad ethical appeal was the same, whether it was voiced by the Quaker Isabella Ford, or Margaret McMillan ("Educate every child as if it were your own"), or by the free-thinker Charles Glyde: "I wish to treat all poor as I would my own father, mother, sister, or brother."[51] In the early nineties this ethical appeal gave fervour, self-confidence and stamina to the movement; later, when it was taken out of its direct social context and transformed into platform rhetoric by such men as Snowden and Grayson, it was to smudge political understanding and weaken the movement. But in 1892 this authentic moral revolt was one of the first indications to a close observer that the ILP had come to stay: "It is of the people—such will be the secret of its success." The letter is from Tom Maguire to Edward Carpenter:

Now the mountain, so long in labour, has been delivered of its mouse—a bright active cheery little mouse with just a touch of venom in its sharp little teeth. . . . Our mouse though young in the flesh is old in the spirit, since to my own knowledge this is its third reincarnation. . . .

You will find in your travels that this new party lifts its head all over the North. It has caught the people as I imagine the Chartist movement did. And it is of the people—such will be the secret of its success. Everywhere its bent is Socialist because Socialists are the only people who have any message for it.[52]

ii.

NO MAN HAD WORKED harder for this than Maguire. Of poor Irish-Catholic parentage, singled out by the priests for his intelligence, he had found his own way to secularism at the age of 16, joined the Democratic Federation at 17, was finding his feet as an open-air propagandist and a lecturer in the debating clubs and coffee taverns in his 18th year.[53] J. L. Mahon was in Leeds for a period in 1884, and struck up a friendship with him. When the split in the SDF took place, Maguire sided with Morris and was placed on the Provisional Council of the League. He commenced the work of building a small Leeds branch, while also giving aid to Bland, Minty, and Pickles in Bradford.[54] By October 1885 there were sixteen Leeds socialists in good standing: most were young industrial workers, unemployed or on short time.[55]

He went through the whole gamut of experiences which made up the lives of the "pioneers"; the open-air work, the occasional big meeting for Morris or Annie Besant, the attacks—especially from his old Catholic associates ("we shall live their narrow fury down," he wrote to Mahon[56]), the weekend outings when propaganda and pleasure were combined,[57] the excitement when the first premises were opened, the songs and camaraderie of the fervent sect.[58] A poet, and a man of great intellectual vigour and curiosity, he was naturally drawn to William Morris's side of the movement. But more than most Socialist Leaguers, he knew that the early propaganda was too abstract to achieve a wide popular appeal. As early as 1884 he singled out the Eight Hours' Day demand as of prime importance;[59] although—as a photographer's assistant—he was not a trade unionist himself, he was directing the Socialist League, in 1885, towards work among the miners and the ASE.[60] From the maturity of his late twenties he looked back tolerantly upon these years. "We were kindly, well-disposed young chaps," he wrote, whose object was "the Internationalisation of the entire world." As time went by, and no progress was made (after four years' propaganda the League branch was only 30 strong), the socialists began to divide:

> Some thought that we might advantageously limit the scope of our ideal to the five continents, while directing our operations more immediately to our own locality. Others were strongly of the opinion that our ideal was too narrow, and they proposed as the object of the society the internationalisation of the known and undiscovered world, with a view to the eventual inter-solarisation of the planets. . . . They entirely ignored the locality to which, for the most part, they were comparative strangers.[61]

The division so parodied followed closely the division between the anarchists and parliamentarians in the national Socialist League. In the wrangles of 1887 and 1888, the Leeds branch sided with the parliamentarians; after 1888, while the Leeds and Bradford Leagues maintained their link with the national body, sold their quota of *Commonweal*, and regarded William Morris with undiminished affection, they took less and less notice of London goings-on. They subscribed now to Keir Hardie's *Miner*, 2s. 6d. was scraped together for the Mid-Lothian election fund; and while Maguire still contributed poems and articles to *Commonweal*, he also maintained a link with Mahon, who had now broken with the League and who produced in 1888 his blueprint for a labour party, *The Labour Programme*.[62] After the Bradford TUC of the same year, the Yorkshire Socialist Leaguers directed their energies towards the two main objectives: the conversion of the trade unions, and propaganda for an independent party of labour. "A definite step is now being taken towards the formation of a Socialist Labor Party in Leeds," declared a handbill of autumn 1888, which announced lectures by Maguire on "The Need of a Labour Party," and by Tom Paylor, on "The Lesson of the Trades Congress."[63] When Mahon and H. A. Barker launched their Labour Union, Maguire and Pickles (of Bradford) were among the signatories.[64] After Maguire's death, a correspondent in the *Yorkshire Factory Times* commented on the breadth of his reading and the volume of propaganda work which he undertook in these years—"Three lectures each Sunday, and two, and occasionally three, in the course of the week, in addition to articles, poems, and letters to the press."

The propaganda gained growing audiences in the coffee taverns, Radical clubs, and at the "open-air spouting place"—Vicar's Croft. But the Leeds Trades Council was a stronghold of the Liberal skilled unionists, and—except in the ASE—no headway could be made. The breakthrough, when it came, came in spectacular fashion. Some bricklayers' labourers, attending an open-air meeting, stayed on to discuss their grievances ("rather aimlessly") with Paylor and Sweeney. The Leaguers offered their clubroom for a committee meeting of the men on the next Sunday. On 30 June 1889 3,000 labourers attended a meeting at which they were addressed by Maguire, Paylor, and other socialists; 200 names were handed in for the new union; a committee elected; within a week several thousand labourers were on strike for a ½d an hour (from 5d, to 5½d); within five weeks the union was 800 strong, and the strike had ended in victory.[65] A week later the great Dock Strike in London began.

It is a comment upon the divorce between the skilled unionists and the unskilled that the labourers turned to the socialists rather than to the Leeds Trades Council, on which the skilled building unions had long been represented. From the outset the skilled unionists in Leeds regarded the socialist intervention with undisguised hostility, while even the *Yorkshire Factory Times* published a grumbling, suspicious editorial.[66]

The socialists for their part were elated, and were not above rubbing salt in the wound: "We are endeavouring to organise the unskilled labourers in all branches of industry in the town, since the aristocrats of labour take no steps in organising them."[67] But no one anticipated the nearly incredible surge of unskilled agitation which engulfed the West Riding in the next twelve months. Trade was brisk, and Maguire repeatedly urged the workers to seize their opportunity; in December he was addressing a demonstration of the newly formed Leeds section of the Gasworkers and General Labourers Union (embracing already gasworkers, maltsters, draymen, general labourers, dyers, and claiming a membership of 3,000) and urging them to press home their advantage while the employers "could not afford to tarry,"[68] a month later he was exhorting a meeting of clayworkers and brickyard labourers "to go with the flowing tide."[69] Mattison, the young skilled engineer, helped out the Gasworkers as secretary; he recalled later the shock of surprise when Will Thorne came up to help, with his heavy navvy's boots and knotted red handkerchief.[70] Week after week, Maguire, Paylor, Sweeney, Cockayne, and Turner attended demonstrations, assisted strikes, presided at the formation of new unions: tramway workers, blue dyers, corporation workers, plasterer's labourers, paviour's labourers, mechanic's labourers, axle workers. In October 1889 900 girls struck at Messrs. Arthur's tailoring works, against the deduction of 1d. out of every 1s. earned in payment for motive power on their sewing-machines; despite the selfless assistance of Isabella Ford[71] and Maguire, and the ambiguous support of the Trades Council,[72] the strike ended after the sixth week in a sad collapse.[73] But the defeat scarcely checked the advancing wave of unionism. In late October 1889 the Leeds Tailors' Union (catering at first chiefly for Jewish workers) was formed, with Maguire in the chair.[74] The Tailoresses' Union continued to grow, with the particular assistance of Isabella Ford. When some 3,000 tailoring workers went on strike, Maguire was adviser, organiser, and poet, writing for them "The Song of the Sweater's Victim," "the singing of which by several hundred Jews in their broken English may be better imagined than described.":

> ... every worker in every trade,
> In Britain and everywhere,
> Whether he labour by needle or spade,
> Shall gather in his rightful share.[75]

In March these new unions still remained outside the Trades Council, and had grouped in a new body called the "Yorkshire Labour Council."[76] The first May Day in Leeds was celebrated by this Council, in association with the Gasworkers. The procession alone was estimated at 6,000, headed by the banner of the Leeds Jewish Tailors, Pressers, and Machinists; a band playing the "Marseillaise"; 1,100 Jewish tailors; 900 slipper-makers; 800 gasworkers; dyers, maltsters, teamsters, and labourers. Between the slipper-makers and the gasworkers there marched the smallest and proudest contingent—40 members of the Leeds Socialist league. Maguire presided at the main platform, where the demonstration was swelled by several thousand, and a resolution passed endorsing the "necessity of an Eight Hour Day . . . as the first step towards the abolition of national and industrial war; the overthrow of race hatred; and the ultimate emancipation of Labour."[77] The Annual Report of the Leeds Trades Council for 1890 mentions neither May Day nor the gas strike, but recorded the Council's resolution in October (on a small majority vote) "that a general Eight Hour's legislative measure is impracticable."[78]

Maguire, Paylor, Mattison—all were in their early twenties when this sudden elevation from the status of a sect to that of leaders and advisers to the unskilled of half a populous county took place. They had no national advisers. Morris was retiring in disgust from the anarchist playground which the London League was becoming; anyway, he was writing *News from Nowhere*, which his Leeds followers read eagerly in the odd half-hours spared from union organising[79]—although he found time to deliver his last notable address for the League, on "The Class Struggle," in Leeds in March 1890. It is a noble and far-seeing lecture, but its only practical proposal was that a General Strike for socialism might be the best next step—for which advice Maguire and Paylor moved a hearty vote of thanks.[80] Forty miles away, at Millthorpe, Edward Carpenter watched events with awe; he had no advice to offer, and his influence upon the Leeds socialists made itself felt in other ways.[81] Cunninghame Graham helped with a fleeting visit, as did Thorne. The only national figure who kept his finger on events in Leeds was Maguire's old friend, J. L. Mahon of the Labour Union; and his reputation was much tarnished by the failure of the London Postmen's Union.[82] The Leeds and Bradford socialists were virtually detached from London and thrown upon their own resources; in May 1889 they held a joint demonstration at the famous Chartist meeting spot, Blackstone Edge, with the Lancashire branches of the SDF;[83] in July of the same year a Yorkshire Socialist Federation was set up.[84] But their own resources were not slender. The years of seemingly fruitless propaganda, when the joint forces of Leeds and Bradford socialism had tramped like a group of youth hostellers, spreading "the gospel" in villages and singing Morris's songs in country lanes,[85] had not been wasted. Maguire and Jowett, in their very early twenties, both showed astonishing maturity; they had gained a fund of experience, a clear theory of politics, and a self-confidence and élan, which prepared them for those vintage years, 1889–92, when (in Ben Turner's words) "It was not alone a labour of love, but a labour of joy, for the workers seemed awake."[86]

The climax to Leeds new unionism, and the final proof of the ability of Maguire's small group, came in the gas strike (or lockout) of June–July 1890. The rapid organisation of the previous winter had won, without a struggle, sweeping gains for the men, including the eight-hour day. In the summer of 1890, when the demand for gas fell off, the Gas Sub-Committee of the Liberal-dominated municipal council, determined to counter-attack with all the forces at its command, and to enforce the withdrawal of certain concessions.[87] A short, but violent and extremely ill-tempered, struggle ensued. The Gas Committee alienated general working-class and much middle-class sentiment by its stupid and high-handed tactics, particularly its elaborate attempts to displace local men by blacklegs imported (often under false pretences) from great distances and at great cost to the rate-payers. Worse, it made itself ridiculous in a hundred ways; the villain in the public eye was its chairman, Alderman Gilston, well known for his Radical Home Rule speeches and his claims to be a "friend of the working classes"; another Liberal councillor set Leeds laughing by his renderings of "Rule Britannia" for the entertainment of blacklegs temporarily housed in the Town Hall crypt. Ridicule grew as those few blacklegs who were transported to the gasworks turned out to be incapable of performing the work, or asked to be sent home at the town's expense. At the height of the struggle, a ludicrous procession moved through the surging crowds in the town centre; several hundred blacklegs, headed by cavalry, surrounded by a double file of police, and a file of military, and followed by the Mayor and magistrates. As they passed beneath the Wellington Road railway bridge, coal, sleepers, bricks, bottles, and assorted missiles were hurled down by pickets and sympathisers upon the civic procession. Arriving in the new Wortley gasworks in a "very excited and exhausted state," the blacklegs at once held an indignation meeting in protest against their inadequate protection. Then—when pickets climbed on the walls to shout—they fled over the rear walls "by the dozen" until only 76 remained inside. For several days the town was like an armed camp. On one side, Hussars with drawn swords patrolled the streets in defence of the Liberal Gas Committee; on the other, railwaymen, corporation workers, and even (it would seem) individual policemen, combined to give information to the pickets. When the strikers returned, with almost complete victory, it was estimated that the affray had cost the town £20,000.[88]

Maguire and Paylor, and their leading converts among the gas-workers, Walt Wood and Cockayne, bore the brunt of the struggle. They tried

to get the crowd into peaceful ways, but blood was shed nevertheless. In the morning after the first night of the riots, it was a sight to see the leaders of the union telling the members off to duty, arranging picketing work, and getting the men who had been deceived ... off home.[89]

Maguire, rather than Thorn, deserved the copy of *Capital* which Engels gave to the victor of the struggle.[90] Moreover, in the height of the struggle he saw his political opportunity, and struck home hard. He addressed both of the mass demonstrations on the two Sundays of the strike, and drove home the lesson of the independence of labour. If the Leeds Gas Committee persisted in their course, he said, "the Liberal party of the town would get such a knockdown blow as they would never recover from." How long (he asked) are the working classes of this town "going to return people to the Council who, when returned, use the forces of the town against the working classes?"[91] From this point on, many skilled unionists in Leeds began to turn away from Liberalism.[92]

If the first strong link in the chain which led to the ILP was forged in the gas strike, it also led to the breaking of the last link which bound the Leeds socialists to the Socialist League. The occasion was a quarrel in the local club. "Those of us who had to do with the gasworkers, in response to the men's wishes and in accordance with our ideas of policy, considered a Labour Electoral League should be formed," Maguire wrote to Carpenter. "Our Anarchist friends, who were conspicuous by their absence in the gas fights, told the people that no policy should be entertained but physical force"; "I admit the Labour Electoral move is not all to be desired, but it seemed the next immediate step to take in order to keep the Labour unions militant, and to emphasise the conflict of the workers and the employers."

The incident disgusted him: "As usual with Socialists when they fall out, all kinds of personal attacks and insinuations have been the order of the day."[93]

The majority of the Leeds socialists went out with Maguire, to be followed, shortly after, by the Bradford Socialist League. Both groups formed socialist clubs, and soon, as a more stable form of organisation, these adopted a Fabian disguise; over the next year a rash of Fabian Societies spread across West Yorkshire, until the London Fabians became quite uneasy at the threatened permeation.[94] But the Fabian Society offered no more prospect for turning the mass industrial unrest into political channels than had the Socialist League; and it was only with the formation of the Bradford Labour Union that the political wing of the movement got under way. "I thought of a new move," recalled James Bartley, then a sub-editor on the *Workman's Times*, who initiated the first meeting:

On Sunday, April 26th, 1891, I took the first steps for putting it into operation. That particular Sunday . . . was a bright sunshiny day. I went to Shipley . . . in order to consult Mr W. H. Drew. . . . He was attending anniversary services at Bethel Baptist Chapel, but during a lull in the proceedings I called him out to the chapel-yard. Here we talked over the situation.[95]

When the Bradford Labour Union was finally founded in May it was under the heading Independent Labour Party. "Suddenly a name was coined that hit off the genius of the English people," Maguire later said. From this moment it "went like wildfire."[96] Why was its birthplace Bradford and not Leeds?

iii.

LEEDS WAS TO PROVIDE a remarkable example of arrested development. Despite its early vigour, the movement met repeated barriers; the first authentic

ILP councillor in Leeds was not elected until 1906, when Jowett had already done fourteen magnificent years of service on the Bradford Council—eight miles away! But if we note the social and industrial contrasts, some of the reasons become apparent. Leeds was not as close-knit a community as other West Yorkshire towns: its industries were more diverse. The unskilled male workers were in general successful in improving their conditions as a result of the new unionism, and some of their discontent was dispersed: the gas strike was short, sharp, and victorious where that at Manningham Mills was long, humiliating, and a defeat. Social antagonisms were modified by the interpolation of many intermediate strata between the mass of the workers and employers, including those skilled workers who owed a traditional allegiance to Lib-Labism.

It is this last fact, above all, which accounts for the failure of the Leeds ILP to gather the momentum of Bradford. Although the new unions affiliated to the Trades Council after the gas strike, and the Yorkshire Labour Council was dissolved,[97] the old guard on the Trades Council maintained a controlling influence. In September 1891 they seemed to be drawing together, with a successful mass demonstration addressed by Mann and Tillett; and a Labour Electoral Union was sponsored by the Council, on independent lines.[98] But the Trades Council insisted on maintaining the right of veto over the Labour Union, and the old guard sought to exercise this in the Liberal interest; finally, in 1892, it severed its connection with the Union, which became the Leeds ILP.[99] Hence the impressive unity between Trades Council and ILP which was the leading feature of developments in Bradford, Halifax, and the heavy woollen district was never to be found in Leeds.

This political friction was only to be expected in a centre where the Trades Council had a history covering a quarter-century, and the leaders of the skilled unions had a place in the Liberal firmament. But the problem was aggravated by socialist errors and accidents of person. In 1890 Maguire's old friend, J. L. Mahon, returned to Leeds. Maguire had defects as a political leader—he was without personal ambition and incapable of political guile. In the intervals between storms (when necessity drove him to the front) he preferred to advise from the background.[100] He allowed Mahon—who shared none of his dislike of the limelight—to assume the leadership of the Leeds movement; perhaps he was glad to be relieved of the responsibility he had borne for so long.

Mahon was a man of great ability: the idea of Labour Unions was largely his. He had done stalwart service for the Socialist League in the past. But now his many defects were gaining on his virtues. He was vain, incurably quarrelsome, and given to intrigue, and he inspired neither loyalty nor trust. It would be tedious to recount the rows that gathered around him between 1890 and 1893. He wrangled inside the Gasworkers' Union:[101] he was prominent in a sensational row between the Gasworkers and the Trades Council over the School

Board election of November 1891:[102] he allowed himself to be drawn into a long and unsavoury public quarrel with John Judge, the leader of the old unionists.[103] Finally, he allied himself wholeheartedly with Champion's attempt to "nobble" the ILP in 1892. He flaunted Tory "sympathies" in an attempt to shock Liberal working men from their allegiance.[104] With Champion's money, and under Champion's day-to-day direction, he stood as Independent Labour candidate for South Leeds in September 1892—a by-election which ended in riot and anticlimax, but which did as much as anything to raise the well-justified taunt of "Carlton Club money" which hung around the ILP at its foundation conference.[105] "What a cunning chap he is," Carpenter wrote to Mattison—"I can't say I like him. I wonder how Maguire feels about it all."[106] But Maguire's opinions are not recorded. Mahon and Champion between them nearly succeeded in smashing the ILP on the eve of its foundation; and yet Maguire's old friendship for Mahon, and his hatred for personal rancour and intrigue, led him to retreat into his shell.[107]

In the woollen districts the development was quite different. Here the origins were less spectacular; but when the movement began in earnest, the entire trade-union movement swung round behind it. In 1886 that other remarkable young Yorkshire socialist, Ben Turner, could only get two other members for a Huddersfield branch of the SDF.[108] The Bradford League, in its early years, depended a good deal upon speakers and guidance from Leeds; it paid serious attention to the trade unions only after the Bradford TUC of September 1888.[109] The extant minute-books of the Bradford Trades Council have a hiatus between July 1889 and January 1893. As the former minute-book closes, the Trades Council claims to represent 3,000 workers, mainly outside the textile industry. Its secretary, Sam Shaftoe, is a prominent unionist of the old Lib-Lab school, and the Council is still negotiating humbly with the Liberal Association for a member on their School Board Eight. When the latter minute-book commences, the Council claims 10,000 members, Drew of the weavers is on its executive, Shaftoe has disappeared, Cowgill—an ILPer from the ASE—is secretary, and the Council is functioning in close alliance with the ILP.[110]

Three events dictated this transformation; the publication of the *Yorkshire Factory Times*, the influence of the Leeds unskilled agitation, and the events surrounding the Manningham Mills strike. Andrews, the proprietor of the *Cotton Factory Times*, started the Yorkshire journal largely as a commercial venture; it was his policy to employ the local union men as correspondents, and Drew, Bartley, Turner and Gee were placed on the staff, with Burgess as the first editor. Its influence achieved in a few months what the painstaking efforts of organisers had failed to achieve in years. Its dramatic effect in the woollen districts, as propagandist for trade unionism, has been described in the vivid pages of Ben Turner's reminiscences.[111] Bad masters were exposed, grievances aired, successes advertised. With the textile workers on the move, the unskilled struggles in Leeds spilled over into the towns and villages to the West, swelling the tide. Maguire, Paylor, Turner, Mattison, organised the gasworkers and clay-workers at Halifax, where 9,000 were claimed at a demonstration in the autumn of 1889.[112] Railwaymen were organised in other towns. In December 1890 the Manningham strike commenced.

This strike, which at its peak involved nearly 5,000 workers and which dragged through a bitter winter until the end of April 1891, has often been described. Here we may select only certain features for comment. (1) Contrary to the general impression, it was not the most-depressed but the better-paid workers—velvet and plush weavers—who initiated the strike. The several thousand unskilled women and girls who later thronged the streets came out in sympathy or were forced out by the firm in order to embarrass the strike fund.[113] (2) Sympathy was aroused for the strikers, not only by their inexperience and pitiful plight, but also by the explanation of S. C. Lister that it was necessary to bring down their wages to continental standards, and peg them to the rate paid at his mills in Crefeld. This "continental threat" the *Yorkshire Factory Times* took up as "a distinct challenge to all the textile workers in the two counties of Lancashire and Yorkshire."[114] (3) The outstanding organisers of the strike—Turner, Drew, and Isabella Ford—were proclaimed socialists; Turner, living in Leeds, was in constant contact with the Leeds socialists, although his earlier experiences in West Yorkshire, where he had received generous assistance from Liberal unionists of the old school, led him to take up a mediating role. (4) It was the repeated attempts by chief constable, watch committee, town clerk, and Mayor to prevent the strikers and sympathisers from holding meetings, at first in halls, and then in customary open-air meeting places (thus provoking the famous riots in Dockers' Square) which, willy-nilly, forced to the very forefront the question of independent political action. It was this struggle which induced the strikers to fetch up Ben Tillett for a great protest meeting; and he voiced their sentiments when he declared that "at election times the people can teach would-be Caesars—town clerks and Mayors and watch committees—a salutary lesson."[115] After the strike was defeated, the *Factory Times* commented: "The operatives have from the first been fought not only by their own employers at Manningham but by the whole of the monied class of Bradford. From the highest dignitary down to the lowest corporate official 'law and order' has been against them."[116]

"In future," warned Drew, when presenting the balance sheet of the strike, "capitalists will have to reckon with whole communities of labour rather than sections."[117]

This, then, was the background to Bartley's discussion with Drew in the yard of the Bethel Baptist chapel. Even so, the formation of the Bradford Labour Union was only one in a chain of similar attempts, each of which had been re-absorbed within the Liberal Party;[118] and at any time in the next year the Labour Union might have met with the same fate. Its programme, like that of the Colne Valley Labour Union, was largely a list of radical-democratic demands, adapted from Mahon's *Labour Programme* of 1888 which clearly provided the model.[119] Despite the admonition, "Workmen, Remember November" placarded in the streets from the time of the Manningham strike, only one Trades Council nominee was successful in the 1891 municipal elections, and he was the staunch old unionist, Shaftoe, who—when he had done his duty by securing guarantees from the Council for the right of public meeting—fell back into the Liberal Party, which rewarded him with nomination to the bench.[120] Moreover, the Bradford and Colne Valley Labour Unions had the utmost difficulty in finding suitable candidates to nurse the constituencies. Tillett and Mann were up to their necks holding the Dockers' Union together, and beating off an employers' counter-attack; Shaw said the Bradford working men should choose one of their own number, and not run after the "tall hats and frock coats."[121]

At length Blatchford was persuaded to nurse East Bradford, only to withdraw, without an apology to the electors, when the launching of the *Clarion* absorbed all his time.[122] Tillett was persuaded to stand for Bradford West only when presented with 1,000 electors' signatures, and after a deputation from the Labour Union had visited the Dockers' Annual Congress.[123] Mann, when invited by Colne Valley, held aloof longer; he was wondering about permeating the Church; he had his eye on the ASE; he was doubtful about parliamentary action; he thought the Colne Valley men should get down to trade unionism and municipal action before they talked of Parliament.[124] The Yorkshire men had to solve their problems on their own.

In truth, it was a miracle that the Labour Unions survived into 1892, and multiplied so fast. This could not have been done without a resolute and capable local socialist leadership, aided by the inflexibility and stupidity of the local Liberal employers. It was a longer step than we realise from the running of occasional Labour candidates for council or school board, even against official Liberal nominees, to the formation of an independent party, pledged to a socialist programme. The Labour Union men was assisted by the uncompromising advocacy of Blatchford and Burgess; by the proportional representation system operating in local board elections, which enabled them to win spectacular and morale-building victories;[125] but above all, by the advance of the Trades Council movement.

The Trades Councils, even more than the Labour Unions, were the organisational unit upon which the West Yorkshire ILP was based. Among Trades Councils re-formed or formed at this time were Halifax (1889), Huddersfield (1890), Keighley (1890), Brighouse (1892), Spen Valley (1891), the Heavy Woollen District (Dewsbury & Batley, 1891); the Yorkshire Federation of Trades

Councils—the first county federation—was founded in 1893.[126] In almost every case, these were formed by socialists and new unionists with the direct aim of promoting independent political action; in some cases, the Trades Council formed the local ILP as its political arm.[127] The socialists no longer sowed their propaganda broadcast or at thinly-attended meetings; they directed it first and foremost at the unionists, urging them to take political action, at first in the field of local politics.

> Men of an antagonistic class (declared Maguire, addressing a demonstra-
> tion of 2,000 gasworkers and labourers at Dewsbury in July 1891), were
> sent upon their various public bodies to manage their town's affairs. Men
> who polluted rivers and filled the air with smoke from their chimneys
> were sent to their Council chambers to carry out the Acts of Parliament
> to prevent the pollution of rivers and the air.[128]

Since the Trades Councils were young, the socialists encountered little opposition. At Bradford, Shaftoe was too good a trade unionist to stand aside from the tide of new unionism; he played his full part, speaking often alongside Paylor, Turner, and Drew, becoming secretary of the newly formed Woolcombers' Union, and although he was known to oppose the ILP he held his silence during Tillett's 1892 candidature.[129] At Halifax the Liberals delivered themselves into the hands of the ILP by an act of crass stupidity. Beever, the President of the Trades Council, had been converted to socialism and was taking an active part in the local Fabian propaganda in late 1891, but another prominent and influential member, Tattersall, was still a member of the Liberal executive. In 1892 both Beever and Tattersall were sacked, one after the other, by the same firm; the reason given, "they did not want anyone in their employ who was engaged in setting labour against capital."[130] It was well known in the town that the most influential partner in the firm was also a leading member of the local Liberal caucus, and the indignation in the town was so intense that testimonials were raised, demonstrations held, a Labour Union formed—the month after Tattersall's dismissal—on the initiative of the Trades Council, and a month later Keir Hardie was addressing a mass meeting which resolved that "the time has come when a national and independent Labour Party must be formed."[131] Two months later again, in November 1892, Beever, Tattersall, Lister, and one other ILP candidate were swept on to the town council, while in January 1893, in the ILP's first parliamentary by-election, Lister, the local squire, mine-owner, and Fabian, who had come to socialism by way of Marx's *Capital* and Tom Maguire, polled 3,028 votes against the Liberal 4,617 and the Tory 4,219.

Indeed, this last incident points the pattern which can be seen throughout the West Riding. At Leeds the Liberal Gas Committee. At Colne Valley, the sitting Liberal member, Sir James Kitson—the "Carnegie" of the West Riding, whose firm ex-Royal Commissioner of Labour Tom Mann described as having "worse conditions ... than could be found in any other engineering firm in ... Leeds."[132] At Halifax the Liberal employer, sacking the Trades Council leaders. In a dozen boroughs and urban districts Liberal councillors refusing trade-union demands for "fair contracts" or artisan dwellings. In Holmfirth the Liberal Association which rejected the eight-hour day to the disgust of the miners' delegates who forthwith resigned.[133] In Shipley the Liberal caucus, where three men were "ruling the roost," which held down Radical contendents.[134] In Bradford the worsted-spinning Liberal Nonconformist MP and the Liberal Watch Committee. In every case social and industrial agitation on questions in the immediate, everyday experience of the working people, confronted the face—sometimes complacent, sometimes oppressive, sometimes just plain stupid—of established Liberalism. As the people recoiled in confusion and anger, the socialists seized their opportunity and founded the ILP.

iv.

HOW FAR WAS the Yorkshire ILP an authentic socialist party? How far was it a late product of Liberal-Radicalism, carried by a temporary tide of industrial and social unrest into independent political channels? The evidence is conflicting. Lister, in his 1893 contest at Halifax, went out of his way to emphasise that he was a labour, and not a socialist, candidate.[135] Calculations at Halifax and Bradford suggest that a fair number of votes were drawn from former Conservative electors, but undoubtedly the majority came from Liberal electors or from young men voting for the first time.[136] In 1897 Tom Mann fought a by-election at Halifax, polling 2,000 votes. In an after-the-poll speech he paid tactful and generous tribute to Lister, but

> most excellent man as he was ... his particular appreciation of Socialism, his method of advocating Socialism, his speaking of it as advanced Liberalism ... was one of the chief reasons he had succeeded in getting the number of votes he had. (Cheers.) In his judgement the Socialist movement generally, and the Independent Labour Party particularly, did not at the last fight reach that particular stage when the issues were sufficiently clearly defined.... He contended that there were more Socialists in Halifax today than there were when Mr Lister polled 3,800. (Cheers.)[137]

The first years of the Halifax ILP bear out this judgment; endless bickering and defections in the 600-strong branch called upon the time of Hardie, Mann, and even the Annual Conference and revealed how many disgruntled Liberals and even Tories had been swept into the movement in 1892.

No doubt this was true elsewhere, and helps to explain a certain decline in support in the late nineties. It is true also that socialist demands were sometimes tacked on to liberal-democratic demands in an almost ludicrous manner, to disarm opposition or as a casual afterthought.[138] But this is only half the truth, and the less important half. The Yorkshire ILP was a party of youth; its leaders— Maguire, Ben Turner, Jowett—were young; the men and women who staffed the Labour unions and clubs, the Labour churches, the trade unions and Trades Councils, were often in their twenties. And the young people were socialists— ardent followers of Hardie, Morris, Blatchford, Tillett, Mann. When Blatchford accepted the East Bradford nomination he was uncompromising in his socialist advocacy: "The earth and all that the earth produced—the tools they used, the land and all the capital belonged to the people." The *Yorkshire Factory Times* commended this doctrine in its editorial, as "the foundation upon which the Independent Labour Party must be built. It is a rock, and is irremovable. It is as firmly fixed as the earth itself. It is a line of demarcation over which neither Liberal nor Tory may pass and retain his creed."[139]

It was this socialist conviction which prevented the Bradford men from surrendering to Liberal blandishment, when Tillett was offered a straight fight with the Tory in West Bradford.[140] The young socialist delegates gave an overwhelming rebuff to Mahon's attempt to draw the socialist teeth of the ILP at its first conference. In October 1894 the delegates at the Yorkshire Federation of the ILP were dissuaded from voting for a change of name to the "Socialist Labour Party" only by the advocacy of Maguire who (at 29) was "as old a Socialist as any in the room."[141]

In private—it is true—Maguire had his doubts. There were troubles enough in the early ILP—enough to make him wish to concentrate on his writing for the *Factory Times* and *Labour Leader,* or to prefer a part in the unemployed agitation to "your damned party politics and silly quarrels."

> People call themselves Socialists [he wrote to a friend], but what they really are is just ordinary men with Socialist opinions hung round, they haven't got it inside of them. . . . It's hard, very hard; we get mixed up in disputes among ourselves . . . and can't keep a straight line for the great thing, even if we all of us know what that is.[142]

No doubt, as a confirmed atheist, he distrusted the spell-binding "Come to Jesus" appeal which the new men like Snowden were bringing into the movement.[143] His early maturity seemed to be giving way to a premature middle-age, hastened by illness and perhaps by the lurking awareness that he was soon to "be eternally elbowed out of place after one small scrappy peep at the big show." Not yet 30, he was to be found more and more often drinking in the Leeds Central

ILP Club, telling stories of the "old days" like an old-timer, and entertaining the company with anecdotes and songs. He continued his part in the unemployed agitation, concealing from everybody the fact that he was practically one of the unemployed himself. Early in March 1895, in his thirtieth year, he collapsed with pneumonia; his comrades found him without food or fire in the house; he died on 8 March, refusing the services of a priest: "I will stand or fall on the last twelve years of my life and not on the last five minutes." His funeral was attended by a demonstration almost as large as those of 1889–90, in which Jewish tailoring workers and Irish labourers, gasworkers and ILP councillors, all joined. With his death a phase of the movement comes to an end.[144]

The young men of the Yorkshire ILP owed much to Maguire. He had been the point of junction between the theoretical understanding of the national leaders, the moral teaching of Morris and Carpenter, and the needs and aspirations of his own people. Nothing in history happens spontaneously, nothing worthwhile is achieved without the expense of intellect and spirit. Maguire had spent his energies without restraint. A poet of real talent, his feelings had been assaulted by the filth of Leeds; the rag, shoddy, and wool-combing industries, with their toll of disease and the dread anthrax. His bitter experiences while organising the tailoresses were recorded in his *Machine Room Chants*; sometimes in the moving tales of poverty: "No, I wouldn't like to die, sir, for I think the good Lord's hard / On us common workin' women; an' the like o' me's debarred / From His high, uncertain heaven, where fine ladies all go to. / So I try to keep on living, though the Lord knows how I do." Sometimes in humorous sketches of the problems of the organiser:

> They say I am cutting the other girls out
> Who work for their bread and tea—no doubt;
>   But, thank you! England's free,
>   Te-he!
> I will do as I like as long as I dare,
> What's fair to me is my own affair,
> And I'll please myself anyhow—so there!
>   Says the Duchess of Number Three.
> And the Number Three Department girls
> They copy her hat and the cut of her curls—
>   'Tis a touching sight to see,
>   Dear me!
> Her slightest word is their sacred law,
> They run her errands and stand her jaw,
> Content to find neither fault nor flaw
>   In the Duchess of Number Three.

If many of the Yorkshire young people had in fact got socialism "inside of them," then something of its quality—the hostility to Grundyism, the warm espousal of sex equality, the rich internationalism—owed much to Maguire. It is time that this forgotten "provincial" was admitted to first-class citizenship of history, and time also that we discarded the theory of the spontaneous combustion of the Yorkshire ILP.

Notes on the South Leeds Election

ON THE RESIGNATION of the Liberal member for South Leeds in August 1892, J. L. Mahon at once wrote to Champion for his support in financing an Independent Labour Candidate in a three-cornered contest. "I am rather sick of helping backboneless people into Parliament," Champion replied (27 August 1892). However, after various possible candidates load been approached without success (Mann, Hammill, Clem Edwards, Solly), Champion urged Mahon to stand himself. Champion saw his own part as that of an authoritative Parnell, and wrote to Mahon (5 September 1892): "If as I am rather inclined to do, I go in for taking hold of the ILP and running it for all it is worth, I mean to have as lieutenants men who won't scuttle at the first shot and will agree with me that our only chance is to go for the Liberals all along the line without gloves. It is possible, given pluck to put out 50 Liberals at the next election by running men in 10 seats and voting Tory in the other 40. That will cause some little fuss, and will probably put in a Tory Govt. holding power at the sweet will of the ILP. But it will make the Labour question in general and 8 hours in particular what the Irish question has been made by similar tactics."

While Champion scoured the London clubs for money, Mahon implemented this policy and mounted a campaign on aggressively anti-Gladstonian lines. From his letters Champion would appear to have been suffering from delusions of grandeur: he wrote of his conversations with Chamberlain; his financial resources; his "personal adherents" in various towns; his intention of sending the Liberals "back to opposition"; of buying control of the *Workman's Times;* of "exposing" all new union leaders who refused to speak for Mahon. He sent a strong-arm man from Liverpool (14 September 1892): "the handiest man with his fists of my acquaintance . . . very good tempered doesn't drink, and never hits anybody first. But he knows his business and will half kill the biggest Irishman in Leeds in two minutes." Votes were not a serious consideration—"the main thing is to stoke up the anti-liberal feeling for the future." When Keir Hardie came up to help Mahon, Champion wrote (20 September 1892), "Please assure him from me, that if he will come and see me on his arrival in London, I shall be able, and willing, to render him independent of any attacks he may meet in his Constituency for helping you."

Mahon's election manifesto was a long anti-Gladstonian harangue, culminating in a series of Radical (but not socialist) demands. The provocation offered
to Liberal electors was only too successful. Mahon's main election meeting was
packed with Gladstonian supporters—with the Irish most prominent; neither
the candidate, nor Tom Maguire (the Chairman), nor H. H. Champion himself,
could gain a hearing; and the meeting ended in violent riot (*Leeds Mercury, Sheffield Daily Telegraph,* 19 September 1892). Three days later Mahon was disqualified from standing owing to an error in his nomination papers, and the incident
ended in general ill-will.

Champion and Mahon remained in correspondence and confidently
expected to dominate the first ILP Conference: on 4 November 1892 Champion was writing: "There will practically be none there—outside the local
men—but my men." Even Hardie was marked down as "going on all right. . . . If
he goes on as he is, I would help him and forgive him his 'in-and-out-running'
just after the election." Mahon, for his part, was advising Yorkshire audiences
to support those in favour of Chamberlain's "Labour Programme" unless the
Liberals brought out a better one (*Keighley News,* 10 December 1892). His final
action in the Yorkshire ILP was to denounce John Lister's candidature at Halifax
in February 1893. This curious combination of Parnellite tactics, Tory money,
arbitrary intrigue, and apparently "pro-Tory" interventions, helps to explain the
setback suffered by the Leeds ILP, the bitterness of feeling between old and new
unionists on the Leeds Trades Council, and the profound suspicion with which
some Socialists (who knew of Champion's and Mahon's strategy) regarded the
first year of the ILP.

THOMPSON PUBLISHED THIS ARTICLE IN THE *NEW LEFT Review* I/15 (May–June 1962) as "a chapter from a book shortly to be published." The book, of course, was *The Making of the English Working Class.* Thompson explains the eighteenth-century "common Englishman" as "not so much democratic, in any positive sense, as anti-authoritarian. He felt himself to be an individualist, with few affirmative rights, but protected by the laws against the intrusion of arbitrary power." Then comes the French Revolution, the English Jacobins, and Tom Paine and the *Rights of Man*, "a foundation text of the English working-class movement." "The English Jacobins pleaded for internationalism, for arbitration in place of war, for the toleration of dissenters, Catholics and free-thinkers, for the discernment of human virtue in 'heathen, Turk or Jew.'" They sought, by education and agitation, to transform "the mob" (in Paine's words) from "followers of the camp" to followers of "the *standard* of liberty."

The Free-born Englishman

When reform agitation resumed in 1816, it was not possible, either in London or in the industrial North or Midlands, to employ a "Church and King" mob to terrorise the Radicals. From time to time, between 1815 and 1850, Radicals, Owenites, or Chartists complained of the apathy of the people. But—if we leave out of account the usual election tumults—it is generally true that reformers were shielded by the support of working-class communities. At election times in the large towns, the open vote by show of hands on the "hustings" which preceded the poll usually went overwhelmingly for the most radical candidate. The reformers ceased to fear "the mob," while the authorities were forced to build barracks and take precautions against the "revolutionary crowd." This is one of those facts of history so big that it is easily overlooked, or assumed without question; and yet it indicates a major shift in emphasis in the inarticulate, "sub-political" attitudes of the masses. We must look in many directions to find reasons for this change—the Jacobin propaganda of the 1790s, the painful experiences of the Napoleonic Wars, effects of industrialisation, the growing discredit of the monarchy (culminating in the Queen Caroline agitation of 1820), increasing popular alienation from the established Church, the educative propaganda of Cobbett and of the cheap Radical press after 1815, the ambiguous influence of the Irish immigration (which—while a source of new tumults—was never a source for tame "Church and King" mobs).

The shift in emphasis is perhaps related to popular notions of "independence," patriotism, and the Englishman's "birthright." The Gordon Rioters of 1780 and the "Church and King" rioters who destroyed the houses of wealthy dissenters in Birmingham in 1791 had this in common: they felt themselves, in some obscure way, to be defending the "Constitution" against alien elements who threatened their "birthright." They had been taught for so long that the Revolution settlement, embodied in the Constitution of King, Lords and Commons, was the guarantee of British independence and liberties that a kind of reflex had been engendered—Constitution=Liberty—upon which the unscrupulous might play. And yet it is likely that the very rioters who destroyed Dr.

Priestley's precious library and laboratory were proud to regard themselves as "free-born Englishmen." Patriotism, nationalism, even bigotry and repression, were all clothed in the rhetoric of liberty. Even Old Corruption extolled British liberties; not national honour, or power, but freedom was the coinage of patrician, demagogue and radical alike. In the name of freedom Burke denounced, and Paine championed, the French Revolution: with the opening of the French wars (1793), patriotism and liberty occupied every poetaster:

> Thus Britons guard their ancient fame,
> Assert their empire o'er the sea,
> And to the envying world proclaim,
> One nation still is brave and free—
> Resolv'd to conquer or to die,
> True to their KING, their LAWS, their LIBERTY.

The invasion scare of 1802–3 resulted in a torrent of broadsheets and ballads on such themes, which form a fitting background for Wordsworth's smug and sonorous patriotic sonnets:

> It is not to be thought of that the Flood
> Of British freedom, which, to the open sea
> Of the world's praise, from dark antiquity
> Hath flowed, "with pomp of waters, unwithstood."

"Not to be thought of," and yet, at this very time, freedom of the press, of public meeting, of trade union organisation, of political organisation and of election, were either severely limited or in abeyance. What, then, did the common Englishman's "birthright" consist in? "Security of property," answered Mary Wollstonecraft in her *Rights of Men:* "Behold . . . the definition of English liberty." And yet the rhetoric of liberty meant much more—first of all, of course, freedom from foreign domination. And, within this enveloping haze of patriotic self-congratulation, there were other less distinct notions which Old Corruption felt bound to flatter and yet which were to prove dangerous to it in the long run. Freedom from absolutism (the constitutional monarchy), freedom from arbitrary arrest, trial by jury, equality before the law, the freedom of the home from arbitrary entrance and search, some limited liberty of thought, of speech, and of conscience, the vicarious participation in liberty (or in its semblance) afforded by the right of parliamentary opposition and by elections and election tumults (although the people had no vote they had the right to parade, huzza and jeer on the hustings), as well as freedom to travel, trade, and sell one's own labour. Nor were any of these freedoms insignificant; taken together, they add up to a "moral consensus" in which authority at times shared, and of which at all times it was bound to take account.

Indefinite as such a notion of "moral consensus" may be, this question of the *limits* beyond which the Englishman was not prepared to be "pushed around," and the limits beyond which authority did not dare to go, is crucial to an understanding of this period. The stance of the common Englishman was not so much democratic, in any positive sense, as anti-authoritarian. He felt himself to be an individualist, with few affirmative rights, but protected by the laws against the intrusion of arbitrary power. And this indeed was the central paradox of the 18th century, in both intellectual and practical terms: constitutionalism was the "illusion of the epoch." Political theory, of traditionalists and reformers alike, was transfixed within the whiggish limits established by the 1688 settlement, by Locke, by Blackstone, in much the same way as the most diverse groups in the Soviet world today must argue out their differences within the terms and conventions of traditional Marxism. For Locke, the chief ends of government were the maintenance of civil peace, and the security of the person and of property. Such a theory, diluted by self-interest and prejudice, might provide the propertied classes with a sanction for the most bloody code penalising offenders against property; but it provided no sanction for *arbitrary* authority, intruding upon personal or property rights, and uncontrolled by the rule of law. Hence the paradox, which surprised many foreign observers, of a bloody penal code alongside a *liberal* and, at times, meticulous administration and interpretation of the laws. The 18th century was indeed a great century for constitutional theorists, judges, and lawyers. The poor man might often feel little protection when caught up in the law's toils. But the jury system *did* afford a measure of protection, as Hardy, Horne Tooke, Thelwall and Binne discovered. Wilkes *was* able to defy King, Parliament and administration—and to establish important new precedents—by using alternatively the law courts and the "mob." There was no *droit administratif*, no right of arbitrary arrest or search. Even in the 1790s, each attempt to introduce a "continental" spy system, each suspension *of habeas corpus*, each attempt to pack juries, aroused an outcry beyond the reformers' own ranks. If any—faced by the records of Tyburn and of repression—are inclined to question the value of these limits, they should contrast the trial of Hardy and his colleagues with the treatment of Muir, Gerrald, Skirving and Palmer in 1793–4 in the Scottish courts.

This constitutionalism coloured the less articulate responses of the "free-born Englishman." He claimed few rights except that of being left alone. No institution was as much hated, in the 18th century, as the press-gang. A standing army was distrusted, and few of Pitt's repressive measures aroused as much discontent as the erection of barracks near the industrial towns. The profession of a soldier was held to be dishonourable. "In arbitrary Monarchies," wrote one pamphleteer in 1793, where the Despot who reigns can say to his wretched subjects, "Eat straw," and they eat straw, no wonder that they can raise Armies of human Butchers, to destroy their fellow creatures; but, in a country like Great Britain, which at least is *pretended to be free*, it becomes a matter of no small surprise that so many thousands of men should deliberately renounce the privileges and blessings attendant on Freemen, and voluntarily sell themselves to the most humiliating and degrading *Slavery*, for the miserable pittance of sixpence a day.

Resistance to an effective police force continued well into the 19th century. Moreover, not only freedom from intrusion but also equality before the law was a source of popular congratulation. Sensational reading matter, such as the *New Newgate Calendar; or Malefactor's Bloody Register*, recorded with satisfaction instances of the noble and titled brought to. Tyburn. Local annalists recorded smugly such cases as that of Leeds' "domineering villanous lord of the manor" who was executed in 1748 for killing one of his own tenants in a fit of temper. And, in hostility to the powers of any central authority, we have a curious blend of popular and parochial defensiveness. Local rights and customs were cherished against the encroachment of the State by gentry and common people alike; hostility to "the Thing" and to "Bashaws" contributed much to the Tory-Radical strain which runs through from Cobbett to Oastler, and which reached its climax in the resistance to the Poor Law of 1834.

This notion of the rule of law as the effective defence of the citizen against arbitrary authority was accepted by even the extreme reformers. The London Corresponding Society, in an Address of 1793 sought to define the difference in status between the English commoner and the commoner in pre-revolutionary France: "Our persons were protected by the laws, while their lives were at the mercy of every titled individual. . . . We were MEN while they were SLAVES." But this defensive ideology nourished, of course, far larger claims to positive rights. Wilkes had known well how to strike this chord—the champion defending his individual rights passed imperceptibly into the free-born citizen challenging King and Ministers and claiming rights for which there was no precedent. In 1776 Wilkes went so far as to plead in the House of Commons for the political rights of "the meanest mechanic, the poorest peasant and day labourer," who—

has important rights respecting his personal liberty, that of his wife and children, his property however inconsiderable, his wages . . . which are in many trades and manufacturers regulated by the power of Parliament. . . . Some share therefore in the power of making those laws which deeply interest them . . . should be reserved even to this inferior but most useful set of men.

The argument is still that of Ireton (or Burke) but property-rights are interpreted in a far more liberal sense; and Wilkes rounded it off with the customary appeal to tradition and precedent: "Without a true representation of the Commons our constitution is essentially defective . . . and all other remedies to recover the pristine purity of the form of government established by our ancestors would be ineffectual."

"Pristine purity," "our ancestors"—these are key phrases, and for 20 years arguments among reformers turned upon nice interpretations of these terms. *Which* model was pure and pristine, to *which* ancestors should reformers refer? To the founding fathers of the United States, breaking free from the trammels of precedent, it seemed sufficient to find certain truths "self-evident." But to Major John Cartwright (1740–1824) publishing his pamphlet *Take Your Choice* in the same year as the Declaration of Independence (1776), it seemed necessary to shore up his case for annual parliaments, equal electoral districts, payment of members, and adult manhood suffrage, with reference to Saxon precedent. The "good, grey major" defined as early as this the main claims of advanced political reformers, from 1776 to the Chartists and beyond. And from these claims he never swerved. Incorruptible, incapable of compromise, eccentric and courageous, the Major pursued his single-minded course, issuing letters, appeals, and pamphlets, from his seat in Boston, Lincs, surviving trials, tumults, dissension and repression. It was he who sallied forth after the Napoleonic Wars, to found the first reform societies of a new era, the Hampden Clubs. But although the Major's principles and proposals outlived his own long lifetime, his arguments did not.

In a moment, we shall see why. (The answer, in two words, is Tom Paine.) But we should first note that in the 20 years before the French Revolution a new dimension was *in practice* being added to the accepted procedures of the constitution. The Press had already established indefinite rights independent of King, Lords and Commons; and the agitation surrounding Wilkes' *North Briton* revealed both the precariousness of these rights and the sensitivity of a large public in their defence. But the second half of the 18th century sees also the rise of the Platform—the "extra-parliamentary" pressure group, campaigning for more or less limited aims, mobilising opinion "without doors" by means of publications, great meetings, and petitions. A new cog was added to the complicated machinery of constitution; Erskine and Wyvill, using the familiar mechanical imagery of checks and balances, called for "Clock-Work Regularity in the movements of the People." Major John Cartwright went further—the more fuss stirred up, for the most far-reaching demands, among all classes of people, the better:

On the old maxim of teaching a young archer to shoot at the moon [he wrote to Wyvill] in order that he may acquire the power of throwing his arrow far enough for practical purposes, I have always thought that a free discussion of the principle of Universal Suffrage the most likely means of obtaining any Reform at all worth contending for.

For the Major—although he couched his arguments in terms of precedent and tradition—believed in methods of agitation among "members unlimited." In the dark winter of repression, 1797–9, the gallant squire of Boston issued a reproof to the caution of the pusillanimous North Yorkshire reformer. "I am but little afraid of your Yeomanry," he wrote to Wyvill, "but your *Gentlemen* I dread.... It is fortunate for me that hitherto all the *Gentlemen*, except one, have been on the *other side*. My efforts, therefore, have not been maimed by their counsels, and I have on all occasions spoken out,

> I feel as if nothing but strong cordials, and the most powerful stimulants, can awaken the People to any thing energetic.... Unless our appeals convince all understandings, and the truths we utter irresistibly seize on the heart, we shall do nothing.... If you should, in order to get on at all, be compelled to propose mere expedients short of such energetic appeals, I hope in God you will be rescued from the situation by some strong-minded men at your Meeting.

Similar constitutional arguments might, then, conceal deep differences in tone and in means of propaganda. But all reformers before Paine commenced with "the corruptions of the Constitution." And their degree of radicalism can generally be inferred from the historical precedents cited in their writings. The aristocratic Whig Supporters of the Bill of Rights were content to enforce the precedent of the settlement of 1688. The advanced Society for Constitutional Information, founded in 1780, whose pamphlets by Dr. Jebb, Cartwright, and Capel Lofft provided Thomas Hardy with his first introduction to reform, ranged widely—to the Magna Carta and beyond—for precedents, and drew upon both Anglo-Saxon and American example. And, after the French Revolution, theorists of the popular societies dealt largely in Anglo-Saxon "tythings," the Witenagemot, and legends of Alfred's reign. "Pristine purity," and "our ancestors," became—for many Jacobins—almost any constitutional innovation for which a Saxon precedent could be ramped up. John Baxter, a Shoreditch silversmith, a leader of the L.C.S. and a fellow-prisoner on trial with Hardy, found time to publish an 830-page *New and Impartial History of England* (1796) in which Saxon precedent is almost indistinguishable from the state of nature, the noble savage, or the original social contract. "Originally," Baxter supposed, "the constitution must have been free." History was the history of its corruption, "the Britons having been subdued first by the Romans, next by the Saxons, these again by the Danes, and, finally, all by the Normans." As for the Revolution of 1688 it "did no more than expel a tyrant, and confirm the Saxon laws." But there were plenty of these laws still to be restored; and, next to universal suffrage, the ones which Baxter liked best were the absence of a standing army, and the right of each citizen to go armed. He had arrived, by industrious constitutional arguments, at the right of the people to overthrow the constitution.

Nevertheless, as Christopher Hill has shown in his study of the theory of the "Norman Yoke," these elaborate and often specious constitutional controversies were of real significance. Even the forms of antiquarian argument can conceal important differences in political emphasis. From the anonymous *Historical Essay on the English Constitution* (1771) to the early 1790s, the more advanced reformers were marked out by their fondness for citing Saxon precedent. Long before this Tom Paine had published his *Common Sense* (1776) whose arguments were scarcely conducive to the appeal to precedent:

A French bastard landing with an armed banditti and establishing himself King of England, against the consent of the natives, is, in plain terms, a very paltry, rascally original. It certainly hath no divinity in it. . . . The plain truth is that the antiquity of English monarchy will not bear looking into.

But this was published on American soil; and, as we shall see, it was only after the French Revolution and the publication of *Rights of Man* that such iconoclasm was heard in England: "If the succession runs in the line of the Conqueror, the nation runs in the line of being conquered, and ought to rescue itself from this reproach." Meanwhile, the theory of the "Norman Yoke" showed astonishing vitality; and even had a revival, in Jacobin circles, after 1793, when Paine was driven into exile and his *Rights of Man* was banned as seditious libel.

This was, in part, a matter of expediency. Paine's prosecution revealed the limits of freedom permitted within the conventions of constitutionalism. To deny altogether the appeal to "pristine purity" and "our ancestors" was actively dangerous. When Henry Yorke, the Sheffield reformer, was on trial in 1795, his defence turned upon this point: "In almost every speech I took essential pains in controverting the doctrines of Thomas Paine, who denied the existence of our constitution. . . . I constantly asserted, on the contrary, that we had a good constitution," "that magnanimous government which we derived from our Saxon fathers, and from the prodigious mind of the immortal Alfred." Even John Baxter, whose "Saxons" were Jacobins and *sans-culottes* to a man, felt it expedient to dissociate himself from Paine's total lack of reverence: "Much as we respect the opinions of Mr. Thomas Paine . . . we cannot agree with him, that we have no constitution; his mistake seems to arise from having carried his views no further than the Norman Conquest."

E. P. Thompson and the Making of the New Left

But it was more than expediency. According to legend, Saxon precedent provided precedents for a constitutional monarchy, a free Parliament based on universal manhood suffrage, and the rule of law. In coming forward as "Patriots" and
constitutionalists, men like Major Cartwright and Baxter were attempting to take
over the rhetoric of the age. It seemed that if matters were to be posed as bluntly
as Paine had posed them in *Common Sense*, then reformers would be forced to
disengage from the constitutional debate altogether, and rest their claims upon
reason, conscience, self-interest, "self-evident" truths. For many 18th-century
Englishmen whose minds were nurtured in a constitutionalist culture the idea
was shocking, unnerving, and, in its implications, dangerous.

And yet it was necessary that this rhetoric should be broken through,
because—even when tricked out in Baxter's improbable Saxon terms—it
implied the absolute sanctity of certain conventions: respect for the institution of monarchy, for the hereditary principle, for the traditional rights of the
great landowners and the Established Church, and for the representation, not
of human rights, but of property rights. Once enmeshed in constitutionalist
arguments—even when these were used to advance the claims of manhood suffrage—reformers became caught up in the trivia of piecemeal constitutional
restoration. For a plebeian radical movement to arise it was essential to escape
from these categories altogether and to set forward far wider democratic claims.
In the years between 1770 and 1790 we can observe a dialectical paradox
through which the rhetoric of constitutionalism contributed to its own destruction or transcendence. Just as students in the Communist world today who read
Lenin find in his writings a devastating criticism of aspects of Soviet reality, so
those in the 18th century who read Locke or Blackstone's commentaries, found
in them a devastating criticism of the workings of faction and interest in the
unreformed House of Commons. The first reaction was to criticise the practice
in the light of the theory; the second, more delayed, reaction was to bring the
theory itself into discredit. And it was at this point that Paine entered, with
the *Rights of Man*.

The French Revolution had set a new "precedent": a new constitution had
been drawn up, in the light of reason and from first principles—which threw
"the meagre, stale, forbidding ways of custom, law, and statute" into the shadows.
And it was not Paine, but Burke, who effected the first major evacuation of the
grounds of constitutional argument. The French example, on one hand, and the
industrious reformers quarrying for pre-1688 or pre-Norman precedent, on the
other, had made the old ground untenable. In his *Reflections on the French Revolution* Burke supplemented the authority of precedent by that of wisdom and
experience, and the reverence for the constitution by reverence for tradition—
that "partnership . . . between those who are living, those who are dead, and
those who are to be born." The theory of checks and balances upon the exercise

of specific powers is translated into the moody notion of checks and balances upon the imperfections of man's nature:

> The science of constructing a commonwealth . . . is not to be taught *a priori*. . . . The nature of man is intricate; the objects of society are of the greatest possible complexity: and therefore no simple disposition or direction of power can be suitable either to man's nature, or to the quality of his affairs. . . . The rights of men in governments are . . . often in balances between differences of good; in compromises sometimes between good and evil, and sometimes between evil and evil.

Radical reformers "are so taken up with their theories about the rights of man, that they have totally forgotten his nature." "By their violent haste and their defiance of the process of nature, they are delivered over blindly to every projector and adventurer, to every alchymist and empiric."

The argument is deduced from man's moral nature in general; but we repeatedly glimpse sight of the fact that it was not the moral nature of a corrupt aristocracy which alarmed Burke so much as the nature of the populace, "the swinish multitude." Burke's great historical sense was thought to imply a "process of nature" so complex and procrastinating that any innovation was full of unseen dangers—a process in which the common people might have no part. If Tom Paine was wrong to dismiss Burke's cautions (for his *Rights of Man* was written in reply to Burke), he was right to expose the inertia of class interests which underlay his special pleading. Academic judgement has dealt strangely with the two men. Burke's reputation as a political philosopher has been inflated, very much so in recent years. Paine has often been dismissed as a mere populariser. In truth, neither writer was systematic enough to rank as a major political theorist. Both were publicists of genius, both are less remarkable for what they say than for the *tone* in which it is said. Paine lacks any depth of reading, any sense of cultural security, and is betrayed by his arrogant and impetuous temper into writing passages of a mediocrity which the academic mind still winces at and lays aside with a sigh. But the popular mind remembers Burke less for his insight than for his epochal indiscretion—"the swinish multitude"—the giveaway phrase which revealed another kind of insensitivity of which Paine was incapable, a blemish which vitiates the composure of 18th-century polite culture. In all the angry popular pamphleteering which followed it might almost seem that the issues could be defined in five words: Burke's two-word epithet on the one hand, Paine's three-word banner on the other. With dreary invention the popular pamphleteers performed satirical variations upon Burke's theme: *Hog's Wash, Pig's Meat, Politics for the People: A Salmagundy for Swine* (with contributions from "Brother Grunter," "Porculus" and *ad nauseam)* were the titles of the pamphlets and periodicals. The stye, the swineherds, the bacon—so it goes on. "Whilst ye are . . . gorging yourselves at troughs filled with the daintiest wash; we, with our numerous train of *porkers*, are employed, from the rising to the setting sun, to obtain the means of subsistence, by . . . picking up a few acorns," runs an *Address to the Hon. Edmund Burke from the Swinish Multitude* (1793). No other words have ever made the "free-born Englishman" so angry—nor so ponderous in reply.

Since the *Rights of Man* is a foundation text of the English working-class movement, we must look at its arguments and tone more closely. Paine wrote on English soil, but as an American with an international reputation who had lived for close on 15 years in the bracing climate of experiment and constitutional iconoclasm. "I wished to know," he wrote in the Preface to the Second Part, "the manner in which a work, written in a style of thinking and expression different to what had been customary in England, would be received." From the outset he rejected the framework of constitutional argument: "I am contending for the rights of the living, and against their being willed away, and controlled and contracted for, by the manuscript-assumed authority of the dead." Burke wished to "consign over the rights of posterity for ever, on the authority of a mouldy parchment," while Paine asserted that each successive generation was competent to define its rights and form of government anew.

As for the English Constitution, no such thing existed. At the most, it was a "sepulchre of precedents," a kind of "Political Popery"; and "government by precedent, without any regard to the principle of the precedent, is one of the vilest systems that can be set up." All Governments, except those in France and America, derived their authority from conquest and superstition: their foundation lay upon "arbitrary power." And Paine reserved his particular invective for the superstitious regard in which the means for the continuation of this power was secured—the hereditary principle. "A banditti of ruffians overrun a country, and lay it under contributions. Their power being thus established, the chief of the band contrived to lose the name of Robber in that of Monarch; and hence the origin of Monarchy and Kings." As for the right of inheritance, "to inherit a Government, is to inherit the People, as if they were flocks and herds." "Kings succeed each other, not as rationals, but as animals. . . . It requires some talents to be a common mechanic; but to be a King, requires only the animal figure of a man—a sort of breathing automaton."

> The time is not very far distant when England will laugh at itself for sending to Holland, Hanover, Zell, or Brunswick for men, at the expence of a million a year, who understood neither her laws, her language, nor her interest, and whose capacities would scarcely have fitted them for the office of a parish constable.

The hereditary system in general was consigned to the same oblivion: "An hereditary governor is as inconsistent as an hereditary author."

All this was blasphemy. Even the sacred Bill of Rights Paine found to be "a bill of wrongs and of insult." It is not that Paine was the first man to think in this way: many 18th-century Englishmen must have held these thoughts privately. He was the first to dare to express himself with such irreverence; and he destroyed with one book century-old taboos. But Paine did very much more than this. In the first place he suggested—although in a confused, ambiguous manner—a theory of the State and of class power. In *Common Sense* he had followed Locke in seeing Government as a "necessary evil." In the 1790s the ambiguities of Locke seem to fall into two halves, one Burke, the other Paine. Where Burke assumes Government and examines its operation in the light of experience and tradition, Paine speaks for the governed, and assumes that the authority of Government derives from conquest and inherited power in a class-divided society. The classes are roughly defined—"There are two distinct classes of men in the nation, those who pay taxes, and those who receive and live upon taxes"—and as for the Constitution, it is a good one for—"courtiers, placemen, pensioners, borough-holders, and the leaders of the Parties . . . ; but it is a bad Constitution for at least ninety-nine parts of the nation out of a hundred."

From this also, the war of the propertied and the unpropertied: "When the rich plunder the poor of his rights, it becomes an example to the poor to plunder the rich of his property." By this argument, Government appears as Court parasitism: taxes are a form of robbery, for sinecurists and for wars of conquest: while "the whole of the Civil Government is executed by the People of every town and country, by means of parish officers, magistrates, quarterly sessions, juries, and assize, without any trouble to what is called the Government." So that—at this point—we are close to a theory of anarchism. What is required is less the reform than the abolition of Government: "The instant formal Government is abolished, society begins to act."

On the other hand, "society," acting through a representative system as a Government, opened up new possibilities which suddenly caught fire in Paine's mind while writing the crucial fifth chapter of the Second Part of *Rights of Man*. Here, after extolling Commerce and industrial enterprise, clouting colonial domination (and—later—proposing international arbitration in place of war), hitting out at the penal code ("legal barbarity"), denouncing closed Charters, Corporations, and monopolies, exclaiming against the burden of taxation, he came to rest for a moment on the sins of the landed aristocracy:

> Why . . . does Mr. Burke talk of this House of Peers, as the pillar of the landed interest? Were that pillar to sink into the earth, the same landed property would continue, and the same ploughing, sowing, and reaping

would go on. The Aristocracy are not the farmers who work the land . . . but are the mere consumers of the rent.

And this led him on to far-reaching impressionistic proposals for cutting the costs of Government, army and navy; remitting taxes and poor rates; raising additional taxation by means of a graduated income-tax (rising to 20 shillings in the pound at £23,000 p.a.); and paying out the moneys raised or saved in sums to alleviate the position of the poor. He proposed family allowances; public funds to enable general education of all children; old-age pensions—"not as a matter of grace and favour, but of right" (for the recipients would receive back only a portion of what they had contributed in taxation); a maternity benefit, a benefit for newly wedded couples, a benefit for funerals for the necessitous: and the building in London of combined lodging-houses and workshops to assist immigrants and unemployed.

> By the operation of this plan, the poor laws, those instruments of civil torture, will be superseded. . . . The dying poor will not be dragged from place to place to breathe their last, as a reprisal of parish upon parish. Widows will have a maintenance for their children . . . and children will no longer be considered as encreasing the distresses of their parents. . . . The number of petty crimes, the offspring of distress and poverty, will be lessened. The poor, as well as the rich, will then be interested in the support of Government, and the cause and apprehension of riots and tumults will cease. Ye who sit in ease, and solace yourselves in plenty . . . have ye thought of these things?

This is Paine at his strongest. The success of the First Part of *Rights of Man* was great, but the success of the Second Part was phenomenal. It was this part—and especially such sections as these—which effected a bridge between the older radicalism of the Whig "commonwealthsman" and the radicalism of Sheffield cutlers, Norwich weavers and London artisans.

Reform was related, by these proposals, to their daily experience of economic hardship. However specious some of Paine's financial calculations may have been, the proposals gave a new constructive cast to the whole reform agitation. Cartwright formulated the specific demands for manhood suffrage which were to be the basis for a hundred years of agitation (and Mary Wollstonecraft, with her *Rights of Women*, initiated for the second sex an even longer era of struggle). Paine, in this chapter, set a course towards the social legislation of Liberal and Labour administrations in this century.

Few of Paine's ideas were original, except perhaps in this "social" chapter. "Men who give themselves to their Energetic Genius in the manner that Paine does are

no Examiners"—the comment is William Blake's. What he gave to English people
was a new rhetoric of radical egalitarianism, which touched the deepest responses
of the "free-born Englishman" and which penetrated the "sub-political" attitudes
of the urban working people. Cobbett was not a true Painite, and Owen and the
early Socialists contributed a new strand altogether; but the Paine tradition runs
strongly through the popular journalism of the 19th century—Wooler, Carlyle,
Hetherington, Lovett, Holyoake, Bradlaugh, *Reynold's News*. It is strongly challenged in the 1880's but the tradition and the rhetoric are still alive in Blatchford
and in the popular appeal of Lloyd George. We can almost say that Paine established a new framework within which radicalism was confined for nearly a hundred years, as clear and as well-defined as the constitutionalism which it replaced.

What was this framework? Contempt for monarchical and hereditary principles, we have seen:

> I disapprove of monarchical and aristocratical governments, however
> modified. Hereditary distinctions, and privileged order of every species . . .
> must necessarily counteract the progress of human improvement. Hence
> it follows that I am not among the admirers of the British Constitution.

The words happen to be Wordsworth's—in 1793. And Wordsworth's also
the retrospective lines which recapture more than any other the optimism of
these revolutionary years when—walking with Beaupuy—he encountered a
"hunger-bitten" peasant girl:

> . . . and at the sight of my friend
> In agitation said, "Tis against *that*
> That we are fighting," I with him believed
> That a benignant spirit was abroad
> Which might not be withstood, that poverty
> Abject as this would in a little time
> Be found no more, that we should see the earth
> Unthwarted in her wish to recompense
> The meek, the lowly, patient child of toil,
> All institutes for ever blotted out
> That legalised exclusion, empty pomp
> Abolished, sensual state and cruel power,
> Whether by edict of the one or few;
> And finally, as sum and crown of all,
> Should see the people having a strong hand
> In framing their own laws; whence better days
> To all mankind.

This optimism (which Wordsworth was soon to lose) radicalism clung to tenaciously, founding it upon premises which Paine did not stop to examine: unbounded faith in representative institutions; in the power of reason; in (Paine's words) "a mass of sense lying in a dormant state" among the common people, and in the belief that "Man, were he not corrupted by Governments, is naturally the friend of Man, and that human nature is not of itself vicious." And all this expressed in an intransigent, brash, even cocksure tone, with the self-educated man's distrust of tradition and institutes of learning ("He knew by heart all his own writings and knew nothing else," was the comment of one of Paine's acquaintances), and a tendency to avoid complex theoretical problems with a dash of empiricism and an appeal to "Common Sense."

This, with its strengths and weaknesses, contributed much to working-class radicalism. But Paine's writings were in no special sense aimed at the working people, as distinct from farmers, tradesmen and professional men. His was a doctrine suited to agitation among "members unlimited"; but he did not challenge the doctrines of capitalist enterprise and of *laissez-faire*. His own affiliations were most obviously with the unrepresented manufacturing and commercial classes; with men like Thomas Walker, partner in his bridge-building enterprise, and leading Manchester reformer; with the Constitutional Society rather than the L.C.S. His proposals for a graduated income tax anticipate more far-reaching notions of property redistribution; but it is clear that they were aimed at the landed aristocracy, where the hereditary principle involved in the custom of primogeniture gave him offence. In terms of political democracy he wished to level all inherited distinctions and privileges; but he gave no countenance to economic levelling. In political society every man must have equal rights as a citizen: in economic society he must naturally remain employer or employed, and the State should not interfere with the capital of the one or the wages of the other. The *Rights of Man* and the *Wealth of Nations* should supplement and nourish each other. And in this also the main tradition of the 19th-century working-class radicalism took its cast from Paine. There were times, at the Owenite and Chartist climaxes, when other traditions seemed to become dominant. But after each relapse, the substratum of Painite assumptions seemed to remain intact. The aristocracy were the main target; their property might be threatened—even as far as Land Nationalisation or Henry George's Single Tax—and their rents regarded as a feudal exaction dating from "a French bastard" and his "armed banditti"; but—however hard trade unionists might fight against their employers—industrial capital was assumed to be the fruits of enterprise and beyond reach of political intrusion. Until the 1880s, it was—by and large—within this framework that working class radicalism remained transfixed.

It is true that there is in Paine a glibness and literalness of mind which was reproduced by bis English Jacobin followers in the 1790s and which—with the more sophisticated optimism of William Godwin—was bitterly rejected and caricatured by disenchanted reformers when French revolutionary Convention passed, by way of Terror, into Bonapartism. The critique and the caricature, expressed with the combined genius of Burke, Wordsworth, Coleridge, have dominated the judgments of many contemporary scholars, themselves exposed to similar experiences of revolutionary disenchantment in the past 25 years. And more recently, in a projection backwards of Cold War apologetics, the men of the Enlightenment, for whom Paine was the outstanding English publicist, are seen as rootless, disoriented intellectuals, whose naive faith in human perfectibility and disregard for traditional sanctities and for the institutional continuity of the "social organism" opened the way to "totalitarianism."

Against this new historical myth it is necessary to repeat once again the simplest truths. Paine and his English followers did not preach the extermination of their opponents, but they did preach against Tyburn and the sanguinary penal code. Paine himself was brought under the shadow of the guillotine for pleading for the life of the French King. The English Jacobins pleaded for internationalism, for arbitration in place of war, for the toleration of dissenters, Catholics and free-thinkers, for the discernment of human virtue in "heathen, Turk or Jew." They sought, by education and agitation, to transform "the mob" (in Paine's words) from "followers of the *camp*" to followers of "the *standard* of liberty."

They spoke also for the democracy of representative institutions, and against the oligarchy of property. Nor is there the least reason to suppose that without their agitation the middle and working classes would have been graciously admitted to a share in power according to some self-acting principle of institutional and organic continuity. On the contrary, the evidence runs the other way. We cannot say what the consequences would have been if Paine's followers had effected a revolution in this country; but we can say that it was Burke who said that the *Rights of Man* called for the "refutation . . . of criminal justice," and that it was the adherents of God and King and Law who employed repression, Botany Bay, and imprisonment against the "totalitarians." Finally, it is extraordinary that after 160 years it is still possible to find historians referring in a facile way to the French "Terror," as if it was the spontaneous generation of false philosophical and moral principles, and was unrelated to the threat of counter-revolution and conquest at the hands of a European reaction in which English diplomacy and the English Navy played a leading part.

This is not to dismiss the charges against some English Jacobins, of doctrinaire notions and shallow moral experimentalism, whose most notable expression is in Book III of Wordsworth's *Excursion*. These have often been the vices of the "Left." Paine had little historical sense, his view of human nature was facile, and his optimism ("I do not believe that Monarchy and Aristocracy will continue seven years longer in any of the enlightened countries in Europe") is of a kind which the 20th-century mind finds tedious. But so great has been the reaction in our own time against Whig or Marxist interpretations of history, that some scholars have propagated an absurd substitution of historical roles: the persecuted are seen as forerunners of oppression, and the oppressors as victims of persecution. And so we have been forced to go over these elementary truths. It was Paine who put his faith in the free operation of opinion in the "open society": "Mankind are not now to be told they shall not think, or they shall not read." Paine also who saw that in the constitutional debates of the 18th century "the Nation was always left out of the question." By bringing the Nation *into* the question, he was bound to set in motion forces which he could neither control nor foresee. That is what democracy is about.

Notes

INTRODUCTION

1. "Grundyism" refers to a tendency to be overly fearful of what respectable people might think.

2. E. P. Thompson, "Homage to Tom Maguire" (pp. 263–288 of this volume). The Social Democratic Federation founded in 1881 was an early Marxist group. The Socialist League was founded in 1884, by Morris, Eleanor Marx, and Edward Aveling.

3. This is not a critical review of Thompson's New Left writings; it is rather more an appreciation, a tribute by a former student, comrade, and friend. Critical commentary on Thompson, his life and writings abounds. So much so that Bryan Palmer, in one of the first studies of Thompson, *E. P. Thompson: Objections and Oppositions* (London, Verso, 1994), detected what he saw as "an uncomfortable respect for Thompson's histories" and a "nagging denigration of his accomplishments"; Palmer saw it as "fundamentally political" (1–2). This continues.

4. E. P. Thompson, *William Morris: Romantic to Revolutionary* (London: Lawrence & Wishart, 1955).

5. Thompson, *The Making of the English Working Class* (London: Penguin, 1968).

6. Thompson, "Homage to Tom McGrath," *TriQuarterly*, 70, Fall 1987, p. 117.

7. His colleague, the late historian Eric Hobsbawm, remembered Thompson this way: "He was the only historian I knew who had not just talent, brilliance, erudition and the gift of writing, but the capacity to produce something qualitatively different from the rest of us, not to be measured on the same scale." Hobsbawm, "E. P. Thompson," *The Guardian*, 30 August 1993.

8. E. P. Thompson, *Writing by Candlelight* (London: Merlin Press, 1980).

9. Several of these are collected in Thompson, *Customs in Common* (London: Merlin Press, 1991).

10. Mary Kaldor, "E. P. Thompson," *The Independent*, 25 November, 2013.

11. "E. P. Thompson," interviewed by Mike Merrill, *Visions of History* (New York: Pantheon, 1976), 7.

12. E. P. Thompson, "Revolution" (p. 159 of this volume).

13. Nikita Khrushchev (1894–1971) was First Secretary of the Communist Party of the Soviet Union during the Cold War. On February 25, 1956, he made his "secret speech" denouncing Stalin.

14. Stuart Hall (1932–2014), a Rhodes scholar at Oxford and from Jamaica, became an editor of *Universities and Left Review* (*ULR*) and the *New Left Review* (*NLR*). He suggests that the name "New Left" was borrowed from the French, the "nouvelle gauche," an independent current in French politics "associated with Claude Bourdet, a leading figure in the French Resistance." Hall, as much as Thompson a spokesman for the New Left, describes it "as the coming together of two related but different traditions—one that of dissident, libertarian, communism, the other an 'independent socialist,' the latter not so much generational as postwar, that is, not so personally reflecting the Second World War experience." Hall, "The Life and Times of First New Left," *New Left Review*

61 (January–February 2010). See Chris Rojek, *Stuart Hall* (Cambridge, United King-don: Polity, 2003); "Stuart Hall (1932–2014) and the 'First' New Left, Life and Times," in *Out of Apathy: Voices of the New Left Thirty Years On*, ed. Robin Archer et al. (London: Verso, 1989), 13.

15. David Morley and Bill Schwartz, "Stuart Hall," *The Guardian*, 10 February 2014.

16. Peter Sedgwick, "The Two New Lefts," in David Widgery, *The Left In Britain, 1956–1968* (London: Penguin, 1976), 131. The first New Left is simpler to define than the second. The first, however, has been diminished, perhaps mistakenly, by the interna-tional events of 1968. In Britain, the anti–Vietnam War movement, the Vietnam Soli-darity Campaign (VSC) in particular, was significant; there was a youth movement of sorts, student sit-ins, notably at the LSE, but also at Warwick, one in which Thompson was involved. There were community groups, various papers, and many ultra-left grou-plets. The *New Left Review* maintained a modest readership but was not an organ of the movement. The terms "non-aligned" and "independent" distinguish the New Left from other peace movements in the 1950s, some of them supporters of, or "aligned" with, the Soviet Union. The New Left maintained an independence of all regimes.

17. Hilary Rose, *Genes, Cells and Brains: The Promethean Promises of the New Biology* (Lon-don: Verso, 2012), 3.

18. The word *anti-hierarchical*, however, elides the issues of gender. Jean McCrindle, who left the Communist Party in 1956 and then joined up with the New Left as a student at St. Andrews University in Scotland, reflected that the "women's silence seems quite incredible." McCrindle quoted in Lynne Segal, "The Silence of Women in the New Left," in Robin Archer et. al., eds., *Out of Apathy, Voices of the New Left Thirty Years On*, 107. See McCrindle, "The Hungarian Uprising and a Young British Communist," *His-tory Workshop Journal* 62 (2006). The issue of "Women in the New Left" is discussed by Sheila Benson, Dorothy Wedderburn, and Lynne Segal, in *Out of Apathy, Voices of the New Left Thirty Years On*, 107–16. Thompson as historian-teacher was quite knowledge-able on subjects of gender. Anna Davin, a founder of the History Workshop, a student of Thompson's at Warwick, remembers: "Thompson taught the course on industrial-ization, and of course told us about people and their lives and culture. He introduced us to the classic work of Ivy Pinchbeck on *Women Workers and the Industrial Revolution* [1930]. Women were always there in his account, working, singing, rearing children, taking part in bread riots, writing poetry, or—like the early feminist and revolutionary, Mary Wollstonecraft—demanding change." Conversation with CW, September 2013.

19. Thompson, "Homage to Tom Maguire," (p. 267 in this volume).

20. Ibid., (p. 265 in this volume).

21. Thompson, "Where Are We Now?," (p. 246 in this volume).

22. Thompson, *William Morris*, 620.

23. J. H. Goldthorpe et al., *The Affluent Worker* (Cambridge: Cambridge University Press, 1968).

24. Labour MP Anthony Crosland, in his book *The Future of Socialism* (London: Jonathan Cape, 1956), projected a capitalism "modified almost out of existence," one that re-quired a reworking of almost all of Labour's commitments, including "Common own-ership." See Part 1, chaps. 1 and 2.

25. Peter Townsend (1928–2009) was a founder of the Child Poverty Action Group and author of *The Family Life of Old People* (Hoboken, NJ: Wiley, 1955); see Brian Abel–Smith and Peter Townsend, *The Poor and the Poorest* (London: G. Bell & Sons, 1965).

26. Richard Hoggart, *The Uses of Literacy* (Oxford: Oxford University, 1970), 52.

27. Thompson rejected easy "poverty = protest" formulas.

28. Theodosia Jessup and E. P. Thompson, *There Is a Spirit in Europe: A Memoir of Frank Thompson* (London: V. Gollancz, 1947).

29. George Orwell, *On the Road to Wigan Pier* (San Diego, CA: Harcourt, 1958).
30. Fred Inglis, ed., *E. P. Thompson: Collected Poems* (Tarset, UK: Bloodaxe Books, 1999), 18.
31. Conversation with CW, September 2013.
32. Saville Papers, Hull History Center, Thompson to Saville, n.d.
33. Ibid., n.d.
34. Conversation with CW, September 2013.
35. Julian Harber, "Who Was EPT? The man, the historian, the teacher, the comrade," Celebrating 50 years of E. P. Thompson's *The Making of the English Working Class*, paper presented at People's History Museum, Manchester, UK, April 13, 2013. This hospitality, these open houses, seem lost on various critics who seem conflicted by the Thompsons' homes. I remember jaws dropping when Dorothy invited all (nearly a thousand people) at the 1993 New York memorial meeting to visit, if possible. The Wick Episcopi house was routinely alive with long- and short-term guests; it was a place for tutorials and seminars and meetings of all sorts, our Thompson's post-graduates in the "Crime Group," including the authors of *Albion's Fatal Tree*, met there. International visitors and students were especially welcome, as they were at the Thompsons' stone cottage in North Wales. Stephen Roberts, one of Dorothy's students, writes, "It was in the discussions that were happening at the Thompsons' country house, Wick Episcopi, that Dorothy found most stimulation. All of her postgraduates entered this extraordinary world of scholarly generosity and cooperation. Scholars flowed through Wick with their latest drafts to discuss or with news of an interesting archival find." Stephen Roberts, "Memories of Dottie, Dorothy Thompson (1923–2011)," *Labour History Review* 76/2 (August 2011): 165–66. Tony Judt's sour complaints ("Goodbye to All That," *New York Review of Books*, September 21, 2006) about the Thompsons' "leafy perch in Middle-England" is particularly ill-informed, impelled one must suspect by something other than the Thompsons' lifestyle.
36. David Goodway, "Dorothy Greenald, Books Took Her from Factory Floor to Political Literacy," *The Guardian*, 14 April 2002. She was married to Joe Greenald, to whom *The Making* is also dedicated.
37. Conversation with CW, September 2013.
38. Peter J. Conradi, *A Very English Hero: The Making of Frank Thompson* (London: Bloomsbury Publishing, 2012), 15.
39. Ibid., 67–68.
40. Neville Kirk, "Setting the Standard: Dorothy Thompson, the Discipline of History and the Study of Chartism," in Roberts, "Memories of Dottie: Dorothy Thompson," 2.
41. Eric Hobsbawm, "The Historian's Group of the Communist Party," in *Rebels and the Causes: Essays in Honour of A. L. Morton*, ed. Maurice Cornforth (London: Lawrence & Wishart, 1978), 28.
42. Saville Papers, n.d
43. Roberts, "Memories of Dottie: Dorothy Thompson," 164.
44. Fred Inglis, *Richard Hoggart* (London: Polity, 2014), 99.
45. Neville Kirk, "National Chartist Leadership, Some Perspective,"in *The Duty of Discontent, Essays for Dorothy Thompson*, ed. Owen Aston et al. (New York: Mansell, 1995), 10. Also Sheila Rowbotham, "Dorothy Thompson: The Personal Is Political", *New Left Review* I/200 (July–August 1993).
46. Roger Fieldhouse, "Thompson, the Adult Educator," in *E. P. Thompson and English Radicalism*, ed. Richard Fieldhouse and Richard Taylor (Manchester, UK: Manchester University Press), 28.
47. Conradi, *A Very English Hero*, 268–69. The Cairo Parliaments were unofficial assemblies of soldiers initiated by rank-and-file soldiers.

48.   "I recall a resolute and ingenious civilian army, increasingly hostile to the conventional military virtues, which became—far more than any of my younger friends will begin to credit—an anti-fascist and consciously anti-imperialist army. Its members voted Labour in 1945: knowing why, as did the civilian workers at home. Many were infused with socialist ideas and expectations wildly in advance of the tepid rhetoric of today's Labour leaders." Thompson, "A State of Blackmail," *Writing by Candlelight*, 131.

49.   Inglis, *Richard Hoggart*, 76.

50.   Peter Searby, "Edward Thompson as Teacher, Yorkshire and Warwick," in *Protest and Survival: Essays for E. P. Thompson*, ed. John Rule and Robert Malcolmson (New York City: New Press, 1993), 16.

51.   Saville papers. n.d.

52.   Thompson, "Homage to Tom Maguire," (p. 266 in this volume).

53.   Ibid., 288.

54.   John Saville, *Memoirs from the Left* (London: Merlin Press, 2003), 104.

55.   Sheila Rowbotham, *Dreams and Memories* (London: Virago, 1983), 342.

56.   Recording, Dorothy Thompson at E. P. Thompson Memorial, New York, December 12, 1993. In Cal Winslow's possession.

57.   Thompson quoted in Merrill, *Visions of History*, 8, 21.

58.   Inglis notes that "Thompson finds in the staid transcripts not only the honest fight of the oppressed, allegiance to whom was his first historical principle as well as his method, but also a light shining from the blind justice of the day and still burning through the rigged evidence and fixed witnesses of the courts." *Collected Poems*, 11.

59.   In my own research relating to South Coast smugglers, the accused were routinely convicted—many to be hanged in chains—on the basis of the testimony of informers, stewards, and enclosing land owners. See Cal Winslow, "Sussex Smugglers," in E. P. Thompson et al., *Albion's Fatal Tree: Crime and Society in Eighteenth-Century England*, rev. ed. (London: Verso, 2011), 119–166. Also see E. P. Thompson, *Whigs and Hunters: The Origins of the Black Act* (New York: Pantheon, 1975).

60.   Sheila Rowbotham writes: "Early women's history owed a great deal to the history from below which the Ruskin Workshops had helped to develop.... It was of course to be at the Ruskin History Workshop in autumn 1969 that a small group of us resolved to call the first Women's Liberation Conference. Women's history was thus closely connected to the beginnings of the women's movement. Sally Alexander and Anna Davin both played an important role in organizing the first conference, which was held at Ruskin in late February 1970." Rowbotham, "Some Memories of Raphael," *New Left Review* I/221 (January–February 1997).

61.   Robin Blackburn writes that Thompson would "furnish a model for some women's history and black history... itself requiring revision or development in their light," in "Edward Thompson and the New Left," *New Left Review* I/201 (September–October 1993).

62.   John Barrell, *The Darkside of the Landscape: The Rural Poor in English Painting 1730–1840* (Cambridge: Cambridge University Press, 1980), 73.

63.   Ibid., 1, 5.

64.   Ibid., 73.

65.   Fieldhouse, "Thompson, the Adult Educator," 31.

66.   Andy Croft, "Walthamstow, Little Gidding and Middlesbrough: Edward Thompson, Adult Education and Literature," *Socialist History Journal* 8 (1995): 29.

67.   Fieldhouse, "Thompson, the Adult Educator," 67.

68.   Thompson quoted in Searby, "Edward Thompson as Teacher, Yorkshire and Warwick," wrote: "This sort of class must be kept alive.... Any other course might mean the abandonment of working-class education in favour of (an easier job for the tutor!) the further isolation of an elite."

69. Fieldhouse, "Thompson, The Adult Educator," 31–33; E. P. Thompson, "Against Aca-
     demic Standards." Adult Education Papers, vol. 1, no. 4, University of Leeds, July 1950,
     unpublished. Julian Harber kindly provided me with a copy of this paper. Hilary Wain-
     wright places Thompson's views on education in "a profoundly egalitarian tradition."
     See her "Democratizing Knowledge," in *Arguments for a New Left: Answering the Free-
     Market Right* (Hoboken, NJ: Wiley-Blackwell, 1994), 77. Thompson takes the tradition
     of adult working-class education (in "Education and Experience," Special Collections,
     Brotheron Library, Leeds University) back beyond Tawney et al. to the French Revo-
     lution, Wordsworth, then Lawrence and finally Jude, the young stonemason, with his
     utopian visions of education at Christminster, "a true protagonist of intellectual and
     cultural values."

70. John Henry Newman (1801–1890) was an Oxford academic and leader of the Oxford
     Movement of Anglicans, which wanted to return to more traditional forms of worship.

71. Thompson, "Against Academic Standards," 25–26.

72. Ibid., 25.

73. Ibid., 31–32.

74. David Goodway, "The Making of *The Making,*" in Fieldhouse, 62.

75. Ibid., 62.

76. Searby, "Edward Thompson as Teacher, Yorkshire and Warwick," 13.

77. Ibid.

78. Ibid., 12.

79. Fieldhouse, "Thompson, the Adult Educator," 38, 39.

80. Thompson quoted in Merrill, 13.

81. Thompson, *The Making,* 14.

82. Eric Hobsbawm, "Edward Palmer Thompson," *Proceedings of the British Academy* 90
     (1995): 521–39.

83. New preface,, *The Making,* 1980 edition, 14.

84. *Guardian,* December 26, 2013.

85. Iain Boal, unpublished paper in Cal Winslow's collection.

86. Thompson, *The Making,* 213.

87. Thompson, "The Long Revolution," (p. 195 in this volume).

88. Thompson, *The Making,* 231.

89. Ibid., xiii.

90. In the years *The Making* was being written, the New Left reached its high point, then
     rapidly declined. One result, ironically, was that even though *The Making* was not
     "aimed at an academic audience," there it found its greatest success.

91. Thompson, *The Poverty of Theory and Other Essays* (New York: Monthly Review Press,
     1978), i.

92. Ibid., i.

93. John Saville, "The 20th Congress and the British Communist Party," in *The Socialist
     Register 1976,* ed. Ralph Miliband and John Saville (New York: Monthly Review Press,
     1976), 7.

94. Ibid., 7.

95. Ibid., 21.

96. Thompson, "Through the Smoke of Budapest," (p. 37 in this volume).

97. Ibid.

98. Dorothy Thompson, New York City memorial speech. Stuart Hall called 1956 "the
     breakup of the political ice-age, which defined for people of my generation the bound-
     aries and limits of the tolerable in politics," in "The Life and Times of the First New
     Left," *New Left Review* 61 (January–February 2010).

99. Thompson, "Through the Smoke of Budapest."

312 Notes to pages 23–26

100. Dorothy Thompson, "On the Trail of the New Left," *New Left Review* 1/215 (January–February, 1996), 96.
101. Ibid.
102. Thompson, "A Place Called Choice," in Inglis, E. P. *Thompson: Collected Poems*, 55–67.
103. Conradi, *A Very English Hero*, 123.
104. James Hinton, *Protests and Visions, Peace Politics in 20th-Century Britain* (London: Hutchinson, 1989), 171.
105. Doris Lessing, *Walking in the Shade, 1949–1962* (New York: Harper Perennial, 1998), 216.
106. Thompson refers here to the book *The God That Failed*, ed. Richard Crossman (New York: Harper & Row, 1963). *Encounter* was an Anglo-American journal published in Britain in 1953 by Stephen Spender and Irving Kristol; it was harshly anti-communist and later revealed to be funded by the CIA.
107. Thompson was in fact quite modest about his own abilities: "I am not a systematic thinker of any kind and only attempt it in the sense of defending the truth of a noble and collapsing tradition until the thinkers come along and rebuild it." Saville Papers. Thanks to David Howell for sharing with me a draft of an article forthcoming in *Contemporary British History*.
108. Stuart Hall and Raphael (then Ralph) Samuel came from Oxford to *ULR*, founded the Partisan Café, and later would be a founder of the History Workshop.
109. Peter Sedgwick, a libertarian socialist and member of the first editorial board of *ULR*, also suggested that the New Left was more "a milieu than a movement," an insight meant to be critical but worth considering. See "The Two New Lefts," in *The Left in Britain, 1956–1968*, ed. David Widgery (London: Penguin, 1976), 135.
110. The two journals merged for a variety of issues—political, organizational, and financial. The editorial board was greatly expanded; Stuart Hall became the first editor. A glance at the early issues shows variety in content, fiction, poetry, drawing, and reviews, as well as in the featured political material. Its connection to the "movement" is clear: the September 1960 issue, for example, focuses on the United States; includes a letter from C. Wright Mills; urges readers to take *NL* literature to Scarborough for the Labour Party conference. Forty New Left Clubs are listed on the back inside cover.
111. Saville Papers, n.d. Thompson himself was ambivalent concerning the Labour Party (he would join, then resign several times), but unlike others was quick to support independent candidates, as in the 1959 Lawrence Daly campaign and the 1966 Richard Gott campaign. Gott stood in Hull on an anti–Vietnam War platform.
112. The word used to describe Labour supporters and politicians who supported NATO.
113. "Socialist Humanism." Thompson indicted the Stalinist Party, as it exists in the Soviet Union, but importantly, "how it is mimicked in the national Parties internationally, including by 'King Street,'"(headquarters of Communist Party in Britain) The ideology of Stalinism and its anti-intellectualism is "embodied in the rigid forms of 'democratic centralism' of the Communist Parties. These remove the centre of moral authority from the individual conscience and confer it to the leadership of the Party. Even in Britain, extremes of loyalty, identification of the Party with personal and social aspirations, reveal themselves in attitudes towards the critic, who threatens to break the 'unity of the Party'of intense hatred."
114. Hinton, *Protests and Visions*, 171.
115. Saville Papers, 31 March (ca. 1958).
116. Hall, "The Life and Times of the First New Left," *New Left Review* 61 (January–February 2010): 7.
117. Conversation with author, September 2013. Peter Sedgwick wrote this unique account of the New Left in 1964; "There was the building, for instance, situated a stone's throw from Marx's old rooms in Soho, whose various floors were given over to the multiform

functions of the New Left's cultural apparatus; its nether storeys housed the Partisan, 'London's left-wing coffee house' (a similar establishment opened later in Manchester), whose dramatic, brutalist décor and white megawatt downglare diffused a curious alienation effect upon the customers; the basement was more subdued, though still Spartan enough, a dining room and resort for poetry and folksong; the first floor began life as the frantic publicity HQ for the first Aldermaston march and subsequently became an odd little socialist library, full of literary garbage from the thirties, review copies of books just out, exchange copies of fraternal publications, and some true incunabula of Left lore. Here meetings and at least one exhibition (a heaped conspectus of cuttings and souvenirs from the thirties) took place. The upper-most floor held the editorial-cum-administrative office for the publications and groupings of the movement; the latter included the Universities and Left Review Club (1957–8; re-christened New Left Review Club from 1959 on), which used to attract hundreds to weekly meetings and discussions in the larger basements of Central London, and further regular meetings were held by such autonomous sections as the Education, History of Socialism, Left Scientists, Social Priorities, and Literature groups, the International Forum, and the London Schools Left Club, a self-governing unit for youngsters still at school. Between thirty and forty local left Clubs ran on a modest scale outside London, mostly either in the Southeast or in the Industrial North (including Scotland). Sporadically through these years, there were hopes and hints of an informal New Left International, small but alive and identifiable. The Universities and Left Review Club's *Cry Europe* meeting, which packed St. Pancras Town Hall on Bastille Day 1958, united on its platform representatives of the West German anti-nuclear mass campaign and the French neutralist Left, spokesmen from the crushed Hungarian revolution and the rising anti-fascist generation of Spain, and staff members from the established Left and Liberal press (*Observer, New Statesmen, Herald*). And all through its existence, the New Left sensed that it had allies abroad: the French PSI, the flickering Marxist revisionism of Eastern Europe, and the entire gamut of sociologue radicalism in the United States from C. Wright Mills to Riesman, were all announced (or else announced themselves) as fraternal delegates in the thronged convention of ideas that met in permanent session, with a limitless agenda, up to the crisis of the movement." See Widgery, *The Left in Britain, 1956–58*, 132.

118. Stuart Hall, "The Life and Times of the First New Left," *New Left Review* 61 (January–February 2010).

119. Dorothy Thompson, "On the Trail of the New Left," 99

120. Conversation with author, September 2013.

121. Quoted in Richard Taylor, *Against the Bomb, The British Peace Movement, 1958–1965* (Oxford: Clarendon Press, 1988), 49.

122. Thompson, "Countermarching to Armageddon," *New Left Review* I/4 (July–August 1960). On the significance of the CND, Doris Lessing wrote, "I think the Aldermaston Marches have not been given enough attention as a unique social phenomenon. Just consider: for half a dozen years, every year, in springtime, hundreds of thousands of people from all over Britain, Europe, America, even distant parts of the world, converged on Aldermaston and for four days walked to London, spending nights in schools and halls, welcomed or not by the towns or villages they came through, exciting the world's press, mostly to hostile reporting, making friends, learning, enjoying themselves—people who could never have met otherwise. Scientists and artists, writers and journalists and teachers and gardeners, politicians, every kind of person, met, walked together, talked—and often remained friends afterwards." Lessing, *Walking in the Shade*, 307.

123. Michael Bess, *Realism, Utopia, and the Mushroom Cloud* (Chicago: University of Chicago Press, 1993), 264.

124. Hinton, *Protests and Visions*, 172.
125. Ibid.
126. The unilateralists in the Labour Party won at the 1960 Scarborough Conference. However, their position was reversed the following year.
127. Thompson, "The New Left," (p. 121 in this volume).
128. Thompson, "The Long Revolution (Part 1)," (p. 211 in this volume).
129. Kenneth O. Morgan, *Britain since 1945, The People's Peace* (Oxford: Oxford University Press, 2001), 179; David Howell, letter to author.
130. Ken Alexander, "Power at the Base," in Thompson, *Out of Apathy*, 243–86.
131. David Howell, "The Ideology of Labourism," in *John Saville: Commitment and History; Themes from the Life and Work of a Socialist Historian*, ed. David Howell, Dianne Kirby, and Kevin Morgan (London: Lawrence and Wishart, 2011), 178. Howell suggests Labourism is an ideology that looked to parliamentary methods for the redress of grievances and the long-term solution to working class problems.
132. Thompson, "The New Left," (p. 122 in this volume).
133. Hinton, *Protests and Vision*, 53.
134. Letter to Rafael Samuel, quoted in Goodway, "The Making of *The Making*," 8.
135. "Revolution", *Out of Apathy*, (pp. 157–158 in this volume).
136. Ibid.
137. Jean McCrindle, "Lawrence Daly," *The Guardian*, 29 May 2009.
138.. Lawrence Daly, "Fife Socialist League," *New Left Review* I/4 (July– August 1960).
139. Thompson, "A Special Case," 72.
140. David Kynaston, *Modernity Britain: Opening the Box, 1957–59* (London: Bloomsbury Publishing, 2013), 335–36. There is a photo of Ernest Rodker, with beard, in Lessing, *Walking in the Shade*.
141. Jean McCrindle, "Lawrence Daly," *The Guardian*.
142. Conversation with author, August 2009.
143. Thompson, *The Making of the English Working Class*, 110.
144. Thompson, "Homage to Tom Maguire," (p. 287 in this volume).
145. Thompson, "Commitment in Politics," (p. 116 in this volume).
146. Thompson, "The Long Revolution," (p. 200 in this volume)
147. Dorothy Thompson, "On the Trail of the New Left," 98.
148. Thompson, "Socialist Humanism," (pp. 48–87 in this volume).
149. Madeleine Davis, "E. Thompson, Ethics and Activism," paper delivered at "The Global E. P. Thompson" conference, October 3–5, 2013, Weatherhead Center, Harvard University, Cambridge, MA.
150. Thompson, "Socialist Humanism," (p. 50 in this volume).
151. Ibid.
152. Thompson, "Commitment in Politics, (p. 115 in this volume).
153. Dorothy Thompson, "On the Trail of the New Left," 100.
154. Ibid.
155. Dorothy Thompson also argues that these ideas "blossomed again in the eighties" in END and reminds readers that it was at an IWC conference that C. L. R. James first spoke when he came to Britain ("On the Trail of the New Left," 95). Mike Rustin writes: "The New Left was successful, for some years, as a multidimensional expression of these emergent presences in British culture. Its strength was that it sought to unify, in a common project, a great diversity of experiences and issues, without seeking to reduce them to formulae or subject them to organizational discipline." *Out of Apathy, Voices of the New Left Thirty Years On*, 124.
156. Perry Anderson, *Arguments within English Marxism* (London: Verso, 1980), 120. Peter Sedgwick had written much the same in 1964: "Not the faintest murmur of this

movement now remains" ("The Two New Lefts," 134). "Where Are We Now" takes up the argument with Perry Anderson in the 1963 dispute. Some readers will remember the disagreements continued. Here, I confess to thinking that simply considering the cast of characters involved in the first New Left (the writers for *The New Reasoner* and *Universities and Left Review*, for example, and their cumulative contribution to the left of our times) makes Anderson's contention of thinness nothing short of breathtaking. Similarly, one finds Anderson, in "The Left of the Fifties," *New Left Review* I/29 (January–February 1965), complaining that the New Left "made almost no attempt to analyze the evolution of the Eastern Bloc, or the emergence of a worldwide Euro-American neo-colonialism." For what it may be worth now, I think readers will find this not quite the case. Considering the issue of "analyzing the character of the Eastern Bloc," it must be said that a great amount of ink has been spilled on this topic. This is certainly the case with the Trotskyists, yet the results, aside from splits, expulsions, etc., and having missed the boat on the events of 1989–1991 entirely, are of scholastic interest at best, more probably belonging in the dustbin.

157. Thompson, *The Poverty of Theory*, 245–301.
158. Blackburn, "Edward Thompson and the New Left."
159. See Thompson, "The Poverty of Theory or An Orrery of Errors," in *The Poverty of Theory and Other Essays*, (New York: Monthly Review Press, 1978) for an extended discussion of Marxism and some of its problems.
160. See Kate Soper, *Troubled Pleasures, Writings on Politics, Gender and Hedonism* (London: Verso, 1990), 90.
161. Thompson, "Where Are We Now?" (p. 246 in this volume).
162. Thompson, *The Poverty of Theory and Other Essays*, ii.
163. Thompson, "A Special Case," *Writing by Candlelight* (London: Merlin, 1980), 76.
164. Thompson, *Whigs and Hunters*, chap. 10.
165. Thompson, "C. Wright Mills: The Responsible Craftsman," *Peace News*, 29 November 1963, quoted in Sedgwick, "The Two New Lefts," 131.

SOCIALIST HUMANISM

1. This is the general view of most Trotskyists: it would also appear to be the view of Khrushchev, in his famous "revelations."
2. For example, "People who pass as orthodox Marxists have turned our ideas of movement into a fixed dogma to be learnt by heart and appear as pure sects" (1891).
3. A comparison of the European communist press of thirty years ago with the Stalinist press which reached its apotheosis in the incredible *For a Lasting Peace, For a People's Democracy*, shows the loss of moral and emotional energies, the replacement of man by resounding abstract nouns. Compare also our "Daily Worker" with the Chartist or early socialist press. If millions are spent on armaments, people must be shown that it raises the price of beer and fags; an appeal to their moral conscience is "idealist" or—if attempted—phony and tongue-in-cheek. Hence also the dwindling appeal of Communism to young people, whose moral and intellectual idealism is not engaged.
4. Cf. Engels to Bloch: "Political, legal, philosophical theories, religious ideas . . . exercise their influence upon the historical struggles and in many cases preponderate in determining their form."
5. I have argued this in my *William Morris*, esp. pp. 827–841.
6. See Ken Alexander in *The Reasoner*, No. 1: "G. D. H. Cole and Others."

THE NEW LEFT

1. While we disagree sharply with much of the theory and tactics of the leadership of the Socialist Labour League, we regard the attempt of the Labour Party Executive to suppress its ideas by means of administrative proscription as contemptible. An open Trotskyist organisation has as much right to claim a place within the federal structure of the Labour Party as, for example, the Fabian Society; and the concern expressed by the Labour bureaucracy for "democracy" and the Party's constitution are belied by the undemocratic and unconstitutional means which it is adopting (as in Leeds) to enforce the ban.

REVOLUTION

1. The quotations here are taken from Stalin's *On the Problems of Leninism* (1926), but the influence of this concept is to be found far outside the Communist tradition.

THE COMMUNISM OF WILLIAM MORRIS

1. Republished together with a collection of interesting letters of Morris to J. L. Mahon in *William Morris, the Man and the Myth* by R. Page Arnot, 1964.
2. This may refer to "Some Bourgeois Idols" or "The Commercial Hearth," in *Commonweal*, April 1886, and 8 & 15 May 1886.
3. A position which has recently received a fresh and penetrating appraisal in Mr. Raymond Williams's *Culture and Society*.

HOMAGE TO TOM MAGUIRE

In collecting material for this essay I am indebted to Mrs Florence Mattison (the widow of Alf Mattison), Miss Norah Turner (daughter of Sir Ben Turner), and Mr A. T. Marles, first secretary of the Leeds Fabian Society, for help, information, and the loan of documents. Among other debts I must mention the kindness of the librarians or officials of the Brotherton Library, Leeds; the Bradford Trades Council; the Bradford Independent Labour Party; and the Colne Valley Labour Party.

1. J. Clayton, *The Rise and Decline of Socialism in Great Britain* (1926), p. 82.
2. Of 115 delegates, 24 came from Bradford, 8 from Leeds, 6 from Huddersfield, 3 from Halifax, and 8 from other parts of West Yorkshire. *Report of the First General Conference, ILP* (1893).
3. Of 305 branches listed in the 1895 Directory, 102 were in Yorkshire, followed by Lancashire (73), Scotland (41), London (29). Of Yorkshire's share we find Bradford (29), Colne Valley (11), Spen Valley (9), Leeds (8), Halifax (8), Huddersfield (8), Dewsbury (5). *ILP Directory* (Manchester, 1895).
4. For Champion, see especially H. Pelling, *The Origins of the Labour Party 1880–1900* (1954), pp. 59–64. For Mahon, see E. P. Thompson, *William Morris, Romantic to Revolutionary* (1955), pp. 614–16, where, however, the direct influence of Mahon's "Labour Union" model upon the Yorkshire labour unions is underestimated. For forerunners of the "independent labour" pattern, see above, p. 271, note 1, and his "Land and Labour League," *Bulletin of the International Institute of Social History*, Amsterdam, 1953.
5. For Northumberland, see Thompson, *op.cit.*, pp. 517ff. For Bolton, see Dona Torr, *Tom Mann and His Times* (1956), i, pp. 251ff.
6. Census figures: Leeds (1851) 172,000, (1901) 429,000; Bradford (1851) 104,000, (1901) 280,000.

7.   See Joan Thomas, *History of the Leeds Clothing Industry* (Yorkshire Bulletin of Economic and Social Research, 1955), chapter 2.

8.   Ben Turner, *About Myself* (1930), pp. 78–79. Turner had made contact earlier with the SDF and had been attached to a London branch.

9.   Amongst the voluminous local literature, the following are of value in marking the "independent" tradition: G. J. Holyoake, *History of Co-operation in Halifax* (1864); Owen Balmforth, *Huddersfield Industrial Society* (Manchester, 1910); and the reminiscences of John Hartley (*Todmorden & District News*, July 1903) and Joseph Greenwood (*Co-Partnership*, September 1909)—both of the strong Hebden Bridge Society.

10. Garside, born 1843, had a long record in the ASE, radical politics, and co-operative productive ventures, before his election to the County Council for Slaithwaite in March 1892: *Yorkshire Factory Times* (hereafter referred to as *YFT*), 26 February 1904.

11. Shaftoe, secretary to the Bradford Trades Council, was a skep and basket-maker; Bune, the Leeds secretary, was a brush-maker. In 1880 the Bradford TC represented Warpdressers, Stonemasons, Joiners, Plumbers, Lithographers, Engineers, Letterpress Printers, Tailors, Moulders, Hammermen, Dyers, Brush-makers, Skep & Basket-makers, Coach-makers, and Coopers. But six monthly meetings in 1881 were abandoned with "no quorum" or "desultory conversation." (Bradford TC Minutes, 24 September 1880 *et seq.*) The Leeds TC had 33 societies affiliated in 1883; 25 in 1887. (*Annual Report*, 1894, p. 3.)

12. Circular, dated 1887, in Shaftoe Cutting-book (in possession of the Bradford TC).

13. Turner, *op. cit.*, p. 93.

14. J. Lawson, *Letters to the Young on Progress in Pudsey* (Stanningley, 1887); F. Peel, "Old Cleckheaton," in *Cleckheaton Guardian*, 25 January to 4 April 1994.

15. B. Wilson, *The Struggles of an Old Chartist* (Halifax, 1887), p. 40.

16. See Jowett's foreword to F. Brockway, *Socialism over Sixty Years* (1946), pp. 13–24.

17. W. Cudworth, *Condition of the Industrial Classes of Bradford & District* (Bradford, 1887).

18. See, e.g., *Halifax Guardian* for 12 articles on "The Slums of Halifax" commencing 17 August 1889. Tom Maguire contributed a series of articles on "Insanitary Leeds" to the *Leeds Weekly Express*, and see also Maguire and other contributors to *Hypnotic Leeds* (Leeds, 1893), edited by A. Marles.

19. Turner's election address for Batley in 1893 in Turner, *op. cit.*, p. 171; 1893 Manifesto of Leeds ILP in T. Paylor, *Leeds for Labour* (Leeds, 1905), etc.

20. In 1885, 18,312 half-timers worked in the worsted industry alone, 92 per cent in Bradford district (Cudworth, *op. cit.*, p. 10); in 1898, 6,887 half-timers were employed within the Bradford borough boundaries, and 4,086 within Halifax (*The Trade Unionist*, November 1898). On the question of the local exemption standard see the evidence of R. Waddington, secretary of the Half Time Committee of the NUT before the *R.C. on Labour*, 1892, xxxv, Group C, 3662 *et seq.*; and of G. D. Jones, 3855 *et seq.*

21. An old Birstall lady recalled: "The mill-owners were very cute in dodging factory inspectors. . . . They had a big whisket handy in the sheds, and when they expected the inspector, we young girls were popped underneath the baskets until he had gone." *Heckmondwike District News*, 14 August 1926.

22. Cudworth, *op. cit.*, p. 20.

23. In 1885 North America did not feature among Batley's markets but was the second export market for Bradford's worsteds. *R.C. on Depression of Trade and Industry* (1886) I, pp. 75, 78.

24. Evidence of Mark Oldroyd of the Dewsbury and Batley Chambers of Commerce, ibid, iii, 14, 105–7.

25. Evidence of H. Mitchell of the Bradford Chamber of Commerce, ibid., ii. 3764 *et seq.* The export of raw material and semi-raw material (tops) was compensating for the decline in worsted stuffs.

26. Ibid., ii. 6494 *et seq.*
27. The amount of the decline was an endless source of controversy; but friendly and unfriendly sources agree upon the fact. Cudworth, *op.cit.,* p. 41: "During the past ten years deductions have been made in wages and quietly submitted to by the workpeople." See *YFT,* 20 September 1889 (Leeds wage tables, 1872–89); 10 July 1891. *R.C. on Labour,*1892, xxxv, C, evidence of Gee, Turner and Drew, *passim,* especially 5092, 5124, 5389–5411, 5675; 5554 (family wage); 5469, 5548–49 (Manningham Mills). For a summary of evidence presented by the weavers' leaders before the Royal Commission, see Tom Mann, *An Appeal to the Yorkshire Textile Workers* (Huddersfield, 1893).
28. Minutes of power-loom overlookers in possession of Bradford Trades Council; Minutes of Card Setters and Machine Tenters in possession of existing union.
29. It is important to note that even on the crest of the new union wave, with the assistance of the *Yorkshire Factory Times,* only 2 in 9 of the Huddersfield weavers were organised; 1 in 13 in the heavy woollen district; and 1 in 16 in the Bradford district. *R.C. on Labour,* 1892, xxxv, C; evidence of Gee (4790); Drew (5455–58); Turner (5682–3); see Drew's comment (5499): "when people get down to the pitch to which the textile operatives are in the W. Riding, they have very little heart for anything [and] . . . cannot afford even . . . the subscription."
30. Bradford TC Minutes, 29 November 1876. See also Walter Bateson, *The Way We Came* (Bradford, 1928), for the assistance given to the dyers by Shaftoe, who "worked alongside of them as if he was a dye–house worker himself, and not a member of . . . an exceptionally skilled trade—skep-making."
31. B. Turner, *Heavy Woollen Textile Workers Union* (YFT, 1917), pp. 61–63.
32. The best accounts are in Brockway, *op. cit.,* chapter 2, and M. McMillan, *The Life of Rachel McMillan* (1927), *passim.*
33. The comparison with the cotton industry, with its strong unionism among the male spinners, and the union leaders' opposition to the Legal Eight Hour Day, is instructive.
34. See the evidence of J. H. Beever, secretary of the Halifax Trades Council, when questioned by Mundella at the Royal Commission: "Well, supposing you lost the trade?—Which I do not think probable. Suppose you did and you had passed an Act of Parliament, what would you do then?—Past experience does not send us in that direction." *R.C. on Labour,* 1892, xxxv, C, 10,040–47.
35. Minutes of the Election Committee for Messrs Greening and Stansfeld, 1868 (in our possession).
36. John Lister, "The Early History of the ILP Movement in Halifax," MSS. in the Mattison Collection, Brotherton Library; and Election Manifesto and copy of *Halifax Free Press* in the same collection.
37. *Christian Socialist,* September 1884.
38. K. Marx and F. Engels, *Selected Correspondence* (1943 edn.), p. 469.
39. Ben Wilson, *op. cit.,* was published in 1887; J. Burnley's Chartist novel, *Looking for the Dawn* (Bradford,1874); Frank Peel, *Risings of the Luddites, Chartists and Plugdrawers* (Heckmondwike, 1888). A gentleman named Aurelius Basilio Wakefield, onetime secretary to the Leeds committee of the Labour Representation League, was indefatigable in the 1870s and 1880s, delivering lectures on Ernest Jones.
40. C. L. Robinson, first ILP councillor in Bradford, had imbibed Chartist principles as a boy, was an admirer of Ernest Jones, and founder of a Republican Club in Bradford in 1870 (*YFT,* 15 January 1904). See also Tattersall, *YFT,* 22 July 1892; Ben Riley, *YFT,* 17 June 1904; Ben Turner, *About Myself,* pp. 28–29, 66; Philip Snowden, *An Autobiography* (1934), i. pp. 18–19.
41. *YFT,* 22 July 1904.

42. Ben Turner came to regard himself as an undenominational (or perhaps Benturner-ite?) Christian, but he never "belonged" to any church (information from Miss Norah Turner). For Gee, see *YFT*, 15 July 1892.

43. *YFT*, 5 February 1904, and *Labour Leader*, 20 April 1901, for biographies of Wood and Bland.

44. At the mass execution of Luddites in 1813, the prisoners sang Methodist hymns on the scaffold. The outstanding West Yorkshire Chartist leader, Ben Rushton, was an expelled local preacher.

45. See *YFT*, 17 July 1891: "Ben is a deep Christian—an earnest, everyday Christian. . . . He is at home teaching trades unionism or preaching the religion of Christ."

46. When Tillett at first refused to stand, J. Bedford (of the General Railway Workers), E.D. Girdlestone, and G. B. Shaw were each invited to stand. *YFT*, 15, 22, and 29 May 1891.

47. *Bradford Observer*, 9 and 13 June 1892.

48. Ibid., 14 June 1892; Brockway, *op. cit.*, pp. 40–41.

49. *Bradford Observer*, 16 January 1893.

50. *Dewsbury Reporter*, 8 June 1895.

51. *YFT*, 14 October 1904.

52. Isabella Ford (ed.), *Tom Maguire, A Remembrance* (Manchester, 1895), p. xii.

53. Ibid., pp. ix–x, xiii: Mattison Letterbook.

54. For the early history of the Leeds and Bradford Leagues, see also Thompson, *op. cit.*, pp. 488, 491–94, 496.

55. Correspondence of the secretary, Socialist League, in the International Institute of Social History, Amsterdam; Maguire to Mahon, October and November 1885.

56. Ibid., September 1885.

57. See E. Carpenter, *My Days and Dreams* (1916), pp. 134–35; Mattison Notebooks.

58. "The Socialist League stood definitely for a brotherhood built on pure comradeship. . . . The Paris Commune and Chicago Martyrs anniversaries we used to look forward to. . . . Songs and speeches were a feature of those gatherings." W. Hill to A. Mattison, n.d., in Mattison Letterbook.

59. *Christian Socialist*, September 1884.

60. See Maguire, "The Yorkshire Miners,"*Commonweal*, November 1885.

61. *YFT*, 4 November 1892.

62. *Commonweal*, 28 April 1888; Thompson, *op. cit.*, pp. 614–15. Jowett was advocating an independent Labour Party in 1887 *(Bradford Observer*, 8 February 1887).

63. Handbill in Mattison Collection.

64. Thompson, *op. cit.*, pp. 615–16.

65. Maguire's notes in *Commonweal*, 10 August and 16 November 1889; Thompson, *op. cit.*, pp. 618–20; *YFT*, 2 August 1889. Tom Paylor was at this time an insurance agent, Sweeney a boot and shoe worker.

66. It complained at the new unions which accepted as leaders "outsiders who may have some other object in view than the sole interest of the workers. Joined by a few malcontents from other associations these are organizing attacks on the old and tried officials of the Congress." *YFT*, 30 August 1889.

67. *Commonweal*, 6 July 1889.

68. *YFT*, 13 December 1889.

69. Ibid., 20 December 1890.

70. *Leeds Weekly Citizen*, May 1931.

71. I. O. Ford came from a wealthy Quaker family at Adel Grange, near Leeds. She had helped Miss Paterson with the Women's Provident League. In the summer of 1888 she assisted the Weavers' Union during a strike in Leeds, and from that time forward was associated with all the new union struggles involving women. *Report and Balance Sheet*

of the West Riding Power Loom Weavers Association, September 1888; and *YFT,* 1 November 1889.

72.   *YFT,* 1 November 1889, and, for Sweeney's criticisms of the Trades Council officials, 10 January 1890.

73.   *YFT,* 25 October 1889 to 27 December 1889.

74.   Ibid. 1 November 1889.

75.   *Tom Maguire, a Remembrance,* p. xvi; slide of the song in Mrs. Mattison's possession.

76.   *YFT,* 7 and 28 March 1890.

77.   Ibid., 9 May 1890; *Leeds Weekly Citizen,* May 1931.

78.   Leeds TC *Annual Report* for year ending 31 May 1891, p. 6.

79.   It appeared in instalments in *Commonweal* throughout 1890.

80.   *Leeds Mercury,* 26 March 1890; Thompson, *op. cit.,* pp. 632ff.

81.   On 12 March 1890, in the midst of the new union struggles, Carpenter was writing to Mattison: "An interesting book has turned up, by Havelock Ellis, called *The New Spirit*— on Whitman, Tolstoi, Ibsen, Heine, & others. Everything seems to be rushing on faster & faster. Where are we going? Niagara, or the Islands of the Blest?" Mattison Collection.

82.   See Thompson, *op. cit.,* pp. 652–53. Mahon and Donald addressed the first demonstration of the Leeds gasworkers, *YFT,* 13 December 1889.

83.   *Commonweal,* 4 May 1889; *Leeds Weekly Citizen,* 29 April 1929.

84.   Ibid., 10 August 1889.

85.   See F. W. Jowett, *What Made Me a Socialist* (Bradford, n.d.).

86.   Turner, *About Myself,* p. 80.

87.   For the full case of the Gas Committee and the union's reply see the letters exchanged between Ald. Gilston and Tom Paylor in the *Leeds Mercury,* 27 and 28 June 1890.

88.   The best accounts of the strike are to be found in the *Leeds Mercury; Commonweal* also carried (very strident) reports written by an anarchist.

89.   *YFT,* 5 February 1904; *Tom Maguire, a Remembrance,* p. xv.

90.   W. Throne, *My Life's Battles* (1925), pp. 131f.

91.   *Leeds Mercury,* 30 June 1890.

92.   Arthur Shaw of the ASE, President of Leeds Trades Council in 1894 and 1896, relates how—before the gas strike—he "worked with ardour and perseverance for the success of the Liberal Party." During the strike he witnessed a Liberal Councillor and "professed friend of Labour" entertain the blacklegs with "Britons never shall be slaves." Other Liberals provided them with beer and tobacco, while at the same time the Leeds gasworkers were provided with military, as another mark of Liberal friendship. "This decided me. I vowed I would never again assist either of the Political Parties." J. Clayton (ed.), *Why I Joined the Independent Labour Party* (Leeds, n.d.).

93.   *Tom Maguire, a Remembrance,* p. xi.

94.   By the end of 1892 there were Fabian Societies at Batley, Bradford, Copley (near Halifax), Halifax, Holmfirth, Huddersfield, Leeds, and Sowerby Bridge; Castleford and Dewsbury were added before May 1893. *List of Members* (Fabian Society, October 1892) and *Tenth Annual Report* of Fabian Society, April 1893. A correspondent in the *Labour Leader,* 20 April 1901, notes that the Bradford Socialist League "afterwards merged into the Bradford Socialist Society and finally became a branch of the Fabian Society." The Halifax Fabian Society was especially effective in its propaganda; see Lister MSS. History.

95.   *Labour Leader,* 13 April 1901.

96.   *Dewsbury Reporter,* 13 October 1894.

97.   At the same lime the Leeds TC changed its name to the Trades and Labour Council.

98.   Leeds Trades Council, *Annual Report,* 1892, pp. 1–2, 6. This was the successor to the Labour Electoral Association which had been founded after the gas strike, with Maguire

as secretary and the formidable old unionist, Judge, as treasurer. *YFT,* 18 July 1890, and for Judge, 1 July 1892.

99.   *Annual Report,* 1893, p. 5.
100.   "I'll retire into the corner and write poetry," he declared after the gas strike (*Tom Magu-ire, a Remembrance,* p. xii). See also letter quoted in Thompson, *op. cit.,* p. 703 n. 1: "Tom . . . sinks his own individuality and allows other people to run away with his ideas," etc.
101.   Mahon was elected paid assistant secretary of the Yorkshire District of the Gasworkers on a slender majority vote in July 1891. *YFT,* 10 July 1891.
102.   *YFT,* 20 November 1891.
103.   Ibid., 26 February 1892.
104.   Information from Mr A. T. Marles.
105.   See Note on the South Leeds Election, pp. 315–16.
106.   Edward Carpenter to Alf Mattison, 2 October 1892, Mattison Collection.
107.   On the occasion of the first National Conference of the ILP Carpenter wrote to Matti-son (13 January 1893): "(I see that old fraud Mahon has got there—Champion too!) I am glad you didn't yield to Mahon about going, and Tom M. I think in his heart cannot be sorry that *you* were elected." Mattison Collection.
108.   Article by Turner in *Yorkshire Evening News,* 1924, in Mattison Cutting-book.
109.   Obituary of Paul Bland, *Labour Leader,* 20 April 1901.
110.   Bradford TC Minutes, in possession of Bradford Trades Council.
111.   Turner, *Heavy Woollen Textile Workers Union,* pp. 65–67: "The paper opened up a new vista. We scoured Yorkshire textile areas for members, and the Union grew from a few hundreds to a few thousands." See also Paylor on its effect, in *YFT,* 25 December 1891.
112.   *Commonweal,* 19 October 1889; John Lister, a learned antiquarian, was later to write: "I learned many useful, practical lessons from some of these 'agitators' who . . . knew far more about the industrial history of our country than I." Lister MSS. History.
113.   *YFT,* 19 December 1890, 16 January 1891.
114.   *Ibid.,* 6 February 1891. But a German manufacturer wrote to the *Bradford Observer* from Crefeld and claimed that their average wages were *higher* than those in Lister's mills.
115.   Ibid., 24 April 1891.
116.   Ibid., 1 May 1891.
117.   Ibid., 17 July 1891.
118.   The Bradford Trades Council was "considering" contesting East Bradford with a Labour candidate in 1885 (TC Minutes, 10 February 1885). But in 1888 the Liberal Association could only be persuaded with great difficulty to admit a Trades Council nominee to the "Liberal Eight" for the School Board. (Minutes, 6 November, and entries to 4 December 1889.) However, a Labour Electoral Association had been formed in 1888, and socialists like Bland, Cowgill, Conellan and Bartley were making themselves felt on the Council. But the LEA was hamstrung by Liberal–Socialist disagreements, and Jowett, who was secretary, let it die. *Labour Leader,* 20 April 1901; Brockway, *op. cit.,* p. 31.
119.   For Mahon's *Programme,* see Thompson, *op. cit.,* p. 615, note 2. For the Bradford La-bour Union programme, see *Labour Union Journal,* 30 June 1892. For Colne Valley, see Mann, *op. cit.*
120.   Bills and election leaflets in Shaftoe Cutting-book.
121.   *YFT,* 29 May 1891.
122.   Ibid., 15 and 22 January 1892.
123.   *Minutes of 2nd Annual Congress of Dockers &c.* (September 1891), pp. 25–26. The signa-tures have been bound and are preserved by the Bradford Trades Council.
124.   Minutes of Colne Valley Labour Union (in possession of C.V. Labour Party). For an example of Mann's views on the priority of trade union and municipal work over par-

liamentary, see the *Trade Unionist & Trades Council Record,* 5 September 1891; for an example of a reproof aimed at Mann, see editorial, "Tom Mann and the Representation of Labour," *YFT,* 28 August 1891.

125. E.g., at Huddersfield in February 1891, when Balmforth topped the poll in the School Board elections.
126. *YFT,* 10 February 1893.
127. The Heavy Woollen District Trades Council was formed in July 1891, with Ben Turner as secretary, and in only two months was intervening in local elections. Minutes, 15 September 1891 (in possession of Miss Nora Turner).
128. *YFT,* 10 July 1891.
129. *Bradford Observer,* 14 June 1892.
130. *YFT,* 1 July 1892. The firm was Clayton, Murgatroyd & Co.
131. Lister MSS. History and cuttings in Mattison Collection, and *YFT,* 20 November 1891.
132. *Trade Unionist & Trades Council Record,* 7 November 1891.
133. *YFT,* 7 August 1891.
134. Ibid., 14 August 1891.
135. Election Manifesto and Lister MSS. History; *Halifax Free Press,* January 1893.
136. Snowden, *op. cit.,* p. 69: "The ILP was attracting in the main the young men who were not yet voters."
137. *Halifax Guardian,* 6 March 1897.
138. In February 1894 a resolution was passed at the Yorkshire Federation of Trades Councils urging the government to "take up at once the question of the nationalisation of the land, minerals, railways, and all the means of production and distribution, as a means of helping to solve the unemployed question." *YFT,* 16 February 1894.
139. *YFT,* 10 July 1892.
140. See Burgess in the *Labour Leader,* 20 April 1901.
141. *Dewsbury Reporter,* 13 October 1894.
142. *Tom Maguire, a Remembrance,* p. vi.
143. Snowden, *op. cit.,* p. 82.
144. *Tom Maguire, a Remembrance;* T. Maguire, *Machine Room Chants* (1895); J. Clayton, *Before Sunrise* (Manchester, 1896); miscellaneous cuttings in Turner and Mattison Scrapbooks, and Mattison Notebook.

Index